"Academic research on the far right has traditionally focused on such movements in Western Europe and North America. This volume shifts the focus to cover the entire American continent, addressing differences, similarities and connections. Of particular interest is the role of US governments and conservative movements to promote and support far right and authoritarian regimes and movements in Latin America. This is an important contribution".

Tore Bjørgo, *Director, Center for Research on Extremism (C-REX), University of Oslo, Norway*

"This volume could not be more timely. The resilience of an extreme nationalist right throughout the Western Hemisphere is an abiding fact of the twenty-first century. It manifests itself in terms of political economy, in the 'culture wars' (these days look at the transnational attacks on 'woke' gender-based thinking) and in electoral politics. This right's resilience derives from two sources—the self interest to preserve its privileges among wealthy classes, and from a sense of being 'left behind' or 'replaced' on the part of a cultural and economic 'precariat'. But it also depends on a right-wing infrastructure that well predates contemporary controversies. Illuminating these enduring sources of the political right is the great virtue of this collection. The ten country-by-country studies in *The Right in the Americas* tie today's extreme right ascendency to its predecessors and their continuing and often shape-shifting role, and to the uninterrupted influence of US hegemonic power. For readers, for political thinkers and for political actors, the book is a caution against facile convictions of the right's vulnerabilities and about the limitations of short-term political thinking and strategies".

Lawrence Rosenthal, *Chair, Berkeley Center for Right-Wing Studies, USA*

"The ascent of the new right, in particular in its extreme variants, has raised red flags around the world, especially in our Hemisphere. It results from the crisis affecting democracy, particularly at its traditional sources, which has been unable to catch up with new demands and has lost space vis-à-vis these emergent forms. This is why this book is important, the authors in their respective fields explore the roots and the new processes explaining the right's ascent in national case studies that cover significant geographical areas, presenting their similarities and substantial differences. The authors transcend the frontiers of politics and address economic, social and cultural issues, offering analyses from diverse perspectives that this volume manages to reconcile. One of its merits rests in the authors' ability to challenge old understandings, reworking arguments that address the complexity of contemporary crises, as well as having perceived the inroads that new technologies are opening in the ideological dispute; allowing

political actors to even capture discursive and organizational tools from their adversaries".

Hernán Ramírez, *Research Professor, Universidade do Vale do Rio dos Sinos (UNISINOS), Brazil*

"In line with the wave of conservative groups, neoliberal sectors, and anti-communist and neo-fascist organizations that have nurtured the right-wing and the European New Right during the current century in the Americas, we have also noted a strong activism from various social and political actors, and the strengthening of governments that reinforce the worldview and the values that define this sector of the international political geometry. In that landscape, this text represents an excellent and important collective effort of academics from various countries of the Americas that present the particularities of varying right-wing lineages and discover the elements that unify them, especially, throughout the 20th and 21st centuries. Altogether, these works reveal a broad right-wing geopolitical strategy, a process in which the United States keeps playing a central role, as the source from which key ideas emerge and networks with a decisive influence are strengthened along the continent. The book is an obligatory reference for those who wish to understand the development of a broad front of actors that compete with the left for the economic, political and social powers in the Americas. In the contest for hegemony in the continent, the right persists on showing its capability for reorganizing and for exercising the government, and for that, they utilize old narratives and mechanisms of political articulation, but they also succeed in incorporating unprecedented discursive and programmatic repertoires, that prove appealing to large social sectors".

Tania Hernández, *Director, Permanent Seminar on the Right in Mexico, National Institute of Anthropology and History (INAH), Mexico.*

THE RIGHT IN THE AMERICAS

The Right in the Americas discusses the origins, development, and current state of conservative and right-wing movements in ten countries in the Americas.

The growth of the right is one of the most important issues of the moment in global politics. Within the context of democracy erosion, rejection of traditional politics, and economic uncertainty, right and extreme-right actors are capable of offering misguided answers and hope to a significant part of a country's population, who will trust their promises and bring them to power with their vote. This dynamic has repeated itself in an astonishingly consistent pattern across the Americas. This book analyses eight Latin American countries—Argentina, Brazil, Chile, Colombia, Honduras, Mexico, Uruguay, and Venezuela—along with Canada and the United States, two G7 countries. It demonstrates that conservatism is in fact a hemispheric phenomenon, promoted and invigorated by the regional hegemon—the United States of America—both as government and as civil society. Beyond this regional scope, the peculiarities of each case study are explored in detail, providing solid historical background, while at the same time uncovering their commonalities and cross-pollination.

This study will be of great interest to scholars of conservatism, right-wing politics, comparative politics, and North American and Latin American politics.

Julián Castro-Rea is Professor in the Department of Political Science at the University of Alberta, Canada.

Esther Solano is Professor of International Relations at Federal University of São Paulo, Brazil.

Fascism & the Far Right
Routledge Studies in Fascism and the Far Right

Series editors
Nigel Copsey, Teesside University, UK and Graham Macklin, Center for Research on Extremism (C-REX), University of Oslo, Norway.

This book series focuses upon national, transnational and global manifestations of fascist, far right and right-wing politics primarily within a historical context but also drawing on insights and approaches from other disciplinary perspectives. Its scope also includes anti-fascism, radical-right populism, extreme-right violence and terrorism, cultural manifestations of the far right, and points of convergence and exchange with the mainstream and traditional right.

Titles include:

The Nazi Party and the German Communities Abroad
The Latin American Case
João Fábio Bertonha and Rafael Athaides

Nazi Occultism
Between the SS and Esotericism
Stéphane François

The Rise of the Radical Right in the Global South
Edited by Rosana Pinheiro-Machado and Tatiana Vargas-Maia

Global Identitarianism
Edited by José Pedro Zúquete and Riccardo Marchi

The Politics of Memory in the Italian Populist Radical Right
From Mare Nostrum to Mare Vostrum
Marianna Griffini

Love, Hate and the Leader
A Fascist Childhood
Trevor Grundy

Memory in Hungarian Fascism
A Cultural History
Zoltán Kékesi

The Right in the Americas
Distinct Trajectories and Hemispheric Convergences, from the Origins to the Present
Edited by Julián Castro-Rea and Esther Solano

For more information about this series, please visit: www.routledge.com/Routledge-Studies-in-Fascism-and-the-Far-Right/book-series/FFR

THE RIGHT IN THE AMERICAS

Distinct Trajectories and Hemispheric Convergences, from the Origins to the Present

Edited by Julián Castro-Rea and Esther Solano

LONDON AND NEW YORK

Cover image: 'American Bug' by Alina Tousseeva © 2023

First published 2024
by Routledge
4 Park Square, Milton Park, Abingdon, Oxon OX14 4RN

and by Routledge
605 Third Avenue, New York, NY 10158

Routledge is an imprint of the Taylor & Francis Group, an informa business

© 2024 selection and editorial matter, Julián Castro-Rea and Esther Solano; individual chapters, the contributors

The right of Julián Castro-Rea and Esther Solano to be identified as the authors of the editorial material, and of the authors for their individual chapters, has been asserted in accordance with sections 77 and 78 of the Copyright, Designs and Patents Act 1988.

All rights reserved. No part of this book may be reprinted or reproduced or utilised in any form or by any electronic, mechanical, or other means, now known or hereafter invented, including photocopying and recording, or in any information storage or retrieval system, without permission in writing from the publishers.

Trademark notice: Product or corporate names may be trademarks or registered trademarks, and are used only for identification and explanation without intent to infringe.

British Library Cataloguing-in-Publication Data
A catalogue record for this book is available from the British Library

Library of Congress Cataloging-in-Publication Data
Names: Castro Rea, Julián, editor. | Solano, Esther, editor.
Title: The right in the Americas: distinct trajectories and hemispheric convergences, from the origins to the present / edited by Julián Castro-Rea and Esther Solano.
Description: First edition. | New York: Routledge, 2023. | Series: Fascism and the Far Right | Includes bibliographical references and index. | Identifiers: LCCN 2023004688 (print) | LCCN 2023004689 (ebook) | ISBN 9781032402741 (hbk) | ISBN 9781032386959 (pbk) | ISBN 9781003352266 (ebk)
Subjects: LCSH: Conservatism–America–History. | Radicalism–America–History. | Right and left (Political science)–America–History. | Right-wing extremists–America–History. | America–Politics and government.
Classification: LCC JC573.2.A6 R56 2023 (print) | LCC JC573.2.A6 (ebook) |
DDC 320.52097–dc23/eng/20230324
LC record available at https://lccn.loc.gov/2023004688
LC ebook record available at https://lccn.loc.gov/2023004689

ISBN: 978-1-032-40274-1 (hbk)
ISBN: 978-1-032-38695-9 (pbk)
ISBN: 978-1-003-35226-6 (ebk)

DOI: 10.4324/9781003352266

Typeset in Times New Roman
by Deanta Global Publishing Services, Chennai, India

To my mother Elsa, with unlimited love
JCR

To Alexandre, the love of my life
ES

CONTENTS

List of Figures   *xi*
List of Tables   *xii*
List of Contributors   *xiii*
Foreword   *xviii*
   Karin Fischer

Introduction: The right in the Americas   1
   Julián Castro-Rea and Esther Solano

PART I
THE AMERICAS AS RIGHT-WING TRANSNATIONAL SPACE   **17**

1 United States: The Mecca of conservatism in the Americas
    and its international projection   19
    Julián Castro-Rea and Kyle Beattie

PART II
GENESIS AND DEVELOPMENT OF RIGHT-WING ACTORS   **55**

2 Argentina: Democracy, authoritarianism, and the pursuit of order   57
    Ernesto Bohoslavsky and Sergio D. Morresi

3 Canada: The evolution, transformation, and diversity of
    conservatism   76
    Frédéric Boily

4 Colombia: Matrices, tensions, and contexts for explaining the origin and change of right-wing politics 88
Laura Camila Ramírez Bonilla

5 Honduras: The problem of the origin of political ideas on the right 110
Gustavo Zelaya Herrera

6 Mexico: The right, from opposition to power and back 126
Mario Virgilio Santiago Jiménez

7 Uruguay: The political right and some landmark moments in history, from the foundational anti-Jacobinism to the re-emergence of the militaristic far right 140
Gerardo Caetano

PART III
CONTEMPORARY EXPRESSIONS OF THE RIGHT 165

8 Brazil: The New Right and the rise of Jair Bolsonaro 167
Camila Rocha, Esther Solano and Jonas Medeiros

9 Chile: Orthodoxy and heterodoxy on the right 190
Stéphanie Alenda, Carmen Le Foulon and Julieta Suárez-Cao

10 Venezuela: Democracy as market, or how the right-wing opposition confused the two in its quest for power 217
Barry Cannon and Ybiskay González

PART IV
CONCLUSIONS 237

11 The right in the Americas: Concluding remarks 239
Julián Castro-Rea and Esther Solano

Index *243*

FIGURES

1.1	United States: Top 20 largest foundations by total giving, 2015. *Source:* Adapted from Foundation Center, 2015.	42
1.2	United States: Major conservative think tanks and their connections to the military industrial complex. *Sources:* Armstrong, 2014. [original figure, Creative Commons Attribution-ShareAlike 4.0 International License]; Beattie, K.A. (2022). [adapted figure].	44
1.3	Americas: State funding of religion index, 2014-present. *Source:* Association of Religion Data Archives, et al. "Religion and State (RAS) Project" (1990-2014).	45
9.1	Chile: Sensibilities by party. Source: Authors' elaboration.	200
9.2	Chile: Leaders' sensibilities by degree of religiosity, age group, and gender. Source: Authors' elaboration.	201
9.3	Chile: Positions on rights of sexual minorities by sensibility and party. Source: Authors' elaboration.	203
9.4	Chile: agreement with decriminalisation of abortion by sensibility and party. Source: Authors' elaboration.	204
9.5	Chile: Agreement with eliminating profit in education by sensibility and party. Source: Authors' elaboration.	206
9.6	Chile: Agreement with establishing a new constitution by sensibility and party. Source: Authors' elaboration.	207

TABLES

1.1	United States: Attempt or successful overthrow of a government in the Americas, 1945–present	34
1.2	United States: Countries in the Americas with active NED projects and funding, 2019	35
4.1	Colombia: Programmatic principles of right-wing parties according to their most recent statute	97
4.2	Colombia: Contexts, tensions and matrices of origin and transformation of the right	103

CONTRIBUTORS

Stéphanie Alenda is Associate Professor and Director of Research of the faculty of Education and Social Sciences at Andrés Bello National University, Chile. She holds a PhD in Sociology from the University of Lille 1 and a master's degree in Sociology from the EHESS, Paris. She is the current President of the Research Committee on Political Sociology (IPSA RC06/ISA RC18) (since 2018). Her areas of expertise are party organisations, right-wing politics, political elites, and activists. Her work has been published in prestigious scientific journals. She has recently edited: *Anatomía de la Derecha Chilena. Estado, Mercado y Valores en Tiempos de Cambio* (2020). She is a member of the Red de Politólogas #NoSinMujeres.

Kyle Beattie is a researcher of Political Science and an instructor of English as a Second Language. He obtained his BA in Political Science from Humboldt State University and his MA in Teaching: TESOL from the University of Southern California. Currently, he is a PhD student at the University of Alberta, Canada, in the Department of Political Science, specialising in International Relations and Comparative Politics. His doctoral dissertation focuses on the field of corruption studies

Ernesto Bohoslavsky obtained his PhD in Latin American History at Universidad Complutense de Madrid and currently is an Associate Professor in Latin American Contemporary History at Universidad Nacional de General Sarmiento, Argentina. Bohoslavsky is researcher at Consejo Nacional de Investigaciones Científicas y Tecnológicas, Argentina. He specialises in Latin American History, with a focus on the twentieth century. He has conducted research on right-wing ideologies, parties and intellectuals in Argentina, Brazil, Chile, and Uruguay, using a comparative and transnational history approach. His recent publications include *Las derechas* *ibero-americanas. Desde el final de la Primera Guerra hasta la Gran Depresión. Mexico City*, 2019 edited with David Jorge and Clara Lida.

Frédéric Boily is Professor, Campus Saint-Jean, University of Alberta. He specialises in Canadian political ideologies, specifically conservatism and populism in Alberta and Quebec. He is the author of several books, most notably: *Le conservatisme au Québec. Retour sur une tradition oubliée* (2010). This book received the Donald Smiley award (2011), from the Canadian Political Science Association. His most recent books include: *La droite en Alberta. D'Ernest Manning à Stephen Harper* (2013); *Stephen Harper. La fracture idéologique d'une vision du Canada* (2016); *John A. Macdonald. Les ambiguïtés de la modération politique* (2017), *La Coalition Avenir Québec. Une idéologie à la recherche du pouvoir* (2018) and *Trudeau. De Pierre à Justin. Portrait de famille de l'idéologie du Parti libéral du Canada, nouvelle postface de l'auteur* (2019).

Gerardo Caetano is a Historian and Political Scientist. PhD in History, *Universidad Nacional de La Plata*, Argentina. He is full Professor and Researcher, *Universidad de la República*, Uruguay and former President of the Supreme Council of FLACSO (2012–2020). He was head member at the Directive Committee of CLACSO (2009–2015), researcher at the National Research System, Uruguay (level III), member of the academies of Letters and Sciences of Uruguay, the Spanish Royal Academy and the Argentinian History Academy. He has been professor at bachelor and postgraduate courses, national and international levels, and member of numerous international scientific organisations and editorial committees of worldwide renowned publications. He has published numerous books and articles in his specialities. His work has obtained various academic awards in Uruguay and abroad.

Barry Cannon (PhD, Dublin City University, 2005) lectures on politics in the Sociology Department of Maynooth University, Ireland. His research focuses on Latin American politics, especially the Left and the Right in the region, on populism as concept and practice and on the crisis of democracy. He has published in a number of key journals, including *Third World Quarterly*, *Latin American Politics and Society*, *Democratization and New Political Science*, among others. He co-edited, with Patricia Rangel, no. 126 of (Barcelona) *d'Afers Internacionals on the Latin American Right*. His most recent book is *The Right in Latin America: Elite Power, Hegemony and the Struggle for the State* (2016)

Julián Castro-Rea (PhD, Université de Montréal) is Professor, Department of Political Science, University of Alberta, Canada. He was a member of Mexico's Foreign Service, where he was distinguished with the Genaro Estrada Award, also research professor at Centre for Research on North America (CISAN), National Autonomous University of Mexico (UNAM). For over 30 years of academic career, Julián Castro-Rea has been a prolific researcher and committed instructor.

He has authored or co-authored 10 books, 19 refereed articles, 23 refereed book chapters, among many other diverse contributions. Some recent publications include: "My Girlfriend Became Neo-Nazi: The Right's Presence and Activity in the Internet", *Center for Right-Wing Studies Working Papers*, May 2019; « Right-Wing Think Tank Networks in Latin America : The Mexican Connection », *Perspectives on Global Development and Technology* (Leiden), no. 17, 2018; "Escrever com a direita: os best sellers da direita no espanhol e sua promoção nas redes transnacionais" in Bohoslavsky, Ernesto et al, eds., *Pensar as direitas na América Latina*, São Paulo: 2019; pp. 143–160 and "Requiem pour l'État révolutionnaire : l'influence de l'ALÉNA sur la réforme du secteur de l'énergie au Mexique", in Dorval Brunelle ed., *L'ALÉNA à 20 ans : un accord en sursis, un modèle en essor*, Montreal, 2014; pp. 193–211.

Karin Fischer, historian and sociologist, is Senior Lecturer and head of the Global Sociology and Development Research Unit at the Institute of Sociology at Johannes Kepler Universität, Linz, Austria. Her research focuses on neoliberal transformation, global commodity chains, and uneven development in historical and transnational perspective. She has published widely about transnational neoliberal networks and think tanks in Latin America. Her recent books include: *Clases dominantes y desarrollo desigual: Chile entre 1830 y 2010,* 2017; and as co-editor *Capitalism in Transformation: Movements and Countermovements in the 21st Century*, 2019; *Globale Warenketten und ungleiche Entwicklung. Arbeit, Kapital, Konsum, Natur*, 2021; *Globale Ungleichheit. Über Zusammenhänge von Kolonialismus, Arbeitsverhältnissen und Naturverbrauch*, updated edition 2022.

Ybiskay González is a sociologist from Venezuela and completed her PhD in Politics at the University of Newcastle, Australia, in 2018. She is currently a casual academic staff at the University of Newcastle. She has published about Venezuela in the *Bulletin of Latin America, Revista CIDOB d'Afers Internacionals*, and in the book *Populismus: Diskurs –oHegemonie –eStaat*, edited by Kim Seongcheol and Agridopoulos Aristotelis

Carmen Le Foulon is a researcher and Coordinator of the Public Opinion Program at Centro de Estudios Públicos, Chile. She holds a PhD in Political Science from Columbia University. Her areas of expertise are legislative behaviour, representation, gender politics, public opinion, and voting behaviour. Her work has been published in prestigious scientific journals. She is a member of the Red de Politólogas #NoSinMujeres.

Jonas Medeiros is a social scientist and a researcher at the Brazilian Centre for Analysis and Planning (CEBRAP), where he is a member of the Law and Democracy Nucleus (Núcleo Direito e Democracia). He holds a PhD in Education from the State University of Campinas (UNICAMP), Brazil, and currently researches public sphere, social movements, and critical theory. He co-authored

Escolas de Luta ["Combative Schools"] (Brazil, 2016) and co-edited *Ocupar e Resistir: Movimentos de ocupação de escolas pelo Brasil* (2015–2016) ["Occupy and Resist: School Occupation Movements across Brazil"] (Brazil, 2019).

Sergio D. Morresi is Associate Professor in the Politics Department of the National University of Litoral (UNL) and a researcher at the Argentinian National Research Council. His work focuses on political theory, especially neoliberal and conservative political thinkers, and contemporary Latin American history. He is author of *La nueva derecha Argentina y la democracia sin política* (2008), *Mundo PRO: anatomía de un partido fabricado para ganar* (2014, with A. Belloti y G. Vommaro) and editor (with G. Vommaro) of *Saber lo que se hace: política y expertise en Argentina* (2011) and *"Hagamos equipo". PRO y la construcción de la nueva derecha argentina* (2015). He also contributed with various articles in academic journals.

Laura Camila Ramírez Bonilla holds a PhD and a MA in History from El Colegio de México. She also has a BA in Political Science and a MA in Political Studies from the National University in Colombia. Currently, she teaches at the Department of History at Universidad Iberoamericana, Mexico City, where she was appointed, from 2019 until 2021, director of the bachelor's programme in History. Her primary lines of research are: (1) Catholic church, society, and politics in the second half of the twentieth century. (2) peacebuilding. (3) history and mass media (mostly television) in Mexico and Colombia. She is the author of the book *Entre altares y mesas de diálogo. El episcopado colombiano en acercamientos de paz con grupos armados ilegales (1991-2006)* (2015)

Camila Rocha holds a PhD and a master's in Political Science from Universidade Federal de São Paulo, where she also obtained her bachelor's degree in Social Sciences. She was awarded the prizes for best doctoral thesis by the Brazilian Association of Political Science and the University of São Paulo in the area of Human Sciences, and has several publications on political behaviour and contemporary political culture. She is currently a researcher at the Brazilian Centre for Analysis and Planning (CEBRAP).

Mario Virgilio Santiago Jiménez is a professor and researcher at the José María Luis Mora Research Institute, Mexico. He has taught courses on the historiography of Mexico, the political history of Mexico in the twentieth century, new political history, and recent history. He has also presented communications in national and international academic spaces and has published articles in different magazines on Mexican and Argentine right-wings. He is a member of the Working Group "Contemporary Right-wings: Dictatorships and Democracies" (CLACSO) and is founder of the Permanent Seminary of Contemporary History and Present Time of Mexico

Esther Solano is Professor of International Relations at Universidade Federal de São Paulo, Brazil and teaches in the Master programme on Latin America and the European Union at the University of Alcalá, Spain. Among other publications she has recently edited in Brazil are: *Is there a way out? Critical essays on Brazil* (2017), *Hate as politics* (2018), and *Brazil in collapse* (2019).

Julieta Suárez-Cao is Associate Professor at the Institute of Political Science of the Pontifical Catholic University of Chile. She holds a PhD in Political Science from Northwestern University. Her areas of expertise are political parties, women's representation, electoral systems, and subnational politics. Her work has been published in prestigious scientific journals and she has co-edited two books: one on multi-level party systems and the other on politics and gender. She is one of the coordinators of the Red de Politólogas #NoSinMujeres.

Gustavo Zelaya Herrera. He obtained a degree in Philosophy from the National Autonomous University of Honduras (UNAH). During his 32-year career in higher education, he has been professor of Latin American Thought, Honduran Thought, Central American Thought, Axiology and Political Philosophy. He coordinated the Philosophy Career of the Faculty of Humanities and Arts at UNAH for several periods. He has delivered several lectures at Central American philosophy conferences on issues of national identity and the history of ideas. He was invited by Trinity College in Hartford, Connecticut to expound on José M and his political influence (2018). His published works include: *The Legacy of the Liberal Reform*, Honduras, 2001; *José Cecilio del Valle and Utilitarianism*, Honduras, 2014; *Thinking Philosophy*, co-authored with Dr Irma Becerra, 2014; *Political Ethics*, co-authored with Irma and Longino Becerra, 2016; Essays on Honduran political thought published in magazines and in the *Anthology of Contemporary Honduran Critical Thinking*, CLACSO, 2019. He was recognised with the Rey Juan Carlos I Historical Studies Award for contributing to the historical knowledge of Honduras, awarded by the Government of Spain, September 14, 1994.

FOREWORD
Karin Fischer

With the arrival of the new millennial Chile celebrated the tenth birthday of the transition to democracy. On my first visit to the country in the summer of 2000 I expected a celebratory mood. Instead, it seemed like a grey veil had been cast over the city of Santiago and its inhabitants. This veil was not like the layer of smog that covers the Chilean capital during the winter months. It was the invisible shadow of the dreadful 16 years of the Pinochet dictatorship which had a lasting impact on the mentality of Chileans and the culture of the country. Neoliberal beliefs and principles had permeated not only the economy and the political sphere, including the former opposition, but also large parts of civil society. If there is something like "neoliberal hegemony" on the Latin American continent, it would be here I thought.

Chile was an early "experimental laboratory" for the implementation of neoliberal ideas, years before Margaret Thatcher and Ronald Reagan heralded the global historic turn. In the course of a "pacted transition", the regime ensured that the legal framework and the structure of the neoliberal state were kept in place.

Apart from such constitutionalisation, the former state cadres and their supporters intensified their work in the "trenches of civil society". Only a few weeks after the installation of the first democratic government (and the electoral defeat of the regime's presidential candidate), they founded a new think tank, for example. Backed by a robust knowledge infrastructure that combines academics in private universities, professional experts in think tanks, and friendly media channels, they continued to influence policymakers and the public at large. Together with their allies in business the forces of the right managed to safeguard the neoliberal model (Fischer, 2015; Madariaga, 2020).

Hegemony is a tricky term. Applying the Gramscian understanding of "hegemony" to a context in which neoliberal economic adjustment was imposed from above and implemented under reliance on brutal military dictatorships is certainly misleading. Gramsci's understanding of hegemony requires a fair amount of integration of inferior classes and a certain degree of public consent. If the regime had to rely on unconstrained force, repressive authority, and extreme violence to advance neoliberal adjustment policies like in Chile, there can be talk about popular consent in propaganda material only. But Gramsci's dual concept of consent and coercion at the same time can be considered invaluable explaining the strategies, the flexibility, and the persistence of the right. Firstly, it broadens our perception of politics. Politics is more than party politics and government policy, electoral processes, and the attainment of state power. Secondly, a holistic view of different spheres of power—the military, the state, civil society—illuminates the flexibility with which the right responds to different political constellations. Finally, looking at the right-wing forces in the "trenches" of civil society directs us to observe historical continuities that can be obscured by the primary focus on election cycles and changes in government.

The chapters of this book document the diversity of the right both in ideological and organisational terms. Contrary to expectations of orthodoxy and ideological uniformity the right is characterised by a high degree of contextual adaptability and variability. Identifying categories for the different ideological currents already can be considered an elusive task. Some authors of this book differentiate between (neo-)conservatives, (neo-)liberals, conservative liberals or liberal-conservatives. When classifying political parties, they refer to right-wing, moderate, centre-right, and radical or extreme-right parties. Such heterogeneity makes it almost impossible to speak of the right in singular. Therefore, some authors prefer to speak of "political families": the Catholic, now Christian family, including other churches and religions, especially evangelicals; the conservative liberal and the neoliberal family; each of these assemblages integrates a set of subcurrents. Taken together, they oscillate between fragmentation and unity, and differ in tones and agendas in response to specific political and historical conjunctures. The key themes of the right—law and order, religion, social discipline, hierarchy, authority, nation, family, individual freedom, private property rights, racial stereotypes—represent a rich mix, some of resonant traditional ideologies, others with a wider popular connotation. They can be woven together to make a set of discourses which are then harnessed to the practices of the right (or right-wing factions) and the class forces they aspire to mobilise and to represent (Hall, 1979: p. 180).

However diverse the family members are, they have a strong unifying bond: that is, firstly, the war against "communism" (or optionally socialism, collectivism, statism) and against anything that might pave the way to it; secondly, the war against anything perceived as an attack on the institutional pillars of church, military, and class privileges, and, thirdly, that any kind of political regime was and is preferable to a left-wing—in their perception "communist"—government. "Anti-communism" is an enduring political weapon, in some places elevated to the status of a holy war, whether or not the Soviet Union exists (Weld, 2020). Put differently, the right can be defined by the axes that it disputes vis-à-vis its opponents (such as the role of the State or the social order), and by the defence of privileges to the detriment of the demands of full democracy, i.e., political, and social rights for the masses. Whichever "family" one feels to belong to, and however the code of values is defined, and society is conceptualised, they all agree on one thing: a (neo-)liberal economic order based on private property and an interventionist political programme in favour of free enterprise and entrepreneurship (Mirowski and Plehwe, 2015; Slobodian, 2018). In practical political terms this means: low taxes, restrain the power of trade unions, welfare-state retrenchment, and no state interference into ownership control and business matters (except rescue by the state when necessary). This is a universal consensus between conservatives and (neo-)liberals, between the centre-right and the extreme right.

As mentioned, the ways and means to achieve these goals and maintain them are manifold. Practices range from military interventions, paramilitary activities, and killings to electoral campaigns and movement tactics. This is also true for the projection of conservative/right-wing ideas from the United States to Latin America in the context of the global cold war: US strategies follow coercion, force, repression on the one hand, and winning consent mediated via civil society institutions on the other. Regardless of which party is in power, the US government has actively supported military coups against "undesirable" governments in its "backyard". At the same time ideological interventions and civil society strategies have been launched with support from the US establishment. The Rockefeller Report from 1969 recommended financially and organisationally supporting the spread of evangelical churches and Pentecostal movements in Latin America in order to combat liberation theology, for example. The US Congress decided to send missionaries and provided millions of dollars for the construction of Mormon temples (Keely, 2015). Twenty years later in 1988, the Council for Inter-American Security launched "Santa Fe II" as a guide for the new president. The document continues with the anti-communist rhetoric of its predecessor from 1980. "Santa Fe I" had been dedicated to Ronald Reagan and had proclaimed "World War III" with Latin America as one of the two principal sites (Hepple, 2011). Santa Fe II distinguished between "temporal governments", i.e., elected officials, and "permanent governments" which consist of the armed forces, the judiciary and civil society organisations such as business organisations, trade unions and educational institutions. The authors claimed that Marxist intellectuals (still) dominated the civil society and recommended increasing the budget of the United States Information Agency in order to initiate a "cultural war" against "Gramscian Marxism". The mentioned civil society organisations should serve as a basis for this and be transformed into weapons against rampant etatism, nationalism, and communism in Latin America (for a Spanish translation of the document, see *Equipo Envío*, 1988).

Such reversal of Gramscian thought in support of extending working-class influence also reached Latin America, above all contemporary Brazil where "anti-communist warriors" sparked a "cultural war" against the Worker's party and left-wing intellectuals at the turn of the millennium. Turning Gramsci's approach upside down and unafraid to learn from the "enemy", one of their protagonists claims in (intentional?) disregard of factual power relations that the left has successfully achieved cultural hegemony exercised via NGOs, media, publications, education, and arts. He accused the military government (1964–1985) of being "focused only on combating armed subversion and lazily evading the duty of cultural struggle" (Carvalho, 2008, cited in Burgos, 2019: p. 159, translated by the author). Similar to the United States, aggressive "freedom fighters" in alliance with older right-wing groups and think tanks mobilised a mass of supporters via social media. Much like what we know from Donald Trump's Twitter account, there has been no restriction on the use of violent and disruptive language, defamation, and fake news (Amaral, 2015).

The persistence of the right and their current upswing from the United States to Brazil, from Hungary to India, should motivate us to "look behind the surface phenomena". This is what Stuart Hall called for in his famous essay on what he already called "Thatcherism", published four months before Margaret Thatcher won the elections. When researching the right, historical determinism is to be avoided, as is an elite bias. Rightist strategies should be studied in a movement–countermovement perspective, and the right and the dominant classes do not per se control the course of political development, let alone history. "We mustn't underestimate the capacity for resistance and struggle", as Hall (1979) said, but "we must find the points of intervention' and 'if we are correct about the depth of the rightward turn, then our interventions need to be pertinent, decisive and effective" (p. 174). This applies unchanged and especially for today.

The full dimensions of the shift to the right continue to evade a proper analysis. Systematic scholarly engagement with the right has not gone far. In fact, it is difficult to speak of the existence of a field of study in itself. Different manifestations of the right such as classical fascism and contemporary forms of the extreme right, military dictatorships in Latin America, and neoliberalism are intensively studied. The respective research communities are, however, hardly connected with each other. Transnational or hemispheric, interdisciplinary, and longitudinal studies are widely missing. Engaging in a transregional dialogue is therefore a highly productive endeavour to which this book makes an important contribution.

References

Amaral, M. (2015) The right's new clothes. *Brazil Wire*, 29 July. English translation by Angela Milanese. http://www.brasilwire.com/the-rights-new-clothes/ [Accessed 18 October 2022].

Burgos, R. (2019) La derecha y Gramsci: Demonización y disputa de la teoría de la hegemonía. In *Gramsci – La teoría de la hegemonía y las transformaciones políticas recientes en América Latina. Actas del Simposio Internacional Asunción, 27–28 de Agosto de 2019*. Asunción, Centro de Estudios Germinal, pp. 145–187.

Equipo Envío. (1988) Santa Fe II: El imperialismo ante América Latina. *Revista Envío* 90, Diciembre. https://www.envio.org.ni/articulo/580 [Accessed 18 October 2022].

Fischer, K. (2015) The influence of neoliberals in Chile before, during, and after Pinochet. In Mirowski, P. & Plehwe, D. (eds.), *The road from Mont Pèlerin. The making of the neoliberal thought collective*, 2nd ed. Cambridge, MA and London, Harvard University Press, pp. 305–346.

Hall, S. (1979) The great moving right show. In Davison, S., Featherstone, D., Rustin, M., & Schwarz, B. (eds.), *The great moving right show and other essays*. Durham, Duke University Press, pp. 172–186.

Hepple, L. W. (2011) Lewis Tambs, Latin American geopolitics and the American new right. *School of Geographical Sciences, University of Bristol*. http://www.bristol.ac.uk/media-library/sites/geography/migrated/documents/lewis.pdf [Accessed 18 October 2022].

Keely, T. (2015) Medellín is 'fantastic': Drafts of the 1969 Rockefeller Report on the catholic church. *The Catholic Historical Review* 101 (4), pp. 809–834.

Madariaga, A. (2020) *Neoliberal resilience: Lessons in democracy and development from Latin America and Eastern Europe*. Princeton, Princeton University Press.

Mirowski, P., & Plehwe, D. (eds.) (2015) *The road from Mont Pèlerin. The making of the neoliberal thought collective*, 2nd ed. Cambridge, MA and London, Harvard University Press.

Slobodian, Q. (2018) *Globalists. The end of empire and the birth of neoliberalism*. Cambridge, MA, Harvard University Press.

Weld, K. (2020) Holy war: Latin America's far right. *Dissent Magazine*, Spring. https://www.dissentmagazine.org/article/holy-war-latin-americas-far-right [Accessed 18 October 2022].

INTRODUCTION

The right in the Americas

Julián Castro-Rea and Esther Solano

Paraphrasing the introductory phrase of Karl Marx's *Communist Manifesto*: "A spectre is haunting the Americas—the spectre of the right". While Donald Trump's tenure as President of the United States (January 2017–January 2021) and its aftermath were the most visible expressions of this trend—in particular in the English-speaking world—many countries in the Western Hemisphere have recently trod a similar path. From Argentina to Chile, from Peru to Brazil, democratically elected governments rolled back the so-called "Pink Tide" of left-leaning governments that swept the region by the turn of the twenty-first century.

Why did it happen? How is it at all possible that governments that upheld the needs and priorities of popular sectors were overturned largely because those very popular sectors turned their back on them? Why did the populace choose political options that would inevitably implement—some of them beyond the first time—policies that are detrimental to the interests of the majorities? How do these political options manage to present themselves as a credible alternative, as a new hope for the citizens? Which repertoires, propaganda, narratives, symbolic and rhetoric mechanisms do they use for this purpose? These are some of the questions that will drive this book, and will be answered by understanding the sources of right-wing movements and the causes of their recent success.

Moreover, this book acknowledges that right-wing movements, parties, leaders, and thinkers in any given country do not act and prosper in isolation from each other; they rather identify one another, even across borders, exchange ideas and strategy, and overall cooperate for the better achievement of their goals.

The growth of the right is, we are convinced, one of the most important issues of the moment in global politics. While in this respect the European experience has been extensively studied, comparatively few works have gathered a broad reflection on the right in Latin America, and even less on the Americas as a whole.

DOI: 10.4324/9781003352266-1

Among these works we can highlight the following, in the order when they were published:

Conservative Parties, the Right, and Democracy in Latin America, edited by Kevin J. Middlebrook (2000), explores the conditions under which political institutions are capable of promoting economic and social elites' accommodation to democracy. Alliances between upper-class groups and the armed forces have historically been a major cause of military intervention in Latin America, therefore disrupting democracy, while countries with electorally viable national conservative parties have experienced significantly longer periods of democratic governance since the 1920s. The contributors to Middlebrook's book examine the relationship between the right and democracy in Argentina, Brazil, Chile, Colombia, El Salvador, Peru, and Venezuela during the 1980s and 1990s. The authors focus particularly on the challenges that democratisation may pose to upper-class groups; the political role of conservative parties and their electoral performance during these two crucial decades; and the relationships among conservative party strength or weakness, different modes of elite interest representation, and economic and social elites' support for political democracy.

Patricia Swier and Julia Riordan-Gonçalves, in their volume *Dictatorships in the Hispanic World: Transatlantic and Transnational Perspectives* (2013), study dictatorships in the Spanish-speaking countries in the twentieth century from a comparative and interdisciplinary approach. Some of the themes, explored through a transatlantic perspective, include testimonial accounts of violence and resistance in prisons; hunger and repression; exile, silence, and intertextuality; the modification of gender roles; and the role of trauma and memory within the genres of the novel, autobiography, testimonial literature, the essay, documentaries, puppet theatre, poetry, and visual art. By looking at the similarities and differences of dictatorships represented in the diverse landscapes of Latin America and Spain, the authors provide a panoramic view of the dictatorship that moves beyond historiographical accounts of oppression and engages actively in a more broad dialectics of resistance and a politics of memory.

Juan Pablo Luna and Cristóbal Rovira Kaltwasser, in their edited volume *The Resilience of the Latin American Right* (2014), comparatively explore the reasons why the right in Latin America managed to not only survive but remain influential during the "Pink Tide" period. In a context of pronounced social inequality, which plays against the right's restrictive view of equality, the Latin American right resorted to three strategies in order to keep politically relevant: (1) interest representation through non-electoral means, (2) creating electoral movements with no partisan appearance, and (3) party building. They seem to agree with Middlebrook (2000), in the sense that reliable right-wing political channels for representation of elite interests are necessary for the survival of democracy in the region.

In a similar note, Barry Cannon's *The Right in Latin America: Elite Power, Hegemony and the Struggle for the State* (2016) explains the discursive, policy and strategic responses employed by the right in response to the rise of the left in Latin America at the turn of the twenty-first century. This response not only plays at the time of elections, but it is also present at the social and cultural levels; taking advantage of the right's supporters' deep economic, political, social, cultural, and international influence.

Mike González, in his book *The Ebb of the Pink Tide. The Decline of the Left in Latin America* (2019), discusses the setbacks that the Latin American leftist governments have suffered, thus opening the gate to "reactionary challenges". He identifies the problems that the left has confronted in the region, and its weaknesses, wondering if the 'Pink Tide' is on the wane.

A historical analysis of the issue is offered in *Latin American Dictatorships in the Era of Fascism: The Corporatist Wave*, by António Costa-Pinto (2019). The author focuses on the wave of dictatorships that emerged in Latin America during the 1930s and the transnational dissemination of authoritarian institutions in the era of fascism. Costa-Pinto revisits the study of authoritarian alternatives to liberal democracy in 1930s Latin America from the perspective of the diffusion of corporatism in the world of interwar dictatorships. He explores what drove the horizontal spread of corporatism in Latin America, the processes and direction of transnational diffusion, and how social and political corporatism became a central set of new institutions utilised by dictatorships during this era. These issues are studied through a transnational and comparative research design to reveal the extent of Latin America's participation during the corporatist wave which by 1942 had significantly reduced the number of democratic regimes in the world.

In his *Conservative Party-Building in Latin America: Authoritarian Inheritance and Counterrevolutionary Struggle* (2021), James Loxton explores the origins of conservative parties in Latin America by examining new parties formed between 1978 and 2010. The most successful cases, he finds, shared a surprising characteristic: they had deep roots in former dictatorships. Through a comparative analysis of failed and successful cases in Argentina, Chile, El Salvador, and Guatemala, Loxton argues that this was not a coincidence. Successful parties inherited a range of resources from outgoing authoritarian regimes that, paradoxically, gave them an advantage in democratic competition. The author also highlights the role of intense counterrevolutionary struggle as a source of party cohesion. In addition to making an empirical contribution to the study of the Latin American right and a theoretical contribution to the study of party-building, Loxton advances our understanding of the worldwide phenomenon of "authoritarian successor parties"—parties that emerge from authoritarian regimes, but that operate after a transition to democracy.

More recently, *The Right and Radical Right in the Americas: Ideological Currents from Interwar Canada to Contemporary Chile*, edited by Tamir Bar-On and Bàrbara Molas (2022), examines the history and contemporary manifestations of the right and radical right throughout the Americas. The right and radical right have come in diverse ideological currents, which have undergone historical changes. Their strategies need to be contextualised in respect to the country and region.[1]

The book that the reader has in her hands, in turn, aims at making four main contributions beyond previous works: (1) understanding current right-wing politics from a Hemispheric point of view, that is, considering the interaction among right-wing movements and organisations across national borders in all countries in the Americas (including Canada and the United States); (2) studying comparatively ten national specific cases from North, Central, and South America; (3) joining theoretical analysis with empirical research on the right, and (4) gathering together established academics from different countries and scientific disciplines who are working on the study of the right in the Americas.

We need to make clear here our understanding of the concepts of conservatism and the political right. These concepts, even if they have a long pedigree, have recently been contested as being useless. Parties in modern democracies, the argument goes, have an interest in presenting themselves to the electorate as non-ideological, moderate, inspired by the common good (and common sense) alone when defining their platforms and their resulting public policies. As a result, parties tend to migrate away from the edges to the centre of the political spectrum and fight for it, becoming "catch-all parties", thus making the classic right–left distinction increasingly irrelevant.

Some specific authors have also contested the usefulness of the left–right distinction, elaborating on the alleged "end of ideologies" at the end of the Cold War. From a liberal perspective, Francis Fukuyama argues that there is no alternative left to neoliberalism; because socialism, its main adversary, collapsed and disappeared as a credible option (Fukuyama, 1993). A different version of the "end of ideologies" argument is offered by Anthony Giddens, who believes that the distinction between left and right is meaningless because it is possible and even necessary to follow a "third way" of politics that promotes progressive solutions to social dilemmas while at the same time accepts the prevailing economic structures (Giddens, 1994).

This book adopts a wholly different position. We believe, and will attempt to demonstrate in each national case considered, that the terms "conservative", "right", and "left" are still extremely relevant as general indications of what a political party or movement stands for. Even if each particular political group or actor displays a unique blend of ideological features, it is still possible, and quite useful, for political analysis, to determine if a given group or actor is essentially conservative or not, if it leans to the right or to the left. Of course, in order to make this claim credible, a discussion of the deep meaning of these concepts is in order, showing how they can be useful as heuristic tools to make sense of current political realities.

Let's start with conservatism. At a very general, intuitive level, conservatism means a disposition to conserve. It is a mental syndrome that leads people to accept social realities as they are, be it because they seem unchangeable to them, because the observer feels powerless to affect them, or simply because they look okay overall from the observer's standpoint.

It is easy to understand that many societies and political orders in the past actively encouraged a conservative outlook among their members; so being conservative was not really a choice for, say, a peasant in the European Middle Ages. Therefore, true conservatism exists only where people have a choice to believe or not that social and political realities deserve to be changed and that change can actually be operated.

Conservatism is thus a modern concept, which truly entered the vocabulary of politics and political science in the nineteenth century. The term itself was invented originally in French (*conservateur*), to refer to those philosophers and politicians who fought to preserve the old institutions, the heritage of civilisation and the values of natural justice against the onslaught of the Revolution: Guizot, Chateaubriand, Bonald, de Maistre. Conservatism was then naturally associated with the defenders of the rights and privileges of monarchy and aristocracy within the French National Assembly before and after the Revolution. However, all those thinkers had something in common: they had been influenced by Irish eighteenth-century political thinker Edmund Burke, who can perhaps be considered the father of modern conservatism. This is maybe ironic, since Burke himself disliked the term, preferring to declare himself a defender of *preservation*, which would make him a "preservative" instead!

In our view, the word that better encapsulates the essence of conservative thought is *pessimism*. Indeed, conservatives are pessimistic about human nature: they see people as intrinsically selfish and potentially evil, thus in need to be restrained if the social order is to be preserved. They also distrust human ability to understand the world's physical and social realities—a distrust that is often guided by a religious belief in an omniscient supreme being. From this perspective, any human attempt at guiding ill-understood social or natural processes is ludicrous at best, when not plainly dangerous and even blasphemous. The wisest way of action according to this view is to yield to what is and exists, assuming there are compelling reasons for that even if they are not fully understood by the limited human mind. Within that overview, a good leader will acknowledge the limited ability we all have for modifying reality, and guide people along the received institutions and traditions from the past.

To make this point clearer, we can call Thomas Hobbes to our help. For Hobbes, human beings in the state of nature would fight with each other to death in order to make their selfish goals prevail (Hobbes, 1651). The institution of the state is therefore justified as a necessary condition to avoid this constant fighting, in order to impose by force some basic rules of peace and coexistence. The state must be dreaded rather than loved by the populace, as it is the surest way of making its laws being respected. Therefore, we would argue, Hobbes is the modern intellectual whose ideas lay at the heart of present-day conservatism.

There is another basic feature of conservative thought: its idea about the meaning of equality. As a reflection of their worldview, for conservatives inequality is but another aspect of the natural order of things, something that cannot and should not be modified. From the conservative standpoint, it is preferable to take advantage of existing inequalities to encourage competition that will reward the more deserving among us, thanks to our effort and merit. Competition among individuals is for conservatives the engine of social progress.[2] Institutions, starting with the state, must then protect the space for competition to flourish, while refraining from any attempt at intervening in favour of any individual or social group.

Perhaps an example may better illustrate this point. As Alain Noël and Jean-Philippe Thérien suggest (Noël and Thérien, 2008: pp. 18–19), the debate over affirmative action is quite telling about the conservative views on equality, and how they may collide with the rest. For conservatives, affirmative action is outrageous because it gives advantage to some people and groups over the rest of society, when it comes to hiring or targeting who will benefit from specific government programs. Conservatives do not buy the argument that some people— for example, women, racialised minorities, people with disabilities—have been systematically disadvantaged, thus deserving a little head start in order to have access to opportunities for meaningful advancement. Not only is this advantage unfair, conservatives would say, but it is also dangerous to the extent that it may create distortions in the labour market, public spending, and general equilibrium of society at large. Conservatives do not necessarily oppose equality, but they would rather support an equality based on merit and deservedness, as opposed to entitlement and substantive results.

It is also necessary to differentiate between the two main variants of conservatism: fiscal and social. Fiscal conservatism refers specifically to a preference for limited taxation and state activism, particularly in the economy; which in practice translates into a fondness for market solutions to all governance needs. A fiscal conservative will have a tendency to believe that state-run programs or entities are intrinsically wrong, although they might sometimes be a necessary evil. This is because private enterprise is, according to them, the natural, more efficient way of managing anything, to the extent that it is based on the values all conservatives cherish: individualism, self-sufficiency, competition, selective rewards for effort, etc.

In sum, fiscal conservatism refers to conservatism as applied to the realm of economics. Social conservatism, in turn, means an adherence to traditional values for coexistence in civil society such as religion, family, and nation. Social conservatives thus reject everything that they believe may challenge those values; such as atheism, homosexuality, gay rights, secularism, abortion, immigration, and its impacts on the demographic makeup of a society, use of minority languages, etc.

How about the concept of right? Once again, the word and the idea are French in their origins (*droite*). They come from the physical arrangement of the first National Assembly, created in June 1789—that is, at the outset of the Revolution— to jointly represent the interests of the Crown, landed nobility, the Church, and the common people. After the first meetings, a pattern emerged spontaneously within the room where the Assembly gathered: partisans of the privileges of nobility and royal institutions migrated to the right of the hall, while partisans of equality and reforms sat on the left (Noël and Thérien, 2008: p. 14). These literal, spatial metaphors soon acquired political meaning, and have ever since been employed to classify parties, individuals, and movements.

"Right" has become ever since a term to both position a political actor relative to another one, and qualify the intensity of a conservative conviction. Indeed, once the transition from monarchy to republic was completed in France, the right became synonymous with politicians and thinkers in favour of the re-establishment of monarchic institutions, the status quo, or even moderate change. However, during the 1890s, socialism emerged as a legitimate political option and occupied the left of the political spectrum. All other republicans, moderate or not, were pushed to the right. This period was also the beginning of the extended use of the right–left dichotomy in other countries, gradually acquiring common currency through the twentieth century.

Interestingly, the right took advantage of the accidental distribution of political factions in the first Assembly to exploit the semantic connotations existing in more than one language. In English, what is "right" is also what is true and correct. In French, *droit* means straightforward (i.e. not twisted, phoney) as well as being synonymous with law. In Spanish, *derecho* is also another word for law, and it equally means straight, frank, and honest. Next time you go to Mexico, order your liquor at the bar *derecho*, and you will get an unaltered, not-mixed-with-anything dose of your favourite spirit.

In contrast, the word "left" has much less favourable implications. The Latin word *sinistra* originally meant "left" (still used in Italian with the same meaning) but took on meanings of "evil" or "unlucky" during the classical Latin era. This double meaning survives in European derivatives of Latin, and in the English word "sinister". Moreover, in English, left is what remains, what is expendable (as in "leftovers"). In French, being *gauche* means being clumsy, awkward, even inappropriate—a meaning that is matched by the Spanish expression *tener dos manos izquierdas* (to have two left hands). Readers who are proficient in other languages may perhaps confirm that similar positive connotations exist for the word "right" and negative implications for "left" in different linguistic traditions.[3]

In order to avoid the trap of relativism when defining the right—that is, we know what it is only in reference to something else, as in the original spatial metaphor in the National Assembly—Noël and Thérien built on D. D. Raphael's distinction of common contrasting ideas of distributive justice: one that stresses merit and deservingness, another insisting on equal worth and needs. This is the basic distinction between the right and the left: even if both ideological syndromes declare their support to the idea of equality, whereas the right understands the term as the opportunity given to each individual to prove her value and reap the benefits of her salience, the left sees equality as the substantive result of social interaction, which every human being has the right to enjoy. We see right up the convergence of conservatism and the right, with similar notions about the meaning of equality.

This way, a right-wing individual aiming for equality will insist that the institutions provide an even playing field where people can compete, and display their abilities (intelligence, hard work, scholarly background, etc.) to achieve success.

The resulting differences will only be natural, rewarding some people over the rest for their achievements. A left-wing person, in contrast, perceives society as so mired with structural obstacles for fair competition to ever occur; therefore she will only see equality where there is an attempt to evening out the end results (redistributive programs, progressive taxation, affirmative action, etc.).

This definition makes already apparent the compatibility between conservatism and a right-wing mentality. As explained, conservatives see differences among human beings as not only natural but desirable; they will thus embrace the right-wing appreciation for competition and reward to effort. There is a clear correspondence between the conservative and right-wing visions of society and human nature.

Finally, we must acknowledge that the right comes in very different historical packages, rather than a single version of it, even within a single country. While this distinction makes sense from a historical perspective, comparative political science requires a unified definition that "travels well" from one case to the next one. We decided to respect this methodological and disciplinary difference in the chapters herein contained, in order to preserve the diversity of perspectives in this regard.

To conclude the exploration of relevant concepts, we must also address a term that is often used in studies of conservatism and the right: populism. Populism consists in the artificial division of society into two distinct categories: the people and the elite (Derks, 2006). The people are that section of the population who rightfully belong to the nation, who therefore should be the ones who steer the boat of government, the economy, and society. The elite is all the rest, both the individuals who actually lead the state and those who are complicit with them either because they benefit from that concentration of power or because they are deluded. Populism offers to take back the power from the elite and put it back in the hands of the people, usually under the guidance of a charismatic leader who is able to read and implement "the people's will".

Populism is not an ideology; it is a political tool that can be used by any political ideology, left or right, conservative or progressive. Of course, it all depends on how the categories of people and elite are defined. Left-wing populism would define them in socioeconomic terms, stressing the concentration of wealth and power in the hands of a few, to the detriment of the working masses. Right-wing populism, in turn, would define the categories in nationalist (cultural or ethnic) terms, according to which the people are those who were born in the state's territory, speak the majority language, and belong to the predominant ethnic group. The elite would thus be the politicians and bureaucrats who stand in the way of the direct exercise of power by the majoritarian group, and those who benefit from their control and decisions: immigrants with diverse cultural backgrounds, poor people enjoying government support, academics who justify this state of things, etc.

This way, populism has become a useful tool in the hands of the right, which can thus divert attention from its defence of socioeconomic inequality to the vindication of the "authentic citizen", splitting class solidarity in the process and attracting votes from the masses.

Hoping that our basic concepts are properly explained by now, we move on to explore the reasons why conservatism and the right have become popular political options recently. Several authors are studying present-day democratic decline or even regression (Brown, 2019; Przeworski, 2019)). Post-democracy, illiberal democracy, and de-democratisation are some of the concepts used to define a procedural, formal, or electoral democracy where representative institutions fulfil the election ritual but are totally captured by a neoliberal rationality with predatory and violent characteristics that leads to unequal societies, where rights and liberties are undermined. Strong economic crises, new sociability structures, globalisation dynamics, politics in the internet, all these elements make more evident for citizens the growing "democratic charade". Most traditional left parties or social democracies are not capable of responding to the social anxiety and anguish so present in our societies (Worth, 2013). New right-wing or even extreme-right parties, with authoritarian tendencies presenting themselves as anti-system, outsiders, or anti-mainstream, manage to address this social anger and frustration (Vlandas and Halikiopoulou, 2019).

Within this context of democracy erosion and rejection of traditional politics, right and extreme-right actors are capable of misguidedly offer answers and hope to a significant part of a country's population, who will trust their promises and bring them to power with their vote. This dynamics repeats itself in an astonishingly consistent pattern across the Americas.

Besides, the comparative analysis that this book shows a series of other regularities across country cases, namely:

(a) Conservative and right-wing ideologies and political organisations in the Americas have a long pedigree. They appeared from the moment each country achieved independence, usually during the nineteenth century, often including in their program a reactionary element (return to the old regime) plus an element of social reorganisation guided by conservative and right-wing principles.
(b) The core social support to conservative and right-wing actors is a country's elite and other privileged sectors; including, but not limited to, large business and landowners, churches, some sections of the middle classes, and the military brass.
(c) Conservative and right-wing actors are generally wary of democracy, to the extent that their limited popular appeal makes them struggle to gather enough votes to be elected. Therefore, they prefer some kind of oligarchy, censitary democracy, or outright authoritarian regimes that guarantee the defence of their interests and principles, by force if necessary.
(d) Economic and social inequalities increased under right-wing governments throughout the twentieth century.
(e) Democratic transitions experienced in most Latin American countries by the end of the twentieth century offered a new opportunity to the right to be

electorally competitive, thanks to the adoption of neoliberalism as a novel guide for public policy.
(f) Over time, however, negative impacts of neoliberalism temporarily shut down right-wing actors from power. They nonetheless managed to survive thanks to non-partisan interest representation, party building, and the support of international networks of solidarity and civil society organisations with ideological affinity.
(g) Right-wing actors were able to return to power thanks to the crafty use of post-ideological, pseudo democratic, and populist strategies, thus creating a competitive right-wing movement adapted to the realities of the twenty-first century.

Contents of this book

This volume deals with ten distinct case studies corresponding to as many sovereign countries in the Americas. They are the following, in alphabetical order: Argentina, Brazil, Canada, Chile, Colombia, Honduras, Mexico, the United States, Uruguay, and Venezuela. Chapters have been authored or co-authored by a total of 18 scholars, most of them with several years of experience in academia, affiliated to recognised institutions from different locations in the Americas and Europe, trained in social science disciplines such as history, sociology, and political science. We are convinced that this collection provides a rich source of information, a sound reference about each specific country and a wide array of perspectives on the development of conservatism and the right in the Americas.

There are no common methodological or epistemological criteria followed by the contributors to this book. Most authors decided to explore the origins of conservatism in the country they deal with, reaching back to the nineteenth century, but in some cases (Brazil, Chile, and Venezuela) the focus is on the short term. The information to support the analysis was drawn from historical sources, statistical databases, discourse analysis, and interviews. This is so because, given the complexity of the phenomenon under study and its multi-causal nature, we relied on the expertise of each specialist to account for the main axes to understand each case study, from a group of common concerns and topics.

The analysis is launched with a discussion on the Americas as right-wing transnational space. Julián Castro-Rea and Kyle Beattie show how the United States not only is the country in the Americas where the political right and conservatism have developed superior strength and diversity, but is also the hub of propagation of right-wing ideas throughout the hemisphere and of support to movements that embody them. This trend achieved its pinnacle during Donald J. Trump's presidency (2017–2021). The chapter first presents a cultural and historical overview, as a background to explain why the United States provided such a fertile ground for the growth of right-wing and conservative ideas and movements; before exploring their projection to the rest of the Americas on the back of money, foreign policy, military interventions, soft power, and overall organisational support.

The following six chapters explore the genesis and development of right-wing actors in selected countries. In their chapter about Argentina, Ernesto Bohoslavsky and Sergio Daniel Morresi explain how for decades Argentina lacked a stable and autonomous political right, able to play by the rules of democracy. The absence of a politically competitive right-wing party during most of the twentieth century has been identified as the source of Argentina's traditional political challenges: coups d'état, lack of élite commitment with democracy, and little or no capacity to process social conflicts via republican institutions.

The authors detail how economic and cultural élites in that country, even if internally fragmented, nonetheless systematically identified themselves with a peculiar blend of liberal-conservative tradition that rejected social, political or cultural inclusion of popular sectors, embracing a hierarchical order, in tense coexistence with democratic principles as their structuring axis. Liberal-conservatives did not hesitate to resort to undemocratic and illiberal practices to maintain their privileges, occasionally even collaborating with their right-wing rivals: Catholic nationalists (culturally reactionary, politically authoritarian, and economically against free markets and favouring a strong state). However, by the end of the twentieth century the élites learned to coexist within the liberal democratic framework. Their disruptive potential was thus limited, allowing the growth of right-wing political movements with more independent agendas and enhanced electoral appeal.

Frédéric Boily examines the Canadian right from three angles: firstly, its long history, secondly, its qualitative transformation during the 1980s, and thirdly, its regional diversity. An exploration of its roots shows that the Canadian right by the end of the nineteenth century radically differs from its expression by the 1980s, when a neoliberal fashion led it in a different direction. This turn is more clearly seen in Western Canada, especially in Alberta, but it can also be observed in other provinces such as Ontario. In Québec, meanwhile, the right shares some affinities with its counterparts in other provinces, but it remains state-focused and determined to defend Québec's cultural singularity.

Laura Camila Ramírez Bonilla provides key elements to analyse the origins and transformations of the right in Colombia from a historical perspective. She offers historical context, and explains sources and tensions that have shaped the power struggle within this ideological syndrome; from the creation of the Colombian Conservative Party (*Partido Conservador Colombiano*) by the mid-nineteenth century until the electoral triumph of the Democratic Centre Party (*Partido Centro Democrático*) by the first decades of the twenty-first century. Ramírez Bonilla provides a panoramic view, which highlights the diversity, internal fractures, complex alliances, and confrontations within Colombia's right-wing movement. This chapter argues that conservatism, both as a value system and as a partisan option, and the Catholic religion, as a belief system and network of socio-cultural institutions, are constant elements of the Colombian right. This does not mean that these elements are static components, always seeking the same objectives. It rather means that the conservative and religious roots, planted since the nineteenth century, have produced varied identities, contrasting political agendas, and different results.

Analysing the case of Honduras, Gustavo Zelaya Herrera shows the impact of liberal and Enlightenment ideas in the worldview of historical figures in that country. Eventually split between conservative and liberal, the differences among these figures are not so much due to ideological matters but to the way those ideas were translated into public policy. Later on, they added positivist principles as another utilitarian element to their political theory and practice. This fusion of Enlightenment, liberalism, and positivism was predominant during the nineteenth century. Starting the following century, steps towards the creation of the first Honduran political parties, the Liberal and the National parties, were taken. Since 1980, both organisations seem to embrace neoliberalism. In practice, however, they steer away from this ideological syndrome; because when they are in power the state, construction, services and procurement contracts, tax exemptions, etc. become a bounty for economic and political clienteles.

In his chapter, Mario Virgilio Santiago Jiménez describes the development of the right in Mexico from the end of the 1910–1917 revolution and the year 2020. He identifies the existence of three ideological families that have shaped a spectrum: the Catholic, the liberal conservative, and the neoliberal. Although these families have practically coexisted during the entire period covered in this chapter, each one has occupied a predominant place at different historical periods: the post-revolution (1920–1945), revolutionary nationalism (1946–1975), and the neoliberal consensus (1975–2015). Finally, it is suggested that, although a left-wing coalition is now governing Mexico, the three right-wing families are still alive and well in Mexican political culture.

The chapter dealing with Uruguay, written by Gerardo Caetano, identifies historical moments of development of the right in that country. They span from the original anti-Jacobin ideologies in the nineteenth century, the re-emergence of an extreme right with militaristic components, until the recent creation of the *Cabildo Abierto* (Open City Council) party, a "black swan" in current Uruguayan politics reviving the old "liberal conservatism" of the right in that country. This chapter seeks to identify the historical dimension and the scope of this new actor in Uruguayan politics, evaluating the reasons for its emergence and the uncertainty about its future.

The last three case studies deal with contemporary expressions of the right in the Americas. Camila Rocha, Esther Solano, and Jonas Medeiros show how Brazil's New Right activism had flooded the streets and the social networks years before Jair Bolsonaro's ascension to the presidency in January 2019. This process promoted the emergence of new leadership and new forms of expression and organisation, as well as new ideas that started circulating with great strength in the Brazilian public sphere, inspired by libertarianism and condemnation of an alleged "left-wing cultural hegemony" within the country. As a background, the authors describe the activities of Brazil's right-wing in previous decades, assessing its links with the recent New Right. They also explain how, in the midst of political transformations occurring in the country, a new constellation of actors and ideas was formed, which over time largely contributed to the political turn to the right that Brazil experienced and the subsequent ascent of Jair Bolsonaro to power.

Stéphanie Alenda, Carmen Le Foulon, and Julieta Suárez-Cao explore how intellectual traditions and ideological influences after 1973 helped shape the contemporary Chilean right. These influences are manifested in three distinct political families: a subsidiary right, heir of the liberal-Catholic tradition, a libertarian orthodox right, revamped during the 1973–1990 military dictatorship, and a solidary right, related to the social-Christian lineage. Based on a survey applied to almost 700 right-wing party cadres, the authors of this chapter built categories of right-wing elites along the state-market axis. They demonstrate that the subsidiary approach keeps predominating among right-wing party leaderships. Differences are more apparent along the sociocultural axis than along state-market differences. Beyond political values, party allegiance also shows significant results. *Evópoli*, Chile's new centre-right organisation, displays more progressive sociocultural values than other parties on the right. Finally, the authors reveal that within the coalition between new and conventional parties on the right—denominated *Chile Vamos*—there is disagreement between a core group displaying pro-market and conservative moral values, and a heterodox cluster of members supporting state-centred and morally liberal positions.

Ybiskay Gonzalez and Barry Cannon demonstrate how right-wing groups in Venezuela have made use of the democracy/authoritarianism dichotomy in their discourse against "Chavista" governments in order to broaden their coalition and polarise the country, while at the same time hiding their neoliberal and conservative distinctive features. Their empirical information is drawn from discourse analysis of texts found in public documents and interviews with major political figures of the opposition. The authors' analysis considers discourse as an articulating practice within a system of meaning, which depends on and is specific to each society and its struggles for hegemonic control. This chapter also highlights the heterogeneity of right-wing groups in Venezuela, building from a historical review that includes the origins of "Chavista" governments, the opposition and its tactics against the government, as well as antagonistic relations between these two factions.

Acknowledgements

We owe a heartfelt recognition to the authors of this book's chapters who, despite the long wait and difficult times that the trying coronavirus pandemic brought upon us, have done an excellent, professional job. The translators and proof-readers Kyle Beattie and Daniel Tranter-Santoso helped us so much in a timely and efficient manner. This is a collective project that without the enthusiasm of each and every one of the contributors would not have seen the light. We are proud to submit here to the readers the final result of this arduous joint collaboration.

Notes

1 Besides these works published in English, we were also able to identify a number of titles dealing with the topic published in other languages: Torrico (2017), Traverso (2017), Forti (2021), Stefanoni (2021), and Torrico (2021). However, these works either address the rise of the global right in general or in Latin America alone. None of them adopts the hemispheric approach that we do in this volume.
2 As one conservative character in the feature movie *No* put it: "People must believe that anyone may become rich in a society. Please note: anyone, not everyone. And when every individual wants to be that anyone, things go well" (Larrain, 2013).
3 In Russian, the adjectives правый or правильный both mean correct or right. The corresponding noun is право, law, the verb is править, to rule or to correct. All these words have the same root: прав, the rules, associated with правда, the truth. In contrast, the left is левый. Besides its spatial meaning, the word also means "unlawful or illegal". For instance "to go to the left" (ходить на лево) is a colloquial way of saying "to have sex outside of the marriage"! In Persian, right (درست) means proper, true, correct, appropriate and good. The associated word راست means right, straight. Left (چپ), in contrast, can be translated as negative manners and thoughts. If someone is cranky in Iran, she or he gets up from the left rib; if a wife is not nice to her partner she has fallen to the left with him. If someone gives you a dirty look they look at you left! My sincere thanks to Alina Tousseeva and Heidi Zahiri for having shared these linguistic and idiomatic remarks with me.

References

Bar-On, T., & Molas, B. (eds.) (2022) *The right and radical right in the Americas: Ideological currents from Interwar Canada to contemporary Chile*. Lanham, Lexington Books.

Brown W., (2019) *In the ruins of neoliberalism. The rise of antidemocratic politics in the west*. New York, Columbia University Press.

Cannon, B. (2016) *The right in Latin America: Elite power, hegemony and the struggle for the state*. New York, Routledge.

Costa-Pinto, A. (2019) *Latin American dictatorships in the era of fascism: The corporatist wave*. Abingdon and New York, Routledge.

Derks, A. (2006) Populism and the ambivalence of egalitarianism. How do the underprivileged reconcile a right wing party preference with their socio-economic attitudes? *World Political Science Review* 2 (3), 175–200.

Forti, S. (2021) *Extrema derecha 2.0. Qué es y cómo combatirla*. Madrid, Siglo XXI.

Fukuyama, F. (1993) *The end of history and the last man*. New York, Avon Books.

Giddens, A. (1994) *Beyond left and right: The future of radical politics*. Stanford, Stanford University Press.

González, M. (2019) *The ebb of the pink tide. The decline of the left in Latin America*. London, Pluto.

Hobbes, T. (1651) *Leviathan: Or the matter, forme, of a common-wealth ecclesiastical and civil*. New Haven, Yale University Press (2010 ed.).

Larrain, P. (2013) *No* (Feature Movie), Sony Pictures.

Loxton, J. (2021) *Conservative party-building in Latin America: Authoritarian inheritance and counterrevolutionary struggle*. New York, Oxford University Press.

Luna, J. P., & Kaltwasser, C. R. (eds.) (2014) *The resilience of the Latin American right*. Baltimore, Johns Hopkins University Press.

Middlebrook, K. J. (ed.) (2000) *Conservative parties, the right, and democracy in Latin America*. Baltimore, Johns Hopkins University Press.

Noël, A., & Thérien J.-P., (2008) *Left and right in global politics*. Cambridge, Cambridge University Press.
Przeworski, A. (2019) *Crises of democracy*. Cambridge, Cambridge University Press.
Stefanoni, P. (2021) *¿La rebeldía se volvió de derecha? Cómo el antiprogresismo y la anticorrección política están construyendo un nuevo sentido común (y por qué la izquierda debería tomarlos en serio)*. Buenos Aires, Siglo XXI.
Swier, P., & Riordan-Gonçalves J., (2013) *Dictatorships in the hispanic world: Transatlantic and transnational perspectives*. Madison, Fairleigh Dickinson University Press.
Torrico, M. (ed.) (2017) *¿Fin del giro a la izquierda? Gobiernos y políticas públicas*. Mexico City, FLACSO.
Torrico, M. (2021) *Giro a la derecha. Un nuevo ciclo político en América Latina*. Mexico City, FLACSO.
Traverso, E. (2017) *Les nouveaux visages du fascisme*. Paris, Textuel.
Vlandas, T., & Halikiopoulou D., (2019) Does unemployment matter? Economic insecurity, labour market policies and the far-right vote in Europe. European Political Science 18, 421–438.
Worth, O. (2013) *Resistance in the age of austerity. Nationalism, the failure of the left and the return of god*. Halifax, Fernwood.

PART I

The Americas as right-wing transnational space

1
UNITED STATES

The Mecca of conservatism in the Americas and its international projection

Julián Castro-Rea and Kyle Beattie

Introduction

This chapter will attempt to demonstrate that the United States not only is the country in the Americas where the political right and conservatism have developed superior strength and diversity but is also the hub of propagation throughout the hemisphere of right-wing ideas and support to movements that embody them. This trend achieved its pinnacle during Donald J. Trump's presidency (2017–2021). The chapter will first present a cultural and historical overview, as background to explain why the United States provided such a fertile ground for the growth of right-wing and conservative ideas, before exploring their projection to the rest of the Americas on the back of money, foreign policy, military interventions, soft power, and overall organisational support.

Political culture in the United States

The most distinctive feature of political culture in the America is *exceptionalism*, that is to say, the perception shared by the vast majority of citizens that their country is unique and superior to the rest of nations around the world. A series of important consequences for public awareness and behaviour result from this core feature, which have remained historically constant: exacerbated nationalism, messianism, conviction of moral superiority, racism, xenophobia, voluntarism, militarism, and constitutional fundamentalism.

In a study entitled *Fascism. Why Not Here?* Brian E. Fogarty (2009) develops the thesis that the observer can identify in the collective psyche of the United States a series of features similar to the prevailing state of mind of Germans at the time of Hitler's rise to power: romanticism, nationalism, populism, racism, and authoritarianism.[1]

DOI: 10.4324/9781003352266-3

However, Fogarty's thesis, certainly provocative yet impeccably argued and supported with solid evidence, is hardly groundbreaking. During the US Constitutional debates of the 1780s, the lesser-known writers of the anti-Federalist papers argued that the US Constitution as it was written would lead the United States towards a military empire (Philadelphiensis, 1788). Since 1935 US writer Sinclair Lewis, in his novel *It Can Happen Here*, had already highlighted some deep features of his country's political culture, arguing that a fascist regime was not a remote possibility. Closer to us, Philip Roth's novel *The Plot against America* (2004) and Joe Conason's essay *It Can Happen Here: Authoritarian Peril in the Age of Bush* (2007) develop a similar argument. Few analysts took those warnings seriously, until Trump brought the discussion about developing fascism in the United States a disturbing possibility.

Another permanent feature of US political culture on both the left and the right is love for conspiracies, something that Richard J. Hofstadter (1964) called a "paranoid style" of doing politics. This means that political events, especially whenever they are major or catastrophic, are often attributed to vested interests acting in secret coordination. Unrelated events or facts are linked into a grand narrative that "exposes" the true intentions of conspiracy's masterminds. While conspiracies reflect the human tendency to find patterns in scattered events in order to make better sense of them (Brotherton, 2015), conspiracies are recurrent in US public discourse, becoming even more pronounced as of late among President Trump's followers because the president himself is also fond of the "paranoid style" (Muirhead and Rosenblum, 2019).

Historical background: Conservative origins of the United States and subsequent developments

Trump's election as president of the United States in November 2016 surprised many political analysts and political scientists. Because of Trump's controversial personality and extreme views on several policy issues, the overwhelming majority of the social sciences community reacted with surprise and incredulity when the election results were announced, attributing the victory mostly to an accident, that is, the unintentional aggregation of an uncalculated protest vote. Moreover, the Trump phenomenon was brushed aside as something temporary, as it was claimed that citizens in that country would soon realise their mistake and would fix it either with impeachment or elections.

Of course, we know now that the Trump wave was something deeper, stronger, and more lasting than initially met the eye. It is important to identify here the reasons why this was so, namely the undercurrents of US politics that fuelled the wave, because they are intimately connected with the development of right-wing politics in that country.

The Trump phenomenon is the result of the convergence of at least four factors: the historical origins of the United States and its subsequent developments, some salient features of that country's political culture as already stated, the activation of right-wing movements over the past few decades, and a novel strategy for political campaigning. This chapter will focus on the first three factors, as they are germane to understanding the political right in that country.

From its inception, the United States has provided a fertile ground for conservative ideas, although this reality has usually been ignored by mainstream historiography, trapped in the assumption that the country represents the triumph of liberalism and modernity (Brinkley, 1994).

The so-called "Revolution of Independence" was not a true social revolution as understood in the social sciences literature (for instance, Skocpol, 1979), to the extent that it did not radically transform the social structure and distribution of power and resources existing in the British Thirteen Colonies. In fact, the movement was rather the struggle of local elites against British colonialism, mainly aimed at preserving and enhancing their privileges. Inspired on conservative values, not only independence was justified alleging the breach of British constitutional principles by colonial authorities, but numerous practices and legal principles established by the British were preserved: property system, slavery, White privilege, the rights of the landed class, etc. To a large extent, according to some interpretations, the independence revolt was "a counter-revolution, a conservative movement that the Founding Fathers fought to preserve their liberty to enslave others" (Horne, 2014), given the impending abolition of slavery within the British empire.

Moreover, James Madison, recognised as the main drafter of the current US Constitution, was not in favour of unlimited democracy, along with other fellow Founding Fathers. A wealthy slave master himself, Madison devised ways of protecting the rich minority and property rights within the Constitution (MacLean, 2017: p. 8). That way, the political institutions that were created for the new state also retained an important dose of conservative elements. Notable cases in point are the Senate, originally not only appointed but also favouring less populated states, and the Electoral College to choose the president, giving the privileged minority the institutional tool to modify majoritarian popular will (Dahl, 2001).

John C. Calhoun, at some point Vice-President and Senator, attempted to push the protection of the privileged classes from the vagaries of democracy even further. Politically and intellectually active from the 1820s on, Calhoun can be seen as the forefather of a tradition of conservatism distinct to the United States. According to him, property owners—particularly people like himself, slave-based plantation owners—must be shielded from the intrusion of government powers lest freedom is lost. Governments are vulnerable, he pursued, to the collective push of the masses, who would force politicians to implement programmes in their favour paid with taxes collected from the more well-off. This situation, in Calhoun's mind, made the masses the oppressors of property owners, an unfair condition that needed to be reversed. He supported the powers of states as the original sovereignty-holders, maintaining that the federal government was their creation, simply because state governments are more easily controlled by the propertied classes. His absolutist, intransigent stance on this matter became the doctrinal basis for Southern states' secession claims, which in turn fuelled the US Civil War in the 1860s (MacLean, 2017: pp. 1–10).

Over time, new versions of conservative and right-wing ideologies would develop, adding new layers to the founding influences, thus producing a complex and variegated movement. Some thinkers, and the events that led them to prominence, must be mentioned because of the lasting influence they had over the conservative ideologies.

In the 1930s, Austrian economist Friedrich A. Hayek moved to the United States, hired as professor by the University of Chicago. Author of the popular book *The Road to Serfdom* (originally published in 1944), Hayek imported to the United States his own brand of economic theory, which laid the foundations of neoliberalism.

Coined in 1938, the term *neoliberalism* refers to the belief that the liberal order in a society is the result of the deliberate action of states. There is no such thing as "the invisible hand", markets must be created with regulations and law enforcement. Law creates the framework where freedom is possible, adapting institutions to the emergence of new conditions. However, the state has to limit itself to defend the principles of freedom, not give orders; leaving civil society and the market to make their own decisions. Paradoxically, neoliberalism believes that the state has the duty to create the market, but once this is done the state has to refrain from interfering with market mechanisms (Van Horn and Mirowski, 2009). Moreover, for neoliberalism economic freedom is more important than political freedom. Freedom means mostly the capacity for realisation of individual wants and desires. Neoliberal freedom is then the ability of the individual to do as she pleases in economic activities, thus maximising her profits and consumption. The market is actually a better reflection of people's will than elections. Similarly to Calhoun, neoliberals distrust democracy, as it may become a tool to empower the state to tamper with the market.

James Buchanan, influential right-wing public intellectual based at the University of Virginia, managed to effectively graft neoliberalism into the US political tradition. He crafted a libertarian discourse inspired on Calhoun's ideas, according to which government intervention in the economy with redistribution purposes effectively steals from the productive classes to maintain a government elite and unworthy social parasites (MacLean, 2017; Elrod, 2018).

Despite its deep historical roots, the right-wing movement struggled to position itself as the predominant political ideology in the United States from the 1930s to the 1970s. The emergence and consolidation of the Welfare State made Keynesianism and its government intervention, socially responsible approach the predominant guiding principle for public policy. The Cold War consolidated a policy of containment of communism, rather than its outright defeat. Keynesianism domestically and containment internationally became the two pillars of what Robert B. Horwitz (2013: p. 6) calls "establishment conservatism" or moderate Republicanism, prevalent until the late 1970s. Richard Nixon, Republican president commonly considered a hardliner, in fact represents the predominance of establishment conservatism; as he famously declared in 1971: "We are all Keynesians now" to justify his economic policies while engaging in nuclear weapons talks with the Soviet Union and rapprochement with China.

However, not all conservatives were comfortable with this moderate approach. A new strain of anti-establishment conservatism, blending market libertarianism, socially traditional Christian values, and aggressive militarism to defeat communism started to breed. McCarthyism, with their emphasis on anti-communism and traditional US values, undoubtedly gave an impetus to this new brew. Perhaps the most lasting legacy of that era is the influential periodical *National Review* (nationalreview.com) founded by William F. Buckley in 1955, articulating and promoting anti-establishment conservative values (Horwitz, 2013: p. 8). Still printed over six decades, this biweekly magazine has become a reference, a greenhouse, and a clearing house where anti-establishment conservative ideas and writers are tested and developed before they reach the larger public and mainstream political debate.

The anti-establishment conservative movement was able to briefly prevail within the Republican Party with the selection of candidate Barry Goldwater for the 1964 presidential elections, prompted by conservative Christian preachers such as Billy Graham. Soundly defeated, Goldwater was unable to discard establishment conservatism and revert the prevailing liberal consensus. But in time the seed that the movement behind him planted would eventually grow.

The recent surge of the right

Despite the decades-long Keynesian setback, the right in the United States exponentially developed its strength and influence over the past 40 years, in successive leaps and bounds. It is fair to say that Donald Trump was the unintended beneficiary of the concerted efforts that the right-wing movement in the United States has deployed since the early 1970s to recover the hegemonic position in that country's domestic politics. Indeed, Trump took advantage of a vast political movement, both ideological and institutional, which advanced in successive waves, adding new ingredients to make it more politically effective. This movement, which in a nutshell can be called *backlash politics*, could be divided in five distinct stages, each stage approximately matching a decade. There is abundant scholarly literature about each one of these stages. Due to space restrictions, in this chapter we will only offer an overview of the main features and contribution to the conservative movement that each one of these waves made.

The first wave, launching the era of backlash politics, is represented by the now-famous "Powell Memorandum". On August 23, 1971, corporate lawyer Lewis F. Powell Jr. wrote a confidential memorandum to Eugene B. Sydnor Jr., Chairman of the US Chamber of Commerce's (USCC) Education Committee. In that memorandum, entitled "Attack of American Free Enterprise System", Powell (1971) outlined a comprehensive plan to revert a situation that he alarmingly diagnosed as a "broadly based and consistently pursued...assault on the enterprise system". He wrote: "the time has come indeed, it is long overdue for the wisdom, ingenuity and resources of American [sic] business to be marshalled against those who would destroy it".

He thus outlined a series of actions that he thought should be carried out to confront the situation. First of all, a coordinated, multi-firm, long-range strategy, led by the United States Chamber of Commerce (USCC), ought to be implemented. The strategy must reach universities, the media, electoral politics, the judiciary.[2] The combined effort would certainly require a substantial amount of funds that corporations must provide generously. USCC could coordinate the efforts, going through a restructuring that would make it more efficient in performing the task.

The Chamber and the business community took his advice seriously and ended up creating institutions (foundations, NGOs, think tanks, etc.) to contribute to the programme's implementation. Most importantly, that call for action was the origin of the large foundations that, over the following decades, would fund with their deep pockets the efforts of the right to implement Powell's ambitious programme: Ollin, Bradley, Scaife Mellon, and, above all, Koch Foundations (Mayer, 2016). Notably, these private foundations have bankrolled the push for privatisation of public services starting in the 1980s (Phua, 2001).

The first wave was also at the origin of the proliferation of think tanks, those factories of ideas that would educate the US public into conservative values. Six think tanks stand out among the hundreds of them, because of their contribution to the conservative cause: American Enterprise Institute, Heritage Foundation, Hoover Institution, Manhattan Institute, Cato Institute, Hudson Institute, and the Council on Foreign Relations.

The second wave of backlash politics was the emergence of the religious right, with the creation of the *Moral Majority* movement in 1979, followed by the *Christian Coalition* ten years later (Martin, 1996). These movements directly appeal to people's religious beliefs and values as a guide for political action and would give the right new momentum through the 1980s and beyond (Woodrum, 1988). The wave would catapult Pat Robertson, Bill Reid, and other televangelists to national prominence; thanks to their ability to mobilise the vote for the right usually based on single issues: opposition to abortion, to gay rights, promotion of religious freedom, etc. (Green and Guth, 1988).

The third wave corresponds to the emergence of climate change as a major policy issue worldwide, and the impacts it had on the United States. The US right sharply reacted to the United Nations Conference on Environment and Development (also known as Earth Summit, held in Rio de Janeiro, Brazil in June 1992) with the launch of a movement to deny the existence of climate change and its human roots. The movement questioned the science behind climate change, thus creating a political discourse hostile to science, rationalism, and policy-oriented expertise in general (Plehwe, 2014; Dunlap and Jacques, 2013). Measures devised to fight the environmental emergency were presented as mere excuses for government overreach and overtaxation, and attacked as a leftist political agenda[3] (Conway and Oreskes, 2010; Trapenberg Frick, Weinzimmer and Waddell, 2014).

Later on, right-wing think tanks, organised as well-funded networks, coordinated efforts to attack environmental policies from many angles (Goldenberg, 2012; Goldenberg, 2013). Of course, this opposition slowed down government response against climate change (Cann, 2015).

Subsequent backlash politics waves would incorporate new expressions of the right to the cumulative growth of this political movement. Both George W. Bush's terms in office (2001–2008) brought forward the fourth wave: the rise of neoconservatism to the summit of political power in the United States. Inspired on the ideas of Leo Strauss and his disciples—notably gathered around the influential think tank American Enterprise Institute—neoconservatism is a philosophical and ideological defence of Western civilisation, seen as a source of eternal truths and timeless values (Brinkley, 1994: pp. 420–422). According to that view, the West and, particularly, the United States have the right and indeed the duty to promote those values domestically and abroad. This heavily normative approach had major consequences in the promotion of unilateralism, militarism, and exceptionalism in US foreign policy (Parmar, 2005; Stahl, 2016: pp. 174–197).

The fifth wave consisted in the rise of right-wing populism in 2009, with the emergence of the so-called *Tea Party* movement (Williamson et al., 2011; Burack and Snyder-Hall, 2012). This movement, a response to Barack Obama's election as president and to the programme he implemented to confront the economic crisis, added some powerful ingredients to the existing conservative mix:

(a) populism—the rhetorical division of society between the elite and the people, both defined in a manipulative way, blended with hypernationalism and xenophobia—as a major mobilising force (Rosenthal and Trost, 2012; Rosenthal, 2020),
(b) *astroturfing*, or pseudo popular mobilisation sponsored by large corporations, the conservative media and wealthy foundations (Fang, 2013; Meagher, 2012),
(c) constitutional fundamentalism, also called originalism or popular constitutionalism, meaning the reinterpretation of the allegedly true spirit of the US Constitution by common people rather than law specialists, in order to serve a conservative agenda (Whittington, 2011; Whittington, 2013; Siegel, 2008; Kramer, 2004; Zietlow, 2012; Forbath, 2006). Constitutional reinterpretation includes expansive understandings of the first (freedom of expression) and the second (right to bear arms) constitutional amendments. The Federalist Society, an advocacy right-wing legal think tank, vigorously promoted conservative views on law drafting and interpretation (Scherer and Miller, 2009; Riehl, 2007; Gerchik, 2002) also influencing appointments of federal judges and Supreme Court justices (Baum and Devins, 2017).

The sixth, contemporary wave is of course the rise of Donald J. Trump to the presidency. Even if he did not contribute to any of the previous waves and was not even a Republican militant before he became that party's candidate, Trump managed to surf over the conservative movement thanks to his ability to bring together the different components of the movement. He benefitted from the ideological environment created by Powell's successful call to arms. He enlisted the Christian right as a pool of staunch supporters. Trump also successfully wooed climate change denialists, by supporting their claims to pursue fossil fuel development in the interest of the economy. Equally, he certainly benefitted from the surge of right-wing populism initiated by the *Tea Party*, bringing the populist appeal to new heights.

In his version of populism, Trump crafted "the people" according to the main themes of the right-wing movement. He defined it as all those individuals who have somehow felt the impact of recent economic, social, and political transformations: the unemployed, victims of the 2008 crisis, war veterans neglected by the government, victims of violent crime, White heterosexual males (favourite target of identity movements), etc. Strange as it may seem, this rhetorical definition of "the people" also includes nationalist entrepreneurs, owners of small, medium, and even large business operations. Of course, this definition is also strongly nationalist and ethnocentrist: in order to be legitimate member of this "people" you must have been born in the United States, be a citizen of that country, be Christian, be conservative in ideology, or not belong to an ethnic, cultural, or racial group suspiciously at odds with the dominant majority.

In contrast, the "elite" is, according to Trump, that broad and fuzzy human group that either directly benefits from the status quo or contributes to its preservation: professional politicians, beneficiaries of social programmes, globalising entrepreneurs, union leaders, left-wing scholars, mainstream media, etc. Again, strange as it may seem, contributing to the "elite" are, by exclusion, all those individuals who do not meet the requirements to belong to "the people": undocumented migrants, people coming from non-Christian countries, refugees, those who have never served in the military, those people who do not worship the country's nationalist symbols, etc.

Therefore, in Trump's populist rhetoric, the project is to return all power to its legitimate owner, the people as he defines it, pushing back the devious and opportunistic elite encroached in Washington ("draining the swamp", as he put it during his campaign). In order to achieve this mission, portrayed as heroic, all means are valid, the elite does not even deserve the benefit of an explanation. Because he did not belong to the circles of political power before running for president, Trump was able to present himself as the independent champion of the common people. That is why his candidacy aroused the enthusiasm of previously marginalised people, who suddenly feel vindicated and validated with the populist rhetoric, even if it seems simplistic, manipulative, and ethnocentric even to the casual observer.

Contradiction with neoliberal distrust of democracy

However, Trump departs from the right-wing movement that preceded his election in two important aspects. First, his government not only displaced but also discredited the neoconservative approach to foreign policy. Indeed, his government signed a peace agreement with the Taliban and initiated the process of withdrawing US troops from Afghanistan and Iraq, it shunned the UN and its agencies—formally withdrawing from UNESCO and WHO, for example—and overall diminishing his country's central role in international affairs. Secondly, Trump's nationalist approach to economic matters challenged neoliberal globalisation. His insistence on fixing trade balances and agreements in order to guarantee the predominance of US interests is at odds with the basic neoliberal rule of free market competition.

Moreover, Trump added another element to the right-wing toolbox: the efficient use of online social media for political campaigning, more specifically, the design of customised political messages to reach potential sympathisers according to their preferences. Hired by Trump's campaign managers, private corporation Cambridge Analytica obtained access to the private information of millions of US-based Facebook users. Making use of that information—the "likes", websites visited, chat groups, online purchases, etc.—the corporation was able to create profiles of the voters, sending them electoral propaganda virtually personalised. Following this procedure, it is estimated that Trump's campaign sent over 75,000 different versions of customised messages, adapted to the tastes, preferences, and values of each voter. That way, millions of people were led to believe that Trump was on the same political page as them, which naturally incited the enthusiasm for his candidacy come election day. Manipulative use of social media has been ever since adopted as a common practice in the right-wing movement toolbox for spreading their message out.

By the end of Trump's mandate, the cultural background and the institutional context that give strength to the right not only persist, but they have allegedly been reinforced. Of course, there have been internal disagreements along the way, but overall, the right-wing movement has been able to ward off destructive blows and maintain differences arising among its members hidden from public sight. The internet has become the new frontier for political campaigning (Castro-Rea, 2019) and lobbying (McNutt and Marchildon, 2009); the right is more present than ever in that medium and will likely find a politically effective way of circumventing the increasingly restrictive rules for online political campaigning and exercising political influence.

US support to right-wing actors in the Americas

Ever since the promulgation of the Monroe Doctrine in 1823, US activity in the Americas has promoted and protected that country's political and economic interests in the region: mainly securing access to consumer, procurement, and investment markets, and protecting geopolitical and military objectives. From that perspective, stability is sought rather than democracy; the latter can be sacrificed in the altar of the former if circumstances require. In contrast with the rhetoric justifying it, the net impact of such activity has been to support right-wing, authoritarian political actors (governments, parties, pressure groups, etc.).

In fact, when it comes to the US promotion of interests abroad the de facto "right-wing" encompasses the traditional Washington Establishment composed of both Democrats, Republicans, and the corporate and military industrial complexes that support them internationally, also known as the *power elite* (Mills, 1956). This is because, when it comes to US policy and activities in the Americas, it largely makes no difference whether the US federal government is led by Democrats or Republicans; the same net effect of supporting the elite's agenda internationally can be detected over the years (Livingstone, 2009; Guilhot, 2005). This support to right-wing actors, in particular across the Americas, is due to these actors' historical predisposition to take a favourable stance towards US economic, political, and military interests. If some governments in the Americas claiming to be "left-wing" actually turn out to defend these same US interests, Washington will normally not publicly criticise them and allow them to continue in their position unimpeded. Such was the case, for example, with Ollanta Humala in Peru (2011–2016) and Michele Bachelet in Chile (2006–2010, 2014–2018) in recent years. Thus, the primary objective behind supporting these governments appears to be utilitarian, aimed at stability and a more efficient advancement of critical US interests.

US activity in the hemisphere goes well beyond open military interventions, like the ones reported in the press or discussed by historians. On an everyday basis, there is a multifront activity that flies under the radar of public attention, carried out by government agencies, para-governmental institutions, NGOs, individuals, or networks coordinating two or more of these actors. This activity may be carried out directly by US-based right-wing actors, or even by other political actors in that country that domestically do not identify with the right. However, the net impact will be to further the right-wing agenda internationally. The rest of this chapter is dedicated to explaining the different levels and nuances of US support for international right-wing causes through brief overviews of each area of activity and selected case studies that demonstrate how this support functions at various levels across multiple types of organisations.

Government agencies involved in relations with the Americas

One thing that is important to recognise when looking at the support given to various right-wing causes across the Americas is the different types of approaches that are used in order to achieve these objectives. It is thus useful to divide the approaches used by different government agencies into what international relations scholars and diplomats sometimes call *soft* and *hard* approaches (Sharp, 1973; Perkins, 2016; Perkins, 2004). The soft approach relies upon US-funded aid programmes and scholarship programmes that attempt to influence populations through social issues such as education and health. Alternatively, within the hard approach you will find the use of spies, paramilitaries, private contractors, and even the US military in certain cases (Panama, Grenada, Mexico, Cuba, etc.). Below, we will explore both approaches and the government agencies most often behind their use.

Soft approach: Using aid programmes, propaganda, and control of public image and information to influence populations

The soft approaches in US support of right-wing governments and other political actors in the Americas usually consist of activities or strategies that are aimed at what George W. Bush infamously called part of his success in Iraq when addressing the UN General Assembly in 2005, namely that he had helped in assuring that the Iraqi, "hearts and minds are opening to the message of human liberty as never before" (Dickinson, 2009). These strategies often consist of education and health initiatives or the training of people on certain types of heavy machinery or farm equipment. This all may sound quite beneficial, even noble, until one realises that up until the current period (1) the education initiatives are partly designed to help mould, select, and train the latest generation of technocrats poised to rule their respective countries on behalf of US political, economic, and military interests (Quigley, 1981; Snow, 2010); (2) the funding of health programmes is often used to carry out controversial experiments, such as eugenics-like forced or coerced sterilisation on Indigenous women in Peru (Del Aguila, 2006), or to simply create an ineffectual healthcare industry as in Bolivia (Tejerina et al., 2014). Another classic strategy is simply funding a good programme that works and is helping and then use the threat of defunding that programme as a bargaining tool later. This has been a preferred negotiation tactic of the Trump administration most recently, for example, in particular with the funding of international institutions.

A further method of exploiting aid agencies as generators of influence is by awarding contracts and business start-ups to particular networks of individuals during or after the aid programme. This has been shown to limit the growth of some local businesses while promoting the growth of other particular businesses (Bah et al., 2011). Thus, aid programmes are often not what they seem; they come with strings attached, strings that benefit particular interests. As we look at the following three examples of government agencies that are notorious for this type of activity, the reader must keep in mind that many of the people working in these organisations may be well intentioned. It is not the desire of the authors to suggest otherwise, rather that institutional norms and modes of operation within an organisation often prevail over the wishes of individuals.

USAID

USAID was originally created in 1961 as an act of Congress and later maintained by an executive order of President Kennedy. It has subsequently been funded every year by Congress, albeit to different degrees. It claims, and appears, to benefit developing nations through humanitarian, educational, and commercial based forms of aid. However, upon review of the literature that has developed over the last few decades, researchers have shown that USAID has multiple problems with internal evaluations, unintended consequences, corruption, and even a form of economic or cultural warfare that promotes neoliberal policies at the expense of the well-being of local populations.

A principal issue for USAID is its own lack of internal evaluation and unbiased critiques of its performance, which in turn negatively affects its policymaking decisions (Clapp-Wincek and Blue, 2001; Chapman and Quijada, 2009). A second issue is the tendency for USAID to only benefit a certain number of businesses with their programmes and thus leave other businesses, usually small businesses, at a disadvantage for not receiving the aid, which usually comes in the form of loans, machinery, education, and investment opportunities (Bah, Brada, and Yigit, 2011). Tied in with this, a third problem for USAID is how it has become ever more intertwined with neoliberal policymaking (Klak, 1992) and in many instances has made countries more dependent on foreign aid rather than independent (Hearn, 1998). A fourth major problem for USAID is its own dependence on the current congressional and presidential political alignment for funding (Goldstein and Moss, 2005). A fifth issue is the broader NGO/development industrial complex that has been created around the concept of aid, USAID contractors (Roberts, 2014), and their tendency to move towards "NGO-isation" (Hearn, 1998), all of which have helped tarnish the industry's image due to allegations of corruption.

By far the worst problem stemming from the work of USAID is its support for anti-democratic right-wing regimes or opposition movements, which nearly rivals that of the World Bank (Valverde, 1999). This kind of support has been the case in Colombia for decades, infamously under the military juntas of Argentina (1976–1983) and Chile (1973–1990) during the last century, under Alberto Fujimori (1990–2000) in Peru, and under the Bolsonaro administration in Brazil (2019-2022).

In recent years, USAID has politically and/or financially supported right-wing opposition movements within left-wing controlled countries such as the Jeanine Añez regime in Bolivia (USAID, 2020), the Venezuelan opposition led by Juan Guaidó (USAID, 2020), and the Nicaraguan opposition embodied in evangelical Pastor Saturnino Cerrato and Juan Sebastián Chamorro (Norton, 2020; Cerrato and Chamorro, 2020). By regularly giving support to opposition groups, these aid organisations claim to be supporting noble causes such as "democracy", "free speech", and "transparency", but appear to be simply supporting favourable political groups while undermining their rivals. While in the past century this could be explained away by Cold War strategy and keeping communism at bay, the only potential explanation in our current decade is a desire to maintain the course of neoliberal market trends by politically manipulating the hemisphere if necessary. In this century's young history, Bolivia, Venezuela, and Nicaragua are textbook examples of the negative course that USAID might take in a country whose government begins to oppose the United States.

The case of Bolivia is a tragic one that has seen decades of investment into various sectors of the economy including health and anti-drug operations failing to make a lasting impact on the vital statistics of the nation (Tejerina et al., 2014). This sorted history has probably been most comprehensively written about by Larry Heilman (2017) who wrote *USAID in Bolivia: Partner or Patrón?* Heilman struggles with the US 70-year history in Bolivia while explaining many of the high and low points, finally noting that the US aid industry that was originally developed out of the Marshall Plan after World War II slowly morphed over the decades into an anti-communist and pro-neoliberal policy wing of the State Department (Krueger, 2018). The history of USAID in Bolivia was thought to have culminated when USAID was expelled from the country by the Morales government in 2013, only to be invited to return by Añez after seizing power in 2019 and sending Morales into exile. It should be highlighted that this expulsion of USAID came under the Obama administration, which is another piece of evidence alongside annual funding rates that both parties in the US support these types of neoliberal development agendas, albeit through different strategic uses of USAID. There was no apparent difference under the Trump administration either, despite his campaign rhetoric about getting the United States out of foreign entanglements and concentrating on putting "America First". If anything, perhaps due to a decrease in US military activity in the Middle East, there has been an increase in US activity in Latin America when Trump assumed power.

Another example is Venezuela, where USAID was utilised by Trump's administration to support the activities of the opposition and to influence and control local media. USAID has been particularly utilised as the "humanitarian" wing of US foreign policy in this regard in Venezuela. By utilising the cover of humanitarian aid, they are able to administer support in crisis-hit areas, support that can just as easily be shifted to back local leaders favourable to US interests. USAID is so closely linked with military and espionage activity in the region that US Southern Command Col. Armando Hernandez confirmed in 2019, "The U.S. military has a long history of supporting USAID-led aid missions" (Brook, 2019). In other words, while the soft and hard approaches may be separated by different government departments and administrators, the two approaches support one another.

Finally, the current case of Nicaragua provides us with yet more demonstrations of the political operations of USAID that support right-wing political groups. During the student-led protests of 2018 against President Daniel Ortega, USAID was found to have met with student leaders from Nicaragua in Washington DC (Blumenthal, 2020). According to Max Blumenthal, Aaron Mate, and Ben Norton, these students were treated to this networking trip by Freedom House, a non-profit US government–sponsored non-governmental organisation (GONGO), to meet with US government representatives as diverse as USAID and Senator Ted Cruz. The strategic aim was to filter and obtain new young recruits who could promote neoliberal policies, protests, and reforms in their home countries at the behest of Washington's interests. Most recently, current anti-Sandinista right-wing coalition leaders Pastor Saturnino Cerrato and Juan Sebastián Chamorro live-streamed an event on Facebook where they openly discussed the support they were promised by US and EU aid advisors for building a "large movement" to oppose Ortega (Norton, 2020). New young leaders who can potentially lead protests and other movements effectively in the present can likely later in life serve in an important role in making their own countries friendly to neoliberal policies. Most importantly, these few examples help demonstrate a foreign policy pattern largely consistent across both Republican and Democratic governments in using USAID programmes to influence Latin American politics, culture, education, and development. This practice did not end in the last century, but is ongoing to the current day (López, 2020).

Hard approach: Using military, spies (PSYOP), or support of paramilitaries

The hard approach can be used by certain elements of the US government as an ongoing threat or put into use when the soft approach fails. In these cases, when all efforts failed over the years to change the government's stance on a sufficiently vital issue (e.g. petrodollar utilisation) (Gokay, 2005), oil market flows (Clark, 2005), strategic interests, support of Israel (Mearsheimer and Walt, 2007; Fisk, 2019), a harder approach may be implemented to either influence or clandestinely or overtly violently remove a non-favourable government from power and replace it with a favourable government (Perkins, 2004). Within the twenty-first century in the Americas, the prime targets for this type of intervention most likely include Venezuela, Bolivia, Honduras, and Mexico.

This foreign policy appears to be largely static in the United States with both Republican and Democrat administrations and congressmen having participated in these actions. This is because both parties in the United States use slightly different ways to achieve similar goals. This provides the added benefit that when the US people get tired of one administration and its blunders after four or eight years, they can replace it "by the other party which will be none of these things but will still pursue, with new vigour, approximately the same basic policies" (Quigley, 1966). Thus, within the hard approach, both the State Department and the Defense Department take part in different types of strategies to achieve similar, if not identical, goals. While authors may disagree as to their intentions and tactics, the end result must be seen as the same.

Department of State

The State Department is thus represented both within the soft approach through their management of USAID and within the hard approach through their use of well-known agent-provocateurs, velvet revolutions, spook operations, propaganda, and agitation that they utilise to destabilise governments that do not favour their policies. This has been a preferred tactic of both Republican and Democratic administrations at least since the end of WWII, and it has been utilised throughout the Americas, most recently in this century in Venezuela (2002, present), Honduras (2009), Bolivia (2019) and Peru (2022). Velvet revolutions such as these are often used to overthrow governments that would not capitulate to exploitative neoliberal financial demands from the transnational capitalist class. This same tactic of propaganda and agitation has now morphed to a new platform with the use of social media, but it has not stopped; if anything, it has become more refined in this century.

Department of Defense

The Department of Defense is in many ways "the bad cop" persona to the Department of State's "good cop" public face. They act where the Department of State has failed. This is most notable in regard to US foreign relations with virtually every country in the Americas (Livingstone, 2009). It also becomes clearer that while the Democrats may attempt to work more clandestinely through the Department of State, the Republicans often work openly through outright military strikes. Either way, there is no doubt that both parties are implicated in activities happening within both departments, though they may prefer the strategies of one over the other.

CIA

The Central Intelligence Agency (CIA) is a product of policy transfer from the British Empire to the United States during and after World War II. Indeed, the CIA grew out of the Office of Strategic Services (OSS), which worked with British intelligence services during WWII and gained much experiential knowledge. The first successful CIA coup was carried out with the help of British intelligence when they overthrew Mohammad Mossadegh of Iran in 1953 (Jeffreys-Jones, 1997).

As can be seen in Table 1.1, elaborated by the authors tapping from diverse historical records, after this success the CIA quickly put this method into action in many countries across the world. It is much cheaper to use the soft method of agent-provocateurs, spooks, propaganda, and agitation than to mount a costly war. Thus, the countries where a full-scale US invasion or a US-directed exile invasion took place are minimal, while the locations where soft tactics were used are the majority. This is a crucial point to underscore because most people only associate US interventions when violent coups are successful and fail to recognise the vast majority of other instances because they are carried out in a more clandestine manner than open declarations of war. It is also noticeable that the brazenness of intervention has been bolstered starting with President Bush Sr., continuing until Obama, when there is a marked increase in these activities. Here is a list of

TABLE 1.1 United States: Attempt or successful overthrow of a government in the Americas, 1945–present

Country	Year
Guatemala	1954*
Ecuador	1960–1963*
Brazil	1962–1964*
Dominican Rep.	1963*
Cuba	present
Bolivia	1964*
Chile	1964–1973*
Costa Rica	1970–1971
Bolivia	1971*
Jamaica	1976–1980*
Grenada	1963*
Nicaragua	1981–1990*
Panama	1989*
Haiti	1994–1995*
Ecuador	2000*
Venezuela	2002, present
Haiti	2004*
Honduras	2009*
Bolivia	2019*
Peru	2022*

(* indicates successful ouster of a government).

Source: Authors' compilation from different historical records; Blum 2003; Blum 2020.

governments throughout the Americas that have been overthrown since WWII using one or a combination of methods (Blum, 2003; Blum, 2020) found in the hard approach.

Para-governmental institutions

Para-governmental institutions are those that are supported by the government but managed privately and that usually have active members from both the private and public sectors. These institutions actively work in two main areas: *outreach* to filter and select new potential members to grow their ranks, and *inreach* aimed at current members to debate direction and strategy as well as to maintain group cohesion.

National Endowment for Democracy

The National Endowment for Democracy (NED) is another project created as the brainchild of US foreign policy heads in the decades following WWII. Again, it was a slow-moving process that evolved throughout the administrations of various presidents until Congress finally approved official funding for the NED under President Reagan, which continues to this day, albeit with some protest. There have been members on both sides of the aisle in US politics that have both advocated for and against the funding of the NED (Epstein and Fergusson, 1996), usually with slightly different reasoning; yet the NED stands as an institution today with mostly full bipartisan support (Jordan, 2009; NED, 2020b).

According to their website,

> The National Endowment for Democracy (NED) is a private, non-profit foundation dedicated to the growth and strengthening of democratic institutions around the world. Each year, NED makes more than 1,600 grants to support the projects of non-governmental groups abroad who are working for democratic goals in more than 90 countries.
>
> *(NED, 2020a)*

As with most of these organisations, their stated goals often sound quite harmless and even possibly helpful in many instances. This, however, is often simply a façade. While claiming to support growing and supporting democracy in various places throughout the world, the historical fact remains that the NED has many times supported the least democratic elements of certain societies in their bid to influence or overthrow a local government that happened to not currently be in US favour. Here is a list of countries in the Americas where the NED was operating in 2019 along with what activities they are funding (Table 1.2).

It is interesting to note that many of the countries where the NED is spending the most resources are also countries where the United States might prefer an

TABLE 1.2 United States: Countries in the Americas with active NED projects and funding, 2019

Country	# of Projects/Grants	Total for 2019
Argentina	2	$447,164
Bolivia	14	$892,350
Brazil	4	$256,000
Colombia	10	$1,516,847
Cuba	51	$1,767,876
Ecuador	16	$1,436,544
El Salvador	1	$50,000
Guatemala	12	$1,408,089
Haiti	7	$1,123,000
Honduras	7	$814,532
Mexico	12	$1,642,634
Nicaragua	16	$986,858
Panama	1	$200,000
Paraguay	8	$274,000
Peru	7	$303,497
Venezuela	40	$1,039,000

Highlighted countries have funding levels at over 1 million USD.

Source: NED, 2020c.

administration more favourable to US interests, now or in the not-too-distant future. Finally, looking through the lists of projects it is noteworthy that more and more projects are utilising a progressive language centred around equity and social justice. Venezuela for example, which has been on the State Department's radar since Hugo Chávez was swept to power in a historic election in 1999, has many grants attempting to "train" citizens in democratic processes, disseminate "verified" information to the public, and in particular working with the Centre for International Private Enterprise (CIPE). The CIPE grant is specifically designed to re-establish neoliberal business ties and practices between Venezuelan businessmen and the United States.

Multiple authors have written about the NED, have evaluated their strategies for developing democratic institutions, and found them not to have that great of an effect on promoting democracy (Scott, 1999: pp. 163–167). Besides, the potential risks of interfering with the internal politics of other countries outweigh its proposed benefits (Hale, 2003; Scott and Steele, 2005). This is because though NED usually establishes ties within a country, even with good work potentially like helping victims of human rights abuses, the institution will begin to form groups dedicated to teaching about NED's idea of "democracy", "social activism", and "organisation". If they are operating in a country where the government might be hostile to these ideas, they will begin to organise, promote, and defend the opposition to that government (Guilhot, 2005). This can eventually lead to the support of popular uprisings or other coup attempts against the hostile government as witnessed in 2019 with Jeanine Áñez Chavez in Bolivia and presently ongoing with Juan Guaidó in Venezuela. Recently, the Mexican government revealed that NED has contributed over $670,000 to NGOs opposing the construction of the Maya Train, a flagship infrastructure project launched by the current leftist presidential administration (López Obrador, 2020).

Fulbright Program

The Fulbright Program was founded in the year following World War II almost exclusively due to the efforts of Senator J. William Fulbright. In many ways, it is a story of a post-war internationally liberal government–sponsored institution that was merged with private interests like the Rockefeller Foundation and Carnegie Endowment due to funding concerns.

The Fulbright Program is in many ways modelled after the Rhodes Scholars programme[4] established by British colonialist Cecil Rhodes.[5] Indeed, Senator Fulbright was a Rhodes Scholar himself in his early twenties (Jeffrey, 1987), so his inclination to extend this British round-table model of young member recruitment and education (Quigley, 1981) is understandable in hindsight. The round-table model will be discussed in more detail in the following section.

Many of the publicly stated goals of Senator Fulbright around his education exchange programme appear quite noble, including, "increas[ing] its participation in world affairs and to contribute to the cause of peace by breaking down some of the mental barriers of isolationism" (Fulbright, 1961: p. 22). Indeed, Fulbright may have had pure intentions while crafting the programme and is not justified to speculate otherwise. According to the congressional bill that established the Fulbright Program, it was designed to encourage the "promotion of international good will through the exchange of students in the fields of education, culture and science" (Bureau of Educational and Cultural Affairs, 2020). With this commendable vision, it is unfortunate the Fulbright Program's power over educational opportunities and curricula has at times been abused for political ends (Snow, 2010).

Over the years scholars have noted the political effects of the Fulbright Program in various countries (Xu, 1999; Rupp, 1999), and we would contend it exhibits some of the same tendencies as USAID. However, this is accomplished in a different manner, similar to Rhodes' scholarships. As with anything, this educational, cultural, and information exchange can be utilised in many ways and can lead to many different outcomes. This is managed in particular through the education of young burgeoning scholars from different countries through scholarship offers, curriculum creation, influenced by US advisors in foreign countries (Seelke, 2005), and foreign professorship exchanges (Xu, 1999); all contributing to moulding individuals towards promoting US-friendly mindsets favourable to neoliberal policies in their home countries and the world in general (Woods, 1987). Again, this is similar to the approach of Rhodes in terms of masking influence, in terms of the types of individuals who might be recruited for such an endeavour, and in terms of how this type of international education programme is intended to engender a feeling among members towards a "common ideology"[6] (Quigley, 1981: p. 151).

Undoubtedly, the Fulbright Program also benefits many students from around the world (Gonzalez, 2012) and has certainly been a source of much needed intellectual, academic, and professional international exchange. However, it also bears the unmistakable right-wing ideology promoted by the US government abroad and the elitist foundations that fund it, which it attempts to impart on its participants (Snow, 2010). This is the first step in recruitment of young professionals who might then be selected to be introduced to other networks of powerful individuals through the modern-day round-table model explained in the following section.

Round-table groups

The round-table model is probably best detailed by historian Carroll Quigley (1981), who was the archivist for the Council on Foreign Relations for many decades during the twentieth century, in his book *The Anglo-American Establishment*. The model originates with late-nineteenth-century British colonialists in Africa who desired a method of recruiting, training, and later utilising highly skilled individuals who could be relied upon to advance the objectives of the British Empire. This round-table system begins with the recruitment phase and then moves towards a professional-working phase. At this point, a recruit might be selected to be introduced to other powerful members of elite networks in politics, finance, military, business, diplomacy, technology, academia, and science. They may also be selected for certain positions, especially non-elected positions that require no public input, in select corporations, institutions, NGOs, and para-governmental bureaucratic bodies like the World Trade Organization, the World Bank, and the International Monetary Fund (Zweigenhaft and Domhoff, 2011). These networks of individuals (Carroll and Sapinski, 2010) are managed in the western hemisphere through select round-table groups like the Council on Foreign Relations (Quigley, 1981) and the Council of the Americas. These groups essentially act as debating clubs of strategic planning for ruling class interests.

1. Americas Society/Council of the Americas (AS/COA)

The Americas Society (AS) and the Council of the Americas (COA) were both founded by David Rockefeller and President Kennedy between 1963 and 1967 with the goal of organising business and political interests in the United States and Latin America in order to prevent the rise of communism and "the threat of possible nationalisation of their profitable subsidiaries" (Hersh, 1982; Hoeveler, 2020). These two organisations are part of the same mission to bind the peoples of the Americas under a stronger neoliberal business ideology, legal framework, and political structure. The AS is concerned with publicity, outreach, public education, and debate, while the COA acts more like a steering committee for important individuals in the network to discuss ways to support "economic and social development, open markets, the rule of law, and democracy throughout the Western Hemisphere" (AS/COA, 2020). Like the Fulbright Program, most of these goals are reasonable and attractive to the average person, however; the key provision of "open markets" reveals its neoliberal underpinnings.

Indeed, AS/COA was one of the main round-table discussion groups used by elites in the Americas to draft the NAFTA, CAFTA, and FTAA trade agreements. Again, both Democrats (e.g. Thomas F. McLarty, III),[7] and Republicans (e.g. John D. Negroponte)[8] fill the boards of this organisation as well as various types of political and business leaders from across Latin America (e.g. Andrés Gluski,[9] Martin Marron,[10] Nicolas Amaya,[11] Om Arora,[12] and Alexandre Bettamio[13]) (AS/COA, 2020). This partial list of influential Directors of AS/COA helps demonstrate how the neoliberal economic order being promoted by these organisations closely resembles a form of corporatism, where select corporations have the privilege of working cooperatively with government leaders and policymakers, while other companies (usually small businesses) that are not connected to these highly influential networks suffer from unfair competition. The AS/COA is thus a good example of a para-governmental neoliberal organisation that contains members from both public and private industry across the Americas where they can use their positions of influence to promote neoliberal shifts in policy (Hoeveler, 2020).

2. Council on Foreign Relations

The Council on Foreign Relations (CFR) probably represents the most successful example of the British round-table method being imported to the United States and is one of its central axes of power. The CFR was established by John. D. Rockefeller, Woodrow Wilson, and various other industrialists in 1921, and has subsequently been funded by the Big Three older foundations: Carnegie, Ford, and Rockefeller. The latter has been the most influential in the development and direction of the CFR in recent years.

Of all the organisations discussed here, the CFR is perhaps the most bipartisan, which supports our claim that, regardless of the rhetoric, both Democrats and Republicans advance an international right-wing agenda. Highlighting a few names from CFR's member list is revealing of its bipartisan and multi-industry nature: Jami Miscik,[14] Richard N. Haass,[15] Thad W. Allen (Perkins, 2004),[16] Mary Boies,[17] Sylvia Mathews Burwell,[18] Ashton B. Carter,[19] Steven A. Denning,[20] Robert Keohane,[21] Laurence D. Fink,[22] Timothy Geithner,[23] Janet Napolitano,[24] Meghan L. O'Sullivan,[25] Fareed Zakaria,[26] Margaret Brennan,[27] Elliot Abrams,[28] George Clooney,[29] Chelsea Clinton, Dick Cheney, John Kerry, Condoleezza Rice, Paul Wolfowitz, Michael Bloomberg, and Henry Kissinger (Council on Foreign Relations, 2020). These names represent a small fraction of a list that includes a veritable who's who of previous Republican and Democrat administrations and important members of top academia, finance, media, and Hollywood. Understanding the CFR as a hub of interlocking directorates (Sapinkski and Carroll, 2018) is a crucial starting point that gives future researchers of right-wing networks an excellent basis on which to continue more forms of elite network analysis (Rothkopf, 2008; Carroll, 2009; Phillips, 2018).

Our reason for including a sample of such an exhaustive list is to demonstrate just how interconnected many of the figures of the US ruling class are, even though they may appear in public as though they are in opposition. They may indeed oppose one another's methods or strategies, but they largely agree on maintaining and promoting the neoliberal system that has worked so well to their benefit. The CFR thus essentially acts as a type of strategy centre, discussion hub, and steering committee for the US power elite who, though they may disagree publicly on issues that do not threaten their power monopoly, are united in their conservative cause of maintaining their positions of power. And the CFR certainly does not steer all these organisations to no end.

Some terrible right-wing ideas that were cooked up at the CFR include: the Vietnam War, the creation of the International Monetary Fund (IMF) (Domhoff, 2014), George W. Bush's War on Terror, etc. CFR is clearly most focused on contributing to creating and maintaining US hegemony, be it military, financial, cultural, or epistemic.

One thing to notice about how the CFR membership list is structured is that they strive to include individuals who are the heads or directors of large public or private institutions. This allows the CFR to influence the structure, trajectory, and overarching goals within various institutions through these select members, whether these members realise they are being utilised in this fashion or not (McCourt, 2017). The misunderstanding between what people perceive to be "left-wing" or "right-wing" media can also be partially dispelled by viewing the control the CFR exercises over virtually *all* mainstream US media. Research has shown that members of these news organisations are also members of CFR, Bilderberg Group, and/or the Trilateral Commission and that many of the top members of the CFR are involved in different institutions, branches of government, corporations, and academia (Swiss Policy Research, 2017). Thanks to the revelations of Wikileaks, we now know that the CFR has its hands in virtually every mainstream media organisation that exists and is therefore able to influence not only the hegemonic news cycle narrative, but also the political debate between two "sides" they clandestinely control (Chomsky, 1998).[30] Thus, through a continuation of an Operation Mockingbird[31]-type media control and a manufacturing of consent for war and a loss of civil liberties (Herman and Chomsky, 2010), the CFR has much control over politics in the United States and by extension abroad.

Non-governmental organisations

Non-governmental organisations (NGOs) are what could be considered an *extremely soft approach* that can be used to gain influence in certain situations. This influence is normally gained on behalf of whatever group is funding the NGO, be it a public grassroots organisation, a private multinational corporation (MNC), or a government agency. NGO work can be an extremely effective strategy for gaining influence, especially when one is providing something to someone that they otherwise lack. Indeed, this is especially encouraged in the business world to demonstrate corporate social responsibility. Still, the lack of traditional accounting oversight can also make NGOs susceptible to various types of corruption and eventual scandals that can decrease public trust in the NGO sector in general (Gibelman and Gelman, S. R. 2001). If this happens, it will work against the public image of the group funding the violating NGO. It is thus of critical importance for NGOs that they always attempt to maintain a good public reputation and image.

NGOs normally provide some type of service for communities or individuals ostensibly for "free". NGOs thus work on gaining the trust and acceptance of a community, sometimes for altruistic and beneficial reasons, but sometimes as a cover for more nefarious activities. There are many cases of NGOs working towards political or other goals that are not within their permissions in the country where they are working.

Understandably, most NGOs advertise themselves and their accomplishments in a positive manner, whether they are using honest or disingenuous descriptions of themselves, and their work is at times hard to determine. NGO work can be divided into three areas: foundations, think tanks, and religious outreach groups. The following section presents an overview about each of these types of NGOs.

Foundations—increasing influence through the body

We have already referred in this chapter to what we call the Big Three older business foundations: the Ford Foundation, the Carnegie Endowment, and the Rockefeller Foundation. They have all had some influence over US activities in the Americas, especially of the soft power kind. We were unable to find any evidence that more recent right-wing foundations—Ollin, Bradley, Scaife Mellon, and Koch—have any direct political presence beyond the United States. However, there are other US foundations active throughout the Americas promoting right-wing agendas (Figure 1.1).

In our current age, the Bill and Melinda Gates Foundation (BMGF) towers over all other foundations (Foundation Center, 2015). While the twentieth century was shaped and dominated by many of the forces at work within the Big Three, the wealth that created those foundations and funded their operations was primarily accumulated in the nineteenth century; these foundations are thus losing steam. In contrast, in 2015 alone, the BMGF funded over $3.8 billion in different projects and research, much of it centred around vaccines and genetic engineering. Meanwhile, the Big Three combined only spent $834 million that same year. Equally, in total assets, the BMGF has over $40.4 billion, while the Big Three are not even worth half that amount combined. Just as the Big Three did much to favour the spread of the transnational capitalist class in the previous century, so too this century could see a move in that direction. In addition to this, the BMGF is uniquely positioned in the world to be able to influence research efforts, government policy initiatives, and media coverage. The list of countries where BMGF is funding research or linked to governments is quite extensive, as well as the amount of influence the foundation has over different world media.

Foundations are typically philanthropic in their funding and orientation, being storehouses for large fortunes of extremely wealthy individuals or families. Thus, while many foundations do offer many types of charity, they still inherently come from and promote a conservative ideology due to their intimate connections with the ruling class (Parmar, 2002). This is unavoidable even with the most well-intentioned individuals of the elite. Importantly, it should be recalled these philanthropists did not acquire their wealth by caring for others but by seeking to maximise their profits, some of them even resorting to a combination of corrupt, illegal, or immoral business practices.

Think tanks—increasing influence through the mind

Think tanks, compared to foundations, are more focused on research, strategy, and planning than on charity. Think tanks normally employ researchers, strategists, and former members of the public and private sector to help inform analyses of various global issues, within the context of right-wing politics in the Americas, and in particular the type of elitism that dominates US politics.

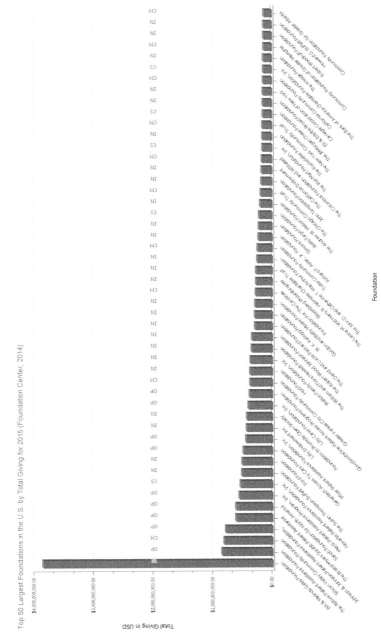

FIGURE 1.1 United States: Top 20 largest foundations by total giving, 2015. *Source:* Adapted from Foundation Center, 2015.

Figure 1.2 shows the connections between conservative think tanks (i.e., the Brookings Institution, the Atlantic Council, and the Institute for the Study of War), with major military contractors (i.e., Lockheed, Booz Allen Hamilton Inc., Northrop Grumman, Raytheon, Boeing, and General Dynamics). Again, at the centre of this network is the steering committee: the CFR.

Karin Fischer and Dieter Plehwe (2013) recently mapped the most important international connections of right-wing think tanks active in Latin America. Formally belonging to, or at least publicly sympathising with, any of these networks is in itself an unequivocal indication of a given think tank's right-wing identity. Another indication is the emphasis given to "the defence of liberty" or "freedom" in its self-identification, essentially understood in neoliberal terms. In fact, the use of these words as identifiers of an organisation's mandate is usually code for being of right-wing identity.

Fischer and Plehwe (2013) were able to identify a myriad of right-wing think tanks active in each and every country of Latin America, articulated by five international coordinations: Atlas Foundation (based in the United States), *Latinoamérica Libre* (US-based), Hispanic-American Center for Economic Research (HACER, US-based), *Red Liberal para América Latina* (RELIAL, based in Germany), and *Fundación Internacional para la Libertad* (FIL, based in Spain). The European coordinations are openly funded by two political parties—Germany's Free Democratic Party and Spain's *Partido Popular*—whereas the ones based in the United States are reluctant to disclose their funding sources.

Churches/evangelism/religious outreach— increasing influence through the spirit

Religion and spirituality have always been powerful forces in human history, and they have certainly shaped the history of the Americas in profound ways. There is also a long-standing connection between religion and conservatism not only due to moral values, but also in views around the preservation of societal stability versus constant progression as liberalism promotes.

Traditionally, most notable in the Americas are the Protestant Christian influence in Canada and the United States and the Catholic influence in Latin America. This divide exists to this day, but major strides have been made especially by Protestant churches throughout Latin America in pulling members away from the Catholic Church and towards their own congregations instead. Most of these congregations carry with them an inherently conservative US-inspired ideology (Mormons, Pentecostals, Jehovah's Witnesses, Seventh Day Adventists, Evangelicals, etc.) based on particular interpretations of the Bible, and, in the case of the Mormons, the Book of Mormon (Butler, 2006).

As the influence of the Catholic Church has waned throughout Latin America there has been an increase in the amount of proselytising by Protestants, many of whom come from the United States. Especially notable in this exercise of evangelism is the Church of Jesus Christ of Latter-Day Saints (Mormons) and the

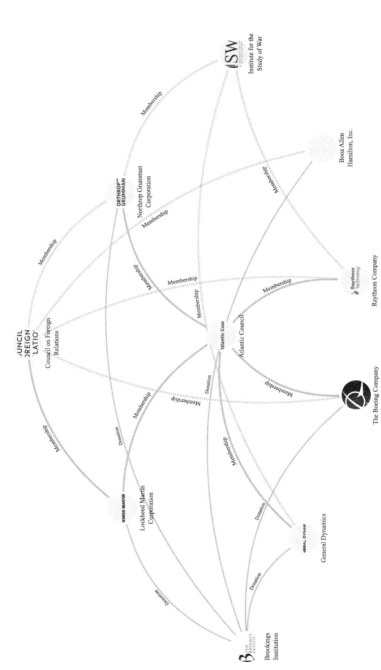

FIGURE 1.2 United States: Major conservative think tanks and their connections to the military industrial complex. *Sources*: Armstrong, 2014. [original figure, Creative Commons Attribution-ShareAlike 4.0 International License]; Beattie, K.A. (2022). [adapted figure].

Jehovah's Witnesses, as they are highly coordinated, top-down mandated organisations that are able to send members all over the world on "missions" to convert people. The Mormons in particular have been active in Latin America for the past century, but only since the end of WWII has their influence been able to spread so widely (Knowlton, 1996).

Mormonism is spread through mandatory missions that are assigned to all young members of the church, called "elders". They are amazingly adept at language and usually study a foreign language thoroughly before going to another country on a mission so as to communicate their ideas more effectively. Though often discriminated against at first for their heterodox views on certain issues, once established in any country, the Mormons have a tendency to create a formidable business network of other individuals who may attempt to promote especially socially conservative causes and can even enter politics (Perry and Cronin, 2012).

Still the Catholic Church does maintain sway in certain countries throughout Latin America. Figure 1.3 shows where state-backed funding for the Catholic Church is dominant in the Americas, most notably Argentina, Peru, and Venezuela.

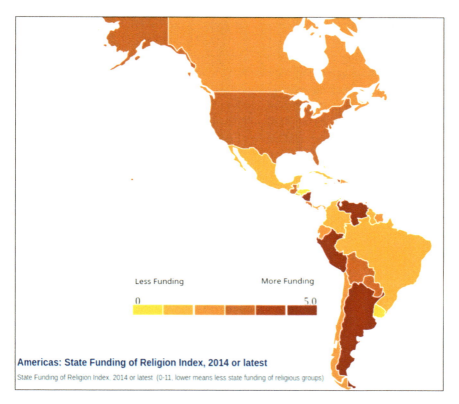

FIGURE 1.3 Americas: State funding of religion index, 2014-present. *Source:* Association of Religion Data Archives, et al. "Religion and State (RAS) Project" (1990-2014).

Networks

Among all of these different institutions and groups mentioned in this chapter, they tend to not only work internally, but also to make partnerships and work together, as illustrated in the case of corporations and think tanks. This means that there are many different interlocking directorates among governmental, non-governmental, and para-governmental institutions, and various other groups.

There are a few organisations that practise organising those groups together such as the Atlas Network mentioned above and the State Policy Network. They have had a huge effect on various different elements of public policy such as oil, tobacco (Smith et al., 2017), and pharmaceutical regulations. Essentially networks act as enablers through funding, supporting new group creation, strategic advice, message coordination, acting as a revolving door between the private and public spheres, echo chamber-builders, and public relations campaign managers.

Conclusions

It should be clear by now that the United States is a central actor in the creation and expansion of conservatism and the right in the Americas. From the birth of that country until the twenty-first century, the United States has upheld conservative and right-wing values, and strived to promote them across the Americas.

A power elite upholding conservative and right-wing values persists in the United States. Their interlocked network traverses a vast percentage of high-consequence positions in government, corporations, military, academia, media, NGOs, think tanks, foundations, and religious institutions. This power elite is inherently conservative in the traditional sense of the word; and promotes US interests, and business-oriented, neoliberal values. With Latin America falling under their perceived "jurisdiction", these networks of powerful organisations and individuals have steered, manipulated, and negatively affected the political environment of not only the United States itself, but of most countries across the Americas as well.

Notes

1 Note that the study was published seven years before Donald Trump's election. Trump is a leader who in his public persona arguably combines all the features that Fogarty identified.
2 Interestingly, two months after writing the memo, President Richard Nixon appointed Powell as justice to the US Supreme Court.
3 Interestingly, however, climate change denial also tapped energy from the postmodernist scepticism about the possibility of achieving objective science, a favourite theme in left-wing discourse. See Latour (2004).
4 "The Rhodes Scholarships, established by the terms of Cecil Rhodes's seventh will, are known to everyone. What is not so widely known is that Rhodes in five previous wills left his fortune to form a secret society, which was to devote itself to the preservation and expansion of the British Empire" (Quigley, 1981: p. ix).
5 "The secret society of Cecil Rhodes is mentioned in the first five of his seven wills. In the fifth it was supplemented by the idea of an educational institution with scholarships,

whose alumni would be bound together by common ideals—Rhodes's ideals. In the sixth and seventh wills the secret society was not mentioned, and the scholarships monopolised the estate. But Rhodes still had the same ideals and still believed that they could be carried out best by a secret society of men devoted to a common cause. The scholarships were merely a façade to conceal the secret society, or, more accurately, they were to be one of the instruments by which the members of the secret society could carry out his purpose. This purpose, as expressed in the first will (1877), was: The extension of British rule throughout the world, the perfecting of a system of emigration from the United Kingdom and of colonisation by British subjects of all lands wherein the means of livelihood are attainable by energy, labour, and enterprise, … the ultimate recovery of the United States of America as an integral part of a British Empire, the consolidation of the whole Empire, the inauguration of a system of Colonial Representation in the Imperial Parliament which may tend to weld together the disjointed members of the Empire, and finally the foundation of so great a power as to hereafter render wars impossible and promote the best interests of humanity" (Quigley, 1981: p. 33).

6 "The effort of the Round Table Group to create a common ideology to unite the supporters of the British way of life appears in every aspect of their work. It was derived from Rhodes and Milner and found its most perfect manifestation in the Rhodes Scholarships. As a result of these and of the Milner Group's control of so much of Oxford, Oxford tended to become an international university. Here the Milner Group had to tread a narrow path between the necessity of training non-English (including Americans [sic] and Indians) in the English way of life and the possibility of submerging that way of life completely (at Oxford, at least) by admitting too many non-English to its cloistered halls. On the whole, this path was followed with considerable success, as will be realised by anyone who has had any experience with Rhodes Scholars. To be sure, the visitors from across the seas picked up the social customs of the English somewhat more readily than they did the English ideas of playing the game or the English ideas of politics, but, on the whole, the experiment of Rhodes, Milner, and Lothian cannot be called a failure. It was surely a greater success in the United States than it was in the Dominions or in India, for in the last, at least, the English idea of liberty was assimilated much more completely than the idea of loyalty to England" (Quigley, 1981: p. 151).

7 White House Chief of Staff and Counsellor to the President and Special Envoy for the Americas under Bill Clinton (1993–1998).

8 Ambassador to Honduras under Ronald Reagan (1981–1985), Ambassador to Mexico under George H.W. Bush (1989–1993), Ambassador to the UN (2001–2004), Ambassador to Iraq (2004–2005), Director of National Intelligence (2005–2007), U.S. Deputy Secretary of State (2007–2009) under George W. Bush.

9 Chief Executive Officer, AES Energy Corporation.

10 Chief Executive Officer, Latin America J.P. Morgan.

11 President, Kellogg Latin America.

12 Regional President, Latin America Pfizer Biopharma Group, Pfizer Inc.

13 President of Latin America Bank of America Merrill Lynch.

14 Chief Executive Officer and Vice Chairman, Kissinger Associates, Inc. 20-year CIA officer, President Bill Clinton's Director for Intelligence Programs at the National Security Council (1995–1996), and President George W. Bush's Central Intelligence Agency's Deputy Director for Intelligence (2002–2005).

15 Middle East advisor to President George H.W. Bush (1989–1993) and State Department Planning Director (2001–2003).

16 Senior Executive Advisor, Booz Allen Hamilton Inc. See Perkins (2004) for more information on Booz Allen Hamilton Inc.

17 Counsel, Boies & McInnis LLP, and on the board of the Center for International Studies, International Rescue Committee, Business Executives for National Security, and the Dean's Executive Committee at Harvard's Kennedy School of Government.

18 President, American University. President Barack Obama's Secretary of Health and Human Services (2014–2017).

19 Director, Belfer Center at the Harvard Kennedy School. President Barack Obama's Secretary of Defense (2015–2017).
20 Chairman, General Atlantic (American equity firm), on the Board of Thomson-Reuters (Canadian media conglomerate). Chairman of the board of trustees of Stanford University and co-chair of the board of directors of The Nature Conservancy. Trustee emeritus of The Brookings Institution.
21 Professor of Political Science at the Woodrow Wilson School at Princeton University, influential academic in the field of International Relations.
22 Chairman and Chief Executive Officer BlackRock
23 President, Warburg Pincus. Geithner served as 75th United States Secretary of the Treasury.
24 President, University of California, former U.S. Attorney (1993–1997), Attorney General of Arizona (1999–2003), Governor of Arizona (2003–2009), and President Barack Obama's first Homeland Security Secretary (2009–2013).
25 Jeane Kirkpatrick Professor of the Practice of International Affairs, Harvard Kennedy School.
26 Host of CNN's Fareed Zakaria GPS. Editor at large of *Time* magazine, and a regular *Washington Post* columnist. Editor of *Newsweek International* (2000-2010) and managing editor of *Foreign Affairs* (1992–2000). Member of CFR, Trilateral Commission, and the Bilderberg Group.
27 Current Moderator of *Face the Nation* on CBS News, Senior Foreign Affairs Correspondent. Former White House correspondent (2012–Present).
28 President Ronald Reagan's Assistant Secretary of State in various capacities (1981–1989), President George W. Bush's Deputy National Security Advisor (2005–2009), President Donald Trump's Special Representative for Venezuela (2019–Present).
29 American actor, film producer, director, and activist.
30 "The smart way to keep people passive and obedient is to strictly limit the spectrum of acceptable opinion, but allow very lively debate within that spectrum—even encourage the more critical and dissident views. That gives people the sense that there's free thinking going on, while all the time the presuppositions of the system are being reinforced by the limits put on the range of the debate" (Chomsky, 1998: p. 43).
31 "The Church Committee's conclusion accurately reflects the problems associated with Operation Mockingbird: "In examining the CIA's past and present use of the U.S. media, the Committee finds two reasons for concern. The first is the potential, inherent in covert media operations, for manipulating or incidentally misleading the American [sic] public. The second is the damage to the credibility and independence of a free press which may be caused by covert relationships with the U.S. journalists and media organisations" (United States. Congress. Senate. Select Committee to Study Governmental Operations with Respect to Intelligence Activities, 1976, p. 178-79).

References

Armstrong, A. (2014) *LittleSis.org.Think tank/defense map for transparify post*. https://littlesis.org/oligrapher/94-think-tank-defense-map-for-transparify-post [Accessed 31 August 2020].

AS/COA, A. (2020) *About AS/COA*. https://www.as-coa.org/about/about-ascoa [Accessed 31 August 2020].

Association of Religion Data Archives, et al. (1990–2014) *Religion and State (RAS) project*. https://www.thearda.com/world-religion/world-maps/?var=fun_4cat.

Bah, E. H., Brada, J. C., & Yigit, T. (2011) With a little help from our friends: The effect of USAID assistance on SME growth in a transition economy. *Journal of Comparative Economics* 39 (2), 205–220.

Baum, L., & Devins, N. (2017) Federalist court: How the Federalist Society became the de facto selector of Republican Supreme Court Justices. *Slate*, 31 January. https://slate.com/news-and-politics/2017/01/how-the-federalist-society-became-the-de-facto-selector-of-republican-supreme-court-justices.html [Accessed 21 July 2020].

Beattie, K. A. (2022) LittleSis.org. Clone: Think tank/defense map for transparify post. https://littlesis.org/oligrapher/8219-clone-think-tank-defense-map for-transparify-post.

Blum, W. (2003) *Killing hope: US military and CIA interventions since World War II*. London, Zed Books.

Blum, W. (2020) Overthrowing other people's governments: The master list. *William Blum*. https://williamblum.org/essays/read/overthrowing-other-peoples-governments-the-master-list [Accessed 31 August 2020].

Blumenthal, M. (2020) US govt meddling machine boasts of 'laying the groundwork for insurrection' in Nicaragua. *The Grayzone*, 24 April. https://thegrayzone.com/2018/06/19/ned-nicaragua-protests-us-government/ [Accessed 31 August 2020].

Brinkley, A. (1994) The problem of American conservatism. *American Historical Review* 99 (2), 409–429.

Brook, Tech. Sgt. Gregory. (2019) DoD, DoS, USAID Work Together to Provide Aid for Venezuelans. *U.S. Southern Command*. [Accessed 31 August 2020]. https://www.southcom.mil/Media/News/Article/1760186/dod-dos-usaid-work-together-to-provide-aid-for-venezuelans/

Brotherton, R. (2015) *Suspicious minds. Why we believe conspiracy theories*. New York, Bloomsbury Sigma.

Burack, C., & Snyder-Hall, C. R. (2012) Introduction: Right-wing populism and the media. *New Political Science* 34 (4), 439–454.

Bureau of Educational and Cultural Affairs. (2020) *History | Bureau of educational and cultural affairs*. https://eca.state.gov/fulbright/about-fulbright/history [Accessed 31 August 2020].

Butler, J. S. (2006) *Born again. The Christian right globalized*. London, Pluto Press.

Cann, H. W. (2015) *Climate change, still challenged: Conservative think tanks and skeptic frames*. Paper prepared for the annual meeting of the Western Political Science Association, Las Vegas, April 2–4, 1–19. http://www.wpsanet.org/papers/docs/wpsa15%20-%20cann.pdf.

Carroll, W. K. (2009) Transnationalists and national networkers in the global corporate elite. *Global networks* 9 (3), 289–314.

Carroll, W. K., & Sapinski, J. P. (2010) The global corporate elite and the transnational policy-planning network, 1996–2006: A structural analysis. *International Sociology* 25 (4), 501–538.

Castro-Rea, J. (2019) *My girlfriend became neo-Nazi. The right's presence and activity on the internet*. Berkeley Center for Right-Wing studies working paper series. https://escholarship.org/content/qt6q68m0sr/qt6q68m0sr_noSplash_5827d6c2994000c1a42673d414c355a4.pdf [Accessed 10 July 2020].

Cerrato, S. and Chamorro, P. (2020) *Artículo 66 on facebook watch*. https://www.facebook.com/Articulo66/videos/610897869483794/ [Accessed 31 August 2020].

Chapman, D. W., & Quijada, J. J. (2009) An analysis of USAID assistance to basic education in the developing world, 1990–2005. *International Journal of Educational Development* 29 (3), 268–280.

Chomsky, N. (1998). The common good.

Clapp-Wincek, C., & Blue, R. (2001) Evaluation of recent USAID evaluation experience. *Center for Development Information and Evaluation*. Working paper number: 320.

Clark, W. (2005) Petrodollar warfare: Dollars, Euros and the upcoming Iranian oil bourse. *Energy Bulletin*, Report number: 2.

Conway, E. M., & Oreskes, N. (2010) *Merchants of doubt: How a handful of scientists obscured the truth on issues from tobacco smoke to global warming*. London, Bloomsbury Publishing.

Council on Foreign Relations, C. (2020) *CFR membership list*. https://www.cfr.org/membership/roster [Accessed: 31 August 2020].

Dahl, R. A. (2001) *How democratic is the American constitution?* New Haven, Yale University Press.

Del Aguila, E. V. (2006) Invisible women: Forced sterilization, reproductive rights, and structural inequalities in Peru of Fujimori and Toledo. *Estudos e Pesquisas em Psicologia* 6 (1), 109–124.

Dickinson, E. (2009) A bright shining slogan. *Foreign Policy*, 22 August. https://foreignpolicy.com/2009/08/22/a-bright-shining-slogan/ [Accessed 31 August 2020].

Domhoff, G. W. (2014) The council on foreign relations and the grand area: Case studies on the origins of the IMF and the Vietnam war. *Class, Race and Corporate Power* 2 (1), 1–41.

Dunlap, R. E., & Jacques, P. J. (2013) Climate change denial books and conservative think tanks: Exploring the connection. *American Behavioral Scientist* 57 (6), 699–731.

Elrod, A. (2018) Property supremacy: Democracy in chains: The deep history of the radical right's stealth plan for America. *New Labor Forum* 27 (1), 127–132.

Epstein, S. B., & Fergusson, I. F. (1996) *National endowment for democracy: Policy and funding issues*. Congressional Research Service, Library of Congress.

Fang, L. (2013) *The machine. A field guide to the resurgent right*. New York, New Press.

Fischer, K., & Plehwe, D. 2013 Redes de think tanks e intelectuales de derecha en América Latina. *Nueva Sociedad* 245, 70–86.

Fisk, R. (2019) [Lecture] Public talk at the University of Alberta.

Fogarty, B. E. (2009) *Fascism. Why not here?* Lincoln, Potomac.

Forbath, W. E. (2006) Popular constitutionalism in the twentieth century: Reflections on the dark side, the progressive constitutional imagination, and the enduring ole of judicial finality in popular understandings of popular self-rule. *Chicago-Kent Law Review* 81 (3), 967.

Foundation Center (2015) *Foundation stats: Guide to the foundation center's research database*. Foundation Center. https://web.archive.org/web/20190825020428/http://data.foundationcenter.org/#/ foundations/all/nationwide/top:giving/list/2015 [Accessed 31 August 2020].

Fulbright, J. W. (1961) The first fifteen years of the fulbright program. *The Annals of the American Academy of Political and Social Science* 335 (1), 21–27.

Gerchik, J. R. F. (2002) Slouching towards extremism: The Federalist Society and the transformation of American Jurisprudence. *Nexus* 7, 45–48. https://heinonline.org/HOL/LandingPage?handle=hein.journals/nex7&div=9&id=&page= [Accessed 21 July 2020].

Gibelman, M., & Gelman, S. R. (2001). Very public scandals: Nongovernmental organizations in trouble. *Voluntas: International Journal of Voluntary and Nonprofit Organizations*, 49–66.

Gokay, B. (2005) The beginning of the end of the petrodollar: What connects Iraq to Iran. *Alternatives: Turkish Journal of International Relations* 4 (4), 40–56.

Goldenberg, S. (2012) Conservative think tanks step up attacks against Obama's clean energy strategy. *The Guardian*, 8 May. https://www.theguardian.com/environment/2012/may/08/conservative-thinktanks-obama-energy-plans [Accessed 21 July 2020].

Goldenberg, S. (2013) Secret funding helped build vast network of climate denial thinktanks. *The Guardian*, 14 February. https://www.theguardian.com/environment/2013/feb/14/funding-climate-change-denial-thinktanks-network [Accessed 21 July 2020].

Goldstein, M. P., & Moss, T. J. (2005). Compassionate conservatives or conservative compassionates? US political parties and bilateral foreign assistance to Africa. *Journal of Development Studies, 41*(7), 1288–1302.

Gonzalez, V. (2012) Rediscovering my Latin American professional identity: A reflection on a fulbright experience. *Journal of International Students* 2 (2), 131–132.

Green, J. C., & Guth, J. L. (1988) The Christian right in the Republican Party: The case of Pat Robertson's supporters. *The Journal of Politics* 50 (1), 150–165.

Guilhot, N. (2005) *The democracy makers: Human rights and international order*. New York, Columbia University Press.

Hale, E. T. (2003) *A quantitative and qualitative evaluation of the National Endowment for Democracy 1990–1999*. Doctoral thesis. Louisiana State University and Agricultural & Mechanical College.

Hearn, J. (1998) The 'NGO-isation' of Kenyan society: USAID & the restructuring of health care. *Review of African Political Economy* 25 (75), 89–100.

Heilman, L. C. (2017). *USAID in Bolivia: Partner Or Patrón?*. FirstForumPress.

Herman, E. S., & Chomsky, N. (2010). *Manufacturing consent: The political economy of the mass media*. Random House.

Hersh, S. (1982) The price of power. *The Atlantic*, 29 September. https://www.theatlantic.com/magazine/archive/1982/12/the-price-of-power/376309/ [Accessed 31 August 2020].

Hoeveler, R. C. (2020) *(Neo)liberalismo, democracia e 'diplomacia empresarial'. A história do Council of the Americas, 1965–2019*. Doctoral thesis. Universidade Federal Fluminense.

Hofstadter, R. J. (1964) *The paranoid style in American politics*. Hoboken, John Wiley & Sons.

Horne, G. (2014) *The counter-revolution of 1776. Slave resistance and the origins of the United States of America*. New York, New York University Press.

Horwitz, R. B. (2013) *America's right. Anti-establishment conservatism from goldwater to the Tea Party*. Cambridge, Polity Press.

Immerwahr, D. (2019) *How to hide an empire: a history of the greater United States*. New York, Farrar, Straus and Giroux.

Jeffreys-Jones, R. (1997) Why was the CIA established in 1947? *Intelligence and National Security* 12 (1), 21–40.

Jordan, J. (2009) After the 2008 Elections: The national endowment for democracy. *Nicaragua Network*. http://www.nicanet.org/wp-content/uploads/2009/04/155james-ned.pdf [Accessed August 30, 2020].

Klak, T. (1992) Excluding the poor from low-income housing programs: The roles of state agencies and USAID in Jamaica. *Antipode* 24 (2), 87–112.

Krueger, C. (2018). Conversing with Lawrence C. Heilman's USAID in Bolivia: Partner or Patrón?. *Bolivian Studies Journal, 23*, 151–187.

Knowlton, D. C. (1996) Mormonism in Latin America: Towards the twenty-first century. *Dialogue: A Journal of Mormon Thought* 29 (1), 159–176.

Kramer, L. D. (2004) *The people themselves: Popular constitutionalism and judicial review*. Oxford, Oxford University Press.

Latour, B. 2004. Why has critique run out of steam? From matters of fact to matters of concern. *Critical Inquiry* 30 (2), 225–248.

Livingstone, G. (2009) *America's backyard. The United States & Latin America from the Monroe Doctrine to the war on terror.* London, Zed Books.

López, W. (2020) EEUU lanza descarado plan intervencionista para tumbar al FSLN. *La Gente: Radio La Primerísima,* 31 July. https://www.radiolaprimerisima.com/noticias/general/287264/eeuu-lanza-descarado-plan-intervencionista-para-tumbar-al-fsln/ [Accessed 31 August 2020].

López Obrador, A. M. (2020) *President of Mexico's daily morning press conference.* [Presentation], 28 August.

MacLean, N. (2017) *Democracy in chains. The deep history of the radical right's stealth plan for America.* New York, Penguin.

Martin, W. (1996) *With god on our side: The rise of the religious right in America.* New York, Broadway Books.

Mayer, J. (2016) *Dark money: The hidden history of the billionaires behind the rise of the radical right.* New York, Anchor Books.

McCourt, D. M. (2017) The inquiry and the birth of international relations, 1917–19. *Australian Journal of Politics & History* 63 (3), 394–405.

McNutt, K., & Marchildon, G. (2009) Think tanks and the web: Measuring visibility and influence. *Canadian Public Policy / Analyse de Politiques* 35 (2), 219–236.

Meagher, R. (2012) The 'vast right-wing conspiracy': Media and conservative networks. *New Political Science* 34 (4), 469–484.

Mearsheimer, J. J., & Walt, S. M. (2007) *The Israel lobby and US foreign policy.* New York, Macmillan.

Mills, C. W. (1981). The power elite [1956]. New York.

Muirhead, R., & Rosenblum, N. L. (2019) *A lot of people are saying: The new conspiracism and the assault on democracy.* Princeton, Princeton University Press.

National Endowment for Democracy, N. (2020a) *About the national endowment for democracy.* https://www.ned.org/about/ [Accessed 31 August 2020].

National Endowment for Democracy, N. (2020b) *History of the national endowment for democracy.* https://www.ned.org/about/history/ [Accessed 31 August 2020].

National Endowment for Democracy, N. (2020c) *Latin America and Caribbean.* https://www.ned.org/region/latin-america-and-caribbean/ [Accessed 31 August 2020].

Norton, B. (2020) Right-wing Nicaraguan opposition boasts of support from US and EU in campaign to oust Sandinista gov't. *The Grayzone,* 7 February. https://thegrayzone.com/2020/02/07/nicaragua-opposition-support-us-eu-coalition/ [Accessed 31 August 2020].

Parmar, I. (2002). American foundations and the development of international knowledge networks. *Global networks,* 2(1), 13–30.

Parmar, I. (2005) Catalysing events, think tanks and American Foreign Policy shifts: A comparative analysis of the impacts of Pearl Harbor 1941 and 11 September 2001. *Government and Opposition* 40 (1), 1–25.

Perkins, J. (2004) *Confessions of an economic hit man.* San Francisco, Berrett-Koehler Publishers.

Perkins, J. (2016). *The new confessions of an economic hit man.* Berrett-Koehler Publishers.

Perry, L., & Cronin, C. (2012) *Mormons in American politics: From persecution to power.* Santa Barbara, ABC-CLIO.

Philadelphiensis, P. (1788) Antifederalist Paper 74.

Phillips, P. (2018) *Giants: The global power elite.* New York, Seven Stories Press.

Phua, K. L. (2001) Corporatization and privatization of public services: Origins and rise of a controversial concept. *Akademika* 58 (1), 45–57.

Plehwe, D. (2014) Think tank networks and the knowledge–interest nexus: The case of climate change. *Critical Policy Studies* 8 (1), 101–115.

Powell, L. F. (1971) *Confidential memorandum: Attack of American free enterprise system.* http://reclaimdemocracy.org/powell_memo_lewis/ [Accessed 24 January 2013].
Quigley, C. (1966) *Tragedy & hope.* New York, Macmillan.
Quigley, C. (1981) *Anglo-American establishment.* G. S. G. & Associates, Incorporated.
Riehl, J. (2007) *The Federalist Society and movement conservatism: How a fractious coalition on the right is changing constitutional law and the way we talk and think about it.* Doctoral thesis. University of North Carolina.
Roberts, S. M. (2014) Development capital: USAID and the rise of development contractors. *Annals of the Association of American Geographers* 104 (5), 1030–1051.
Rosenthal, L. (2020) *Empire of resentment: Populism's toxic embrace of nationalism.* New York, New Press.
Rosenthal, L., & Trost, C. (2012) *Steep: The precipitous rise of the Tea Party.* Berkeley, University of California Press.
Rothkopf, D. (2008) *Superclass: The global power elite and the world they are making.* New York, Farrar, Straus and Giroux.
Rupp, J. C. (1999) The fulbright program, or the surplus value of officially organized academic exchange. *Journal of Studies in International Education* 3 (1), 57–81.
Sapinski, J. P., & Carroll, W. K. (2018) Interlocking directorates and corporate networks. In Nölke, A., & May, C. (eds.), *Handbook of the international political economy of the corporation.* Cheltenham and Northampton, Edward Elgar Publishing, pp. 45–60.
Scherer, N., & Miller, B. (2009) The Federalist Society influence on the federal judiciary. *Political Research Quarterly* 62 (2), 366–378.
Scott, J. M. (1999) Transnationalizing democracy promotion: The role of Western political foundations and think tanks. *Democratization* 6 (3), 146–170.
Scott, J. M., & Steele, C. A. (2005) Assisting democrats or resisting dictators? The nature and impact of democracy support by the United States National Endowment for Democracy, 1990–99. *Democratization* 12 (4), 439–460.
Seelke, C. R. (2005) Overview of education issues and programs in Latin America. *Work.* https://pdf.usaid.gov/pdf_docs/Pcaab686.pdf.
Sharp, G. (1973) *The politics of nonviolent action: The dynamics of nonviolent action.* Manchester, NH, Extending Horizons Books.
Siegel, R. B. (2008) Dead or alive: Originalism as popular constitutionalism in Heller. *Harvard Law Review* 122, 224–228.
Skocpol, T. (1979) *States and social revolutions: A comparative analysis of France, Russia and China.* New York, Cambridge University Press.
Smith, J., Thompson, S., & Lee, K. (2017) The Atlas Network: A 'strategic ally' of the tobacco industry. *The International Journal of Health Planning and Management* 32 (4), 433–448.
Snow, N. (2010) *Propaganda, Inc. selling America's culture to the world.* New York, Seven Stories Press.
Stahl, J. (2016) *Right moves. The conservative think tank in American political culture since 1945.* Chappell Hill, The University of North Carolina Press.
Swiss Policy Research, S. (2017) The American empire and its media. *Swiss Policy Research,* 28 August. https://swprs.org/the-american-empire-and-its-media/ [Accessed 31 August 2020].
Tejerina, H., Closon, M. C., Paepe, P. D., Darras, C., Dessel, P. V., & Unger, J. P. (2014) Forty years of USAID health cooperation in Bolivia. A lose–lose game? *The International Journal of Health Planning and Management* 29 (1), 90–107.

Trapenberg Frick, K., Weinzimmer, D., & Waddell, P. (2014) The politics of sustainable development opposition: State legislative efforts to stop the United Nations' Agenda 21 in the United States. *Urban Studies* 52 (2), 209–232.

United States. Congress. Senate. Select Committee to Study Governmental Operations with Respect to Intelligence Activities. (1976). *Final Report of the Select Committee to Study Governmental Operations with Respect to Intelligence Activities, United States Senate: Foreign and military intelligence* (Book I). US Government Printing Office. https://www.intelligence.senate.gov/sites/default/files/94755_I.pdf

USAID, U. (2020a) *Bolivia: Political transition initiatives.* https://www.usaid.gov/political-transition-initiatives/where-we-work/bolivia [Accessed 31 August 2020].

USAID, U. (2020b) *USAID in Venezuela—frequently asked questions.* https://www.usaid.gov/venezuela/usaid-in-venezuela-faqs [Accessed 31 August 2020].

Valverde, G. A. (1999) Democracy, human rights, and development assistance for education: The USAID and World Bank in Latin America and the Caribbean. *Economic Development and Cultural Change* 47 (2), 401–419.

Van Horn, R., & Mirowski, P. (2009) The rise of the Chicago school of economics and the birth of neoliberalism. In Mirowski, P. & Plehwe, D. (eds.), *The road from Mont Pèlerin. The making of the neoliberal thought collective.* Cambridge, MA, Harvard University Press, pp. 139–180.

Whittington, K. E. (2011) Is originalism too conservative? *Harvard Journal of Law and Public Policy* 29 (34), 29–41.

Whittington, K. E. (2013) Originalism: A critical introduction. *Fordham Law Review* 82, 375.

Williamson, V., Skocpol, T., & Coggin, J. (2011) The Tea Party and the remaking of Republican Conservatism. *Perspectives on Politics* 9 (1), 25–43.

Woodrum, E. (1988) Moral conservatism and the 1984 presidential election. *Journal for the Scientific Study of Religion* 27 (2), 192–210.

Woods, R. B. (1987). Fulbright internationalism. *The Annals of the American Academy of Political and Social Science*, *491*(1), 22–35.

Xu, G. (1999) The ideological and political impact of US Fulbrighters on Chinese students: 1979–1989. *Asian Affairs: An American Review* 26 (3), 139–157.

Zietlow, R. E. (2012) Popular originalism? The Tea Party movement and constitutional theory. *Florida Law Review* 64 (2), 483–512.

Zweigenhaft, R. L., & Domhoff, G. W. (2011) *The new CEOs: Women, African American, Latino, and Asian American leaders of fortune 500 companies.* Lanham, Rowman & Littlefield Publishers.

PART II
Genesis and development of right-wing actors

2
ARGENTINA

Democracy, authoritarianism, and the pursuit of order

Ernesto Bohoslavsky and Sergio D. Morresi

Introduction

During most of the twentieth century, Argentina was subject to military dictatorships and unstable civil regimes emerged from restricted or rigged elections. It could be argued that the instability of the liberal and republican institutions and the acceptance of the army as a semi-legitimate political actor provoked the electoral and ideological weakness of the Argentine right (Di Tella, 1971). According to this approach, the rightist parties failed to impose their leaders and ideas through clean and fair elections because their cultural, geographical, and ideological fragmentation, and their inability to promote hegemonic projects, led them to lose even more electoral appeal and strengthened their distrust towards democracy (Gibson, 1996). In addition, it would be possible to argue that the frailness of the civilian governments and their susceptibility to the pressures of the economic corporations show the economic and social strength of the bourgeoisie (Boron, 2000; Cannon, 2016). Argentina's elites were powerful enough to "capture the state" and control the political game, so they did not need to build political machines to represent their interests (Castellani, 2004). In any case, both perspectives share the idea that—in the face of unforeseen situations that jeopardised the hierarchical order—right-wing leaders rushed to summon the military to undermine the democratic regime and the reformist impulses of the major political parties: the *Unión Cívica Radical* (Radical Civic Union, UCR) and Peronist *Partido Justicialista* (Justicialist Party, PJ).

However, it is not necessary to choose between the two positions that we have just outlined. It is true that the elite could maintain its primacy even when lacking a powerful electoral representation. And it is also true that this absence led to the weakening of the democratic game. As we will show in this chapter, Argentina's economic and cultural elite, although internally fragmented, has systematically

DOI: 10.4324/9781003352266-5

identified itself with a liberal-conservative tradition that coexisted tensely with democratic principles and had no hesitation in using clearly anti-democratic and illiberal practices to maintain its privileges. In this sense, the feebleness of the political right is not caused only by the disdain for politics of a powerful elite; neither can it be reduced to being a consequence of a politically orphan ruling class that resorted to coups d'état as a second-best solution. In our interpretation the elite's search for maintaining a hierarchical order led to the use of diverse tools, and to the pursuit of different paths, some of them contradictory, and many times evidently anti-democratic. For decades, this fact prevented the development of a stable and autonomous political right capable of playing with the rules of polyarchy. However, since the end of the twentieth century, the elite learned to coexist with a liberal democracy that had a limited disruptive potential, thus allowing the growth of political right-wing forces with a more independent agenda.

We understand the political right as a set of ideological and organisational traditions historically situated that have a profound apprehension about the quest for equality and inclusion, which are generally perceived as causing an unjust dispossession (Bobbio, 1995; Lipset and Raab, 1981). Each tradition is articulated by discursive and cognitive processes of understanding and identification, which are characterised by the presence of two central elements: (1) the exclusion of at least one concept that, transformed into anathema, serves as a boundary or as constitutive outside, and (2) a set of ideas acting as a founding myth capable of explaining past actions and justifying present choices and plans, and playing as the reverse of what has been left out. As each tradition has its processes of understanding/identification, the right-wings are not necessarily linked to each other by sympathy, and it is not strange that they fight each other, but they also can establish collaborative relations in certain circumstances. In order to study the Argentinian case, we propose to distinguish two rightist traditions: the nationalism, deeply linked to Catholicism, and the liberal-conservatism (in a Burkean sense).

The nationalist right-wing rejected the inclusion of what it considers to be foreign and erected as a founding myth the idea of a sovereign nation resisting external people or ideas. Generally, the avoidance of the alien is based on the conviction that Argentine identity is inseparable from its Hispanic and Catholic legacy and the certainty that the army and the Church are the only and natural custodians of the "national being". This tradition usually characterises its enemies as an eternal conspirator against Argentina, its religion, economy, and territory (Lvovich, 2006). Concerning the economy, it frequently stands against free markets and in favour of strong state-driven regulations; it also supports the creation/underpin of a hierarchical, Christianised society, organised through elite and corporative agreements. Regarding organisational patterns, they used to form leagues, athenaeums, and even paramilitary bands. Some nationalist parties led by Peronists and ex-military enjoyed momentary or local successes,[1] and several of its members entered into cabinets of elected or de facto governments, in political or educational areas (Lewis, 2001; Rodríguez, 2011). They had a low capacity for political mobilisation because of their ideological authoritarianism and the conviction that multiparty democracy was alien to the national spirit; however, nationalism obtained cultural repercussions such as the imposition of a "revisionist" perspective on national history.[2]

The second great rightist tradition is the liberal-conservative, which rejects the social, political, or cultural inclusion of the popular sectors and embraces a hierarchical republic as a structuring axis. This current includes politicians, businessmen, and intellectuals with sympathies for the liberal organisation of the economy and republican regime. The central figures of this tradition did not have an explicitly anti-democratic discourse but expressed reservations and fears about the "abuses of democracy" (demagoguery, economic, and political populism) and sought to shrink the scope of citizenship or to patronise the *demos*. UCR first and Peronism later were its main enemies, as it appeared as the local version of economic over-regulation, anti-liberal authoritarianism, or a mere prelude to Communism. This tradition was consolidated at the centre of the political and ideological scene in the 1970s, displacing the nationalist tradition with which it had competed and occasionally collaborated before that. The liberal-conservative current found space in both democratic and dictatorial governments, especially in the Ministry of Economy, the Ministry of Agriculture, and the Central Bank (Senkman, 1993). Liberal-conservatives postulated that the critical decisions should be taken by "non-partisans" (usually technocrats, mainly economists) freed from the spurious pressures of organised politics and social interests (as labour unions). Business chambers consistently defended liberal principles in the economy but also manoeuvred to prevent reforms from affecting their advantages in the local market (Sidicaro, 2002). Economic liberalism was compatible with the acceptance or even promotion of authoritarian regimes, restricted political participation (whether qualified voting or other institutional limits to the majority will) since they understood that guaranteeing civic (mainly the economical related) freedom was the only obligation of the State (Vicente, 2015). They used to organise themselves in athenaeums, intellectual circles, or business lobbies. This tradition was not very successful in the polls;[3] its members sought better luck through political interventions of the army to restrict massive political activism or the "waywardness" of reformist governments.[4]

In the first section we summarise some of the main socio-historical Argentine traits and present its most important political actors in analytical perspective. In the second section, we introduce a chronological approach to the nationalist and liberal-conservative traditions between the rise of mass democracy in 1916 and the abrupt end of the Peronist government in 1955. The next section focuses on the most violent and unstable period of Argentine political life that included recurrent and violent dictatorships until 1983. In the fourth section, we move forward to the period between the restoration of democracy into the present (2019); here, we examine neoliberalism as the primary right-wing current in contemporary Argentina as well as its convergence with national-populism. Finally, in the last section, we summarise our findings.

A new, under-populated country

Argentina is today one of the largest countries in the world (its main area is 1,073,500 m²), but its population is only 45 million inhabitants (most of them descendants of Spaniard and Italian immigrants). That disequilibrium between an extended territory and a small demographic volume fed the myth of an immense and unpopulated *Pampa*, despite the fact that it is a highly urbanised and industrialised country with diverse regions and climates (including the Andean Northwest and Patagonia, the subtropical Gran Chaco and Mesopotamia, and an extremely long Atlantic shore). Argentina is also a member of the G20, despite its average GDP (barely the 28th largest economy of the world). Although GDP per capita is relatively high (around $11,600 in 2018), its Gini coefficient is unstable (oscillating between 0.54 and 0.44 in the last 15 years), and the population has gone through several economic crises since the end of the twentieth century until today.

Argentina was part of the former territory of the Viceroyalty of the River Plate created in 1776 by the Spanish Crown. The country declared its independence in 1816 after a political revolution started in Buenos Aires in May 1810. In the following years, the leaders of the new country involved themselves in civil wars between *unitarios* (centralists demanding the primacy of Buenos Aires City) and *federales* (defenders of the provincial autonomies). The extended and bloody confrontation culminated only with the country's reorganisation of 1861. Although Presidents Bartolomé Mitre (1862–1868) and Domingo Sarmiento (1868–1874) pointed out that Argentina was a "liberal born country" (Halperin Donghi, 1988), it is widely recognised that it was only at the end of the nineteenth century that a radical economic and social metamorphosis began, orienting the country in a different direction. In 1879 the government launched a military campaign against the Indigenous groups of the Pampa and Patagonia that almost duplicated the national territory. In the final decades of the century, the Pampa area transformed into a great commodities exporter (mainly meat and wheat), informally but strongly linked to the British economic global networks. The process stimulated the arrival of almost six million European migrants between 1870 and 1914: the growing presence of foreign inhabitants in the country contributed enormously to transform the national demographic and ethnic patterns. After the 1930s, the national economy was transformed by the industrial growth and a more aggressive State intervention. The 1929 crisis and later World War II allowed expanding State action. In the 1960s and 1970s Argentina reached a high industrialisation rate, however, still dependent on traditional commodities exports.

At the beginning of the twentieth century, the oligarchic political regime was ruled by the conservative *Partido Autonomista Nacional* (National Autonomist Party, PAN) that kept almost full control of the political landscape through patronage relations and informally restricted franchise (Sábato, 2001; Botana, 1985). Rural turmoil and urban strikes and agitations as early as the centenary of the May Revolution (1910) showed the problems associated with the demand for democratisation by the UCR and Socialist Party. In 1912, a mandatory and secret male suffrage bill was passed and paved the way for UCR's triumph between 1916 and 1930. The success of the *golpe* of September 1930 that overthrew the UCR president Yrigoyen inaugurated a path of liberal institutions' weakness that lasted more than half a century. Between 1930 and 1983, six coups d'état reached their goals (1930, 1943, 1955, 1962, 1966, and 1976): 22 of those 53 years underwent a military dictatorship. Most of that time, one of the main parties (UCR or PJ) was proscribed. Among the elected presidents (Agustín Justo, 1932; Roberto Ortiz, 1938; Juan Perón, 1946, 1951, and 1973; Arturo Frondizi, 1958; Arturo Illia, 1963; Héctor Cámpora, 1973), only two of them were able to conclude the term.

The military—as in Brazil, Bolivia, and Guatemala—became a key political actor in the country. The Argentine Army underwent a new and efficient professionalisation process at the beginning of the twentieth century, which finally led to its growing autonomy towards the civilian government (Rouquié, 1994). The connections to the Pentagon and the so-called "National Security Doctrine" (Velásquez Rivera, 2002) during the hottest years of the Cold War contributed to legitimate military interventions in political life. This trend almost disappeared during the 1990s when the democratic restoration and the post–Cold War geopolitical shift left no political room for authoritarian and military-controlled governments in Argentina.

Most of the people in Argentina were Catholics. The 1853 Constitution acknowledged Catholicism as the official religion and forced the State to sustain the clergy. Liberal elites had some conflicts with the Vatican at the end of the nineteenth century; however, they were rapidly forgotten, and the Catholic Church returned to the hegemonic bloc in the 1910s. The Argentine Catholic Church was probably the nearest to Rome and stayed firmly close to the most intransigent and fundamentalist principles. The Catholic Church had numerous links with the wealthiest families: high-class women participated in charity Catholic associations and were committed with a traditional gendered pattern behaviour. After the 1930 crisis, the Church insistently spread the political myth that Argentina was a Hispanic-Catholic country (Zanatta, 1996): that myth acted as a counter-image of the liberal and cosmopolitan country that politicians of the late nineteenth century spun. The growing presence of the Church in Argentina became even stronger during Perón's governments in the mid-century, but the love affair between Perón and the Church ended up bitterly during the 1950s. In the 1960s the effects of the Second Vatican Council prompted enormous ideological conflicts within the Catholic world: some of the Catholic activists engaged in Marxism-inspired perspectives, and others assumed very conservative and reactionary points of view on politics, religion, and society.

The first democracy and the fears of the elite (1916–1955)

At the end of the nineteenth century Argentina had an oligarchic regime in which the right to vote was de facto restricted, and the selection of political authorities was carried out within families that also controlled the most important national economic resources (Botana, 1985). This situation changed after a new electoral legislation was passed in 1912, which guaranteed secret and compulsory ballots for adult males. The conservative government initiated the reform process for several reasons. First, to avoid further uprisings of the opponent, UCR, and to modify their decision to not participate in the elections. Second, to separate the main opposition from the anarchists, irreducible in their fight against capitalist exploitation. Third, to modernise State institutions and their relations with society, to better face the challenges of a world in which inter-imperialist tensions promised more significant challenges (Zimmermann, 1995).

The liberal-conservatives of that period acted as sorcerers' apprentices, who unleashed powerful forces that failed to control: they promoted democracy to legitimise their ruling position, but that ended up plunging them into political impotence. The long-awaited modern and unified liberal-conservative party, capable of bringing together the provincial forces behind a unified leadership and principles, was not constituted. Unexpectedly, the electoral laws opened the door to the presidential triumphs of the UCR.

The liberal-conservative disapproval of UCR governments focused on administrative disorder, patronage, disdain for legislative power, and the overruling of provincial autonomies through presidential interventions. For liberal-conservatives, it was necessary to improve the republican order, not to overcome it: the UCR authorities were inept rulers, but democracy was better than those occasional *parvenus*. Even the nationalist Argentine Patriotic League (*Liga Patriótica Argentina*, LPA), the paramilitary organisation created in 1919, did not want to change the political regime, but to close the possibilities open to left activists. LPA added xenophobia and anti-leftism to the liberal-conservative ideological background, paving the way for the emergence of the nationalist right-wing (McGee Deutsch, 1986: p. 225).

Towards the end of the 1920s, a more profound criticism of the democratic regime emerged, the reactionary nationalism, which was not aimed at purifying electoral mechanisms, improving administrative controls, or complying with current legislation, but to put an end to the Argentine decline. High-class intellectuals challenged democracy because they believed that it was indistinguishable from the electoral triumph of the UCR (Echeverría, 2009; Lvovich, 2003; Tato, 2001). This position appeared intensely in the newspapers *La Nueva República* and *La Fronda*, which used racist, classist, and anti-popular speeches. In their perspective, the *radicales* were a new version of Barbarism. These ideas ended up feeding a reactionary nationalist anti-liberal tradition that had its golden age in the 1930s.

Conservative branches of the UCR, popular conservatives, and reactionary nationalists began to work openly in favour of a coup that finally took place on September 6, 1930. Between 1930 and 1943, the two right-wing traditions dominated the government: first the nationalist, between 1930 and 1932, and later the liberal-conservative wing, which dominated between 1932 and 1943.

The nationalists had the conviction that the liberal order was exhausted and nonsense in Argentina. They diagnosed the need to establish an orderly, authoritarian, and integral regime, and considered democracy an ageing, decadent, foreignising regime that lacked the strength necessary to face contemporary challenges. One of the promoters of these ideas was General José Félix Uriburu, who led the coup of 1930 and was dictator until 1932. Uriburu promoted corporatist constitutional reform and the formation of Fascist-like militias. In the 1930s, the nationalists created numerous political groups, but they never managed to unite under a leadership or a party. They oscillated between criticism and the alliance with the conservatives in power (thus, Marcelo Sánchez Sorondo was a national senator while saying that democracy had to be overcome as a political regime). Nationalists began to mobilise lower-class people with social issues in a tone close to that of the Spanish *Falange* (Lvovich, 2006; Rubinzal, 2005; Spektorowski, 1990; Klein, 2001). Groups such as the *Alianza de la Juventud Nacionalista* (Nationalist Youth Alliance, AJN) installed "social justice" as a matter of political turmoil, merging ideas of nationalism, socialism, anti-communism, anti-liberalism, and anti-Semitism. Their speech indicated that there was a causal link between bad living conditions and the economic predominance of foreign interests. They explained Argentina's past and present as the result of a conspiracy that involved the "Sepoy oligarchy", Judeo-Marxist internationalism, British imperialism, and, occasionally, Chilean people (Bohoslavsky, 2009; Lvovich, 2003).

During the 1930s, the liberal-conservative right-wing was made up of politicians from the provinces and rural landowners' chambers, all linked to the old oligarchic regime abandoned in 1916. These groups possessed a remarkable ambiguity regarding the democratic regime. On the one hand, they permanently claimed the republican soul of Argentina and called for elections. However, their practices violated the very nature of political participation due to their use of fraud on a large scale, political violence (including a homicide within the Senate hemicycle), and the harassment of the main party (UCR) for considering it contrary to democracy. An innovative feature of those years is the renewed approach between the Catholic Church and the political authorities. Conservative governments (1932–1943) sought sources of extra-electoral legitimacy by getting closer to the Church. Official support for the organisation of the International Eucharistic Congress in 1934 is one of the best-known expressions of that relation.

Many of the tensions within the rightist traditions' currents emerged explosively with the beginning of the Peronist experience in the mid-1940s, which redefined the previous ideological struggles and identities. Many nationalists felt that Peronism had managed to impose many of its old core ideas: compulsory Catholic education, improvement of workers' welfare, promotion of industrialisation, neutral international politics, and recognition of Franco's government in Spain (Piñeiro, 1997). That is why many nationalists became authorities or representatives of the Peronist regime (1946–1955), a government which selectively discarded some of the nationalism flagships (such as anti-Semitism and the disdain for massive political participation) but put others (as "Social Justice" and the political "third position" against liberalism and communism) in the foreground. Thus, Peronist experience helped with the birth of a popular nationalist right with a more inclusive social concern, usually absent in reactionary nationalism (Besoky, 2016).

Unlike the nationalists, the liberal-conservative right manifested divergent and ambiguous attitudes towards Peronism. Many popular conservatives entered and even led the Peronist Party in various provinces, but others never entirely accepted it (Macor and Tcach, 2003; Nállim, 2014). Indeed, some popular conservatives felt bothered by the Peronist will to expand and take advantage of the political participation of the working classes (and women) and the intensive propaganda. The fact that Peronism robbed them of the sympathy of the Episcopate and the Catholic militants also annoyed them. The call to reform the constitution in 1949, with the objective that President Perón could be re-elected and that the role of the intervening and regulatory State and a more holistic conception of society was established, strengthened the doctrinarians' criticism and helped to strengthen a republican mythology and language. For the liberal-conservative doctrinarians, Peronism lacked moderation and pluralist spirit and, since its beginning, was marching towards some form of totalitarian government and economy that would suffocate people's opinions and private initiative.

Dictatorships, violence, and democracy under surveillance (1955–1983)

In 1955, another coup d'état, in which converged reactionary nationalists, doctrinarian liberal-conservatives, and some popular conservatives, ended with the presidency of Juan Perón. Although in the next three decades the heterogeneous right-wing did not unify, the liberal-conservatives manoeuvred to reach a new hegemony over the nationalist traditions. The successive dictatorships between 1955 and 1983 launched liberal-conservative or neoliberal policies: anti-liberal nationalism no longer played an essential role within the rightist field of those years. The nationalists produced an extremely aggressive press, as well as xenophobic and authoritarian paramilitary bands—some of them linked to Peronist unions in the 1970s—which opted for anti-leftist terrorism. These groups were not numerically relevant, and their role in politics was mainly restricted to violent and intimidating activities.

Between 1955 and 1973, Perón was exiled, and the PJ was banned. So, the Peronists mainly participated in unions or in neo-Peronist parties, but at the same time the dyad between left and right inserted within the party. So, during the 1960s and 1970s, leftist and rightist Peronist political organisations fought against other parties but also between them. After 18 years of proscription, Peronism was allowed to participate in free elections in March 1973, when a proxy candidate (Héctor Cámpora) obtained 50% of the votes. However, it is worth noting that liberal-conservatives obtained almost the same number of votes as the UCR (nearly 21% of the votes), although it occurred in a more fragmented way. This fact showed that there was some popular support base for Argentina's right-wing.

Perón returned to Argentina in 1973 in the middle of a spiral of violence between leftist and rightist Peronists. At first, Perón intended to curb the exalted moods, but in the end, he expelled the main left movements from Peronism and unleashed both the armed forces and right-wing paramilitary gangs to restore order (Franco, 2012). After Perón died in 1974, his widow and successor María Estela Martínez swayed between the support of right-wing popular nationalism and quasi-neoliberal technocratic bets in order to control a chaotic situation (Restivo and Dellatorre, 2005). Nevertheless, the failure of the Peronist economic plans and the continuity of violence paved the way to a new *golpe* in 1976.

Liberal-conservatives and nationalist reactionaries welcomed the new military government, but it was clear that, contrary to what had happened previously, the Peronist right (the national popular right-wing) had no more place. Many right-wing leaders announced their unconditional support for the new dictatorship and served as civil authorities of it.[5] The self-titled "*Proceso de Reorganización Nacional*" (National Reorganisation Process, 1976–1983) was, at first, determined to remain isolated as much as possible so that it would not contaminate itself with politics and prosecute a reconfiguration of the country (Palermo and Novaro, 2003; Quiroga, 2004). The aims announced by the military were not different from the civilian liberal-conservative and nationalist-reactionary goals: defeat the leftists' subversion, re-establish economic order and social hierarchies, and put an end to populist experience. However, the profile of the "reorganised Argentina" was not clear at all. Thus, once the *guerrilla* and the nonviolent left were bloodily crushed, the dictatorship exhausted and lost itself into a labyrinth of impotence (Canelo, 2008).

Liberal-conservatives after 1955 had a smooth relationship with the Church, and had a more individualistic, sceptical, and pessimistic anthropological vision than their precursors of the nineteenth century (Harbour, 1985; Montserrat, 1992; Ostiguy, 2017). Nevertheless, as we have already mentioned, liberal-conservatives form a broad and prolific family. On the one hand, there were the doctrinarian liberal-conservatives, strongly linked with Buenos Aires' elites and great landowners, financial activity, and capital-intensive industries. The doctrinarians did not reach electoral relevance before the 1980s but channelled their ideas almost exclusively through personal contacts with political leaders and professional advisers of the non-Peronist main political parties (the two factions in which radicalism split after 1956) or with high military commanders. The particularities of the Buenos Aires doctrinarian groups led to the formation of a political class oriented to technocracy and, therefore, more permeable to the neoliberal ideas and models, already present since the 1930s (Morresi, 2011). The other liberal-conservative group was the popular conservatives who represented the provinces. Differently from the doctrinarians, they emphasised more traditional discourses, with references to family, Christian values, and history. This faction included old and new conservative parties who were able to act together for two decades because they had two enemies in common: Peronist populism and doctrinarian liberalism in Buenos Aires.[6]

In spite of all the rightist actors sharing anti-Peronism and anti-Communism, they had very different political alternatives in mind. Nationalists insisted on the need for some organic, authoritarian, martial, and hierarchical nation. For liberal-conservatives, the option was a republic, framed within traditional values (effort and temperance as opposed to laziness and dissipation), religious perspective (Western Christian civilisation faced with left totalitarianism), political-economic principles (private property to guarantee freedom against the disrespect for the property of populism), and ethical-political concepts (as Berlinian negative freedom). For rightist actors, democracy should be subordinated to the republic, and masses had to follow moral and cultural norms derived from the Christian-Western spirit. Its elitism expressed not in racist bias, but in "anti-totalitarian" concerns, according to which majorities could lead to the oppression of minorities and the enlargement of State intervention reduces people's margins of manoeuvre.

The republic embraced by the liberal-conservatives is supposedly a tradition bequeathed by the leaders who had placed Argentina among the powerful nations of the world at the end of the nineteenth century. The "old order" functioned as a golden age to which Argentina could return if populism and labour unions were rejected. Thus, to the extent that liberal-conservatives advanced in its domain of the right-wing field in the 1960s and 1970s, they alienated potential support from some right-oriented trade union Peronist leaders, and a dictatorship regime was regularly presented as the only way to impose the necessary order.

A new right for a new democracy (1983–2019)

The occupation of the Malvinas/Falkland Islands in 1982 was the last and desperate attempt of the military to extend a lame regime. However, the defeat of the Argentine troops put the final stitches on the dictatorship known as *Proceso*. As the end of the authoritarian government was relatively abrupt, the liberal-conservatives found themselves poorly prepared for the return of democracy because the enthusiastic support of the right-wing groups for the most homicidal and brutal regime ever seen by Argentina baulked at their electoral allurement. As it became clear that the military authorities were going to abandon power, Álvaro Alsogaray, traditional leader of the Buenos Aires' liberal-conservatism, founded a new party: *Unión del Centro Democrático* (Union of the Democratic Centre, UCEDE) inspired by the Spanish experience of Adolfo Suárez (a former Franco's regime minor figure who led the transition to liberal democracy in the 1970s). UCEDE was aimed at reuniting some cadres of the moribund dictatorship and liberal-conservative figures who had been critical of the regime because they considered it "insufficiently liberal" (Morresi and Vicente, 2020). Unlike previous right-wing political projects in Argentina, the UCEDE was created with an orientation towards neoliberalism, in particular to the German social market economy (Mansilla, 1983; Doman and Olivera, 1989). This neoliberal discourse contrasted with the more traditional and ideologically ambiguous one offered by the popular conservatives. Because popular conservatives (or federalists) chose to focus on the provincial elections, UCEDE was the only nation-based centre-right party to obtain seats in the National Congress in the 1983 elections, allowing visibility of its neoliberal ideas.

UCEDE leaders saw the unexpected triumph of the UCR presidential candidate Raúl Alfonsín as the long-awaited end of the "Peronist threat", a sign that Argentinian people had evolved and rejected the populist siren call. Especially for the younger ones, UCEDE should change too, abandoning the traditional elitist pattern to transform into a modern and competitive organisation, internally democratic and far away from authoritarianism (Arriondo, 2015). At the same time, the growing political and socio-economic fragmentation of Argentina facilitated the neoliberal seduction of the urban middle class, and, by 1987, UCEDE had consolidated as the third political force. This achievement allowed Buenos Aires' liberal-conservatism to lead the rightist political field. In 1988, Alsogaray reunited under his command most of the dispersed federalist parties and movements in a robust *Alianza de Centro* (Centre Alliance, AC) to turn it into a powerful force with real chances of imposing a neoliberal political agenda. The opportunity for realising this objective came unexpectedly in 1989.

Carlos Menem (PJ) won the presidency in 1989 after a populist campaign, which assured that Peronism would repair the UCR's failures with a "productive revolution" and a sharp increase in wages. However, after his victory, Menem embraced pro-market reforms and invited Alsogaray to join the government. Menem's right turn found relatively little resistance, in part due to the disciplinary effect of the hyperinflation crisis that marked the chaotic end of Alfonsín's administration, but also because of the influence of neoliberal ideas throughout the 1980s (Smith, 1990; Heredia, 2015). The entry of AC figures into the Peronist government had ambiguous consequences: Menem's administration did carry the neoliberal agenda driven for years by Alsogaray's party, but the Peronist success produced the electoral decline of liberal-conservatism as an autonomous force.

In the meantime, the social consequences of pro-market economics opened the door for the resurface of a nationalist right. The former military officer Aldo Rico—who had been a prisoner for having mutinied against the Alfonsín government and was pardoned by Menem—founded the *Movimiento por la Dignidad y la Independencia* (Movement for Dignity and Independence MODIN) in 1991. Rico's party grew criticising the neoliberalism and cosmopolitanism of the alliance between "treacherous Peronists" and liberal-conservatives. However, in 1995, Rico joined forces with the Buenos Aires' Peronist governor. Thus, by the mid-1990s, the two Argentine rightist traditions were, in one way or another, inside the Peronist government. This fact was something completely new, as anti-Peronism has been one of the Argentine right's main features since the mid-1940s.

In 1999, an electoral front called "*Alianza*" (Alliance, composed by the UCR and centre-left parties) won the presidency with a campaign centred on the continuity of the market reforms but in a more clean and polite way. The Alliance government collapsed in December 2001 in a wave of social protests pushing for the resignation of the president De la Rúa (Pucciarelli and Castellani, 2014).

The depth of the 2001 Argentine economic and political crisis can be hardly exaggerated. New structures on the right emerged from the organisational decomposition of UCR and PJ. Ricardo López Murphy—former UCR's Minister of Finance—founded the party *Recrear Argentina* (Recreate Argentina) with a neoliberal orientation. Former president Carlos Menem led a faction of PJ towards the right, adding conservative cultural issues to the promise to "go back" to the economic orthodoxy. In the 2003 elections, López Murphy and Menem campaigned with a neoliberal agenda and obtained 18% and 26% of the votes, respectively, results that showed neoliberal support despite the crisis. However, in the second turn, Menem desisted from his candidacy, and another Peronist, Néstor Kirchner, who had campaigned with a more centre-left program, was elected president with only 22% of the vote. Even as Kirchner arrived at the government with feeble support, he began to deploy various initiatives associated with progressive demands accompanied by moderate decisions regarding economic policy (Novaro, 2006; Pucciarelli and Castellani, 2017). In 2007, Cristina Fernández de Kirchner succeeded her husband in the presidency and developed a set of policies oriented against neoliberal heritage, such as the nationalisation of the retirement and pension funds. This left turn at the national level was mirrored with a more energetic opposition from the right.

In this context, Mauricio Macri, a businessman and chairman of a popular soccer team, announced the foundation of a new centre-right party that would later become *Propuesta Republicana* (Republican Proposal, PRO). Despite publicly identifying himself with Peronism, Macri was an outsider coming from the corporate world with a neoliberal agenda and some social conservative positions regarding gender issues. Macri chose to build his party in Buenos Aires city and run for Mayor in 2003. On its electoral debut, PRO triumphed in the first round but was defeated in the second one. Despite this result, the party consolidated into the opposition (Mauro, 2005). In 2007, Macri undertook a more centrist campaign, and PRO finally triumphed in Buenos Aires' elections. PRO was not a new label for an old party, nor was it a split of a traditional movement, but a new player, constructed on the basis of a neoliberal think tank, that confidently stepped onto the territory of established parties to change the manner of doing politics rather than the contents of it (Sikk, 2012; Morresi and Vommaro, 2014).

PRO was from its beginning a different kind of rightist party. Unlike the doctrinarian liberal-conservatives, PRO betted on pragmatism. Its main aim was not to impose an ideological agenda but to win elections. As PRO wanted to seize power through elections, it supported the democratic regime (Morresi, 2015), and its leaders managed to adapt to new demands (thus, for example, they went from condemning homosexuality as a disease to promoting same-sex marriage). PRO also departed from previous rightist parties for not being virulently anti-Peronist.[7] Indeed, PRO nourished itself from a heterogeneous milieu that comprehends liberal-conservative, Peronists and *Radicales* political cadres, corporate and professional figures, and Catholic and NGO activists, a much broader base of recruitment than Argentina's previous rightist experiences (Morresi and Vommaro,

2014). Even as Macri insisted that his party was "beyond left and right", PRO was moving towards an increasingly anti-leftist position, denouncing the perils of the populist path stoked by Cristina Fernández de Kirchner that, in his view, approached Argentina to the Bolivarian "twenty-first century Socialism". From then on, a sort of "red scare" was intermittently activated.

Even as PRO grew, in 2015, it still did not seem prepared to win national elections and faced pressures from the mainstream media to pursue a centre-right Peronist as ally. However, PRO decided to join forces with the UCR and other centre-right minor parties in an electoral front called *Cambiemos* (Let's Change). At the same time, Macri courted the Peronist vote (fragmented among those who supported or opposed the continuity of Kirchnerism) and sought to move away from the traditional right-wing profile through gestures of high symbolic value such as inaugurating a monument honouring Perón. In this way, PRO managed to frame the 2015 election around the opposition between the old and the new (the name "Let's Change" was not accidental) and moved it away from left/right or Peronism/anti-Peronism cleavages (Morresi, 2017). This fact allowed it to prevail in the elections, and Macri became the first right-oriented president in Argentina elected in transparent and fair elections by universal suffrage.

Macri's government performance in its first two years was mediocre at best. However, in 2017, Macri's party managed to consolidate in the midterm elections based on consumer-friendly policies financed through external indebtedness. Nevertheless, other aspects of the incumbents' campaigning deserve observation. *Cambiemos*' discourse, that was moderate and centrist in 2015, moved clearly to the right in a series of issues like security (proposing hardening sentences, repressing social protests, and empowering security forces) and public services (increasing rates far beyond inflation and arguing that those who could not pay should learn to live differently than they were used to be by populist governments). The revalidation of the mandate at the polls enabled Macri to deploy a more aggressive reform agenda. However, *Cambiemos* met with substantial obstacles both in the National Congress and in the streets, where a heterogeneous opposition contested the government initiatives. As a result of the high foreign indebtedness and the absence of reforms, external financing was exhausted, which led the government to devalue the currency, seek IMF support, and take regressive and unpopular economic measures. With very few achievements to show, *Cambiemos* chose to strengthen its identity, adopting a more "republican" grammar and an anti-Peronist discourse, an attitude that helped Peronism to reunite and beat Macri's candidacy for re-election in 2019.

Nevertheless, even if *Cambiemos* was defeated in the polls, it is worth analysing the form in which it led its orientation to the right in the final months of its term, approaching some current European national-populist right (Mudde, 2007; Eatwell and Goodwin, 2018). Indeed, Macri's government campaigned mostly on atavistic fears, as xenophobia (denouncing an inexistent "uncontrolled immigration"), red scare (accusing some Peronist candidates of having been communists serving Venezuela and Cuba), and security panic (encouraging the private use of guns). *Cambiemos*' leaders moved right also on civil rights issues such as abortion and pushed for a positive historical assessment of the last military dictatorship. Because of this strategy, the doors were opened for even more extreme expressions of the right, which until then were very marginal, to find a loophole of action. Libertarians, right-wing nationalists, ultra-conservative Christians, advocates of the military regimes, and even authoritarian and quasi-Nazi candidates were suddenly present in mainstream media, and, in a few months, some of them became legitimate political actors whose ideas deserved consideration in nationally televised debates. Thus, the *Cambiemos*' radicalisation implied moving to the right of most of the public political discussions in Argentina after 2019. Not surprisingly, *Cambiemos*' strategy did not suffice to win the election, but allowed it to obtain 40% of the vote, a remarkable accomplishment in the middle of an economic crisis. It is probably too early to know if *Cambiemos*' radicalisation towards the right will be an ephemeral phenomenon or if, on the contrary, it is a step that inaugurates the coexistence of neoliberalism with illiberal right-wing national-populism.

Conclusions

This chapter showed the changes in the Argentine right throughout the twentieth century until today, as well as its links with democracy. Thus, it can be seen that the nationalist right-wing not only manifested disdain for multiparty democracy but also openly expressed the need to overcome this political regime since it was considered incompatible with the "real country". Consequently, that tradition accounts for a nondemocratic perspective, wary of the assumption of the country's political and ethnic diversity. Opposite to this, the liberal-conservative currents expressed their objections about democracy with a much less authoritarian tone. Ultimately, democracy seemed a necessary evil and one that should be tolerated, but always ensuring that it was adequately protected, whether by strict constitutional rules, the military, or, in recent years, by hyper-sensitised "markets". Instead, they invoked different principles that should be taken to avoid the reification of democracy as a political regime: the danger that the majorities would persecute minorities, the lack of political maturity of the population, the demagoguery of the main parties, and the deformation of economic rules due to undue interference by populist politicians.

Both traditions contained internal tensions deriving from competence for leadership, definition of strategies, economic resources, public attention, and, occasionally, votes. Their conflicts were especially intense when their shared enemy was in withdrawal or defeated (for example, under the successive dictatorships) (Gibson, 1996). When the right-wing traditions faced a powerful common enemy (for example, leftist Peronism in the early 1970s or more recently the Kirchnerism), they lessened their level of confrontation and gave priority to consensual behaviours.

Another fact that seems to be clear from this chapter is that there were variations in the mood of the rightists throughout the century. Sometimes it prevailed the conviction that they were erecting a new order. Optimism and self-confidence were two of the traits linked to right-wing actors at moments. It was the case of the liberal reformists who promoted the new electoral law in 1912, convinced that this would bring a better governed (by them, of course) country, and of the neoliberal intellectuals and politicians of the 1990s, also convinced to be founding a new country, which left behind the statism, isolationism, and inefficiency accumulated in Argentina over half a century. These actors had a greater interest in the future to be built than in the inheritances that should be guarded and maintained. But in other times, the right-wing had the conviction that it was bogged down in a trench from which it had to resist the advance of its adversaries (the UCR, the Peronists, the *guerrillas*, or the State intervention). This was the case for the liberal-conservatives under the UCR governments (1916–1930) or Perón (1946–1955), when they presented themselves mainly as crusaders in charge of restoring the "true" republic, supposedly lost under a demagogic flood. At that time, more than a new order, what was sought was the restoration of a golden age, in which only the self-selected elites could indicate which paths the policy should take.

The electoral victories of the rightist parties after 1912 in Argentina were scarce. The conservative presidencies in the 1930s were possible due to the fraud or the abstentionism of the UCR. The re-election of Carlos Menem in 1995 could be considered a victory for the neoliberal right, but also a Peronist triumph. That is why the triumph of Macri in 2015 appears as a rara avis since it fulfils a long-postponed dream of Argentine right parties: defeating an official (and Peronist) candidate in clean and fair elections.

The absence of an electorally competitive rightist party during much of the twentieth century has been indicated as the origin of long-standing Argentine evils: coups, economic elite's lack of commitment to democracy, little or no capability to process social conflicts within political institutions. As we pointed out, it is difficult—and perhaps impossible or useless—to try to unravel whether the weakness of the right-wing party is the cause of these behaviours or if the process must be understood backward. What we know is that, in the twenty-first century, the Argentine political right has waged and won using liberal democracy rules. In a country with a long history of coups, palatial putsches, and destabilisation processes, it is a novelty that should not be neglected.

Notes

1 One example is *Fuerza Republicana* (Republican Force) led by General Domingo Bussi. Governor of Tucumán during the last dictatorship, Bussi was democratically elected to the same position in 1995.
2 It is possible to distinguish at least two sub-currents inside this family. (b) *Reactionary Nationalism* which rejects both people and ideas considered "not strictly Argentine" (for example, Jews, Liberals, and Communists) and which stands as a myth the idea of a Latin or Hispanic Argentina, founded on "the cross and the sword", with a society

understood in an organic manner and a cultural, ethnic, religious, and socially restrictive conception of the nation; (b) *Popular Nationalism*, which rejects foreign ideas (socialism, liberalism, internationalism, Zionism) but not necessarily the people of foreign origin. This variant stands on the idea of Argentina as a "melting pot" with a destiny of greatness blocked by alien interests and fifth columnists (Buchrucker, 1987; Lvovich, 2006; Besoky, 2018).

3 Its best performances were in provinces as *Corrientes* with the *Pacto Autonomista Liberal* (Liberal-Autonomist Pact, PAL). Only sporadically, and through temporary alliances, liberal-conservatives achieved electoral competitiveness, as was the case for *Fuerza Federalista Popular* (Popular Federalist Force, FUFEPO) in the 1970s. An exception to this rule is the case of the Alliance *Cambiemos* (Let's Change), which triumphed in the 2015 elections (which we will discuss later).

4 We can identify three inner currents within the liberal-conservative family. (a) *Popular Conservatism*, which rejects the autonomous inclusion of the subaltern sectors, but accepts their gradual inclusion in a supervised way, maintaining the hierarchical positions of the local elites. This branch, usually led by traditional provincial parties, does not hesitate to establish patron/client relations, and usually has an ambivalent (or accommodating) position regarding the application of pro-market reforms ('federalist' for Gibson, 1996). (b) *Doctrinarian liberal-conservatism*, which rejects more firmly the political incorporation of popular sectors, mainly when it occurs abruptly and is State-driven, putting at risk the liberal and republican principles of the 1853 Constitution (document which stands as a founding myth). (c) *Neoliberalism*, which admits the inclusion of popular sectors only when it is compatible with the primacy of negative freedom in the Isaiah Berlin's sense, the maintenance of a certain degree of economic inequality, and a more significant State intervention in order to make the real market to approach to the ideal one.

5 As they had already done during the "*Revolución Libertadora*" ("Liberating Revolution", 1955–1958) and the "*Revolución Argentina*" ("Argentine Revolution", 1966–1973).

6 The older was the *Pacto Autonomista Liberal* (Liberal-Autonomist Pact, Corrientes Province), and the newer were *Acción Chubutense* (Action, Chubut Province), or the *Movimiento Popular Neuquino* (Neuquén Popular Movement) or founded by high-rank officers who had exercised as de facto governors as the *Partido Renovador de Salta* (Renovation Party of Salta).

7 Although it is true that PRO captured mostly non-Peronists votes, it is also a fact that it appealed to traditional Peronist voters who were against centre-left Kirchner governments' policies.

References

Arriondo, L. (2015) De la UCeDe al PRO. Un recorrido por la trayectoria de los militantes de centro-derecha de la ciudad de Buenos Aires. In Vommaro, G. & Morresi, S. D. (eds.), '*Hagamos equipo': PRO y la construcción de la nueva derecha argentina*. Los Polvorines, Universidad Nacional de General Sarmiento, pp. 203–230.

Besoky, J. L. (2016) *La derecha peronista*. Doctoral thesis. Universidad Nacional de La Plata. https://www.memoria.fahce.unlp.edu.ar/tesis/te.1280/te.1280.pdf [Accessed 12 October 2022].

Besoky, J. L. (2018) Los muchachos peronistas antijudíos. A propósito del antisemitismo en el movimiento peronista. *Trabajos y Comunicaciones* 47 (57), 1–29. https://doi.org /10.24215/23468971e057 [Accessed 12 October 2022].

Bobbio, N. (1995) *Derecha e izquierda: Razones y significados de una distinción política*. Buenos Aires, Taurus.

Bohoslavsky, E. (2009) *El complot patagónico. Nacionalismo, mitos conspirativos y violencia en el sur de Argentina y Chile (siglos XIX y XX)*. Buenos Aires, Prometeo.
Boron, A. (2000) Ruling without a party. Argentine dominant classes in the twentieth century. In Middlebrook, K. J. (ed.), *Conservative parties, the right, and democracy in Latin America*. Baltimore, Johns Hopkins University Press, pp. 139–163.
Botana, N. R. (1985) *El orden conservador: La política argentina entre 1880 y 1916*, 2nd ed. Buenos Aires, Sudamericana.
Buchrucker, C. (1987) *Nacionalismo y peronismo: La Argentina en la crisis ideológica mundial (1927–1955)*. Buenos Aires, Sudamericana.
Canelo, P. (2008) *El proceso en su laberinto: La interna militar de Videla a Bignone*. Buenos Aires, Prometeo Libros.
Cannon, B. (2016) *The right in Latin America: Elite power, hegemony and the struggle for the state*. New York and London, Routledge.
Castellani, A. G. (2004) Gestión económica liberal corporativa y transformaciones en el interior de los grandes agentes económicos de la Argentina durante la última dictadura militar. In A. Pucciarelli (ed.), *Empresarios, tecnócratas y militares. La trama corporativa de la última dictadura*. Buenos Aires, Siglo XXI, pp. 173–218.
Di Tella, T. S. (1971) La búsqueda de la fórmula política argentina. *Desarrollo Económico* 11(42/44), 317–325.
Doman, F., & Olivera, M. (1989) *Los Alsogaray. Secretos de una dinastía y su corte*. Buenos Aires, Clarín-Aguilar.
Eatwell, R., & Goodwin, M. J. (2018) *National populism: The revolt against liberal democracy*. London, Pelican.
Echeverría, O. (2009) *Las voces del miedo. Los intelectuales autoritarios argentinos en las primeras décadas del siglo XX*. Rosario, Prohistoria.
Franco, M. (2012) *Un enemigo para la nación: Orden interno, violencia y 'subversión', 1973–1976*. Buenos Aires, Fondo de Cultura Económica.
Gibson, E. L. (1996) *Class and conservative parties: Argentina in comparative perspective*. Baltimore, Johns Hopkins University Press.
Halperin Donghi, T., 1988. Argentina: Liberalism in a Country Born Liberal. In: J. Love and N. Jacobsen (eds.) *Guiding the Invisible Hand. Economic Liberalism and the State in Latin America*. New York: Praeger. pp. 99–116.
Harbour, W. R. (1985) *El pensamiento conservador*. Buenos Aires, Grupo Editor Latinoamericano.
Heredia, M. (2015) *Cuando los economistas alcanzaron el poder (o cómo se gestó la confianza en los expertos)*. Buenos Aires, Siglo XXI.
Klein, M. (2001) Argentine Nacionalismo before Perón: The case of the Alianza de la Juventud Nacionalista, 1937–c. 1943. *Bulletin of Latin American Research* 20 (1), 102–121.
Lewis, P. (2001) La Derecha y los gobiernos militares, 1955-1983. In McGee Deustch, S. & Dolkart, R. H. (eds.), *La derecha argentina. Nacionalistas, neoliberales, militares y clericalistas*. Buenos Aires, Javier Vergara Editor, pp. 321–370.
Lipset, S. M., & Raab, E. (1981) *La política de la sinrazón: El extremismo de derecha en los Estados Unidos 1790–1970*. México, Fondo de Cultura Económica.
Lvovich, D. (2003) *Nacionalismo y antisemitismo en la Argentina*. Buenos Aires, Javier Vergara Editor.
Lvovich, D. (2006) *El nacionalismo de derecha: desde sus orígenes a Tacuara*. Buenos Aires, Capital Intelectual.
Macor, D., & Tcach, C. (eds.) (2003) *La invención del peronismo en el interior del país*. Santa Fe, UNL.

Mansilla, C. L. (1983) *Las fuerzas de centro*. Buenos Aires, Centro Editor de América Latina.
Mauro, S. (2005) La campaña electoral por la Jefatura de Gobierno de Buenos Aires: Estrategias políticas e inteligibilidad de la agenda. *Revista Argentina de Sociología* 4, 78–98.
McGee Deutsch, S. (1986) *Counterrevolution in Argentina, 1900–1932: The Argentine patriotic league*. Lincoln, University of Nebraska Press.
Montserrat, M. (1992) *La experiencia conservadora*. Buenos Aires, Sudamericana.
Morresi, S. D. (2011) La larga construcción de la hegemonía neoliberal. In Pérez, G., Aelo, O. H., & Salerno, G. (eds.) *Todo aquel fulgor. La política argentina después del neoliberalismo*. Buenos Aires, Nueva Trilce, pp. 67–78.
Morresi, S. D. (2015) 'Acá somos todos democráticos'. El PRO y las relaciones entre la derecha y la democracia en la Argentina. In Vommaro, G. & Morresi, S. D. (eds.), *'Hagamos equipo'. PRO y la construcción de la nueva derecha argentina*. Buenos Aires, Prometeo, pp. 163–201.
Morresi, S. D. (2017) ¿Cómo fue posible? Apuntes sobre la prehistoria y el presente del partido PRO. In Boron, A. A. & Arredondo, M. (eds.), *Clases medias argentinas: modelo para armar*. Buenos Aires, Luxemburg, pp. 67–85.
Morresi, S. D., & Vicente, M. (2020) Los rostros del liberalismo-conservador: Las polémicas en torno de la gestión de Martínez de Hoz en el ministerio de Economía procesista. In Lvovich, D., (eds.), *Políticas públicas, tradiciones políticas y sociabilidades entre 1960 y 1980. Desafíos en el abordaje del pasado reciente en la Argentina*. Los Polvorines, UNGS, pp. 171–201.
Morresi, S. D., & Vommaro, G. (2014) Argentina. The difficulties of the Partisan right and the case of Propuesta Republicana. In Luna, J. P. & Rovira Kaltwasser, C. (eds.), *The resilience of the Latin American right*. Baltimore, Johns Hopkins University Press, pp. 319–345.
Mudde, C. (2007) *Populist radical right parties in Europe*. Cambridge and New York, Cambridge University Press.
Nállim, J. (2014) *Transformación y crisis del liberalismo. Su desarrollo en la Argentina en el período 1930–1955*. Buenos Aires, Gedisa.
Novaro, M. (2006) *Historia de la Argentina contemporánea: De Perón a Kirchner*. Buenos Aires, Edhasa.
Ostiguy, P. (2017) Populism: A socio-cultural approach. In Rovira Kaltwasser, C., Taggart, P., & Ostiguy, P. (eds.), *The Oxford handbook of populism*. New York, Oxford University Press pp. 73–97.
Palermo, V., & Novaro, M. (2003) *La dictadura militar, 1976–1983: Del golpe de estado a la restauración democrática*. Buenos Aires, Paidós.
Piñeiro, E. (1997) *La tradición nacionalista ante el peronismo: Itinerario de una esperanza a una desilusión*. Buenos Aires, A-Z Editora.
Pucciarelli, A. R., & Castellani, A. G. (eds.) (2014) *Los años de la Alianza: La crisis del orden neoliberal*. Buenos Aires, Siglo XXI.
Pucciarelli, A. R., & Castellani, A. G. (eds.) (2017) *Los años del kirchnerismo: La disputa hegemónica tras la crisis del orden neoliberal*. Buenos Aires, Siglo XXI.
Quiroga, H. (2004) *El tiempo del proceso. Conflictos y coincidencias entre políticos y militares, 1976–1983*, 2nd ed. Rosario, Homo Sapiens and Fundación Ross.
Restivo, N., & Dellatorre, R. (2005) *El Rodrigazo, 30 años después: Un ajuste que cambió al país*. Buenos Aires, Capital Intelectual.
Rodríguez, L. (2011) *Católicos, nacionalistas y políticas educativas durante la última dictadura (1976–1983)*. Rosario, Prohistoria.

Rouquié, A. (1994) *Poder militar y sociedad política en la Argentina II*. Buenos Aires, Emecé.

Rubinzal, M. (2005) *La derecha y la cuestión social en la Argentina. La cuestión obrera en la perspectiva del nacionalismo en Buenos Aires (1935–1943)*. BA dissertation. Universidad Nacional del Litoral. https://www.memoria.fahce.unlp.edu.ar/library?a=d&c=tesis&d=Jte450 [Accessed 12 October 2022].

Sábato, H. (2001) *The many and the few: Political participation in republican Buenos Aires*. Stanford, Stanford University Press.

Senkman, L. (1993) The right and the civilian regimes, 1955–1976. In McGee Deutsch, S. & Dolkart, R. H. (eds.) *The Argentine right: Its history and intellectual origins, 1910 to the present*. Wilmington, Del., SR Books. pp. 119–147

Sidicaro, R. (2002) *Los tres peronismos. Estado y poder económico 1946–55/1973–76/1989–99*. Buenos Aires, Siglo XXI.

Sikk, A. (2012) Newness as a winning formula for new political parties. *Party Politics* 18 (4), 465–486.

Smith, W. C. (1990) Democracy, distributional conflicts and macroeconomic policymaking in Argentina, 1983–89. *Journal of Inter-American Studies and World Affairs* 32 (2), 1–42.

Spektorowski, A. (1990) Argentina 1930–1940 nacionalismo integral, justicia social y clase obrera. *Estudios Interdisciplinarios de América Latina y el Caribe* 2 (1), 61–79.

Tato, M. I. (2001) Crónica de un desencanto: Una mirada conservadora de la democratización de la política, 1911–1930. *Estudios Sociales* XI (20), 143–163.

Velásquez Rivera, É. D. J. (2002) Historia de la doctrina de la seguridad nacional. *Convergencia. Revista de Ciencias Sociales* 27, 11–39.

Vicente, M. A. (2015) *De la refundación al ocaso: Los intelectuales liberal-conservadores ante la última dictadura*. La Plata, UNLP, UNGS.

Zanatta, L. (1996) *Del Estado liberal a la nación católica. Iglesia y Ejército en los orígenes del peronismo (1930–1943)*. Buenos Aires, UNQ.

Zimmermann, E. (1995) *Los liberales reformistas: La cuestión social en la Argentina, 1890–1916*. Buenos Aires, Sudamericana and Universidad de San Andrés.

3
CANADA

The evolution, transformation, and diversity of conservatism

Frédéric Boily

Introduction

This chapter paints an overall picture of the right in Canada from its origins to today, based on three general propositions which will structure the subject as a whole and will make it possible to outline its evolution and identify its important moments.

The first proposition is that the right has a long history in Canada (Boily, 2019). Indeed, if Canada's image on the international scene is that of a progressive country and of Canadian peacekeepers intervening in certain conflicts, we forget that Canada is also distinguished by an important military tradition and that the progressive and internationalist character of Canada comes from a certain "mythology" (Thibault, 2019: pp. 119–127), which developed after the Second World War. But when we look more closely at Canadian political life, we quickly realise that if the Liberal Party of Canada (LPC) was in power most of the time in the twentieth century, this is no longer necessarily the case in the twenty-first century, the Liberals having been in power from 2000 to 2006, the Conservatives of Stephen Harper from 2006 to 2015, while Liberal Justin Trudeau has been in power since 2015. We must not forget that at certain moments in its history, the LPC also leaned to the right, especially between 1993 and 2000, a time when the Liberal government endorsed the prevailing neoliberalism to the point of proposing major cuts in government budgets.

The second proposition is that the Canadian right underwent a profound transformation in the 1980s by adopting the neoliberal ideas in vogue in the United States and Great Britain. As we will see in the second section of the text, the Canadian right, first on the federal scene and then on the provincial political scenes in the 1990s, adapted and transformed by adopting the policies of deregulation and shrinking of the state. It is at this point that the right has in a way converted to the ideas of the economists of the Chicago School, and that government interventionism of the Keynesian type will be put aside in favour of another approach where the state must operate a movement of withdrawal from its action in the economy and society. Keynesian and Rousseauist optimism gives way to the cold Hobbesian and Hayekian reality.

The third proposition emphasises the diversity of the right in Canada. On the one hand, to show its heterogeneity over time, as indicated by the second proposition just stated; on the other hand, to emphasise the diversity existing between provincial right-wing expressions. We must not forget, when we speak of the Canadian right, that the country is not only vast geographically, but that its federal character gives the provinces considerable room for manoeuvre in establishing health and education as well as the opportunity to develop different provincial political cultures. In this regard, the Quebec distinction should be noted, the Quebec right having a particular face in the great portrait of the Canadian right-wing movement due to a particular intellectual and political history. Let us remember for the moment that the Quebec right was deeply marked, before the 1960s, by Catholicism and, to a lesser extent but also in a significant way, by the French right. Thus, we must avoid confusing provincial and federal right-wing movements and be attentive to the distinctions that also exist between the provinces.

It is around these three general propositions that this chapter proposes to show the complexity and diversity of the Canadian right.

The right at the origins: 1867–1965

Let us start with an affirmation: the Canadian right has a long history, a history which is intimately linked to the very beginning of Canada's existence as a country in 1867. Indeed, at the time of the birth of Canada, the political parties as we know them today were still in their infancy (the leftist parties did not yet exist). The party led by John A. Macdonald, Canada's first Prime Minister, was a right-wing party that advocated political solutions from classical conservatism. By that, we mean the conservative right was defined, under John A. Macdonald, by the emphasis placed on the defence of social order, on historical continuity and on the will to preserve what made the singular character of Canada, namely its British heritage.

This is how Canada's first three decades were marked by the right and the Tory tradition. At that time, it was necessary to ensure the preservation of the social and economic order of the entire English Canadian community. "Rooted in the loyalist tradition of the nineteenth century, the thought of Canadian Tories stressed the primacy of the community over selfish individualism" (Massolin, 2001: p. 6). If the community was threatened by internal pressure in the form of an unbridled individualism that undermines the cohesion of the community, it was also threatened by external pressures. These were pressures that came from the United States, particularly in the western part of the country. The question of economic stability was thus at the centre of the concerns of the government of the day, which, through various policies, such as the National Policy (1878), tried to protect the Canadian economy and its manufacturing sector from the influence deemed harmful from its neighbour to the south.

In Canada's first decades (1867–1900), it should also be noted that the Canadian Conservatives saw Canada as an integral part of the British Empire. It is indeed an essential characteristic of Canada to have remained in the lap of the English Motherland and not to have made, as was the case in the United States, a revolution in order to cut ties with England. In the past, this is what made some intellectuals say that the very origins of Canada were conservative, unlike the United States, which was based on revolutionary origins (Lipset, 1990). While this thesis was often contradicted afterwards (Grabb and Curtis, 2010), it nonetheless contains an important kernel of truth, namely that the influence of the conservative right was very present at the origin of Canada and that it continued to deeply infuse Canadian political life in the twentieth century.

Indeed, if the Conservatives lost power to the Liberals of Wilfrid Laurier in 1896 and, afterwards, it was the Liberals who were most of the time in power, the influence of the right continued to be felt even among the leaders of the LPC, who were not left-wing liberals as we understand it today. More interventionist than the Conservatives and more supportive of free-trade in the first decades of the twentieth century, it took a while before they resolutely endorsed an interventionist and Keynesian approach. From 1896 until the mid-1950s, the Conservatives had less impact on Canadian political life.

In the early 1960s, the Conservatives began to be alarmed at what they perceived to be a major identity drift. In their eyes, Canada was indeed denying its conservative (English) origins, those that had allowed Canada to keep its special identity over time. Published in 1965, in his famous work *Lament for a Nation*, George Grant (1965) developed a position representative of the English-speaking conservative right, a right that was alarmed by the transformation, too radical in their eyes, of Canadian identity. According to Grant, Canada simply let itself disappear without real resistance, despite the meagre efforts of the Conservative government of John Diefenbaker (1957–1963) who may have wanted to oppose the United States but without success. Indeed, Grant criticised equally both Conservatives and Liberals for having capitulated before the capitalist and technologist American Empire.

Specifically, Grant believed that Canada had enthusiastically and unreservedly embraced business liberalism imported from the United States and that this would result in the "disappearance" of Canada, which would be absorbed by the US economic and cultural empire. This reaction and this fear of seeing Canada disappear was not, it is true, exclusive to the conservative right but also of the left. On the other hand, what distinguishes the position of the conservative right from that of the left is that it is not only the loss of control over economic instruments that preoccupied the intellectuals of the conservative right, but it was also, and more fundamentally, the very nature of the Canadian national identity which was turned upside down in a direction that moved it away from the traditional definition of Canada.

Another revealing debate to arise in the mid-1960s, which illustrates the position of the Conservative right over Canada's national identity, concerns that of the adoption of the Canadian flag. On the initiative of the Liberal government of Lester B. Pearson, the current maple leaf Canadian flag was adopted in 1965. The adoption gave rise to many political and intellectual position debates typical of the conservative right. Indeed, on the conservative side, it was feared that the adoption of a Canadian flag to replace the Union Jack, which had been the Canadian flag until then, would mean a profound change in Canada's national identity. The national community, it was argued, would find itself cutting its roots with the British tradition that had powerfully forged the country (Igartua, 2006: pp. 182–183).

Thus, in the 1960s, the transformation of the Canadian national identity that had been going on since 1945—what historian José E. Igartua called a Quiet Revolution—had a profound impact also on the intellectual right and right-wing parties. At that time, the classic Canadian right, for which the defence of the national community and its British referents were essential to the definition of Canada, was in decline. The social face of Canada, thanks to immigration, was changing with people coming less and less from Europe, and the resource economy smaller than in the past was gradually giving way to a service economy. This is why, and because the past solutions of the right no longer suited this new environment, the right undertook, from the mid-1960s to the early 1980s, a profound intellectual and political transformation which enabled it to regain power in 1984. Initially resistant to change, the right, in a second phase, was reconciled with the neoliberal logic whose influence was more and more present in Western democracies.

The transformation of the right: From progressive-conservatives to conservatives in Western Canada

As the United States, Canada has been deeply influenced by right-wing neoliberalism. The government of Pierre Elliott Trudeau who returned to power for a last mandate (1980–1984) will be ousted from power by the conservative Brian Mulroney. The conservative program under Mulroney moved away from positions defended by the traditional right that, on certain occasions, could use the state levers to protect the national economy. For example, it was under the conservative government of R. B. Bennet that the Canadian Radio Broadcasting Commission, ancestor of the CBC (1936), was established as well as the Bank of Canada, institutions aimed at ensuring the sustainability of the social order and the national cohesion of Canadian society (Milnes et al., 2015). However, with the arrival of Brian Mulroney to power, the federal government took another direction by adopting the theses conveyed within American republican circles:

> Canada's version of welfare state moved from a policy regime that was rooted in a set of ideas influenced by Keynesian economics, and that focused on social justice, social rights, and financial-resource enhancements, towards a

style intellectually based in "Reaganomics" and supply-side economics and concerned principally with the national debt and deficits, budgetary constraints, and economic stability.

(Prince and Rice, 2007: p. 164).

This is how the new style of the Conservative government turned its back not only on the Keynesianism of the liberal governments, but also put aside the cautious approach, in the conservative sense of the term, which had been that of conservative governments of the past.

In this context, the Mulroney Conservatives gradually made major cuts to the budgets of certain key sectors of the State. For example, they gradually dismantled Crown corporations, such as Petro-Canada and Air Canada, about 15 of which were sold (Wardhaugh, 2007: p. 235). The economic philosophy of the Conservative government was resolutely turned towards the markets as a solution to restart the Canadian economy which had, it is true, been badly hit in the second half of the 1970s. Essentially, the fear of seeing the public finances become out of control motivated the Conservatives to embrace the neoliberal ideas advocating a withdrawal of the state in the economy with, in parallel, a greater confidence put the mechanisms of the market, guarantor, in the eyes of the Conservatives, of Canadian prosperity.

This pro-market orientation was fully revealed with the debate on free trade with the United States. If the Mulroney Conservatives had been rather discreet on this issue during the 1984 election campaign, the dynamics changed once they came to power, and they began talks with the United States to reach an agreement. Building on the good relationship Brian Mulroney was able to establish with President Ronald Reagan, the Canadian Prime Minister emphasised the need to deepen economic relations with his great neighbour to the south.

During the 1988 election the subject of free trade was hotly contested, so much so that it could be described as the "Free trade Election" (Leduc, 2010: p. 371). The Canadian left (Liberals and New Democrats alike) was radically opposed to the Canada-US Free Trade Agreement, ancestor of NAFTA, which had been concluded in October 1987 and subsequently debated in the Canadian Parliament. The idea put forward by the Conservatives was that this treaty to liberalise trade and commerce with the United States would boost the Canadian economy. On the contrary, the opponents saw it rather as a renunciation of Canadian sovereignty in the establishment of distinctive public and social policies. As Liberal Leader John Turner said in one of the most memorable debates in recent Canadian political history:

With one stroke of pen ... you have thrown us into the North-South influence of the United States and will reduce us [...] to a colony of United States because, when the economic levers go, political independence is sure to follow.

(Leduc, 2010: p. 383)

Ironically, when the Liberals returned to power in 1993, this time under the leadership of Jean Chrétien, they would no longer oppose free trade. On the contrary, Jean Chrétien and the Liberals also embraced the pro-market and neoliberal logic; under this government Canadian citizens witnessed major cuts in almost all public budgets. In fact, the fight against the deficit led by the Conservatives had not yielded the expected results in the control of public finances, so much so that when the Liberals took power in 1993, they also had to manage the crisis of public finances. However, this fight was waged from a right-hand point of view, emphasising the need to balance budgets and curb spending deemed excessive. The 1995 budget was particularly austere on the fiscal front with drastic cuts in several areas of government intervention: "The cuts affected everything from the CBC, Petro Canada, and regional development programs to women's shelters and employment insurance benefits, all areas of Liberal traditional support" (Jeffrey, 2010: p. 268). In the early 1990s, the boundaries between the Liberals and the Conservatives were blurred. Liberals, Conservatives and Reformists, as we shall see now, defended the ideas of the neoliberal right by focusing on issues of budget balance and tackling the deficit.

It is indeed in the West of the country that an even more right-wing political party was particularly important. Born in a context of deep dissatisfaction with the Liberals and the Conservatives, the Reform Party led by Preston Manning defended the idea that the reduction of public budgets and the return to balance should be done faster than proposed by all the other political formations (Boily, 2013). Frankly in favour of free trade with the United States, notably because the Alberta oil economy is deeply linked with the United States which is its main export market, the Reform Party found that the conservative proposals of Brian Mulroney did not go far enough in what we can call the "welfare-state retrenchment" (Patten, 2013: p. 66). These positions on the importance of ensuring a favourable economic environment for business were expressed in the party program, the Blue Book (1991), which advocated the principles of economic laissez-faire (Dobbin, 1993).

With the Reform Party, the right also found moral and religious dimensions that the leaders of the Conservative Party of the 1970s and 1980s (Robert Stanfield, Joe Clark and Brian Mulroney) had put aside. On the contrary, the Reform Party, which was anchored in the West of the country where religion had played a more important role in the past with the Social Credit of William Aberhart, wanted to debate same-sex marriages, homosexuality, even abortion (Farney, 2012). Thus, this political formation, resolutely on the right, presented an ideology which married the ideas of the neoliberal right and social conservatism, a mixture which was specific to the right-wing tradition of Western Canada. This is why the party has not had electoral success beyond the four western provinces, this right-wing current having little appeal elsewhere in Canada, even in Ontario where there is a strong right-wing tradition at the provincial level. In Quebec and the Maritime provinces, as we will see in the third section of this chapter, the importance of and the recourse to the state to put in place social policies correcting inequalities are viewed with more benevolence by the electorate and even by right-wing parties.

However, after the merger of the Canadian Alliance (which had replaced the Reform Party) with the Progressive Conservative Party, the Canadian right took a direction closer to the economic interests of the western provinces. With the arrival of Stephen Harper's Conservatives to power, from 2006 to 2015, it was the first time since John Diefenbaker in the late 1950s that a Conservative Prime Minister from the western provinces became head of the federal government. Prime Minister Harper, who was politically socialised in the Reform Party and in Calgary's oil and business circles (Boily, 2007), took up part of the Reformist formula, namely the emphasis on restricting the state's fiscal capacity. For example, it lowered the consumption tax by two percentage points, which hampered the fiscal capacity of the Canadian government to implement far-reaching social policies.

The question concerning the nature of the right and especially that of the depth of the commitments of the Conservatives of Stephen Harper to a resolutely right-wing direction gave rise to many debates during his years in power (Boily, 2016). The policies that his government advocated, inspired by Hayek (Gutstein, 2014), were aimed at ensuring the development of the economy. On the economic side, some observers have argued that the Conservative government has not been able to embrace a resolutely right-wing political agenda: "While balanced budgets, limited government interference in the market, and the pursuit of self-sufficiency through labor market participation remained central commitments, the party's policy in office could be better understood as 'business-friendly' government" (Farney and Koop, 2017: pp. 31–32). If the Conservative government did not go as far as it wanted, this is particularly due to the financial crisis of 2008 that saw the Canadian government inject large sums to support the automakers.

On the other hand, Stephen Harper's Conservatives gave greater prominence to social conservatives even if the latter did not manage to obtain political gains, for example, by stopping same-sex marriages or even reopening the abortion issue. In this sense, Harper made Canada take a moderate turn, as constitutionalist Peter H. Russel (2017: pp. 343–353) affirms, but all the same with important consequences on the evolution of public policies and on the capacity of the state to reverse some aspects of Stephen Harper's legacy (McKenna, 2013).

The diversity of the right in the provinces

Canada is a rather decentralised federation where the provinces enjoy considerable room for manoeuvre in the establishment of economic and social policies. As there were no national unification policies of the type found at the time of the formation of certain European nation-states, each of the provinces was able to retain its cultural and political specificity, which is notably the case of Quebec. Furthermore, the provinces are, according to the division of powers in the 1867 constitution, responsible for education policy, a crucial area if any. This means that there is no single curriculum, for example in terms of history, throughout the Canadian territory. In this sense, we can identify distinctive political cultures (Wiseman, 2006), each structuring a provincial political life, including that of the right. Indeed, what applies to all provincial political cultures also applies to the right.

To be sure, provincial right-wing organisations are not limited to a single whole even if there are undeniable kinship affinities which make it possible to group the parties and the intellectuals under the same label, that of the right. For example, at the turn of the 1990s when the ideas of the neoliberal right made their presence felt very strongly in Canada, we will see that right-wing parties also adopted the vocabulary of deficit and debt reduction while taking up ideas that were present, as we explained in the previous section, in the main federal political parties.

Therefore, this important influence on the federal scene was found in a few provinces, more particularly within provincial political parties in Ontario and Alberta. In these two provinces, as early as 1992 in Alberta and 1995 in Ontario, two right-wing parties took power with the promise to quickly and firmly tackle their provinces' budget deficits. Both parties made the market their creed, and their goal was to create the conditions that will allow entrepreneurs and the industry to grow, what was called "the Alberta Advantage" in that province. This meant that substantial tax cuts would be offered to large companies, followed by the resulting major cuts in education and health (Harrison, 2005). The *Common Sense Revolution*, implemented by Ontario Premier Mike Harris, borrowed the same Alberta paths when "[a] major plank of neo-liberal economics was implemented in the first budget, provincial income tax rates were cut by 30 percent in the hope of stimulating the economy out of its increasingly dire stagnation" (Macdermid and Albo, 2001: p. 192). Again, the Ontario government put into practice the lessons of economic neoliberalism. For them, as for Brian Mulroney, the state is the problem, not the solution. Walking in the footsteps of Hobbes rather than those of Rousseau, the two conservative leaders (Klein and Harris) proposed to reduce the role of the state in the establishment of equalising social policies.

The peculiarity of the Alberta right is that it operates in an oil producing province, with reserves among the largest in the world, which has the effect of giving it a unique face in Canada. For example, the Alberta right (and one could add that of Saskatchewan) is more than elsewhere in the country extremely resistant to any individual carbon tax policy while it shows a will to develop this industry and the network of pipelines to the east of the country. In this sense, the Alberta right vibrates in tune with what observers have called "petro-politics" and that gives current right-wing discourse a very strong anti-environmental tone (Adkin, 2016). In fact, on the environmental policy side, the western provincial conservatives, as well as on the federal scene, trust the technological development and punitive measures for large emitters. This defence of natural resource exploitation, such as petroleum, is also present in the neighbouring province (Saskatchewan), a province which, since the mid-2000s, has been governed by a right-wing party.

Elsewhere in the country, the right shares the creed of the market but generally with less fervour as far as the environment is concerned.

In addition, the Quebec right also presents a distinct face compared to other provinces. Indeed, while the Quebec right, both intellectual and political, has been marked by Catholicism and by nationalism, that of today, while still nationalist, has nevertheless left all religious references aside to defend state secularism (Gélinas, 2007). However, the rise of an independence party, the *Parti Québécois*, which took power in 1976 and called a referendum in 1980, will somehow lead the right parties to be marginalised on the electoral scene. It was not until the 1990s and especially after the second referendum on Quebec sovereignty (1995) that the right witnessed a renaissance on the Quebec political scene (Boily, 2010).

A political party in particular, the Democratic Action of Quebec, embodied with more vigour the orientations of the right with a program of reduction of the size of the state and fight against the unions (Piotte, 2003). In addition, this political formation presented a populist side asserted during the 2007 and 2008 elections with the question of defending Quebec's cultural identity (Boily, 2008). However, the party disappeared after the 2008 election, replaced by the *Coalition Avenir Québec* which participated in two unsuccessful elections (2012 and 2014) before convincingly winning both the 2018 and 2022 elections.

This political group is, in the strong sense, a centre-right coalition that brings together nationalists and people with a right-wing sensitivity who aim to revive the Quebec economy through a fairly interventionist political program focused on entrepreneurship (Boily, 2018). In fact, the place of the state in Quebec society and the economy is an important distinctive element, even for intellectuals deemed to be conservative (Couture and Piotte, 2012). If the Quebec right remains relatively attached to the concept of an interventionist state, in matters of identity the CAQ shows itself more to the right than elsewhere in the country. Indeed, Law 21 which establishes the secularity of the state, indicates that the Quebec right wants to protect the cultural specificity of Quebec and refuses multiculturalism, because it sees it as a danger to the preservation of Francophone culture. On identity issues, the Quebec right lives apart from the large family of provincial rights, whereas in provinces such as Alberta and Ontario, it is issues related to social conservatism that create tensions within their right-wing movements.

Conclusion: The right after the 2019 federal election

Seen from abroad, Canada is said to be a progressive country, allergic to the radical right and more to the left or centrist than in other western democracies. But this reputation is somewhat overrated. Like all Western democracies, the right has had an important influence in the past as in the present and, we can add, will have in the future.

Indeed, the Canadian right is not an imported product but a very Canadian creation whose developments can be followed over time. On the one hand, it does not always present the same face over time; on the other hand, from one province to another the right is not always the same. Can we then find a kind of thread passing through time and across the provinces?

If we want to engage in such an exercise, we will have to say that the Canadian right presents, especially since the 1980s, the same desire to restrict the size and capacities of the state, even in Quebec where, as we said, the right is less antistatist than elsewhere in the country. The Canadian right fears that too much government involvement in the lives of citizens will disrupt the social order in too radical a manner.

What we must now watch is whether the Canadian right, taken as a whole, will allow itself to be seduced by the sirens of identity politics or not and will want to take a turn towards defending the threatened Canadian identity (Kheiriddin, 2021). For the moment, the failure of Maxime Bernier's People's Party of Canada in the last two federal elections (2019-2021) suggests that such a political repositioning operation would be of little benefit to the right. The "Intelligent populism" (Canadian Press, 2019) that Bernier said he wanted to defend did not allow him to have a single candidate elected during the October 22, 2019 and the September 20, 2021 elections, nevertheless obtaining 4.9% of the vote in the more recent election.

That said, following the 2019 federal election, we saw the Conservative Party led by Andrew Scheer, from the west of the country, defend policies relatively similar to those of his predecessor and propose the return to balanced budgets, while the other political parties had abandoned this commitment. The election results (121 MPs and 34.4% of the votes for the Conservative Party) indicate that the Conservatives are very strongly supported in the western provinces (all seats in Saskatchewan, and in Alberta with one exception). Yet, a new leader from Ontario (Erin O'Toole) did not improve the party's electoral appeal during the September 20, 2021, election, earning 119 MPs and 33.7% of the national vote. O'Toole's bet on shifting the party platform towards the centre-right and refurbishing its image (by, for instance, appealing to labour unions) ended in failure. Once again, the right must revisit and reflect on its fundamental orientations, under yet a new leader, Pierre Poilievre (2022), who heralded a populist turn throughout the leadership race. However, the final direction to be taken is yet to be seen.

References

Adkin, L. (2016) *First world petro-politics: The political ecology and governance of Alberta*. Toronto, University of Toronto Press.

Boily, F. (2007) *Stephen Harper. De l'école de Calgary au parti conservateur. Les nouveaux visages du conservatisme canadien*. Québec City, Les Presses de l'Université Laval.

Boily, F. (2008) *Mario Dumont et l'action démocratique du Québec. Entre populisme et démocratie*. Québec City, Les Presses de l'Université Laval.

Boily, F. (2010) *Le conservatisme au Québec. Retour sur tradition oubliée*. Québec City, Les Presses de l'Université Laval.

Boily, F. (2013) *La droite en Alberta. D'Ernest Manning à Stephen Harper*. Québec City, Les Presses de l'Université Laval.

Boily, F. (2016) *Stephen Harper. La fracture idéologique d'une vision du Canada*. Reprint. Québec City, Les Presses de l'Université Laval.
Boily, F. (2018) *La Coalition Avenir Québec. Une idéologie à la recherche du pouvoir*. Québec City, Les Presses de l'Université Laval.
Boily, F. (2019) Transformations in Canadian conservatism. In Fourot, A.-C., Léger, R., Cornut, J., & Kenny, N. (eds.), *Canada in the world. actors, ideas, governance*. Montréal, Les Presses de l'Université de Montréal, pp. 247–269.
Canadian Press. (2019) Maxime Bernier wants to offer intelligent populism. *La Presse .ca*, 11 September. https://www.lapresse.ca/elections-federales/201909/11/01-5240816-maxime-bernier-want-offer-intelligent-populism.php [Accessed 20 October 2022].
Couture, J.-P., & Piotte J.-M. (2012) *The new faces of conservative nationalism in Quebec*. Montreal, Quebec, America.
Dobbin, M. (1993) *The politics of Kim Campbell. From school trustee to Prime Minister*. Toronto, James Lorimer & Company Publishers.
Farney, J. (2012) *Social conservatives and party politics in Canada and the United States*. Toronto, University of Toronto Press.
Farney, J., & Koop, R. (2017) The conservative party in opposition and government. In Lewis, J. P. & Everitt, J. (eds.), *The blueprint. Conservative parties and their impact on Canadian politics*. Toronto, University of Toronto Press, pp. 25–45.
Gélinas, X. (2007) *The Quebec intellectual right and the quiet revolution*. Quebec City, Les Presses de l'Université Laval.
Grabb, E., & Curtis, J. (2010) *Regions apart. The four societies of Canada and the United States*. Don Mills, Oxford University Press.
Grant, G. (1965) *Lament for a nation: The defeat of Canadian nationalism*, 40th anniversary ed. Reprint. Montreal and Kingston, McGill-Queen's University Press, 2005.
Gutstein, D. (2014) *Harperism. How Stephen Harper and his think tank colleagues have transformed Canada*. Toronto, James Lorimer & Company.
Harrison, T. W. Editor. (2005) *The return of the trojan horse: Alberta and the new world (dis)order*. Montreal, Black Rose.
Igartua, J. E. (2006) *The other quiet revolution. National identities in English Canada, 1945–71*. Vancouver and Toronto, UBC Press.
Jeffrey, B. (2010) *Divided loyalties: The liberal party of Canada*. Toronto, University of Toronto Press.
Kheiriddin, T. (2021) Rebuilding the Tories 'big tent' with votes from new Canadians. *National Post*, 2 October. https://nationalpost.com/opinion/tasha-kheiriddin-rebuilding-the-tories-big-tent-with-votes-from-new-canadians [Accessed 22 October 2022].
Leduc, L. et al. 2010. *Dynasties and interludes. Past and present in Canadian electoral politics*. Toronto, Dundurn Press.
Lipset, S. M. (1990) *Continental divide. The values and institutions of the United States and Canada*. New York and London, Routledge.
Macdermid, R., & Albo, G. (2001) Divided province, growing protests: Ontario moves right. In Brownsey, K. & Howlett, M. (eds.), *The provincial state in Canada. Politics in the provinces and territories*. Peterborough, Broadview Press, pp. 163–202.
Massolin, P. (2001) *Canadian intellectuals, the Tory tradition, and the challenge of modernity, 1939–1970*. Toronto, University of Toronto Press.
McKenna, B. (2013). Canada lost when Ottawa cut the GST. *The Globe and Mail*, 24 March. https://www.theglobeandmail.com/report-on-business/economy/canada-lost-when-ottawa-cut-the-gst/article10271589/ [Accessed 22 October 2022].

Milnes, A., Lankin, F., Paikin, S., Lockhart, D., & Paikin, Z. (2015) Let's give RB Bennett his due. *The Globe and Mail*, 20 August. https://www.theglobeandmail.com/opinion/lets-give-rb-bennett-his-due/article26023377/ [Accessed 22 October 2022].

Patten, S. (2013) The triumph of neoliberalism within partisan conservatism in Canada. In Farney, J. & Rayside, D. (eds.), *Conservatism in Canada*. Toronto, University of Toronto Press, pp. 59–76.

Piotte, J.-M. (ed.) (2003) *All right. The ADQ program explained*. Montreal, HMH.

Prince, M. J., & Rice, J. J. (2007) Governing through shifting social-policy regimes: Brian Mulroney and Canada's welfare. In Blake, R. B. (ed.), *Transforming the nation. Canada and Brian Mulroney*. Montreal and Kingston, McGill-Queen's University Press, pp. 164–177.

Russell, P. H. (2017) 15 conclusion. A moderate turn to the right with at least one enduring consequence. In Lewis, J. P. & Everitt, J. (eds.), *The blueprint. Conservative parties and their impact on Canadian politics*. Toronto, University of Toronto Press, pp. 343–353.

Thibault, J.-F. (2019) *Lester B. Pearson. Enlightened realism*. Quebec, Les Presses de l'Université Laval.

Wardhaugh, R. (2007) Brian Mulroney and the West. In Blake, R. B. (ed.), *Transforming the nation. Canada and Brian Mulroney*. Montreal, McGill-Queen's University Press, pp. 225–249.

Wilson, B. G. Loyalists in Canada. *The Canadian Encyclopedia*. https://www.thecanadianencyclopedia.ca/en/article/loyalists [Accessed 22 October 2022].

Wiseman, N. (2006) Provincial political cultures. In: Dunn, C. (ed.), *Provinces. Canadian provincial politics*. Peterborough, Broadview Press, pp. 21–56.

4

COLOMBIA

Matrices, tensions, and contexts for explaining the origin and change of right-wing politics

Laura Camila Ramírez Bonilla

Introduction

The goal of this text is to gather insights into the study of the origins and transformation of right-wing politics in Colombia. From a historical perspective, it seeks to reconstruct contexts, "matrices" (origins), and tensions that have been present in the competition for power across this ideological spectrum. The reader will find a long-term overview that will span the creation of the Colombian Conservative Party, in the mid-nineteenth century, to the electoral triumph of the Democratic Centre Party, in the first decades of the twenty-first century. This text does not identify points of departure and arrival, but turns, recurrences and singularities of the Colombian case.

The first thing to consider is that it is not possible to detect a homogeneous experience of right-wing politics in Colombia, neither ideologically nor operatively. Even the appellation of "right" can be problematic when cataloguing several of the actors and processes that concur in this political scene. Sometimes terms like "conservative", "traditionalist", or "reactionary" can come into play. In that sense, it is necessary to speak of a plural right—the rights—and describe a complex set of patterns, alliances, and tensions, all of which oscillate between the fragmentation and the unity of these groups. From a theoretical and conceptual stance, studying right-wing politics involves identifying shared ideas about order, security, private property, freedoms, morals, social hierarchies, and political power, among other subjects. Nonetheless, historical experience demonstrates variable agendas responding to specific controversies depending on time and space. While historical analysis helps to detect the breakpoints of these ideas and their rearrangements, and also the factors by which these breaks occur, this approach serves to explain the interaction these views have within a "field of action" and the formation of new projects and groups. According to Rodríguez Kauth,

DOI: 10.4324/9781003352266-7

the distinction between political left and right is historical rather than logical, consequently, it has a nominal value, a changing content, an occasional significance, and it is not an unchanging hermeneutical terminology that helps to expose the history of the theory and political praxis

(Rodríguez, 2001: p. 470)

I will use the term "right-wing politics" assuming its historicity and its multiple expression, seeing it as many projects which have been shaped by the alternate persistence and change of specific conditions and incentives. When we speak of plural "rights", I mean both variants and constant resurgence.

Several consistencies originated from the sum of factors that have shaped the plural histories of the right in Colombia, which are conservatism (both as an ideology and a political party), and religion (as a cultural institution and belief system). Both phenomena are what I term enduring "*matrices*". I think this concept helps to avoid a description of static elements, always pointing to the same components. It only throws light on a common reference among the strategies of partisan and ideological competition or antagonisms. I have chosen the word "*matriz*" to name these recurrences due to its more generic notion founded in the dictionary of the Royal Academy of the Spanish Language: "mould of any kind with which something is shaped" (2021).[1] The term has the sense of describing something "foundational" which helps to consider an "origin", which somehow ends up fixing the features of a given object. For this particular case, that perspective means that, although, since the nineteenth century it was possible to speak of conservative and religious roots in the history of the right in Colombia, these have produced dissimilar results. The latter history is marked by the plurality of the political sector and the circumstances that modify its identity. On the other hand, I have called "tensions" to those controversial factors that belong alternatively to the temporal or to the structural, according to their capacity to modify or accentuate values and programmatic agendas in specific contexts.

To this end, the text is organised into four sections. The first attempts a general identification of the contexts that run through the political history of Colombia and of right-wing politics. Secondly, I describe the historical processes belonging to the sphere of conservatism, arguing that this point of view is necessary to identify a "matrix" of the varied rights. The third section delves into the common trajectories between religious institutions and right-wing laden political projects. Finally, a brief fourth section seeks to present an overview of the tensions between these groups and their relations with the wider political system.

Contexts of departure

Three contexts of departure have determined the history of rights in Colombia. First, the emergence of *a bipartisan regime* in an early phase of republican life. Leaving aside the division between Bolivarians and Santanderists, and centralists and federalists—which revealed the profound discrepancies on the models of government after independence—the formal birth of both the Colombian Liberal Party and the Colombian Conservative Party, in 1948 and 1949, respectively, gave entry into a scheme of electoral competition between two political factions that persisted until the twenty-first century and centralised the administration of the government throughout the twentieth century. The exclusion produced by the bipartisan model and its attempts to renew when it faced the erosion of its ideologies, and its actors should be considered a frame of reference in the historical study of political ideologies in Colombia.

Second, a legal milestone: *the Constitution of 1886*. With a centralist model of administration, the political charter established a confessional state and unified control of the public force under a national army. Rafael Núñez, leader of the constitutional change, leaned towards conservatism during his years of government, promoting a legal framework by this ideology.

> The presidential term was extended to six years, and a regime of special powers was established that Congress could grant to the president in addition to his extraordinary powers enshrined in the rule of the state of siege. The death penalty was reinstated, the trade and carrying of firearms were prohibited, and a series of laws were instituted restricting freedom of the press and people gathering.
>
> *(Palacios and Safford, 2002: pp. 458–459)*

With some reforms throughout the twentieth century, the political charter survived until 1991, after the popular election of a constituent that deepened democracy, consecrating the protection of human rights and the environment, the secularism of the State, the guarantee of ethnic and religious diversity, the decentralisation, demilitarisation, reorganisation of the judicial system and the activation of citizens in political participation, among others.

Third, the *political violence* which, under different expressions, has challenged the legitimate and legal monopoly of force in the hands of the State. Leaving aside the civil and regional wars during republican life, it is possible to trace war episodes constantly in the history of the twentieth century, since the "War of thousand days" (1889–1902), confronting liberals and conservatives (the latter facilitating the separation of Panama, in 1903) until the outburst of narco-terrorism at the end of the twentieth century. This trajectory identifies more or less conventional confrontations between two different sides, such as the "Bipartisan violence" of the 1940s and 1950s, or the initial phase of the Internal Armed Conflict (CAI), after the formation of the guerrillas such as the Armed Forces Revolutionaries of Colombia (FARC) and the National Liberation Army (ELN) in 1964. However, over time, asymmetric, unconventional, criminalised violence emerged with a high impact on civilians, such as the "war" against drug cartels and the mutations of the CAI, with the inclusion of paramilitarism and its ties with drug trafficking. The attempt to control this violence by strengthening the military and police forces, through the increase of investment in security and defence, has been one of the common guidelines of right-wing governments in the last two decades.[2] However, the solution of war by peaceful means has also been a debate among the same groups on the right. Three of the most important peace processes were initiatives by right-wing governments: two by the Conservative Party, between 1982 and 1985, under the presidency of Belisario Betancur, one more between 1998 and 2002, with Andrés Pastrana, and a final one with Juan Manuel Santos, a member of the National Union Party (De la U), between the years 2012 and 2016. Curiously, the strongest opposition to the negotiations of the last initiative came from another sector of the right: the Democratic Centre party (CD). Gamboa points out that the peace between Santos and the FARC produced, paradoxically, the strengthening of the political project of Álvaro Uribe Vélez and the CD, likewise, the division of the right as a cohesive community. The fragmentation confronted pro-peace sectors (centre-right) and those opposed to accords with the guerrillas (*Uribistas*) (Gamboa, 2019: pp. 190, 195–196). Since the late 1990s, the subject of peace has been an engine for the political machine, and the discourse of the radical right. In 2002, the independent candidate Álvaro Uribe was elected president, in the first electoral round, embodying a program of rejection of negotiations (that were carried out in San Vicente del Caguán), and the promise of defeating the insurgency through military action.

In these three scenarios, the notion of the State is confronted with reality. As Fernán González indicates, the "partial collapse of the state", "the precariousness of the state", and "the differentiated presence of the state in space and time" lead to question its presence in the national territory and its agency capacity (González, 1997: pp. 236–238). For this article, I am interested in some aspects of the process of the state's construction, such as achieving the means of physical coercion and its constitution as an entity separate from religion—especially from the Church. However, its modernisation, its growing presence, its action in economic policy, and its general operation are subjects worth investigating in detail. I must clarify that, with the exception of the institutional crisis that occurred in the period known as "*La Violencia*", beginning in 1948 with the subsequent establishment of a military dictatorship (1953–1957) and later a transitional military junta (1957–1958), the Colombian political regime will be assumed as democratic. This is because it is a democracy per the formal definition, which recognises the division of powers, freedom of the press, rotation of parties in electoral elections, and the establishment of mechanisms of institutional evaluation. However, something to not overlook is that this regime has coexisted regularly—for more than a hundred years—with repressive actions carried out by the State against civilians and frequent periods of increase in violence (Gutiérrez, 2014: pp. 15–17).

These three contexts, which represent structural problems of construction of citizenship, the modernisation of society, the control over the territory, and the monopoly of coercion, all of which is additionally enmeshed in all sorts of State failures, are essential to read the trajectory of right-wing politics in Colombia up to the present time. This is the arena in which political parties have had to interact since the mid-nineteenth century, in different episodes however, with thorough significance for the overall history of the country.

Conservatism

Conservatism is a clear source to trace the origin of right-wing politics in Colombia. However, some historical references allow considering both similarities and differences between these political projects. The ideas published by José Eusebio Caro and Mariano Ospina Rodríguez in *La Civilización of Bogotá*, on October 4, 1849, not only allowed the creation of the Colombian Conservative Party but also provoked a rupture within the political groups that had participated in independence. The issue was not only political and economic, or to adopt centralism and protectionism, at the base of the claims it was a dispute between civilisation and barbarism according to what was understood by faith: "the morality of Christianity and its civilising doctrines against immorality and the corrupting doctrines of materialism and atheism" (Caro and Ospina as cited by Padilla, 2010: p. 358). Ospina and Caro raised in their postulates strong criticism towards the French Revolution, Jacobinism, and the liberal party founded months ago, altogether. In his opinion, "civilised Europe" had been taken over by impious people coming from factories and universities, materialists, without religion or morals (González, 1997: pp. 178–181).

At the end of 1949, Caro reaffirmed, also in *La Civilización*, seeing a crisis in religious freedom and the education of Catholics under liberal governments, he distrusted democracy, imputing that it manipulated artisans to arm themselves to defend the government. Conservatives advocated rational freedom as opposed to "monarchical, military and demagogic despotism"; they defended the property against the usurpation that the socialists claimed to promote, and "security against arbitrariness" (Jaramillo, 1997). Laguado identifies Latin and ecclesiastical sources in this synthesis of ideas, as well as an exaltation of the Spanish heritage. "If De Maistre was one of the most widely read authors, the papal encyclicals, on many occasions, served as a roadmap" (Laguado, 2006: p. 187). González maintains that "these early controversies are going to mark profoundly political life from that time to the present day" (González, 1997: pp. 183–186). The Jacobin myth radicalised positions and stigmatised the adversary without the possibility of rectifications or variations. This scheme, which justified new warlike confrontations and institutional and legal changes, reached the time of President Rafael Núñez, in the last decades of the century, and the formulation of a new constitution (1886).

Although Rafael Núñez began his political life in liberalism, when he became president of the republic, between 1880 and 1882, he became close to conservatism and the new political coalition called the National Party. In 1884, when he was re-elected as president, he rejected federalism as a system of territorial administration; he attacked press freedom, a lax penal system, and anti-clericalism. The answer to the supposed liberal distortion was the design of a new political charter. The apparent bipartisan alliance, represented by the National Party, ended up being conservative, and established a new administrative, religious, economic, and territorial regime. Furthermore, with the death of Núñez, in 1894, this process was radicalised. The period, known as "La Regeneración", cemented an idea of sovereignty centred on the Nation—with a capital letter—: "conceived as an organic, homogeneous and corporatist unit, above particularisms and regionalisms" (González, 2006: p. 135).

The new century surprised the country amid the "Thousand days' war" (1899–1902), the exhaustion of the political scheme: "National Party—Conservative Party" and the economic crisis (Palacios and Safford, 2002: p. 463). In the same period, the political elites were unable to prevent the separation of Panama. In response to that act, the government exalted Hispanic values, the nobility of the Catholic religion, the Spanish language, public and private institutions, and the patrimonial rights defined by the Spanish Crown in the colonial period as the basis of national identity (Palacios and Safford, 2002: p. 467). Despite the consequences of the war and the independence of Panama, the Conservative Party managed to stay in power for another 30 years.[3] Through a quantitative analysis, Gutiérrez verifies that there were social fractures in the electoral behaviour of the country during that period. Liberal municipalities that had been stable before were concentrated in more urbanised areas of the country, with a higher percentage of the Black population and a warmer climate, and where the Catholic-rural order was weaker. In contrast, and surprisingly, the study reveals that conservative municipalities and grey areas, disputed by political parties, cannot be classified with the same precision (Gutiérrez et al., 2008: pp. 115–119).

The conservative spirit of the Constitution of 1886 prevailed over the reform attempts by the liberal governments in the 1930s. In fact, these attempts were the cause of more radicalisation among the most traditional conservatives. In hand with authoritarian nationalism, counterrevolutionary and restorative voices were heard with intensity. Anti-communism, anti-liberalism, anti-Semitism, anti-democracy and anti-parliamentarism were anchored in the discourse of these ideological currents, not only in Colombia but in the subcontinent. "The positivity was given by the imperatives of 'order, hierarchy, and authority', an organicist conception of society, a vitalist *ethos* at times irrational" (Funes, 2014: p. 158)

In this context, the conservative leader Laureano Gómez occupied a central place. He was President between 1950 and 1951; his vision of the political order was based on Thomist philosophy and the notion of the common good, as well as the belief in Enlightenment as a "ballast of all calamities" (Barrero, 2012: pp. 108–109, p. 83). Democracy, the destiny of the American countries, should be the expression of universal laws defined in the conscience of each agent, which cannot be altered "by a simple vote". Barrero (2012) highlights that respect for human life and dignity were defined as the axes of these laws, with conservatives appearing as the "true democrats of Colombia", according to Gómez, "healthy individualists" and liberals in the "apolitical good sense of the word" (pp. 109, 115).

Convinced, after the Spanish Civil War and the empowerment of Franco, that Hispanicism was the inspiration and source of the cosmology of conservatism, Gómez exalted Christian humanism as the only guarantor of individual freedoms and the only system committed to a hierarchical order of society (Barrero, 2012: p. 112). This condition became expressed in 1953, when he defined universal suffrage as inorganic and in contradiction to the nature of society because of the impossibility of all individuals having the same levels of intelligence. Society, seen as a pyramid, had at its base a "dark and inept vulgarity, where rationality hardly appears to differentiate human beings from brutes" (Laureano Gómez as cited by Barrero, 2012: p. 118). The spirit of countering the dangers of liberalism—which defied the original spirit of the Constitution of 1886—and avoiding the hints of communism, took for granted the radicalisation of conservative imperatives and, thus, the violence of some sectors.

By considering this ideological basis, which evidently is much more extensive than the one presented here and includes characters such as Sergio Arboleda (1822–1888), Gonzalo Restrepo Jaramillo (1895–1966), and Álvaro Gómez Hurtado (1919–1995), there would not be a self-evident definition of conservatism as the "right" in Colombia. After the military dictatorship of Gral. Gustavo Rojas Pinilla (1953–1957) and the establishment of the National Front (1958–1974), which allowed the Conservative Party and the Liberal Party to alternate in the presidency of the republic, the conservatives privileged the pragmatic to doctrine, in defence of a vision of society and its political order.

Conservatism and the recent partisan scheme against the right

From 1958 to the present (2020), the Conservative Party has been elected four times to the Presidency of the Republic. The last occasion was with Andrés Pastrana Arango (1998–2002), who presented the lowest approval ratings of the leaders of the last three decades.[4] The current party statutes, approved in 2015, are poor in ideological terms. The party defines itself as a "political centre organisation" (Art. 1) and presents the slogan of: "the party of solutions". It offers broad, generic frames of reference that seek to deepen democracy, however, that do not allow ideological differences with other political groups (Statutes of the Colombian Conservative Party, April 21, 2015). It is possible to say that the Conservative Party of Laureano Gómez, in the mid-twentieth century, or even that of Ospina Rodríguez, in the nineteenth century, is ideologically closer to the right as a synonym for "order, law, and God", than the structure of the Conservative Party of the twenty-first century. Notwithstanding, political actors and their current programmatic actions are telling of a moderate or centre-right, which in recent years has made its entrance to power consolidating coalitions with other political parties.

The loss of prominence of the Conservative Party in the electoral panorama coincides with two phenomena: on the one hand, the breakdown of the bipartisanship since the end of the twentieth century, and on the other hand, the emergence of new political movements that hold values similar to those of the Conservatives. Since the establishment of the 1991 Constitution, the Conservative Party has not managed to be a majority in the Senate and the House of Representatives, and after the mandate of Andrés Pastrana (1998–2002), its participation in the presidential elections has been tangential. Its candidates have not managed to participate in the second electoral round.[5] On other occasions, the community has accepted to give up on its candidates to integrate multi-party alliances. This last situation arose in the 2006 presidential elections, with Alvaro Uribe's coalition—*Partido de la U*— and in 2018, with the internal division that caused the support for the candidacy of Iván Duque—*Partido Centro Democrático*. That said, this reality is not exclusive to conservatism. In the first decade of the twenty-first century, the traditional political parties experienced, according to Javier Duque (2007), "a double process of shrinking and displacement" (p. 29). Faced with a change in electoral system rules and the emergence of new parties with significant support at the polls, these organisations have tended to restructure and routinise their internal processes— especially, internal democracy (Duque, 2007: pp. 28–29).

In the electoral competition, three relevant parties have embodied the expectations of the current conservative right-wing ideals: the Democratic Centre Party, the Social Party of National Unity (U Party), and the Radical Change Party.[6] Among the three projects, it is the Democratic Centre Party, founded in 2013 under the leadership of Álvaro Uribe Vélez, which is the closest to conservatism that in the nineteenth century structured the conservative ideological platform. The curious fact is that due to the origin of their founders, the three political movements originate from splits in the Liberal Party. None of these organisations defines itself as right-wing,[7] and due to their break with Uribism, during the government of Juan Manuel Santos (2010–2018), the last two oscillate between the centre, the moderate right, and political and economic liberalism. In turn, in the CD party, a moderate sector is identifiable, such as that represented by Iván Duque, and a radical sector, ideologically orthodox, such as the one that characterises former president Uribe, his former minister Fernando Londoño Hoyos or Senator María Fernanda Cabal. In all cases, the scheme attempts to deepen political personalism, as indicated in article 8 of the party legal statutes: "The Democratic Centre party recognizes the former president of the Republic Dr. Álvaro Uribe Vélez as its founding President and maximum leader and counsellor" (Democratic Centre Party Statutes, 2017: p. 6).[8]

In the ideological platform of the CD, three aspects stand out which coincide with the conservative tradition and allow identification of the organisation as part of the right of the political spectrum. First, "it welcomes the definition of the Common Good as a set of conditions in which each individual can achieve his plenitude", a reference that reminds the Thomistic thought defended by Laureano Gómez in his writings in the 1940s and 1950s. Second, it "defends and proclaims the family as a fundamental institution for social coexistence, the progress of the human being and the realisation of His ideals". In the same sense, youth is identified as the patrimony of society and a priority population to be served. The moral agenda, which rejects marriage and adoption of same-sex couples, abortion, euthanasia, and drug-free consumption, and promotes the defence of the nuclear family and child protection, has been at the core of the daily program of the CD. And third, "it will promote private initiative and business development, with the prevalence of State action in pursuit of social welfare and human dignity". According to this programmatic agenda, the guarantee of equal rights and opportunities is based on prosperity given not so much by the overall economy but generated by the private sector. This emphasis is reminiscent of the Conservative Party of the first half of the twentieth century, in its defence of private property and its refusal of agrarian reform. For the Democratic Centre, "investor confidence" and the "austere and decentralised state" were two of the five founding pillars of the party (Losada, 2016: pp. 48-49).[9]

Table 4.1 allows us to synthesise and contrast the most relevant themes on the programmatic agenda of these four political parties, which are close to the right-wing political spectrum.

Based on the analysis of the surveys conducted by the Observatory of Parliamentary Elites in Latin America, between 2003 and 2006, Gamboa (2019) concludes that on a scale of 1 to 10, where 1 represents the left and 10 the right, the Democratic Centre Party obtains an evaluation of 8.16, being the one closest to 10. It is followed by the Conservative Party (7.93), the U Party (7.41), and Radical Change (7.10) (p. 195).

Religion

This "matrix" is at the ideological and historical base of the right in Colombia for three reasons: first, it originates from the alliance that, since the second half of the nineteenth century, consolidated the collaboration between Catholic Church and the Colombian Conservative Party. The proximity of these two entities allowed the ecclesiastical hierarchy to participate actively in the decision-making of the political community; thus, Catholic values were an integral part of the identity of the party. Second, the Constitution of 1886 ratified the religious monopoly in the hands of the Catholic Church, legally establishing a confessional State: "the Catholic, Apostolic, Roman Religion is that of the Nation; the Public Powers shall protect it and ensure that it is respected as an essential element of the social order" (Art. 38). And third, the system of symbols that religion held, especially Christian ones—Catholic or not—is up to the present a medium of political culture. In other words, the religious, even in a secular and confessionally diverse regime, is not only considered an important factor for the majority of the population (Beltrán, 2013: pp. 92–93), but an element susceptible to becoming politicised.

The closeness of the Conservative Party with the hierarchical Church established a sort of pact between the radical right of the twentieth century and integral and intransigent Catholicism. The Concordat of December 31, 1887, not only allied the two organisations officially, but also closed alternatives, both to a regime of separation of spheres—religion from politics—and to the formation of a strictly secular right. The agreement determined, according to article 41 of the Constitution, that religious education was mandatory in public education, with

TABLE 4.1 Colombia: Programmatic principles of right-wing parties according to their most recent statute

Political Party	Self-ideological Definition	Family—Moral	State and politics	Equality—Social Equity	Freedoms	Property	Security
Conservative Party	Centre	Does not mention family, but it speaks of morality in conduct and respect for life from conception.	Of the rule of law.	Exclusion of all discrimination or privilege for ideological, economic, social, sex, or racial reasons.	Freedom of Western tradition. Gender equity.	Right to individual property obtained in a fair title.	Comprehensive human security. Respect for human rights.
Democratic Centre Party	Centre	Fundamental institution for social coexistence, human progress, and the realisation of their ideals.	Community state.	Social welfare. He does not mention the word "equality".	As a source of spiritual development and in the exercise of its individual action.	Promotes private initiative and business development.	Democratic security, civil order, and the rule of law.
U Party	Does not define itself.	Foundation of society.	Social state of law.	Development of equal opportunities and social equity.	Respect for freedom: cultural, ethnic, religious, gender, and opinion.	Does not mention private property.	Does not mention.
Radical Change Party	Does not define itself.	Does not mention.	Community State.	Social equity, greater coverage in health and education, and poverty eradication.	Gender freedom.	Does not mention.	Human security.

Source: Elaborated by the author based on the statutes of the political parties: Colombian Conservative Party Statute (April 2015); Statutes of the U Party (25th November 2012); Statutes of the Colombian Radical Change Party (November 2018); Statute of the Democratic Centre Party (6th May 2017).

observance of the pious practices and the moral precepts of Catholicism. Priests and bishops, with the power to censor, assumed the task of reviewing, authorising, and monitoring teachers, chairs of public institutions, and educational texts. Among other issues, the Concordat endorsed the Vatican's power to appoint archbishops and bishops, granted civil effects to the Catholic couple, and allowed the Church to perform social assistance through the protection of charity. The constitution also enshrined the tax exemption for buildings of worship and administration of the Catholic Church and declared the priestly ministry incompatible with public office. The protection of Catholicism was in the doctrinal base of the party since the nineteenth century. Its function was conceived as a civiliser, addressed to the Indigenous people without faith, to unify the nation, as it has been indicated by Sergio Arboleda (Laguado, 2006: p. 186).

In 1930, the return of the Liberal Party to the presidency ratified the religious issue as one of the factors of tension between the parties. Bipartisan disagreements were violently manifested throughout most of the country. The liberal reforms of Alfonso López Pumarejo (1934–1938), who in 1936 attempted to modernise the Church–State relationship and depoliticise the clergy, were thwarted by conservatism and intransigent Catholicism. "No one disputes that this is a country in which there is moral unanimity of Catholics, and that fact had to be necessarily supported by constitutional norms", said Laureano Gómez (1986). The idea that any constitutional change in religious matters was an accomplice of communism, "secularism" and alienated Colombia from its faith was diffused by the ecclesiastical hierarchy (Arias, 2003: pp. 127, 139). This was expressed in the collective pastoral of 1936: "we said and proved that communism is, on its mental bases, materialistic and atheist; for its purposes, an enemy of God, of the country, of the family and property" (Colombian Episcopal Conference, 1956: p. 428).

The same remarks were repeated in the pastorals of 1948 and 1949, and individual sermons were made inciting violence. "If Congress insists on raising religious problems for us, [...] neither we, nor our clergy, nor our faithful will remain defenceless and passive" (Builes, 1936: p. 1), indicated by Monsignor Miguel Ángel Builes, who declared liberalism a sin. The systematic use of metaphors allowed Builes to promote a genuine contempt for liberals: the Catholic was a "soldier of faith" (Uribe, 2012: p. 156), even if state order and authority were subverted. The increase in violence and the assassination of the liberal leader, Jorge Eliecer Gaitán, on April 9, 1948, radicalised the parties. For the bishops, the collapse of Bogotá was the result of anti-Catholic propaganda and the proselytising of international communism (La Rosa, 2000: pp. 110–111). Religious passions, González argues, exacerbated the climate of political tension. Not even "moral considerations" could stop the chaos that the Church itself contributed to unleashing (González, 1997: p. 297).

Integral and uncompromising Catholicism[10] found in the Conservative Party a way to intervene in politics, both in opinion and collective action. The refusal in this position to admit any modification to the Constitution or the Concordat (which de-centred the role of Christianity in political power) demonstrated: first, a strong conviction in the civic function of ecclesiastical intervention in political life, in other words, to participate in it was seen as a Christian duty. Second, a limited capacity for dialogue that overlooked the tension that other sectors of the Church had with the intransigent right-wing and their vision of social and political order.

In the first aspect, the lay organisation, led by Colombian Catholic Action (ACC), accompanied the anti-liberal and anti-communist crusade of the ecclesiastical hierarchy. (La Rosa, 2000: p. 34).[11] Despite the pontifical precept of not involving political parties or movements, the ACC approached the Conservative Party ideologically and programmatically (Bidegain, 1985: pp. 21–25).[12] Faced with the second aspect, the hierarchy's rejection of Marxist activism stands out. This confrontation awoke among some religious men and women in the late 1940s and was reinforced in the framework of the Second Vatican council and the 1968 CELAM meeting. A "reconfessionalized" State surged from the "co-government" alliance between liberals and conservatives, which ratified Catholicism as the religion of the nation (González, 1997: p. 396). On their side, the ecclesiastical hierarchy was reluctant not only to implement with the mandates of the Council, but also to talk with the so-called "red priests", like the iconic Camilo Torres.

The secular state and religious pluralism versus the right

With the 1991 Constitution, the religious regime took a substantial turn: the establishment of a secular state. This fact, coupled with the expansion of religious pluralism and the gradual disintegration of bipartisanship, impacted the trajectories of the right in Colombia in two ways. First, it mitigated the centrality of the Catholic Church vis-à-vis politics and conservative sectors, fostering a greater secularisation of the public sphere, both normative and institutional. And second, paradoxically, the participation of the evangelical churches in political parties and agendas was accentuated. As part of this, the political representatives of the Christian denominations turned to the right, assuming banners of order, morality, and security that had previously been held by Catholicism in alliance with bipartisanship. The closeness of the Catholic Church to the Conservative Party ceased to be an unquestionable fact and became an individual preference of clergymen and bishops. In 1993, ruling C-027 of the Constitutional Court declared eleven articles of the 1973 Concordat invalid and another five partially unconstitutional.[13] It was in the period of Ernesto Samper (1994–1998) (the last representative of the Liberal Party to assume the presidency) that the congregations of the Evangelical Council of Colombia (Cedecol) and 16 other Protestant churches signed a kind of "concordat".[14]

Faced with a new religious map, the political activity of the Protestant churches began to grow. Beltrán explains that this dynamism was more active among Pentecostals and Neo-Pentecostals than among historical Protestantism. In the latter, social problems are not underestimated; however, they are not considered as a substantial part of their mission of faith. On the other hand, the political activity of evangelicals and churches close to religious fundamentalism and millennialism stands out. They have contrasting views of politics and the role that corresponds to the religious institution, the parish priest, and the parishioner in front of it. These views range from passivity and the idea that the public sector is sinful in the obligation to participate for the future of the community and the exercise of a salvific mission by religious leaders (Beltrán, 2003: pp. 290–295).[15]

After being collectives close to liberalism, several of these congregations turned to the right with the government of Álvaro Uribe (2002–2010).[16] "We identify with him in many things. He defends the biblical model of society, based more on duties than rights. He proclaims the importance of the family nucleus", affirmed a Baptist pastor to the magazine *Semana* (August 26, 2005) when referring to the president. The attempts to criminalise abortion, the debates on the centrality of the nuclear family, and the call for singles to postpone their sexual life are phenomena that prompt the government of Uribe Vélez to coincide with numerous Christian congregations in political life.

Although the previous trend continued in the government of Juan Manuel Santos (2010–2018), the distance between this government and Álvaro Uribe's project marked a turn in the political activity of several of these churches. The plebiscite held on October 2, 2016, by which the President of the Republic sought to ratify the Final Agreement signed with the FARC guerrillas, was the tensest situation during that period.[17] Political analysts have considered that the proselytism of some Protestant pastors could have been decisive in the triumph of "no" in the plebiscite (50.21% of the voters refused to support the peace pact and 49.78% approved it) (Marcos, 2016). Later, the political party "Colombia Justa Libres" was formed on December 11, 2017, as a coalition of Christian pastors and right-wing political leaders.

The discipline of the Christian community and their authentic alignment with conservative political ideas possibly explain part of the phenomenon.[18] According to a 2017 survey done by the National Consulting Centre of Christian parishioners, 37% were willing to vote for the political party that their church supported, while 63% considered it very important that congregations defend their beliefs in the political sphere (Semana, 2nd October 2018). The moral fear, especially focused on gender subjects and the structure of the family, was mixed—and misrepresented—with the suspicion of "concessions" made by the government when they agreed on the demobilisation of the armed group. "Christian morality, family, justice, honesty, excellence, and truth" were defined as the flag of "Colombia Justa" (Gómez and Ospina, 2019). And although the agenda commences with a political fact—peace, and also it diversifies into topics such as health, security, justice, and productivity—Christian morality and a salvific vision of their activity in politics are at the base of his initiative. "*Colombia Justa Libres*" premiered in the 2018 legislative elections, with more than 450,000 votes, which elected three senators and one representative to the chamber. Why is this foray into politics related to the trajectories of the right in Colombia? It is because of the determined support that *"Colombia Justa Libres"* gave the Democratic Centre party in the 2018 presidential elections. The community was part of, in coalition with the Christian "MIRA" party, the "Great Alliance for Colombia", which managed to win the presidency having as candidate Iván Duque (2018–2022).

Tensions

If religion and conservatism can be considered constant "matrices" since the nineteenth century, three more tensions are also to be seen: land, in the first place, and privatisation of violence and liberalism, in second and third places. These are not junctures. I consider these factors that correspond to the structural field, and which affect agendas, actions, and positions of the right in the country.

I will first address the distribution and use of the land. The infructuous attempts to avoid the concentration of land in the hands of few owners by legal, political, and social actions are an issue linked to the history of political elites, as well as to the predominant economic models and the conflicts between the State, the peasants, the landowners, and armed groups outside the law. In addition, in recent years, industrial megaprojects and criminal networks have jointly been the problem. According to ECLAC and official censuses, by the mid-1950s, 55% of landowners in Colombia owned less than ten hectares and occupied around 7% of the surface of the country (IGAC, 2012: p. 55). By the end of the twentieth century, such disparity was accentuated (Machado, 2009: p. 135). "1.33% of the owners owned about 59% of the property area available (…) while 90% only owned 21.4% of the property" (IGAC, 2012: p. 66). Without being simply a mono-causal phenomenon, the bipartisan antagonism of the first half of the twentieth century, based on an oligarchic structure of access to power, prevented the realisation of a social and political transformation of agriculture. Marco Palacios points out that with law 200 of 1936, a "land regime" was constructed which neutralised the most radical demands, but it did not achieve comprehensive agrarian reform. With the revision of the ownership regulations, the division of the liberals, the peasants, and the settlers was evident, while the conservative leaders, defenders of the "sacred right to property", saw their interests protected with a moderate reform (Palacios, 2011: pp. 29, 205–207). What happened to their peasant bases? What political allegiances were in tension over the land issue? Over time, conflicts over land property were compounded by the problem of use. In the 1990s, the competition was no longer only for good quality land for farming, political and coercive control of the territory, war and drug trafficking, money laundering, illegal mining, and multinational projects with high environmental impact were added to the issue, among other factors (Machado, 2009: pp. 134–135).

The second, the privatisation of violence. In the last four decades, criminal structures for the privatisation of violence have, by definition, been counterinsurgent.[19] In the context of the armed conflict, they were built as rural self-defence groups, which, in alliance with drug trafficking cartels, tried to contain the guerrillas. The first of these cases was the group "*Muerte a Secuestradores*" (MAS), founded in 1981 by the Medellín Cartel, in response to the M-19 guerrillas, responsible for the kidnapping of the daughter of drug trafficker Fabio Ochoa. Although this and other organisations lacked a consistent and programmatic ideological corpus, they coincided in their fierce anti-communist struggle, the competition for control of territory—even illegal possession in some cases—and the collaboration with the forces of order, not even to mention their concern of some of them for certain moral canons. Some experts have considered these groups as paramilitaries, filtering in not only into private security and justice systems, but also into "dirty war" regimes at the hands of the State and drug trafficking and, in some cases, legitimate sectors of the population (Reyes, 1991; Romero, 2002: pp. 273, 275; Cruz, 2007: pp. 119–120). The prominence of these illegal groups led to the formation, in 1997, of a national network called the "United Self-Defence Forces of Colombia" (AUC), which entered into a peace process in 2002, under Uribe Vélez's government. Although these armed movements did not have any official affiliation to any political party, their infiltration in the legislative elections of 2002 and 2006, through alliances with regional politicians, allowed them to control part of Congress.[20] Several of these legislators, militants of Uribe, conservatives, and liberals, were prosecuted for conspiracy accused of committing a crime in association with paramilitary groups (Gutiérrez, 2007). The closeness of these violent groups with leaders of the extreme right in some cases, and their sympathy for a right-wing ideology in other cases, has been a controversial and dark issue in Colombia's political trajectory in the last four decades.

And third, the connections of liberalism—and the Liberal Party—with democratic rights. It is not strange that supporters of liberalism have migrated to conservatism, as was the case with Rafael Núñez or José María Samper in the nineteenth century. However, the commercial opening in the 1990s reinforced this trend, responding to views of the economy rather than of a traditional ideology. Uribe Vélez himself, leader of the CD, belonged to the Liberal Party in the 1980s and 1990s. In this route, it is possible to identify, first, trade unions and business organisations adhering to right-wing parties, such as the Colombian Federation of Ganaderos, the organisation Ardila Lule, Asocaña, and Fenalco in the governments of Álvaro Uribe Vélez (2002–2010). And second, the presence of a politically conservative technocracy, formed in economic liberalism, as is the case of Alberto Carrasquilla, Minister of Finance and Public Credit (2003 and 2007), in the Uribe Vélez's administration, reassigned in the same office in 2018 by President Iván Duque (2018–2022).[21] For its part, economic liberalism seems to be the base, since the 1990s, of consensus between conservatives and liberals of the extreme right and centre-right, with few variations. The proposal to reduce state intervention in the economy was accompanied by "investor confidence", the motto of Uribe Velez's administrations, and the signing of a free trade agreement with the United States in 2011. Laguado (2006) highlights the centrality that this tendency has in the works of Óscar Cornblit (1975), Edward Gibson (1996), and Kevin Middelbrook (2000), observing the coalescence of right-wing political projects and upper strata, or economically privileged sectors of society in the political trajectory of Latin America (pp. 169–172). In the case of Colombia, the issue coincides with the concentration of land. Since the nineteenth century conservative leaders became known as powerful landowners in their regions: Sergio Arboleda y Pombo, Mariano Ospina Rodríguez, Rafael Reyes, Guillermo León Valencia, or Álvaro Uribe Vélez.

Faced with each of these elements, the right, in its different variants, has had to assume positions, build agendas, or negotiate with other political sectors. They are factors that have even generated internal controversies. Did reforming land ownership conditions affect the assets of some conservative politicians? What relationship did the acceptance of the private use of weapons and the concentration of land have with the formation of guerrillas and self-defence groups?

Final thoughts

Table 4.2 summarises the overall panorama I have presented so far. I identify contexts that have determined the structures, ideas, and activity of the right-wing in Colombia since the nineteenth century. In this converge bipartisanship, political constitutions, violence, and state weakness. On the other hand, I emphasise three tensions, present in certain historical periods and processes, that have redefined priorities for these political groups up to the present: (a) their relationship with the concentration of land, (b) their commitment to economic and political liberalism, and (c) the privatisation of violence at the hands of self-defence groups and paramilitaries. Finally, in this scheme, two constant "matrices" that run through the history of these communities stand out, contributing identity and values to the political, social, and cultural project: conservatism and religion(s). The integration of new actors and ideas to these "matrices" showed, over time, a difficult path of three projects that, until now, have not finished consolidating in Colombia in the field of praxis: the modernity of society, the separation between religion and politics, and the legitimate monopoly of violence in the hands of the state.

According to "Barometer for the Americas", between 2004 and 2013, the majority of Colombians defined themselves as belonging to the right. On a scale of 1 to 10, where 1 was the left and 10 was the right, the average of the respondents

TABLE 4.2 Colombia: Contexts, tensions and matrices of origin and transformation of the right

Starting Contexts	*Constant "Matrices"*	*Itinerant Tensions*
Bipartisanship	Conservatism,	Liberalism (economic and
Constitution of 1886 and 1991	Religion (Catholic and	political party)
Political violence	Protestant)	Criminal violence
Weak state		Land distribution

Source: Elaborated by the author.

was rated 6.23 (García, Seligson & Rodríguez, 2014: p. 75). The exercise reveals the popular base of this political sector, which has been strong in the presidential elections of the last two decades. Rodríguez found that those who defined themselves as being on the right were, for the most part, older citizens, with a lower level of education, less purchasing power, and belonging to small cities, in stark contrast to the population on the left. This condition casts doubts on the alleged tendency to associate the right-wing with the wealthiest sectors. Those who called themselves followers of the CD were the respondents with the highest rating in the right-hand band, with 7.3% (Rodríguez, 2006: p. 193). The sociodemographic profile is a key subject since it allows hypotheses about the ability to sustain a project from one ideological spectrum or another in the medium term, with the same political success. This is also telling of the need to renew the programmatic platform Ten years later, the Barometer showed that Colombians continued to mistrust democracy, even though they did not declare themselves against it. Since 2004, the survey had not registered "such a low level of satisfaction with the functioning of democracy in the country." The symptoms are not entirely favorable. In 2021, the number of respondents who approve of the execution of a coup doubled (17% to 38%). In addition, 57% are willing to sacrifice the choice of governors in favor of a system that guarantees income and basic services (Plata, Montalvo, Rodríguez & García, 2021: p. 5, 83 and 90).

However, the preference of the Colombian population for right-wing political options is not circumstantial. It responds to a changing historical trajectory, which gave more freedom to conservatism and the Catholic Church, both in its moderate and intransigent versions, to interact with the population and negotiate with the elites in power—or to renew or replace those elites—in spite of other ideological platforms and sociocultural institutions. At the end of the 1950s, when the closeness between liberals and conservatives grew, there was a shift to the centre-right rather than to the centre-left. In the historical overview presented in this text, there were two recurrences that conservatism and religions failed to moderate in the political culture: first, the consolidation of a right-wing political identity that prioritised the rejection of the opponent as a starting point. This is nothing new in the realm of political confrontation. However, in the case of Colombia, in conditions of high-conflict, political groups—of all ideological spectres—got used to despising the adversary or even justifying their elimination. And second, in the same fashion, violence was assumed as a "valid" form of dispute resolution between the most radical sectors of the political factions. The most deeply rooted ideological passions—extreme—were channelled through the armed means. Both the common militant in arms, conservative or liberal, and the guerrilla combatant in the mountains of Colombia or the agents of the State outside the law have acted with exacerbated violence against the opponent, understood as the enemy.

Since 1998, the presidency of the republic has been occupied by communities identified as right-wing—although they define themselves as the centre. The breakdown of bipartisanship, the electoral reforms after 1991, the scaling of the armed conflict, the stigmatisation of left-wing collectivities—because they are considered allies of the guerrillas—and the exaltation of political personalism (represented in the former president Uribe Vélez) have been forceful in reinforcing right-wing trends and their electoral success until 2018. What is the paradox in this historical process? From 1886 the country turned towards conservatism, within the framework of a confessional constitution. At the end of the twentieth century, it also turned to the right, within the framework of a secular, democratic constitution, guarantor of diversity, and equal rights. The balance, however, is interesting. It is because of this balance that understanding its history is necessary. The ideological context does not necessarily reinforce anti-modern values or stagnate the plurality of opinion or dissent throughout society. In the last three decades, a greater secularisation, expansion of spaces for citizen participation, social mobilisation, higher levels of education, and access to alternative means of communication are evident, which in turn coexist with widespread and heterogeneous expressions of the ideological right. There is no single splice pattern between these two realities. Although in the last 20 years the leadership of the right has been mobilised by Uribe Vélez's projects, their presence today does not guarantee the stable permanence of their ideological platform in power either.[22]

The signs of change point to a more accentuated and unpredictable pluralism, which coexists and is in tension with authoritarian forms of political power, caudillismo, populism, and unsurpassed corruption practices. After the peace agreement with the FARC (2017), at least in the big cities, a versatile political dynamism is latent that perhaps the "right–left" contrast scheme does not manage to explain. It is essential to continue with a cartography of electoral behaviour, a historical approach that demystifies the "unprecedented", and a careful look at the social bases of the parties, the middle classes and the political centre.

Notes

1 In Spanish: '*Molde de cualquier clase con que se da forma a algo*'.
2 From 1992 to 2016, "there is a growth cycle in the participation of Defense and Security expenditures as a proportion of the total budget". The record percentage was reached in 2003 with 15.14% (Otero, 2016: p. 49)
3 After the departure from power of Rafael Núñez, in 1892, the National Party continued in the presidency until 1900, when José Manuel Marroquín (1900–1904), from the Conservative Party, took office on account of the coup against Manuel Antonio Sanclemente (1898–1900), within the framework of the Thousand Day War.
4 At its most critical moment, it reached 74% disapproval (December 2001) (Gallup Poll, 2019).
5 The candidates were Noemí Sanín in 2010 and Martha Lucía Ramírez in 2014.
6 The Social Party of National Unity (Partido de la U) was founded in 2005, by Álvaro Uribe Vélez himself, and the Partido Cambio Radical, which comes from a split from the Liberal Party, organised as a party in 2001. Both supported the presidential re-election of Uribe Vélez in 2006. To this list could be added Democratic Colombia, Citizen Convergence, and Alas Equipo Colombia already disappeared from the electoral contest. However, due to their marginal participation in a long-term reading of the party system, they will not be considered.
7 The CD Statutes (2017) state that "The Democratic Centre was born as a centre party within the political spectrum".

8 The exaltation of the former president was more radical in the founding version of the party's statutes. According to article 40, Uribe Vélez will have a seat with "voice and vote in all the governing and representative bodies of the Party". The stamp of the ex-president is evident in the party's logo, which shows the profile of a man with his hand resting on his heart with the phrase "Firm hand. Big heart" (Losada, 2016: p. 49).
9 The other pillars were democratic security, social cohesion, and popular dialogue.
10 Aspe (2008) notes that integralism refers to "full-time Catholics", who had to influence the entire life of the nation to "restore the Christian social order". Intransigence refers to opposition to liberalism, its denial as an ideology, and the attitude of "not allowing oneself to be reduced to the exercise of mere religious and cultural practices" (p. 25).
11 Obedient to the mandate of the bishops, this group distributed its activities among women, youth, and adult men to combat any suspicion of contradiction to the confessional State. The words of Monsignor Juan Manuel González, in 1937, ratified the spirit of the organisation: "If we are all gathered on God's side, our enemies will not be able to do anything against us. We want an organised group in the ACC. In it, we have a hierarchy between those who command and those who obey. We must reach the masses; but to reach them we need militants and leaders", he pointed out to the Catholic Women's Youth (de Cardedal, D. O. G. *Palabras del Excelentísimo Señor*. pp. 12–13).
12 Its creation, in 1933, during the return of the liberals to power, was interpreted by them as an attempt by conservatism to remain in spaces of public power (Arias, 2003: p. 106). It is not surprising that members of the ACC have also been active members of the Conservative Party.
13 The treaty between the Vatican and the Colombian State was not annulled, but it was highly questioned.
14 According to the Pew Research Center, in 2014 74% of Colombians considered themselves Catholic (Catholics are growing faster than the world's population, March 27 2016). In 2010, a survey conducted by the National University of Colombia and the Sergio Arboleda University revealed that 70.9% of the people consulted said they belonged to the Catholic Church, 16.7% to Protestant congregations (Evangelical Christian, Pentecostal, Charismatic Evangelical, Protestant), 4.7% considered themselves atheist or agnostic, 3.5% did not believe in God, and 4.2% were part of other confessions or did not answer the question (Beltrán, 2013: p. 101). The agreement between Samper and the Protestants established the validity of Christian marriage before the law; spiritual assistance in prisons, hospitals, and battalions; and freedom of worship in public educational institutions, among other issues.
15 With the 1991 Constitution, the UC Christian Union stood out, whose representatives participated in the elaboration of the Political Charter, the National Christian Party, the Independent Movement for Absolute Renewal (MIRA in Spanish), and the Civic and Christian Party for the Community (C4). For the legislative and presidential elections of 2018 and the regional elections of 2019, the MIRA remained in force and *Colombia Justa Libres* emerged, collectivities in coalition with the governing party, Centro Democrático. The political reforms of 2003, 2009, and 2018 and the Law of Parties (1475) of 2011 modified the operating scheme of these political organisations, prohibiting double membership, expanding the threshold of votes to obtain legal status, regulating campaign financing and promoting internal democracy and gender equality of parties, among others (Batlle and Puyana, 2013). Based on the electoral results in 2016–2018, experts calculate between one million, five hundred thousand and two million votes (Gómez and Ospina, 2019) (Semana, 2nd October 2018).
16 See: Quevedo and García (2009), and Semana. August 26, 2005. Benditos votos. https://www.semana.com/nacion/articulo/benditos-votos/74470-3 [Accessed October 22, 2022].
17 The "Final Agreement" was the pact signed on September 26, 2016, between the government and the FARC, in Cartagena. In the plebiscite, 50.21% of the voters refused to support the pact and 49.78% expressed their approval.

18 More than 5,000 evangelical churches and up to 11,000 venues throughout the country are registered in the Office of Religious Affairs of the Ministry of the Interior.
19 In this case, we will not refer to the weapons that some members of the Liberal Party and the Conservative Party took during the *La Violencia* period, even if they were outside the law. In particular, from armed groups that confronted liberal guerrillas, in some cases with the approval of state agents, such as the so-called *Pájaros* or the *La Chilavita* organisation.
20 These alliances were known in public opinion as "parapolitics".
21 Carrasquilla is an economist from the Universidad de los Andes (1983), MS (1985), and PhD (1989) in Economics from the University of Illinois. He served as Vice Minister of Finance (2002–2003), Dean of the Faculty of Economics of the Andes (2000–2002), Research Leader at the Inter-American Development Bank (1997–1998), and Technical Manager of the Banco de la República (1993–1997), among other charges. Presidency of the Republic of Colombia. https://id.presidencia.gov.co/gobierno/minhacienda.
22 According to Gallup polls, former president Uribe Vélez has registered decreasing levels of popularity since February 2017. As of April 2018, its negative image was higher than the positive one –38% favourability. The highest peak of popularity of the ex-president was registered in July 2008, with 85% of favourable image, in his second term as president (Gallup Poll, 2019). On June 19, Gustavo Pretro was elected as president of the republic, by a coalition of the left and center left. This is the first time that a candidate from that ideological spectrum has reached the most important position in the government.

References

Arias, R. (2003) *El episcopado colombiano: Intransigencia y laicidad (1850–2000)*. Bogotá, Universidad de los Andes, Instituto Colombiano de Antropología e Historia.
Aspe, M. L. (2008) *La formación social y política de los católicos mexicanos*. México, Universidad Iberoamericana.
Barrero, T. (2012) Laureano Gómez y la democracia. In Mejía, R. S. (ed.), *La restauración conservadora, 1946-1957*. Bogotá, Universidad Nacional de Colombia, pp. 105–128.
Batlle, M., & Puyana, J. (2013) Reformas políticas y partidosemn Colombia: Cuando el cambio es la regla. *Politai: Revista de Ciencia Política* 7 (4), 73–88.
Beltrán, W. (2003) *De microempresas religiosas a multinacionales de la fe*. Bogotá, Universidad de San Buenaventura.
Beltrán, W. (2013) *Del monopolio católico a la explosión pentecostal. Pluralización religiosa, secularización y cambio social en Colombia*. Bogotá, Universidad Nacional de Colombia.
Bidegain, A. M. (1985) *Iglesia, pueblo y política. Un estudio de los conflictos e intereses 1930–1955*. Colombia, Universidad Javeriana.
Builes, M. Á. (1936) *Manifiesto de los prelados de Colombia al pueblo católico*. Bogotá, Imprenta La Rota.
Conferencia Episcopal Colombiana (1956) *Conferencias Episcopales de Colombia*. Bogotá, Editorial el Catolicismo.
Cornblit, O. (1975) "La opción conservadora en la política Argentina". *Desarrollo Económico*, vol. 14, N°5.
Cruz, E. (2007) Los estudios sobre el paramilitaremmo en Colombia. *Anal político* 20 (60), 117–134.
Duque, J. (2007) Institucionalización organizativa y procesos de selección de candidatos presidenciales en los Partidos Liberal y Conservador colombianos 1974–2006. *Estudios Políticos. Instituto de Estudios Políticos, Universidad de Antioquia* 31, 141–181.

Funes, P. (2014). *Historia mínima de las ideas políticas en América Latina*. Mexico city, Colegio de Mexico. http://www.jstor.org/stable/j.ctt14jxngx

Gallup Poll. (2019) *Informe 130*. Bogotá, Colombia. Report number: 130. https://imgcdn.larepublica.co/cms/2019/05/17085310/031800190000-GALLUP-POLL-130.pdf.

Gamboa, L. (2019) El reajuste de la derecha colombiana. El éxito electoral del uribismo. *Colombia Internacional* 99, 187–214. https://doi.org/10.7440/colombiaint99.2019.07.

García, M., Rodríguez, J. & Seligson, M. (2014) *Cultura política de la democracia en Colombia, 2013. Actitudes democráticas en el contexto del proceso de paz*. Bogotá, USAID and Uniandes.

Gibson, E. (1996). *Class and conservative parties. Argentina in comparative perspective*. Baltimore, John Hopkins University Press.

Gómez, G., & Ospina, L. (2019) ¿A qué jugarán los cristianos en las regionales? *El Espectador*, 16 August. https://www.elespectador.com/politica/a-que-jugaran-los-cristianos-en-las-regionales-article-876279/ [Accessed 22 October 2022].

Gómez, L. (1986) *Obras completas*. Bogotá, Instituto Caro y Cuervo.

González, F. (1997) *Poderes enfrentados: Iglesia y Estado en Colombia*. Bogotá, CINEP.

González, F. (2006) *Partidos, guerras e Iglesia en la construcción del Estado nación en Colombia (1830–1900)*. Medellín, La Carreta Editores.

Gutiérrez, É. (2007) Guía práctica para entender el escándalo de la 'para-política'. *Semana*, 4 October. https://www.semana.com/on-line/articulo/guia-practica-para-entender-escandalo-para-politica/84455-3 [Accessed 22 October 2022].

Gutiérrez, F. (2014) *El orangután con sacoleva. Cien años de democracia y represión en Colombia (1910–2010)*. Bogota, Debate.

Gutiérrez, F., Viatela, J. M., & Acevedo, T. (2008) ¿Olivos y aceitunos? los partidos políticos colombianos y sus bases sociales en la primera mitad del siglo XX. *Análisis Político* 21 (62), 3–24. http://www.scielo.org.co/scielo.php?script=sci_arttext&pid=S0121-47052008000100001&lng=en&tlng=es.

Instituto Geográfico Agustín Codazzi (IGAC) (2012) *Atlas de la distribución de la propiedad rural en Colombia*. Bogotá, Imprenta Nacional de Colombia. https://www.researchgate.net/profile/Juan-Munoz-Mora/publication/237428231_Atlas_de_la_Distribution_de_la_Propiedad_Rural_en_Colombia/links/53d7b1680cf2e38c632ddf3c/Atlas-de-la-Distribution-de-la-Propiedad-Rural-en-Colombia.pdf.

Jaramillo, J. (1997) Vicisitudes del pensamiento conservador Colombiano. *Revista Credencial Historia* 90. https://www.banrepcultural.org/biblioteca-virtual/credencial-historia/numero-90/vicisitudes-del-pensamiento-conservador-colombiano.

La Rosa, M. (2000) *De la izquierda a la derecha. La iglesia católica en la Colombia contemporánea*. Bogotá, Planeta.

Laguado Duca, A. (2006) ¿Es posible una teoría general de los partidos conservadores? *Tabula Raza* 4, 167–201. https://revistas.unicolmayor.edu.co/index.php/tabularasa/article/view/1616.

Losada, R., & Liendo, N. (2016) El partido 'centro democrático' en Colombia: Razones de su surgimiento y éxito. *Análisis Político* 29 (87), 41–59.

Machado, A. de J. (2009) *La reforma rural: Una deuda social y política*. Bogotá, Universidad Nacional de Colombia & Centro de Investigaciones para el Desarrollo. http://www.fce.unal.edu.co/media/files/CentroEditorial/catalogo/Libros_Digitalizados/O_reforma-rural.pdf.

Marcos, A. (2016) El voto evangélico, clave en la victoria del 'no' en el plebiscito de Colombia. *El País*, 12 October. https://elpais.com/internacional/2016/10/12/colombia/1476237985_601462.html [Accessed 22 October 2022].

Middelbrook, K. (2000). *Conservative Parties, the Right and Democracy in Latin America.* Baltimore, John Hopkins University Press.

Otero, D. (2016) *Gastos de guerra en Colombia, 1964–2016: 179 000 millones de dólares perdidos.* Bogotá, Instituto de Estudios para el Desarrollo y la Paz – Indepaz.

Padilla, I. (2010) La hispanidad en Colombia en el siglo XIX. Paradoja de la historia, elemento de la subjetividad nacional. In Torregroza, J. & Ochoa, P. (eds.), *Formas de hispanidad.* Bogotá, Universidad del Rosario, pp. 355–366.

Palacios, M. (2011) *¿De quién es la tierra?: Propiedad, politización y protesta campesina en la década de 1930.* Bogotá, Universidad de los Andes y Fondo de Cultura Económica.

Palacios, M., & Safford, F. (2002) *Colombia: País fragmentado, sociedad dividida.* Bogotá, Editorial Norma.

Plata, J.C., Montalvo, D., Rodríguez, J.C., & García, M. (Eds.). (2021) *Cultura política de la democracia en Colombia y en las Américas 2021: tomándole el pulso a la democracia*, Bogotá, TN: LAPOP.

Quevedo, N., & García, H. (2009) Los pastores del Presidente. *El Espectador.* 24 October. http://www.elespectador.com/alvaro-uribe/articulo168504-los-pastores-del-presidente [Accessed 22 October 2022].

Reyes, A. (1991) Paramilitares en Colombia: Contexto, aliados y consecuencias. *Análisis Político* 12. http://biblioteca.clacso.edu.ar/ar/libros/colombia/assets/own/analisis12.pdf.

Rodríguez, J. C. (2006) Izquierdas y derechas en Colombia. Una mirada rápida a los rasgos sociodemográficos del espectro ideológico del país. *Colombia Internacional.* 66, 184–193. https://revistas.uniandes.edu.co/doi/epdf/10.7440/colombiaint66.2007.10.

Rodríguez Kauth, Á. (2001) Izquierda y derecha en política. *Realidad, Revista de Ciencias Sociales y Humanidades* 82, 467–480.

Romero, M. (2002) Democratización política y contrarreforma paramilitar en Colombia. *Política y Sociedad* 1 (39), 273–292.

Sierra, R. (2012) *La restauración conservadora, 1946–1957.* Bogotá, Universidad Nacional de Colombia.

Uribe, Á. (2012) ¿Puede el uso de metáforas ser peligroso? Sobre las pastorales de monseñor Miguel Ángel Builes. In Sierra, R. (ed.), *La restauración conservadora, 1946–1957.* Bogotá, Universidad Nacional de Colombia, pp. 151–169.

5
HONDURAS
The problem of the origin of political ideas on the right

Gustavo Zelaya Herrera

The problem of the origin of political ideas on the right in Honduras

The formation of political ideas in Honduras begins with the introduction of the prevailing currents in Spain between the fifteenth and sixteenth centuries, from a political, ecclesiastical, and educational system that trained the subjects to consolidate the colonial social order according to the values and ideals of the Spanish State.

This dominance extended until the eighteenth century when different events weakened it, for example: the reformist policy of Carlos III; knowledge of political proposals by Rousseau, Adam Smith, and other theorists of that time; Napoleon's invasion of Spain that deepened the crisis of the Spanish colony; and the organisation of the Economic Societies of Friends of the Country that promoted economic development, scientific research, political ideas, and the teaching of useful knowledge. This organisation was also thought of as the place from which the ruler would be enlightened in his management to improve living conditions, a question that would be obtained not with radical transformations, but with the gradual evolution of society (Woodward, 1982; Woodward, 1981; Zelaya Herrera, 2014: pp. 34–39).

During colonial times, the production of ideas was done by the Church, the University of San Carlos de Borromeo in Guatemala, and the University of León in Nicaragua. These were the places of formation of Hondurans such as José Cecilio del Valle (1777–1834), an exponent of Central American enlightenment who believed that everything could be submitted to reason and experience to overcome ignorance and superstition and achieve social progress. Members of the colonial aristocracy also participated, made up of Spanish officials, educated Creoles, members of the church, some merchants, and landowners. This elitist

DOI: 10.4324/9781003352266-8

character is shown in Valle's belief that happiness would be achieved through education and with the installation of governments led by wise men, attached to the law, that provide guarantees for material investment and justice; it is nothing but enlightened despotism (Zelaya Herrera, 2014: pp. 14–17).

Although it was a late cultural phenomenon equivalent to the European Enlightenment, it contributed to forming a critical national consciousness, questioning the colonial system, and allowed that thought to become the enlightened ideology in Honduras.

> Illustration was understood as the best way to get out of disorder and colonial backwardness; a solution that did not necessarily mean radically transforming the government, but the installation of good and wise men in political power, a fundamental idea in Valle, assuming that these men were the ones who could best obey the law. For this they would have to be based on a solid legal body in charge of guaranteeing investment, harmony, and social justice.
>
> *(Zelaya Herrera, 2014: p. 34)*

From this knowledge the independence process was prepared, and the development of thought was favoured without so much monarchical censorship in the midst of a deep political and social crisis between the eighteenth and nineteenth centuries.

The enlightened Creoles were inclined towards the patriarchal relations of the colony; his political ideal was to establish a constitutional monarchy that would preserve the caste system. According to them, society rested on two social classes: the nobles and the commoners, those with the function of leading and making the commoners happy. Ultimately, the Creoles' struggle was for equal privileges, equality of the colony against the metropolis, equality with the traditional oligarchy.

There are phases in the evolution of Honduran political thought that show how predominant liberal and conservative forms emerged during long periods of national history. One phase extends to 1870, influenced by the Enlightenment and the classical liberal ideology of Montesquieu and Locke. That is the foundation of liberals and conservatives, sometimes violently confronted by issues of political power and government, but not because of conceptual differences or fundamental principles, but because of more pragmatic issues; for this reason, it was not uncommon to find liberals and conservatives learning from the same European philosophers; selecting the same theories and applying them as appropriate. Another phase developed from 1870. It is when positivist ideas and Darwin's evolutionism are known. Positivism was the doctrine preferred by the ruling groups to establish and consolidate capitalism, it was the time when railroads, industry, technical skills, and applied sciences were needed.

In general, almost everyone spoke of their time at a time when social science and political science were not well established, but the situation demanded political commitment, moral discourse, journalistic propaganda, and they relied on the discourse of authority to obtain intellectual prestige.

The fundamentals of the nineteenth century: José Cecilio del Valle, Francisco Morazán, and Ramón Rosa

Valle has served as a symbol for liberals and conservatives. He asserted that the ruler's success depended on science, politics, and geography; for this he needed just laws to build conditions of equality among all. He considered education necessary to reduce social differences and, fundamentally, possess the law that regulates and governs political action for the collective benefit: the utilitarian principle that proposes the maximum possible happiness for the greatest possible number. That happiness is achieved from power and in this sense, he proposed two paths:

> from the enlightened monarchy, and the other, from the constitutional republic as the ideal regime ... the enlightened monarch must swear to the constitution, submit to the law, and respond to the town for their performance. Here there would be a fundamental right: the right of rebellion, the right of the people to reject and oppose the will of the monarch. Such a society would manifest itself with purity in ideological struggle and tolerance, in opposition to the censor, to arbitrary authority, against submission and obedience. A finished expression of this struggle would be the existence of the free press as the voice of the people.
> *(Zelaya Herrera, 2004: p. 33)*

Valle aspired to design a State that did not impose any religion because it was a personal matter and proposed free trade for the benefit of agriculture and industry; consequently, the development of the autonomous, free individual, equal before the law, was also an object of this free trade. In other words, he was promoting basic aspects of capitalism; the modern political forms and contents for new modes of exploitation of human labour.

According to Valle, the colonial crisis required reformist measures where different political conceptions, religious tradition, monarchical proposals, and enlightened ideas converged. He considered that the separation from Spain would have to be achieved without bloodshed and with minimal social struggles so as not to risk the independence process. He said that absolute independence was the first right and the foundation of the others and incorporated concepts such as moderation, balance and pauses, such as the conditions to create just laws, education for the majority and economic development. Furthermore, what voting is, and the meaning of popular participation would have to be defined. In this regard, Valle showed great mistrust about universal suffrage and the ability of the people to elect leaders. He argued that the popular decision could be beneficial but also very harmful depending on the education obtained. The people could be virtuous when they can choose freely and with full knowledge of those most prepared in the domain of government and science. He said that

> the vote could make those who, through no fault of their own, have the least aptitude to legislate, govern and judge to the highest destinations; One hundred or two hundred individuals who are not very capable of the functions they exercise will enjoy salaries; and two million or a million and a half men will suffer from their incapacity.
> *(Zelaya Herrera, 2004, p. 72)*

The main thing was to know how to choose the most qualified to govern the least qualified, and this could only be achieved with education as a stage prior to any pro-independence or election process. That meant relegating the role of the people in political decisions and privileging the enlightened in such matters.

For Valle, education was not reduced to a school system designed and directed by the State. The purpose was to train enlightened people, organise life, create other social customs to develop more integral beings; education would also work thanks to the influence of the laws. Therefore science, politics, laws, history, economics, and a stable political order would have to coincide. Enlightened rulers and legislators would know that the objective criterion for distributing social wealth is the principle of general happiness that makes the greatest number of citizens subject to the same form of government. So, there are two components to the best government: wise people capable of calculating the goods and the evils that elaborate the legislative code, and others that put the system in motion. This is the basis of the law of government activity, "The indestructible basis of a solid government is the highest possible good" (Valle in Oquelí, 1981: p. 484).

Valle tried to construct a general theory that included the sciences to apply it to politics and promote social progress through gradual, calculated reforms that avoided violent transformations. The circumstances of his time hampered these proposals. They were moments of political upheaval, the emergence of new economic forms, cultural backwardness, and social instability throughout the region. It was not possible to create conditions for norms of coexistence that would allow building the greatest possible amount of pleasure and distance from pain, as indicated by the utilitarian principle assumed by Valle. Then, the objective of its policy is order and efficiency, which is obtained not so much for the love of humanity; it is achieved with laws, education, and good government (Zelaya Herrera, 2014).[1]

Francisco Morazán (1792–1842), a self-taught man trained in the ideas of the Enlightenment, was elected President of the Central American Federation in 1830. He is considered the first builder of the national state and the first reformer in Central America, who tried to apply enlightened and liberal political ideas.

Morazán thought of organising federal political power from a division of the State into a judicial power, an executive power, and two chambers; that is to say, the modern, liberal State, which could not be implanted since the federation never had peace or resources and was fought from its beginning. His political theses were expressed as freedom of the press, freedom of association, freedom of belief and worship, emancipation of slaves, trial by jury, habeas corpus; guarantees of suffrage, accountability (Morazán, 1992b: p. 290),[2] secular education, civil marriage, and separation of church and state. He tried to put all this into practice through the federal state, although in a document known as the "David's Manifesto" he recognised that federalism had failed due to the hegemony of Guatemala; later he proposed centralism, not as the existence of autonomous states, but as a single state, rectifying his ideas to what he alludes to in his "Testament", where he said:

> I die with the feeling of having caused some evils to my country, although with the just desire to procure its good; and this feeling is increased because when I had rectified my opinions in politics, in the career of the revolution, and I believed I was doing him the good that he had promised me to correct those faults in this way, my life was unjustly taken from me.
>
> *(Morazán, 1992a: p. 101)*

The independence of Central America was not a result of armed clashes, and it is possible that its main effect is noted in the failure of the union of the old provinces of the Captaincy General of Guatemala, in regionalism, in the rise of local oligarchies and the warlordism. That independence in Central America "was not the result of an anti-colonial war, which would have created a real feeling of national solidarity, had as a consequence that society reached the independence era divided by deep interests"; that is to say,

> the struggle for nationality was subordinated to a ... struggle for power, which was clearly manifested after 1821; first in the annexationist project of the Guatemalan oligarchy; then in separatism in places like León and Comayagua; finally in the state political division of the Kingdom of Guatemala. Faced with these tendencies, there were ... weak political currents ... (that) tried to maintain the old unity through the implantation of a political system that was considered adequate.
>
> *(Pinto Soria, 1986, p. 127)*

The representatives of the economic groups involved in this process were interested in replacing the colonialists in power; none tried to transform the economic system to generate stability and make coexistence, solidarity, respect, and warmth possible. In other words, building foundations to overcome poverty and the cultural backwardness of the less favoured did not become a political programme for liberals and conservatives identified with that movement. Rather, it was a question of assuring the new elite an unquestioned exercise of power, a question that was difficult to achieve in part because the political class was very fragile. However, "the central power was always a poor power, unable to permanently finance its own armed force" (Argueta, 2017). It was hoped that the reforms would solve this problem to consolidate those groups in the power of the modern nation; a result of their manoeuvres was the independence of 1821 and then the annexation to Mexico. The independence of Spain was nothing more than a procedure to preserve the political and economic power of groups related to the crown, all resolved with the signing of the independence act to prevent popular participation.

The *independentistas* in the style of Morazán sought to reform individuals as a moment of social progress and achieve the general happiness that would be obtained by disseminating the sciences and the achievements of reason to dominate nature and found the modern state.

After the declaration of independence, that faith in reason would be expressed by Francisco Morazán when, on April 16, 1823, he argued that without education "there will be no equality in people, interests, or property; and we are exposed to let a yoke fall upon us that we can never shake" as cited by Zelaya Herrera (2016). While in power on June 9, 1830, the "Law on the protection of public educational establishments was enacted". He insisted on the importance of education, proposing that the Republic must protect

> the public educational establishments ... until it is placed in a state capable of producing enlightened men who must dictate laws to the Central American people, direct the destinies of the country, direct the domestic differences of their children and command their troops, destined to defend the independence, the integrity of the nation and public liberties.
>
> *(as cited by Zelaya Herrera (2016))*

He also maintained that

> To promote public education and remove all obstacles that retard it, it is the best way to protect freedom ... is to place the present generation on a level with its century and unite it to the enlightened world through ideas and thoughts.
>
> *(Morazán, 1992b: p. 143)*

Not a single one of those civic virtues proposed by Morazán have been present in those who have led the Honduran State, rather have endeavoured to obstruct the public school as a place of democratic training and autonomous thought.

The historical period between 1777 and 1842 where José Cecilio del Valle and Francisco Morazán coincide is where the roots of the conservative and liberal thought of Honduras are found; it is where the political tradition

> blind to changes that improve the lives of the less favoured is being built; interested in the delivery of natural resources, in market-centred competitiveness that nullifies any humanist claim as posed by characters like Francisco Morazán. Rather, in current conditions, when attacking the rights of people is common practice, when impunity, corruption, the sale of regions of the country, makes the formation of culture and national awareness more

complicated, this situation of insecurity and death complicates talking and building coexistence, social inclusion, and humanised life. ... At the core of Morazán thought was ethics as a requirement of social progress, not as rhetoric, but as a historical necessity and thus unmasking the moral ruin of the conservative political tradition.

(Zelaya Herrera, 2016)

Both Morazán and Valle agreed that enlightenment was the best way to get out of colonial disorder, but in Valle it did not mean radically transforming the government, but installing good and wise men in political power, those trained to create and obey the law. In Morazán, illustration was the way to radically transform society and revolutionise the entire state. Valle proposed gradual changes that would be deepened with the education of the people and a just legislation, to order society. Morazán believed in an independence movement that would definitely break with the colonial institutions.

Ramón Rosa (1848–1893) was a kind of heir to the political ideas of Valle and Morazán, politically manifested a combination that seems contradictory of liberal thought and positivism. This set of ideas was promoted from the political power with the participation of Rosa as Minister General of the government, Marco Aurelio Soto (1846–1908), Head of State; and Adolfo Zúñiga (1835–1900), Rector of the Central University. This positivism was known through the Argentines Juan Bautista Alberdi and Domingo Faustino Sarmiento and the Chilean Victoriano Lastarria; 'It is through the latter that the news arrives; and not as mere reflections of Europe, but as recreations of a positivism born in America' (Zelaya Herrera, 2001: p. 16). From those ideas it was thought to organise the State, unify power, education, industry, and science.

After the execution of Francisco Morazán and the failure of the Central American federation, between 1840 and 1876 continuous civil wars broke out in Honduras, there were constant changes of government, intervention of other states, including that of the ruler of Guatemala Justo Rufino Barrios who imposed on Soto and Rosa in power until installing the provisional government on September 2, 1876. It is known as the government of liberal reform. Its clearest objective was to establish the structure of the organised state to insert the country into the world economy and participate in the capitalist market. For this purpose, they organised a mining and agro-export economy, leading the country to monoculture and extractivism practices.

In the Honduran positivist version, religious nuances were not observed as in Comte and a trend full of educational and industrial objectives was developed; they wanted to modernise society and create an educational system that would help form the national consciousness and workers for the system. In their speeches they repeated some classic positivist formulas, such as:

- The conception of history that discovers the social march through three major phases: the theological state, the metaphysical state, and the positive state.

- The conception of science, considering it as eminently practical, utilitarian, experimental; based on the observation of phenomena; thinking of a model of natural and exact sciences, belittling the humanistic disciplines.
- Education, as purely practical, to train men for the industrial workshop.
- The motto "order and progress", giving priority to order, social stability, and institutions; to progress such as that coming from the Anglo-Saxon countries through White immigrants, mining concessions, and the railways. They believed that from the capitalist countries would come the most advanced technique, the aptitude for work, and the best ideas.

In general, like the enlightened liberals, the national positivists tried to make reason and ideas the absolute computer of human life; they explained history as a result of the movement of ideas and not as a contradictory relationship between ideas and things.

They argued that free expression and tolerance for contrary opinions would be the fundamental elements in social progress; that free governments need internal opposition as a guarantee of democracy. They criticised previous institutions and opposed the abuse of power by conservative and liberal groups. For this reason, they affirmed that without freedom of the press and of assembly, without confrontation of opinions, activity and public discussion would not take place, but rather the validity of caudillismo and civil war would be reproduced. Institutions, law, and freedom can only be founded where there is no force against society.

In addition to the existence of economic, political, and geographical obstacles, Rosa encountered cultural obstacles from the colony that had produced conformist people who were willing to follow the caudillos; According to him, within these cultural obstacles were the

> "rudimentary and confused political ideas of the political camps", improperly called conservatives and liberals ... one could not be a conservative since his dogma consists in sacrificing everything to order and stability; Nor could one be liberal since they had only existed in spirit and realisation of the liberal idea required deep-rooted habits of order and work ... a complete, moral, intellectual and political education in all social classes ... a very high degree of development ... and great feelings of patriotism, before which ... the influence of personal, sect and party interests is cushioned.
> *(Zelaya Herrera, 2001: p. 39)*

The combination of positivism and liberalism tried to liquidate the colonialist aftertastes, the idealism of the old political groups and scholastic philosophy, to stop at earthly, obvious, factual matters, studied by physics, chemistry, biology, and sociology, and in this way to lean on economic affairs and create something similar to Comte's positive stage, such as liberal reform.

So: industrialisation, free thought, good government, and open borders to the White immigrant were what would give power, glory, and progress. These elements would drive the modern history of Honduras, they would have reason as their foundation in all circumstances, they would obey the ends of truth, freedom, and general happiness.

The stamp of the banana companies in the politics of Honduras

The development of political ideas from the twentieth century to date cannot be understood without the influence of the banana and mining industries, largely owned by North American capital. These forms of capitalist exploitation will manifest themselves in the different governments, in the liberal and conservative political tradition, until a society is highly dependent on the United States. The first half of the twentieth century is the period of economic and political strengthening of the groups that would govern the country, obtain land concessions, control ports, railways, and political power (Barahona, 2005).[3]

It is probable that one of the most significant effects of the liberal reform process of 1876 is not only the relative economic progress that sought to connect the country with the world market, especially the North American one; Another of its consequences is the formation of politicians with liberal roots who tried to organise the inheritance of that reform. Very important will be Policarpo Bonilla (1858–1926), founder of the liberal party in 1891 and builder of a current of political thought in Honduras; under his influence were Terencio Sierra (1849–1907), Manuel Bonilla (1849–1913), Miguel Dávila (1856–1927), Francisco Bertrand (1866–1926), Rafael López Gutiérrez (1854–1924), Vicente Mejía Colindres (1878–1966), and Tiburcio Carías Andino (1876–1969); all were presidents of the Republic. That was part of "The generation that led the destiny of Honduras in the first half of the 20th century ... political-military leaders that were formed in the shadow of Policarpo Bonilla and the Liberal Party since the revolution of 1892-1894" (Barahona, 2005, p. 46).

These characters are direct actors in the period marked by civil wars, North American military intervention, consolidation of the banana companies, and the establishment of the dictatorial government of Tiburcio Carías Andino that lasted from 1933 to 1948, where the repression of the political opposition intensified, and a certain social order was imposed.

Some political ideas of Policarpo Bonilla

Bonilla is considered the main author behind the Political Constitution of 1895, stating that

> This code ensures the independence of the public powers, the freedom of suffrage by secret ballot, the autonomy of the municipalities, prohibits the death penalty; makes the congress exclusive the power to legislate, declares the sessions of the Legislature annual and its powers cannot be delegated;

it establishes a true immunity for the deputies, the trial by jury for the common crimes and of press and the guarantee of habeas corpus; it prohibits presidential re-election ... and declares the laws of the press, the State of Siege, Amparo and Elections as constitutive.

(Mejía Deras, 1997, p. 273)

In the essay *Estudios Constitucionales* Bonilla stated that

the Fundamental Charter is a true pact between the people and their governors, which confers on these rights, only on condition of fulfilling their obligations. The exercise of public power is distributed and entrusts to a few the right to command, imposing on the greatest number the obligation to obey, it also says that this power is not absolute, that it can only be exercised within the limits that it indicates; and if they are transferred, as in any unfulfilled pact, there is the right of resistance, the only way to prevent the code destined to protect citizens, to ensure the use of their freedoms, from becoming an instrument of oppression.

(Bonilla in Durón, 1996: p. 680)

The essential item in the Political Constitution is respect for human life.

From those ideas of a liberal nature and from the political party founded by Policarpo Bonilla, a group organised by the National Party, apparently more conservative and on the right, will emerge. "It was founded in 1923, by General Tiburcio Carías Andino and journalist Paulino Valladares (1881-1926)" (Barahona, 2005, p. 70); He said that "it must be the party where all the good children of Honduras fit, from the Masons, who are radicals because of their broad scope, to the Catholics" (Barahona, 2005, p. 71). Another intellectual of that time believed that "The National Party represents the neoliberalism of our country, which is a vanguard liberalism" (Barahona, 2005, p. 71).

In these expressions, as in the enlightened thinkers of the independence era, the use of categories typical of liberal ideology is noted, often used uncritically, and disconnected from social processes. This characteristic seems constant in much of the so-called Honduran political thought, whether liberal or right-wing, which repeats formulas and endorses political ideas to give prestige and solidity to the discourse. Despite this, it seems that in liberals and conservatives there are agreements in such a way that they show a fairly homogeneous political thought regarding the form of government, the division of public powers and their relationships, the functions of the ruler, the role of the government, citizen, participatory democracy, and the origin of laws. Possibly their main difference is who should govern and which economic group to represent.

Declaration of principles of the liberal and conservative tradition

The National Party is based on four principles: Common Good, Solidarity, Subsidiarity, and Equity (Partido Nacional de Honduras, n.d.). They affirm that society is where the person is realised and that the personal good should be subordinated to the social good of all. Solidarity is a dynamic principle that unites people and drives them to the common good; the purpose of subsidiarity is to harmonise individual relationships and it is a principle of help when necessary and equity is to give each one what they deserve based on their specific needs. The Vision of this party says: 'We are a majority political party, Christian humanist and inclusive, with an ethical leadership, that promotes changes to transform the country, in democracy, freedom and equal opportunities' (Partido Nacional de Honduras, n.d.). And the Mission: 'We are a democratic political organisation with transformative leaders and with a modern ideological agenda, linked to all social sectors to generate the growth and well-being of the Honduran people' (Partido Nacional de Honduras, n.d.). For political action, he maintains that he makes use of democratic means, respecting the will of the majority.

> It is not subordinated to norms of national or foreign entities that attempt against the sovereignty and independence of the State or that go against the republican, democratic and representative form of government; they seek respect for human rights ... contribute to the construction of a world in which peace, solidarity and respect prevail among peoples ... it is fundamentally humanistic, places man as a primary goal and conceives its full realisation within Honduran society. ... Condemns all privileges, whether it comes from a person, from groups or from certain classes.
> *(Partido Nacional de Honduras, n.d.)*

For its part, the Liberal Party declares its

> 'republican, democratic and representative vocation ... accepts as a legitimate source of public power, the will of the people expressed in free and honest elections rejects continuity ... recognizes the right of the people to insurrection, in defence of the constitutional order and to oppose illegitimate regimes'; puts as a supreme social goal and the full development of the human person and the need to guarantee their rights, equal opportunities in political activity, in access to work and in economic well-being; they propose as a condition of development free public education, the protection of culture; establishes as a 'fundamental principle social inclusion ... economic freedom of initiative, investment; trade, competitiveness, contracting and business, so that economic production responds to the concepts of sustainable development, ensuring the equitable distribution of wealth', transparency and accountability; propose the need to develop participatory democracy and strengthen the protection and security of people. This requires an efficient state that promotes social development. It is pronounced for the self-determination of the peoples. Regarding the Vision, it states that 'The fundamental purpose of the Liberal Party of Honduras is to conquer and exercise Public Power through democratic, representative and

participatory procedures, in order to maintain the integrity of the rule of law and to strengthen it, privileging the human being, guaranteeing freedom, justice, economic and social well-being, as well as the elevation and promotion of education and culture'

(Partido Liberal, n.d.).

It seems that ideological definitions are not a basic issue in these parties, especially when they apply economic programmes and develop proselytising practices. As in other societies, for the Honduran political tradition, what is important is the process of marketing figures and discussing what is fundamental in the media. Ideological precision is not so important, but good propaganda and an opinion poll are. The decision of the party member revolves around the smile and the photograph without considering the content of the speech. There are even public figures lacking in speech but possessors of image. Or political agents involved in scandals, in relations with drug activity and in other legal problems that resolve their issues with good marketing; they try to make people believe that politics and economics are separate. This implies the belief that political theory is not necessary for political praxis.

A quick analysis of both proposals indicates that the content differences are not so serious; that the proposals of these political parties, which in theory represent different ideologies, rather show numerous points of agreement. This is going to be noticed more clearly when it is their turn to govern the country; In fact, they turn the State into a kind of booty that is shared between powerful families and the political clientele, apply the same economic measures, endorse the structural adjustment practices imposed by the International Monetary Fund, and, particularly, deepen the general dependence on to the United States of America.

The hallmark of neoliberalism

From 1950 to 1982 Honduras was involved in a kind of rebirth of democracy and constant coups carried out by the military. Efforts had been made to industrialise the country and there was growing urbanisation; the state acquired a preponderant place to promote economic development. It is important to note that the period is the time of the Cold War and Honduras is promoting intervention in internal conflicts in other Central American countries, thanks to the military support of the United States, in such a way, that the country becomes a military base for the control of the region. Starting in 1982, with democratically elected civilian governments with liberal influence, the country entered a highly repressive phase expressed in a progressive militarisation of security, administrative corruption, forced disappearance of people, and murders of opponents considered to be on the left; In other words, the national security doctrine that privileged the State over the people is put into practice. Here it is important to indicate that leaders from both the Liberal Party and the National Party implemented this doctrine, identified, and justified the internal repression and intervention in Guatemala, El Salvador, and Nicaragua.

As has happened since the first decades of the twentieth century, the context will be determined by the United States when proposing what the path of the national economy should be, "recommending measures such as the opening of the national economy and the promotion of non-traditional exports, a drastic reduction of public spending to reduce the fiscal deficit and the beginning of a privatisation program to dismantle the state companies" (Barahona, 2005: p. 261). In January 1982, a sector of private companies told the government that "It has become evident in recent times the urgency or importance of carrying out deep measures of restructuring and financial consolidation of autonomous companies and decentralised organisations" (Hernández, 1983, p. 110). Thus, the fundamental thing is to free markets, reduce the participation of the State, and obtain economic growth. Between 1990 and 1991 this aspiration was better defined in a historical space determined by the dissolution of the Soviet Union; Thus, the so-called Washington Consensus indicated the fundamental conditions for that growth, conditions that both liberal and conservative governments endorsed.[4] Among other things, the application of these measures meant significant reductions in public spending for social programmes; deterioration in health, public education and labour rights; higher food and housing prices; and increased external and internal debt.

In theory, the system developed in Honduras guarantees equal conditions to people, since it starts from the conditions that the State establishes for everyone, but in the process, some are left on the road, few get rich, and few effective conditions of employment are generated. Brutal inequality, not only economic, but in the field of political decisions, and common interests are no longer promoted, but those who concentrate wealth decide for all and the original role of the liberal individual is crushed by new collective decisions: that of the big private corporations and the oligarchy.

The application of neoliberal measures in Honduras deepens inequalities, lowers income, and increases company profits. Faced with this, the compassionate character of the State emerges, and it implements social aid plans that promote official charity. These social programmes are short-term, not sustainable over time; For this reason, it is made to believe that those responsible for solving the problem are the poor themselves with their work, their savings, and the remittances that they send from abroad and that individual progress depends on them. Thus, any reference to social responsibility is set aside and the role of the State in generating the well-being of all citizens is forgotten. Otherwise, in a society governed by the supposed natural laws of the market, only the fittest can succeed and survive.

With these measures dictated by the International Monetary Fund, the aim is to promote the free market, eliminate regulations, reduce the role of the union, establish production units where there is a guarantee of cheap labour, and stimulate State intervention in favour of capital and of corporations; These set the prices; the demand is decided in marketing campaigns regardless of the content of the products. Very similar to political activity: market practices are transferred to this sphere where only the appearance of the character matters and no speech is generated. The latter seems to be the essence of traditional politics in Honduras in times of neoliberalism: it is a form devoid of content, focused on highlighting the most superficial aspects of life and of the characters who seek to establish themselves as rulers and where the fundamental is image promotion.[5]

Despite the supposed free trade and free market, the country does not manage to develop, rather poverty is accentuated, and a situation of violence and unresolved crime continues, although there is a greater focus of resources on public security issues. However, the financial system increases its profits at a time of economic crisis, in the conditions of forced emigration of people, growth of remittances that have become the most important item of the national economy and a large presence of the drug activity.

From 1990 to date the traditional political parties have taken turns in power; four liberal and four conservative governments have succeeded, including the liberal ruler who led the coup against another liberal government on June 28, 2009; they have all applied the recipes of the International Monetary Fund and have generated more points of agreement even in their electoral practices.

The year 2009 marks a turning point in traditional politics, especially due to the coup d'état and the institutional and social crisis caused by such a circumstance. Among other things, bipartisanship is broken, repression of opposition groups worsens, and new political formations appear. Since that year the liberal party has not been in power and the alternation in power between nationalists and liberals disappears. It could be argued that political forms arise that combine liberal ideas with others that seem socialist, as is the case with the *Libertad y Refundación* party; while the old Liberal Party reaches agreements with the National Party to forge a right that repeats the electoral promises of always: security, employment, education, and fight against poverty. The electoral adjustment programmes of the International Monetary Fund, interested in fiscal and economic stability to guarantee the payment of the foreign debt, continue to be implemented. Such political agreements have allowed the establishment of three periods of nationalist government, highly questioned by accusations of electoral fraud and by suspicions confirmed in October 2019 in a Federal Court in New York, of carrying out electoral campaigns financed by drug trafficking.

If perhaps these political forms have any strength, in addition to the little political culture of their leaders and militants, the main thing is that they could have been in political power or been overthrown by military coups; that is its strength: in a military force that can only act when indicated by the US hegemonic power. In particular, the government of Juan Orlando Hernández, representative of that right, can only be sustained with the support of a liberal faction, finance capital, a sector of private business, the military-police force, and, above all, the United States through the State Department and Southern Command.

This right is facing a serious problem: since June 2009 the crisis has worsened; there is more poverty and repression of social resistance that faces injustice and violence: until now this right has been very comfortable in power, so it has had no impediments to suppress social protest. But the situation has taken on another nuance: the government's involvement with drug trafficking seems to have sparked other unitary efforts to confront that power.

Notes

1 In addition to the influences of Montesquieu on the government as a guarantee of political freedom; Adam Smith's idea of work and free trade as sources of wealth; of the Physiocrats with the thesis of agriculture as indispensable for social welfare; The main theoretical impact received by Valle comes from the utilitarianism of Jeremy Bentham, with whom he corresponded and from whom he made two great proposals: the idea of utility and that of the greatest possible good for the greatest possible number, this is obtained through calculation. For Bentham, the supreme ethical goal of society and of individuals is the greatest happiness for the greatest possible number, so that every right, honest, good act is the one that produces the greatest amount of pleasure or happiness. According to Valle, that should be the guide of legislators. It is about defending welfare and the law in rationality and balance. The general utility should be sought, that of the greatest number of individuals who rely on the law and who seek useful behaviour. This utility also has a moral, legal, and scientific basis, since it disposes humanity towards justice and the continuous perfection of man and must be the regulating principle of the laws. In my book *José Cecilio del Valle and Utilitarianism*, such influence is exposed; see references.
2 He established a decree of accountability on November 21, 1825.
3 Chapter II of Marvin Barahona's book (pp. 48 and following) makes a detailed reference to the development of banana companies and its consequences in the economic and political activity of Honduras, as they are expanding their power by founding banks and factories of different sectors.
4 It was a programme of ten proposals: "(1) Balanced budgets; (2) Control of inflation; (3) Reduction of public spending; (4) Expansion of the tax base; (5) Interest rates determined by the market and positive to encourage savings; (6) Competitive exchange rate to promote investments; (7) Liberalisation of imports; (8) No restriction on foreign direct investment; (9) Privatisation of state companies; (10) State deregulation" (Fiallos in Acosta 2009: p. 191).
5 In this sense, says one author (see previous note), after the 2005 elections: "The ways of organising, managing and operating campaigns and voting will not be the same, that is, the tone and direction of the candidate's speech, their ways of dressing and even smiling, their advertising strategy, will be the field of action of image consultants, campaign technicians and experts from transnational companies specialised in winning elections … without contact with national reality or history, under the sign of the society of the spectacle" (Fiallos in Acosta, 2009: p. 193).

References

Acosta, O. (ed.) (2009) *Las ideas políticas en Honduras. Tránsito del siglo XX al XXI*. Tegucigalpa, Publicación de la Federación de Organizaciones para el Desarrollo de Honduras (Foprideh).
Argueta, M. R. (2017) *La Primera Generación Liberal: Fallas y aciertos (1829–1842)*, 2nd ed. Tegucigalpa, Sistema Editorial Universitario, Universidad Pedagógica Nacional Francisco Morazán.
Barahona, M. (2005) *Honduras en el siglo XX, una síntesis histórica*. Tegucigalpa, Editorial Guaymuras.

Durón, R. E. (ed.) (1996) *Honduras Literaria, tomo II, escritores en prosa*. Tegucigalpa, Editorial Universitaria.
Hernández, A. (1983) *El neoliberalismo en Honduras*, 1st ed. Tegucigalpa: Guaymuras.
Morazán, F. (1992a) *Memorias. Manifiesto de David; Testamento*. Tegucigalpa, Secretaría de Cultura.
Morazán, F. (1992b) *Obras. Volumen I. La organización del Estado de Honduras*. Tegucigalpa, Secretaría de Cultura y Comisión Española del Quinto Centenario, Litografía López, S. de RL.
Oquelí, R. (ed.) (1981). *José Cecilio del Valle. Antología*. Tegucigalpa, Editorial Universitaria.
Partido Liberal de Honduras. (n.d.) *Partido Liberal de Honduras*. https://www.partidoliberal.hn/d [Accessed 2 November 2022].
Partido Nacional de Honduras. (n.d.) *Partido Nacional de Honduras*. https://partidonacional.hn/accion-politica [Accessed 2 November 2022].
Pinto Soria, J. C. (1986) *Centroamérica, de la colonia al Estado nacional (1800–1840)*. Ciudad de Guatemala, Editorial Universitaria de Guatemala.
Woodward, R. L. (1981) *Privilegio de clase y desarrollo económico. Guatemala. 1793–1871*. San José, EDUCA.
Woodward, R. L. (1982) Orígenes económicos y sociales de los partidos políticos guatemaltecos. 1773–1823. In Cáceres, L. R. (ed.), *Lecturas de Historia Centroamericana*. San José, Ediciones del BCIE; 61–85.
Zelaya Herrera, G. (2001) *El Legado de la Reforma Liberal*, 2nd ed. Tegucigalpa, Editorial Guaymuras.
Zelaya Herrera, G. (2014) *José Cecilio del Valle y el utilitarismo*. Tegucigalpa, Editorial Universitaria.
Zelaya Herrera, G. (2016) Francisco Morazán y sus detractores. *El Libertador*, 3 October. https://ellibertador.hn/2016/10/03/honduras-francisco-morazan-y-sus-detractores/ [Accessed 2 November 2022].

6
MEXICO

The right, from opposition to power and back

Mario Virgilio Santiago Jiménez

Introduction

The right is a heterogeneous ideological spectrum, and, therefore, it is mutable and porous. It is not an entity with its own life, but a space of political geometry that is defined by the axes that it disputes vis-à-vis its opponents (the role of the State, the social order, etc.) and above all for the defence of "natural" or "divine" inequality between human beings, which translates into the defence of privileges over rights. Considering this, from a historical perspective, it is almost impossible to speak in the singular of the right and a plural that offers mobility for explanation is preferred; with this, in addition, the genealogical explanation that draws a linear route is renounced and one thinks of branches, traditions, or cultures. Seen in this light, I am inclined to think of the rights as families that do not respect the limits of the social and institutional or of political parties, as well as being heterogeneous and including factions and divisions.

For the Mexican case, then, I propose the existence of three great right-wing families: the Catholic (Christian), heir to nineteenth-century conservatism and defined by the defence of the privileges of the traditional Catholic Church in public life, assuming that private life is their natural space and, in this sense, the organic link between political and religious power is claimed, the hierarchical social organisation taking as reference the ecclesiastical institution, in addition to a single moral code defined by religious dogma; the conservative liberal that is characterised by the defence of social and political hierarchy based on justified reason through (positive) science as the tool to subdue nature, organise society and progress, for which it appeals to the dyad civilisation/barbarism—ideal gear of the evolutionary and racial component—to classify individuals and, therefore, establish a legal framework, as well as projects and public policies; and the neoliberal that shares elements with the conservative liberal, but is distinguished

DOI: 10.4324/9781003352266-9

because its civilising project replaces generalised scientific rationality with faith in the market and its philosophical code is inscribed in a globalisation marked by accelerated advances in communications and technology.

Although they have their roots in the nineteenth century and even earlier, the first two have developed over the last hundred years, taking political form in the twentieth century through four stages: the post-revolution (1920 to 1945); the PRI hegemony (1945–1975); the neoliberal consensus (1975–2015); and the last five years. The third family, with a small presence since the forties, was consolidated between the seventies and nineties of the century.

At this point it is important to note that to paint a historical picture of the Mexican rights in a short space we must make thick lines; therefore, the limits between its components will be noticeable at a distance, but will fade as we get closer, also the brushstrokes—details and nuances—will be lost unless we decide to highlight them, finally, all statements and limits are subject to discussion and nuances. Consequently, far from offering a definitive answer, this text aspires to offer some coordinates to promote reflections and questions about the rights in Mexico.

The post-revolution 1920–1945

With the triumph of the Agua Prieta rebellion in 1920, a faction led by the Sonoran group took over the central government and from there tried and developed a series of practices to reconcentrate the power that had dispersed during the previous decade. In this context of political and economic reconstruction of the country, at least two large right-wing families took shape, the main sign of which was their opposition to what they identified as the project of the Mexican revolution, which is why its members stopped being identified as conservatives and received the ambiguous name of counterrevolutionaries or reactionaries (Ramírez Rancaño, 2002; Garciadiego, 2006: pp. 30–49).

Although the Catholic family was drawn from the confrontation between the Catholic Church and the secular State during the nineteenth century, it was consolidated as an opposition during the religious persecution in the framework of the armed phase of the Mexican revolution, passing through the promulgation of the Constitution of 1917 and reaching its climax during the *Cristero* War (1926–1929) (López, 2011: pp. 35–52).[1] For their part, within the complex Catholic universe, guided by the encyclical *Rerum Novarum* of 1891 and the Social Doctrine of the Church (SDC), many politically active subjects—radical and moderate—saw themselves as defenders of Christian civilisation facing the revolutionary threat.[2]

After the agreements of 1929, a sector reluctantly recognised the role of the State as rector of public life and chose to continue its work on the social level, mainly in the fields of education and the family. However, other more radical sides continued the fight—by armed means and conspiracy—against what they identified as the local version of an international threat whose epicentre was in Moscow (Santiago Jiménez, 2017).

In this period, in addition to confrontations over the introduction of sex education, the so-called "socialist education" and the numerous educational missions promoted by the government, the main objective of the opponents was the repeal of the 1917 Constitution, as it condensed anti-clericalism of revolutionary factions: article 3 established lay education and prohibited religious corporations or ministers from running any school; the 5th, among other points, did not allow the establishment of monastic orders; article 13 prohibited special courts; the 24th established freedom of belief and confined the worship of temples; article 27 prohibited churches from "acquiring, owning or managing real estate" and, in fact, those they had would pass into the domain of the Nation; article 55 annulled the possibility that a minister of some cult would accede to the position of deputy; and finally, article 130 confirmed the separation of the Church and the State, giving the latter the power to monitor religious activity, limit the number of ministers and demand that they be Mexican, in addition to nullifying their political rights.

On the other hand, the international scene allowed many politically active Catholics to see the European totalitarian ideologies referring to national "communism", especially when the rebels led by Francisco Franco defeated the Spanish Republic. There, Falangist Hispanicism gained strength, as did conspiracy theories and sympathy for the Axis powers. Of course, the triumph of the Allies in 1945 and the closeness of the Mexican and American governments reduced the ideological margin for radical expressions (Pérez Montfort, 1992).

Within this framework, within educational institutions, youth groups advised and supported by bishops and Jesuits—all imbued with conspiracy theories— emerged, the objective of which was to "stop the advance of communism" by any means (Contreras Pérez, 2002; González, 2007; González, 2005; González, 2003; Delgado, 2003; López Macedonio, 2007), while other lay groups promoted similar ideas, but with different degrees of belligerence (Ortoll, 1990; Serrano Álvarez, 1989; Solís, 2008). Among the latter, at the end of the 1930s, *Synarchism* was formed, which was a broad movement with rural bases in the Bajío area, which abandoned the armed struggle against the State to become a social movement with electoral aspirations (Meyer, 1979; Serrano Álvarez, 1989).

Another strand of Catholics made up of enlightened middle classes and economic elites, participated in the founding of the National Action Party in 1939. This political body appeared as the defender of democracy against the authoritarian regime and participated in numerous elections in which it was conceived by its opponents as the party of the Catholic hierarchy. The heterogeneous conformation of its militancy was of opponents of the revolutionary regimes, so it was born with a contradiction between Catholics and liberals, as well as with little social drag, resulting in an almost testimonial presence within the political system.[3]

For its part, the conservative liberal family, also with deep roots in the nineteenth century, took shape during the Porfiriato (1876–1911) when an elite was consolidated whose vision of social order was founded on a modern code illustrated with strong organicist components and evolutionists. It was not surprising, for example, that the "Indigenous problem" was treated as a racial issue associated with barbarism—the community, "backward" languages, customs—as well as a disease—laziness, alcoholism—of the living organism that was society. The solution, proposed by the "social doctors" or scientists, ranged from heavy-handed measures—slavery or extermination—to education (Sierra, 1950). Of course, this logic was also applied to Jews, Chinese, and other communities seen as "incompatible races" (Lomnitz, 2010). But the reading was not limited to the ethnic axis since it was easily extensible to other sectors of society such as the workers and peasants—whose condition was explained by their limited individual capacity—as well as to various regions of the country interpreted with the filter of geographic determinism.

Another variant of conservative liberalism was promoted by business elites, especially some of the country's capital and Monterrey, the latter industrial enclave linked to international capitals. In fact, the Monterrey elite became the main business nucleus opposed to the Mexican revolution—at least on the ideological level—promoting, among other initiatives, the creation in 1929 of the Confederation of Employers of the Mexican Republic (*Coparmex*), an organisation that would bring together businessmen against the State (Nuncio, 1982).

Far from being the lone flag of the defeated Porfirian elites, this ideological family included numerous revolutionaries such as Luis Cabrera or Plutarco Elías Calles. The first was a *Carrancista* lawyer who defended the individual agrarian distribution and being on the losing side of the revolution, was classified as reactionary. The second became the "Maximum Chief" of the revolution in 1928, leading the ruling group until 1936, overlapping acts of corruption and turning social justice policies into mechanisms of political control.

The conservative liberal family then included members of the revolutionary governments and their opponents. The former saw themselves as a new elite who had earned their place through fighting and therefore could decide who came to power, while the latter remained anchored to the nineteenth-century code and therefore saw regimes post-revolutionaries and their social justice an imposition without scientific diagnosis that only used the masses for their benefit.

Within this sub-branch, more radical expressions that codified caudillismo and local pride in the key to extreme nationalism with overtones of anti-Semitism also stood out, so they went from small chiefs to ideological threats such as the golden shirts and the followers of Yocupicio and Saturnino Cedillo (Martínez Assad, 2010; Almada, 2009; Gojman de Backal, 2001).

It is also important to note that this set of ideas, although it was typical of the political and economic elite, was nested and promoted in the State Institutes of Sciences and in the National Preparatory School, the flagship educational project of the nineteenth-century liberals. For their part, the lawyers who saw the revolution as a threat to progress founded, in 1912, the Free School of Law where the conservative liberalism of the Porfirian imprint would be maintained. In addition, the ideological code would be the canon of the University of Mexico founded by Justo Sierra in 1910, remaining relatively strong until the 1960s when it was already the National Autonomous University of Mexico (UNAM). In fact, several students, academics, and managers of the university institution participated in the founding of the PAN in 1939, highlighting Manuel Gómez Morín. Hence, throughout the twentieth century, the main drivers of conservative liberalism have been enlightened middle classes, especially lawyers.

In summary, during this stage the Catholic family was undoubtedly the one with the greatest strength, including the majority of the ecclesiastical institutions and large social contingents, while the conservative liberal lost weight and blurred between the defeated elites and the new ruling factions. Furthermore, the turbulent international context allowed opponents of revolutionary regimes to see in European experiences an option for their reality, generating local and nationalist versions of international expressions.

Revolutionary nationalism (1946–1975)

In January 1946 the Party of the Mexican Revolution gave way to the Institutional Revolutionary Party (PRI). The change was not only in name. The statutes of the political body were modified, replacing social justice with progress and democracy. By then, the synchrony of the Mexican ruling elite with the political and economic agenda of the American power, as well as the import substitution model, set new coordinates for the national political geometry, especially for the consolidation of a regime that promoted itself as heir of the revolutionary feat and through this maintained the legitimacy of its decisions. Then came economic success through stabilising development—known as the "Mexican miracle"—which would end up cementing the regime.

In this way, unlike the previous period in which it reached high levels of belligerence, the Catholic family was drastically reduced by the emergence of a generation of ecclesiastical leaders willing to negotiate with the government in turn. This made it evident that the heterogeneity typical of Catholics—secular, clergy, hierarchy, radicals, moderates, etc. —began to generate problems of a different nature, especially of obedience, to which was added the gradual urbanisation—and secularisation—from broad sectors of Mexican society, which led to a dynamic of reorganisation of the Catholic universe (Blancarte, 1992).

In this context, the Protestant and Communist threats gained momentum, although none was new in the imaginary of politically active Catholics. The first one was pointed out since the nineteenth century, but it had acquired new forms in the context of the continental alliance during the Second World War (the Yankee threat); however, since there was not an important Protestant community in the country, it was no more than a discursive ghost. For its part, the "red" or "Bolshevik" threat grew strongly, especially from the 1950s onwards, when anti-communism with a Hispanic-Catholic root was mixed with anti-communism from the Cold War. The latter, thought of in a nationalist way, functioned as a hinge between moderates and radicals within the right-wing Catholic family, as well as a bridge with the conservative liberal family, especially during the 1960s in the heat of the impact of the Cuban revolution.

Thus, for example, the radical groups that originated in the previous period, nested in universities experienced a stage of national expansion and international connection, while their public faces received financing from politicians and businessmen, as well as support from journalists (González, 2007; González, 2005; González, 2003; Delgado, 2003; López Macedonio, 2007; Santiago Jiménez, 2016; Santiago Jiménez, 2015; Herrán Ávila, 2015).

But while some Catholic radicals were tolerated by the governments that saw communist hotbeds in educational institutions, others such as the *Synarchists* were seen as the "fifth column" and persecuted by the government whose corporate arms—confederations of workers and peasants—were considered their own spaces.

However, this anti-communist attunement of politically active Catholics did not completely save the differences within them, and their appearance was modified by the Second Vatican Council (1962–1965), the General Conference of the Latin American Episcopate of 1968 and the growth of the classes' stockings promoted by the government economic project. The SDC became the great unifying centre of the majority of Catholics, while left-wing radicals were inclined towards liberation theology—of relative impact in Mexico thanks to the strength of hierarchical conservatism—and those on the right divided themselves between those that did not know the papal authority and those that remained within the Catholic Church to battle the "red enemy".

The atomisation did not undermine the anti-communism that covered the majority of the Catholic universe and towards the 1970s, when the Luis Echeverría government (1970–1976) reactivated a discourse with strong populist overtones and carried out actions such as visiting Castro's Cuba or receiving exiles from Latin American dictatorships, a rebound began that reached its climax in 1974 with mobilisations against the federal birth control policy.

Despite the permanence and then apparent effervescence of right-wing Catholics, the truth is that this family was far from representing a true opposition to the regime as it was in the previous period. In fact, through anti-communism in a nationalist way, they served as containment and a battering ram for the government at different junctures. For this reason, some stamps such as the participation of the PAN in elections or the foundation of the Jus publishing house—financed by the founder of the PAN Manuel Gómez Morín and operated by the former *Synarchist* leader Salvador Abascal—remained as anecdotes of the strength they had in previous periods.

On the other hand, the conservative liberal family lived through a period of boom at the hand of the capitalist modernisation process that had a strong impulse from the 1940s with the entry of the United States into the war and its demand for supplies and work. In this context, a group of lawyers graduated from the University and headed by the secretary of the government Miguel Alemán Valdés took the latter to the presidency of the republic in 1946. Symbolic leader of the National Confederation of Popular Organisations (CNOP), the corporate arm from the official party that brought together the middle classes, Alemán became the benchmark for a new generation in power characterised by not having participated in the revolution and, therefore, founding its legitimacy in the modernising vision that the enlightened middle classes were supposed to promote (López Portillo, 1995), particularly lawyers.[4]

With his government, he started an ambitious industrialisation project that involved reducing the social justice component, tipping the balance in favour of private capital. Hence, it promoted the modification of constitutional articles, highlighting article 27 on property and allowing the restitution of large tracts of land to former owners and the sale to new businessmen, among whom there were several close to the executive power. Large infrastructure works were also promoted, such as highways, expressways in cities, housing units, and the emblematic University City, which evidenced the relevance for the conservative liberal project of the formation of an enlightened elite far—symbolically and physically—from the bustle of the popular downtown neighbourhoods.

From then on, the authoritarianism of the regime acquired new shades as the modernisation project clearly affected the majority whose claims were ignored or repressed, which led to a turbulent six-year closure that was joined by an economic crisis derived from economic dependency towards the neighbour to the north. In this way, although *Alemanismo* did not return to government in the 1950s and 1960s, it consolidated itself as a current within the hegemonic party, maintaining representation in different spaces and always in connection with economic power. In addition, it was characterised by a furious anti-communism that was echoed in the press and educational institutions; hence, as I pointed out, they occasionally supported anti-communist student groups and professionals.

Conservative liberalism also found a foothold in other niches of the official party but alien to *Alemanismo*, assuming components of a heterogeneous nationalism and claiming the characteristic authoritarianism of the political regime. Furthermore, we must not forget that a part of the PAN leadership was part of this right-wing family despite being in opposition to the ruling party.

Finally, among some businessmen with political interests and educational projects such as the Monterrey Group that founded in 1943 the Technological Institute of Superior Studies of Monterrey (ITESM but popularly known as "Tec de Monterrey") and Raúl Bailleres founder of the Autonomous Technological Institute of Mexico (ITAM), a strand of conservative liberalism found new routes in the proposals of foreign economists. In this way, since the 1940s, a small intellectual and business elite cultivated and promoted neoliberal ideas contrary to the statist spirit of the period. Later, towards the 1960s, the promotion of organisations for the discussion and diffusion of economic liberalism as an option for the regime and a brake on communism grew, but they continued to be an anomaly (Romero Sotelo, 2016).

In the 1970s the scenario changed. The international economic crisis and its impact on Mexico, added to the profile of the Echeverrista government, constituted the perfect setting for the emergence of a long-standing opposition. Thus, in September 1973 a command of the Liga Comunista 23 de Septiembre—a guerrilla organisation made up mostly of urban middle-class youth—failed in the attempt of kidnapping Eugenio Garza Sada, the leader of the Monterrey Group, murdering him on the streets of the northern city. From then on, the gap between the most radical opposition businessmen and the government grew unchecked.

It is important to note that in this period the presence of the military in the front line of politics was tempered with their exclusion from the PRI and then with the electoral defeat of General Henríquez in 1952. From then on, they would only retain spaces of power such as the party leadership (Alfonso Corona del Rosal), some governorships and legislative seats. This, in comparison with other Latin American experiences, is striking, since for more than half a century the armed forces had been an executing arm of executive decisions, but not a decisive factor in themselves.

The neoliberal consensus 1975–2015

Between 1973 and 1990 the Mexican economy was characterised by recurrent crises ending the "Mexican miracle" and wearing down the legitimacy of the regime. This scenario was ideal for the emergence of political and social oppositions of all kinds, as well as for the positioning of the technocratic side within the hegemonic party.

The second half of the 1970s saw the growth of right-wing Catholic radicalism expressed in lay organisations—to a large extent heirs to youth groups of previous decades—as well as the conservatism of the SDC, finding a climax in the visit of Pope John Paul II in 1979. Thereafter, different organised expressions were maintained in the logic of social and political participation, while others were organically linked to the National Action Party.

On the other hand, by 1975 the Monterrey businessmen had reached a great consensus with many of their peers until founding the Business Coordinating Council (CCE), an organisation that would promote the free market in different ways and articulate the efforts of businessmen to pressure subsequent governments. In that period, the bridges between government economics specialists and businessmen were strengthened, as the next generations of area officials began their specialisation in business schools in the United States.

From then on, the figure of organised civil society began to function as a hinge between both sides: while businessmen promoted this figure as a counterweight to the authoritarian regime and financed dispersed expressions, the most radical politically active Catholics formed groups that influenced educational and family issues.

This impulse had as one of its consequences the transformation of the PAN. Indeed, starting in the 1980s, the founding generation of the party gave way to new cadres identified with the newly minted liberalism promoted by some businessmen and academics, as well as with radical activism by secret and public Catholic groups. Thus, *neo-panismo* gradually abandoned the role of a witnessing party to begin competing for government spaces.

In this way, conservative liberalism in its various expressions began to lose presence in Mexican political geometry, which did not mean its disappearance. In fact, many of its features had permeated the contending political cultures.[5] Two moments evidenced the change that was happening in the right-wing families: the 1986 elections in the northern state of Chihuahua and the 1988 presidential one. In the first, the PAN denounced fraud against them and led a media information campaign backed by the Catholic hierarchy and some businessmen, as well as lay-led civil disobedience mobilisations. In the second, the fraud claim was repeated, and the PAN protests were led by the candidate Manuel Clouthier, a businessman from the north with great popular impact. In this way, *neo-panismo* closed the 1980s, strengthened with social bases in different regions of the country, which allowed it to negotiate with the ruling party.

For its part, the PRI also underwent a strong transformation as the nationalist currents gave way to a new one led by young technocratic cadres. In fact, the winning candidate in 1988 was Carlos Salinas de Gortari, representative of that generation and the visible face of a group made up of characters such as Manuel Camacho Solís, Pedro Aspe, Jaime Serra Puche, José Córdoba Montoya, and Luis Donaldo Colosio. It should be noted that the technocrats also gave rise to other currents of the party and an example of this was the appointment of Fernando Gutiérrez Barrios—former chief of staff of the Federal Security Directorate, the state's surveillance and repression department—as secretary of the government.

The interlocution of the *salinista* group with the business leaders and *neo-panism*—through Diego Fernández de Cevallos—marked the consolidation of the neoliberal family, the wear of conservative liberalism and the reconstitution of right-wing Catholicism. An example of the above were the various constitutional reforms and public policies characterised by the liberalisation of the economy, the withdrawal of the State in this matter, and the granting of rights to the Catholic Church.

This coincided with the emergence of Anglo-Saxon neoliberalism (Reagan and Thatcher), the intense anti-communist activism of Pope John Paul II, and the fall of the USSR, so that the new ruling coalition managed to tie its renewal speech with the international agenda. Thus, what was previously shown as the ideology of an isolated elite was gradually installed as common sense throughout the 1990s, with the key moment being the entry into force of the Free Trade Agreement with North America in January 1994. At this point, it is important to note that a sector of the business community was in the media and very soon became a determining factor for the dissemination of the new imaginary. In this way, business organisations played a decisive role alongside the ruling groups, while *neo-panismo* continued to increase its social base and won elections through negotiations with the *salinista* government.

In 1997, the PRI lost the legislative majority for the first time. In this context, through television, the presidential campaign of Vicente Fox, PAN governor of Guanajuato, one of the bastions of Catholic *Panism*, began. Very soon, various business figures gathered around Fox, as well as representatives of civil society organisations promoting the image of the politician-businessman who is closer to the people than to the elite. This long campaign ended in 2000 with the electoral triumph of the PAN known in the heat of the celebration as the "transition to democracy".

In this way, the process that had begun at least two decades earlier placed the neoliberal political and business elite, as well as the most conservative Catholic sectors in federal political power. As of that year, two PAN governments followed one another and the return of the PRI to power; however, the neoliberal consensus had been established as the logic of the ruling elite and massified through the media. Hence the agenda of the different governments and most of the parties[6] will revolve around the legislative reforms that definitively open the Mexican economy.

On the other hand, almost with the beginning of the century, largely due to alignment with US security policy and the need to legitimise the State, a new issue grew to become the centre of the government's agenda: violence. Indeed, especially from 2007 when the PAN president Felipe Calderón Hinojosa[7] declared the "war on drug trafficking" a spiral of violence was unleashed which was fuelled by arms trafficking, the increase in drug trafficking on a global scale, as well as the high levels of inequality in the country. Little by little, this phenomenon repositioned the armed forces as an increasingly central political actor and generated other forms of social mobilisation, especially for relatives of the disappeared.

In this new context, the right-wing Catholic family was backed by the ruling elite and strengthened in historical bastions such as El Bajío, an old *Cristero* area, where in collusion with political and business actors they have claimed demands such as the criminalisation of abortion; however, as it happened before, the internal divisions soon emerged: while a part of the hierarchy was strongly linked to the economic powers, other sectors of the laity were more involved in the dispute for political power than in religious activity, all framed by the international paedophile and corruption scandals within the ecclesiastical institution. This erosion, as well as the penetration of market logic into the Mexican social imaginary, gave way to the emergence of other churches, religions, and creeds with strong conservative signs, especially in moral terms, and a greater capacity to adapt to the new environment.

The neoliberal family, for its part, showed a certain unity over more than a decade, and an example of this was the continuity of officials between PAN and PRI governments, highlighting the figure of José Antonio Meade, who had been Secretary of Energy (2011), Foreign Relations (2012–2015), Social Development (2015–2016), and Finance (2016–2017). However, during the six-year term of the *PRIista* Enrique Peña Nieto (2012–2018), the corruption scandals added to the growing socio-economic inequality, the inability to operate politically by the federal administration, and the levels of violence that were experienced in the country soon wore out the neoliberal consensus for broad social sectors, especially among enlightened middle classes and popular sectors (Kerner and Petersen, 2018).

The last five years

Faced with the political crisis experienced during the Peña Nieto government, numerous opposition or discontented sectors gathered around the figure of Andrés Manuel López Obrador, who separated from the ranks of the PRD and formed his own party called the National Regeneration Movement (MORENA) to contend for the third time to the presidency of the republic in 2018. The Tabasco politician took advantage of the wear and tear of most of the traditional political figures and formed a coalition of forces that positioned him as the candidate to win. The PRI candidate was José Antonio Meade, precisely the official who went through administrations and who faithfully represented the neoliberal elite forged in the administration and far from partisan politics, while the PAN candidate was Ricardo Anaya who condensed the wear and tear of the party by lacking a visible political career, but he presented himself as an ambitious and enterprising young man.[8] However, if we attend to the families that we have described in a general way, we might think that they continue to cohabit in an important part of Mexican politics.

The Catholic family has become the Christian family. It is undeniable that the conservative Catholic hierarchy continues to be a fundamental factor of power in Mexico, so much so that, at least since 2000, no major presidential candidate has eluded the closed-door meeting with the Mexican Episcopate Conference on the campaign trail. However, the crisis referred to in previous lines has allowed the emergence of other parallel churches and religions, especially evangelicals that number approximately 35 million believers in the country. In fact, the disappeared Social Encounter Party (PES) participated in the coalition that brought AMLO to the presidency giving him 1.5 million votes (El Universal, August 2, 2019).

Although with substantial differences in creed and practices, the members of this family continue to dispute a place in public life, pressing for the amendment of the Constitution and their participation in federal government projects. In addition, they maintain strong mobilisations of civil organisations around a classic agenda seen with a moral filter made up of the themes of abortion, gender (feminism, same-sex marriages), and family planning,[9] activating responses in the opposite direction that tried to support and justify social differentiation or discredit the debate; hand in hand with this, the social and political problems surrounding the growing waves of migrants—Central Americans, Caribbean, and Africans—have fuelled an incipient xenophobic nationalism; finally, the complex problem of violence has supported ideas in the imagination of some social sectors such as the criminalisation of victims and the acceptance of the apparent dilemma between security and freedom, leading to the support of restrictive public policies and the condemnation of social mobilisations.

In this sense, Mexico shares some of the central themes of the political agendas in other latitudes and that, therefore, define its political geometries, such as migration, but others have not positioned themselves with the same force or in the same direction as the gender and specifically feminism—which burst into the public debate with unprecedented force, but has not elicited a contrary political reaction—or climate change.

Another striking edge of the current Mexican scenario is that the current government and the MORENA party cross at least two of the referred families. This, far from being strange, responds to the dynamics of the coalition or front that the AMLO group organised to win the 2018 election, as well as the current rearrangement of forces and political geometry. For example, the explicit recognition of religion as a factor of social reconciliation, the promotion of a "Moral Primer" with clear conservative features, flirting with various churches to allow them to take over television channels, or some legislative voices from MORENA condemning legalisation of abortion are traits of the Catholic-Christian family.

On the other hand, Alfonso Romo Head of the Office of the Presidency (2018–2020)—linked to the Monterrey Group—served as the main bridge with the most powerful businessmen, while Esteban Moctezuma Barragán Secretary of Education (2018–2021) and current Ambassador to the United States came from Fundación Azteca part of the business conglomerate headed by Ricardo Salinas Pliego, while some press reports have pointed out that the Secretaries of the Treasury and Foreign Relations—Arturo Herrera (2019–2021) and Marcelo Ebrard—are privately advised and supported by José Antonio Meade (Maldonado, 2019). Without a doubt, the neoliberal family was not extinct.[10]

In any case, the truth is that the most radical factions of the Mexican right-wing opponents of the government in turn lack a social base and clear political projects, so it is unlikely that in the short term they represent a threat. However, the success or failure of the policies—especially economic and security—of the current federal administration could feed various social sectors in search of a charismatic reference that comes from the opposition ranks themselves, or even from the same ruling coalition.

Notes

1 Numerous authors have already written about the Cristero rebellion, such as Jean Meyer, María Alicia Puente Lutteroth, Alicia Olivera, Fernando M. González, Moisés González Navarro and Francis Patrick Dooley, to name a few. Of course, the historiographical debate on this period and from different angles is still in force, as López has pointed out, Damián López (2011).
2 Although many others were part of the revolutionary factions.
3 About PAN there is an extensive academic and journalistic bibliography. The works of: Loaeza (1999), Gómez Mont (2008), Hernández Vicencio (2009).
4 That is why it was not surprising that in the 1940s the works of Justo Sierra, Porfirista minister of education, and of Emilio Rabasa, one of the founders of the *Escuela Libre de Derecho*, were republished and disseminated.
5 Even among some leftists.
6 Including the Party of the Democratic Revolution, which had brought together various leftist currents since the late 1980s.
7 The 2006 presidential election was decided in favour of the PAN candidate with a difference of 0.52%. Leftist candidate Andrés Manuel López Obrador declared that he had

been the subject of a fraud planned by his business and political opponents, whom he identified as "the power mafia" (Díaz Polanco, 2012).
8 In September 2019, during his government report, President López Obrador pointed out that the triumph of the reaction is "morally impossible" because "they are morally defeated".
9 See the works of Federico Navarrete on racism and discrimination in Mexico.
10 In March 2019, President López Obrador decreed "the end of the neoliberal era".

References

Almada, I. (2009) *La conexión Yocupicio: Soberanía estatal y tradición cívico-liberal en Sonora, 1913–1939*. México, El Colegio de México.

Blancarte, R. (1992) *Historia de la Iglesia católica en México, 1929–1982*. México, Fondo de Cultura Económica/El Colegio Mexiquense.

Contreras Pérez, G. (2002) *Los grupos católicos en la Universidad Autónoma de México (1933–1944)*. México, División de Ciencias Sociales y Humanidades – Universidad Autónoma Metropolitana Unidad Xochimilco.

Delgado, Á. (2003) *El Yunque. La ultraderecha en el poder*. México, Ed. Grijalbo.

Díaz Polanco, H. (2012) *La cocina del diablo. El fraude del 2006 y los intelectuales*. México, Temas de hoy.

Garciadiego, J. (2006) La oposición conservadora y de las clases medias al cardenismo, *Istor. Revista de Historia Internacional* 25, 30–49.

Gojman de Backal, A. (2001) *Camisas, escudos y desfiles militares. Los Dorados y el antisemitismo en México (1934–1940)*. México, Fondo de Cultura Económica.

Gómez Mont, M. T. (2008) *Manuel Gómez Morin, 1915–1939 la raíz y la simiente de un proyecto nacional*. México, Fondo de Cultura Económica.

González, F. M. (2003) Los orígenes y el comienzo de una universidad católica: Sociedades secretas y jesuítas. *Historia y Grafía* 20, 151–205.

González, F. M. (2005) Integralismo, persecución y secreto en algunos grupos católicos en México en el siglo XX. In Nassif, A. A. & Sánchez, J. A. (coords.), *El Estado mexicano: herencias y cambios. Sociedad civil y diversidad, Tomo III*. México, Miguel Ángel Porrúa/CIESAS/Cámara de Diputados LIX Legislatura, 229–275.

González, F. M. (2007) Algunos grupos radicales de izquierda y de derecha con influencia católica en México (1965–1975). *Historia y Grafía* 29, 57–93.

Hernández Vicencio, T. (2009) *Tras las huellas de la derecha. El Partido Acción Nacional, 1939–2000*. México, Ed. Ítaca.

Herrán Ávila, L. A. (2015) Las guerrillas blancas: Anticomunismo transnacional e imaginarios de derechas en Argentina y México, 1954–1972. *Quinto Sol. Revista de Historia, Instituto de Estudios Sociohistóricos/ Facultad de Ciencias Humanas–Universidad Nacional de La Pampa* 19 (1), 1–26.

Kerner, D., & Petersen, C. (2018) *Aplauso perdido. Análisis del sexenio de Enrique Peña Nieto*. México, Turner.

Loaeza, S. (1999) *El Partido Acción Nacional: La larga marcha, 1939–1994. Oposición leal y partido de protesta*. México, Fondo de Cultura Económica.

Lomnitz, C. (2010) *El antisemitismo y la ideología de la Revolución Mexicana*. Translated by M. Zamudio. México, Fondo de Cultura Económica.

López, D. (2011) La guerra cristera (México, 1926–1929). Una aproximación historiográfica. *Historiografías. Revista de historia y teoría* 1, 35–52.

López Macedonio, M. N. (2007) *Los Tecos en el México de la primera mitad de los años setenta y su proyección trasnacional anticomunista*. Master's dissertation. Instituto de Investigaciones Dr. José María Luis Mora.
López Portillo, F. (1995) *Estado e ideología empresarial en el gobierno alemanista*. México, UNAM.
Martínez Assad, C. (2010) *El camino de la rebelión del general Saturnino Cedillo*. México, Océano.
Meyer, J. (1979) *El sinarquismo: ¿un fascismo mexicano? 1937–1947*. México, Joaquín Mortiz.
Nuncio, A. (1982) *El Grupo Monterrey*. México, Ed. Nueva Imagen.
Ortoll, S. (1990) Las Legiones, La Base y el Sinarquismo. ¿Tres organizaciones distintas y un solo fin verdadero? (1929–1948). In Quiróz, R. M. (ed.), *La política y el cielo. Movimientos religiosos en el México contemporáneo*. México, Universidad de Guadalajara, pp. 73–117.
Pérez Montfort, R. (1992) *Hispanismo y Falange: Los sueños imperiales de la derecha española y México*. México, Fondo de Cultura Económica.
Ramírez Rancaño, M. (2002) *La reacción mexicana y su exilio durante la revolución de 1910*. México, Grupo Editorial Miguel Ángel Porrúa/Instituto de Investigaciones Históricas-UNAM/Instituto de Investigaciones Sociales-UNAM.
Romero Sotelo, M. E. (2016) *Los orígenes del neoliberalismo en México. La Escuela Austriaca*. México, Fondo de Cultura Económica/UNAM.
Santiago Jiménez, M. V. (2015) Anticomunismo católico. Origen y desarrollo del Movimiento Universitario de Renovadora Orientación (MURO), 1962–1975. In Colllado, C. (coord.), *Las derechas en el México contemporáneo*. México, Instituto Mora, 187–254.
Santiago Jiménez, M. V. (2016) *Entre el secreto y las calles. Nacionalistas y católicos contra la 'conspiración de la modernidad': El Yunque de México y Tacuara de Argentina (1953–1964)*. Doctoral thesis. Instituto de Investigaciones Dr. José María Luis Mora, México.
Santiago Jiménez, M. V. (2017) Las revoluciones rusa y mexicana en la visión conspirativa de grupos secreto-reservados mexicanos: Tecos y El Yunque (1934–1964). *Claves. Revista de Historia, Facultad de Humanidades y Ciencias de la Educación-Universidad de la República* 5, 101–127.
Serrano Álvarez, P. (1989) *La batalla del espíritu: El movimiento sinarquista en el bajío mexicano (1932–1951)*. Master's dissertation. Instituto de Investigaciones Dr. José María Luis Mora, México.
Sierra, J. (1950) *Evolución política del pueblo mexicano*. Fondo de Cultura Económica, México.
Solís, Y. (2008) El origen de la ultraderecha en México: La 'U'. *El Cotidiano. Revista de la realidad mexicana actual, Universidad Autónoma Metropolitana–Azcapotzalco* 23 (149), 25–57.
Vargas, H. (1983 April) Nuestras vidas ejemplares. De Salvador Abascal a Luis Pazos: Estampitas de la derecha mexicana. *Nexos* 64. 2fmedioambiente.nexos.com.mx/?p=4176

7
URUGUAY

The political right and some landmark moments in history, from the foundational anti-Jacobinism to the re-emergence of the militaristic far right

Gerardo Caetano

Introduction

The "new faces of the right"—that complex "post-fascism" that Enzo Traverso (2018) and other authors speak of, with some semantic variations,[1] focusing their analysis primarily on Europe and the United States of Trump—find similar expressions in Latin America, allowing for differences in context and direction. In particular, when attempting to delve into the more comprehensive stream of new currents of thought and actors, the adoption of a comparative perspective enables a renewal of heuristics, enriches questions and approaches, and avoids provincial and essentialist restrictions. Moreover, the study of national cases can in that way be leveraged as a platform to establish approximations. One possible approach is to hold up certain "novel elements" of today's political right to the mirror of its foundational matrix, which serves in many ways as its inspiration. With variations depending on the case, that matrix was forged in the West between the nineteenth century and the first decades of the twentieth century.

Within that framework, comparative studies often find Uruguay to be a "unique" case in the continent, for a number of reasons. At a time of great regime turmoil in Latin America, the country retains its characterisation as a "full democracy" in world rankings.[2] The 2019 elections could be held up as categorical proof of this, given that they resulted in a reasonably "calm" alternation of power between the "progressive" project furthered by three consecutive administrations of the *Frente Amplio* (Broad Front) and a new five-party *Coalición Multicolor* (Multicoloured Coalition), which, under the leadership of the National or *Blanco* Party and its presidential candidate, Luis Alberto Lacalle Pou,[3] defeated the former at the polls. However, the scenario emerging from these elections is not devoid of novelties. One, in particular, has to do directly with the topic at hand: the new governing coalition was quick to admit into its ranks a freshly formed party, founded in

February of the election year. This new party called itself *Cabildo Abierto* (Open *Cabildo*) and is led by General Guido Manini Ríos, who in March 2019 had been removed from his position as army commander-in-chief by former president Tabaré Vázquez. Thus far, the proposals and actions of this novel party or movement[4] align it with other far-right actors in the continent, and it exhibits an undeniably military inspiration. In the October 27, 2020, elections, it secured an important number of seats in parliament, placing it in a position to define which way a vote will swing and to influence government decisions—at least in the initial phases—over the next five years.[5]

In this text I seek to contrast a true "black swan" of the most recent period of Uruguayan contemporary politics with the traditional matrix of conservative liberalism that—with the exception of the authoritarianism of the civilian-military dictatorship (1973–1985) and some of the years leading up to it[6]—tended to predominate in the history of Uruguay's political right. Through this analytical exercise, the central question posed in this text aims to explore in historical terms the limits and scope of the novel elements displayed by this new player in Uruguayan politics, through an examination of the conditions in which it emerged and the uncertainties raised by its more or less predictable future.

The initial ideological matrix of the Uruguayan right: Anti-Jacobinism and conservative liberalism (1890–1933)

None of the processes that left a lasting imprint on the Uruguay of the early 1900s and the modern identities of Uruguayan politics forged during that time constituted a leap in the dark or a sharp break from the past. A good starting point to examine this would be to consider what, in the words of Carlos Real de Azúa (1985), was the "obvious, undeniable weakness that the continent's constellation of power had in nineteenth century Uruguay", a constellation formed "by the economic and social hegemony of the agricultural and commercial sectors and the intertwining of those sectors with the Church and the Armed Forces". The restrictions imposed from outside the country were also very lax. A contributing factor in this sense was the very nature of the implantation of capitalism in Uruguay—weak in its origins and slow to take hold—and the little significance that Uruguayan products had in world and regional markets, even in the framework of a basically agro-export model that fell under the British "informal empire" of the late nineteenth century. That scenario opened up the possibility for certain gestures and policies of a more democratic and popular nature.

The combined weaknesses of the country's oligarchic power and of capitalism contributed to reinforce the presence of the state in civil society and the centrality of its role in Uruguay's social formation. This predominance of the state also furthered the relevance of specifically political mediations in Uruguayan society. Formed early on in the country's history, the two traditional political parties (known as *Blancos* and *Colorados* because of their distinguishing colours, respectively, white and red, with the former also known as the National Party) played a leading role as brokers between the demands raised by a civil society lacking strong corporations and a public space defined almost monopolistically by the state. With an ideological background that included similarities and differences, the *Blancos* and *Colorados* thus engaged in a binary and dialectical relationship that cannot be reduced to the simple liberal/conservative opposition so typical of the rest of Latin America.

This early party dynamics and the fertile conditions for the introduction of attendant ideas were also linked to other factors rooted in the country's history. One such factor was a colonial past that was both politically and culturally weak, especially with regard to the classic scheme of "Indies Christianity" of the Spanish empire. Another constituent factor was the arrival of large waves of European immigrants, which shaped a basically receptive society (characterised by influxes) with Eurocentric profiles. This was compounded by weak territorial, ethnic, and community divisions, in the framework of a prevailing "small-scale" perspective that favoured the construction of a citizenry defined by the political horizon and its actors. In addition, the country was overwhelmingly urban-centric—dominated in particular by its capital city of Montevideo—a factor that facilitated homogenising patterns of social integration.

Based on these fundamental legacies, the great dispute that structured modern Uruguay in political and conceptual terms unfolded as a confrontation between the two great "ideological families" of the early 1900s: on the one hand, solidarist republicanism (under the leadership of the first *Batllismo*)[7] and, on the other, conservative or individualist liberalism (represented almost exclusively by the *Herrerista* sector of the National Party as of the 1920s), formed by a peculiar combination of National Party members who adhered to the individualistic liberalism of the Anglo-Saxon realist school, *Colorado* Party members who opposed Batlle y Ordóñez, and staunch ultramontanist Catholics.

The topic of the debates between republicans and liberals thus provides one of the main analytical focal points for thoroughly understanding the mainstays of democracy and the predominant ideological conceptions in that nascent contemporary Uruguay. Generally speaking, in that early political culture, the notions of what could be considered a social reformist left or centre-left tended to prevail—without fully dominating—over ideas advocated from a primarily liberal conservative right-wing camp, which anathematised *Batllismo* and all its "fellow travellers"[8] as a vernacular expression of Jacobinism. Outside that fundamental opposition, there were only small groups of mostly marginal actors. The social bases of that key confrontation were complex, cut across classes, and were articulated with the rural/urban division. On one side were urban workers and middle class together with some progressive industrialists and small- and medium-sized producers, especially from the larger cities. On the other were the many popular sectors of the urban and rural interior of the country, along with the large landowners, big commerce, the financial sectors, and conservative industrialists. This binary distribution is necessarily schematic, but we could say that the early left–right continuum in the country was projected within a primarily partisan and multi-class format, with its respective "social arms".[9]

As noted, in the foundational ranks of the right, converging actors with a liberal conservative profile—strongly hegemonic at the time—tended to prevail over other types of anti-liberal, extremist, militarist, or caudillo-based right-wing groups. The main sources of inspirations of this predominant conservative liberalism of the original right included the ideas of three key ideological figures: Martín C. Martínez (1859–1946),[10] José Irureta Goyena (1874–1947),[11] and Luis Alberto de Herrera (1873–1959).[12] All of them ultimately came to accept liberal democracy as a regime, albeit with more or less reservations. But that did not stop them from insistently warning against the various dangers of Jacobinism.

Martín C. Martínez, for example, wrote a famous doctrinal piece in 1885 on the subject of the theoretical and practical value of popular sovereignty, in which he explored and reviewed different implications of the political principle of popular sovereignty. He did so from an ideological perspective that was clearly conservative and taking a sociological rather than a legal approach. In that framework, he emphatically rejected the parliamentary system, cautioned repeatedly against the "growing power of the masses, who are generally ignorant and ill-inspired", defended the Anglo-Saxon political tradition against a "blind following of the revolutionary movement in France", which in his opinion the majority of Uruguay's elites had fallen prey to, and called for the construction of "free" and "conservative" institutions, capable of pouring "the frothy and rich liquor of democracy into old wineskins" (Martínez, 1885). And he concluded by saying:

> the mistake of the Revolution was in not explaining the perfect correspondence of the form of government with the social environment. [...] Those of us who blindly follow the revolutionary movement in France have not had the honour of falling into the hands of Napoleons like she has.
>
> *(Martínez, 1885)*

But perhaps the most representative and important voice of this liberal conservatism was José Irureta Goyena, a "sort of secular Bossuet of our active classes", as Carlos Real de Azúa (1985) accurately defined him. His ideological views, his institutional thinking, and his opinions on democracy are illustrated in a famous conference delivered in 1944, on the occasion of his incorporation into the National Academy of Letters, of which he was a founding and renowned member. On that occasion, he declared:

> Liberty and equality complement each other like nuts and bolts; fraternity, in contrast, takes precedence over the ends that the others pursue [...]. The first two are individualistic forces; the latter is essentially socialist. [...] The human soul must necessarily be transformed if we are to change the system. [...] Socialism, communism, anarchism, unionism, are all doctrines that seek to replace the balance of the mystical triangle of "liberty, equality, and fraternity" with the hurricane symbolised by the apex of fraternity. [...] Democracy, which is a form of organisation of public powers, is becoming

the symbol of leftist, subversive, and revolutionary governments, whose task must be to overthrow the capitalist system, which is of bourgeois stock and purely liberal structure.

(Irureta Goyena, 1948)

Against the backdrop of conservative "terror", which re-emerged following the impact of the Russian Revolution of 1917 (Caetano, 2017a; Caetano, 2017b), the discussions regarding the historical interpretation of the French Revolution and the Commune reappeared with full force (Herrera, 2016: p. 256).[13] These debates converged in warning that democracy in its "Jacobin version" could "serve as a banner" to conceal the advent of "leftist governments". How was this caution translated specifically in Uruguayan politics? Irureta Goyena made this crystal clear in a 1918 speech, in which he pronounced perhaps the harshest and most critical judgement against the first *Batllismo*. He associated it with an image of "unrest" and accused it of being "worse than socialism", as in its reformist zeal it resulted in generating "movement for the sake of movement, frenzy, agitation, the Saint Vitus Dance disease inflicted on the conduct of the State" (Irureta Goyena, 1948: pp. 275–276).

In order to complete a general picture of the liberal conservative proposal, it is important to review, at least briefly, some of the ideas of Luis Alberto de Herrera, who was without a doubt the maximum leader and ideologist of the National Party for more than half a century. On this subject, in a passage of his classic doctrinal work *La Revolución Francesa y Sudamérica*, Herrera (2009) wrote:

> [T]he worst revolutionary instincts burrow their way into the spirit of the French masses and the republican regime yields to the threat that emerges, obedient to the impulses of the Jacobin demagoguery in full swing. The country's conservative classes tremble with indignation at the outrageous passivity of the government, not in the conflicts between capital and labor—that can be settled between employers and workers—but in the face of their indifference when it comes to cracking down on the abuses against the fundamental freedoms of the industrial individual.

At the national level, that "passivity", if not "complicity", of "republican" or "Jacobin" governments in the face of the onslaught of "the base appetites of the mob" and its "antisocial tide" was also immediately likened by Herrera (2009)—who often thought as a historian and engaged in politics from a historical perspective—with the actions of reformist *Batllismo*. The National Party leader saw it as the instrument used to break with tradition and the past, to pursue a political and social experiment that, in his view, resulted inexorably in statism, the "dissolution of capitalism", and in "moral anarchy".

While there was some "clamouring" and actions by "agitators"—which incidentally also existed among conservatives—actual threats to the social order in the Uruguay of the first decades of the twentieth century were weak and more rhetorical than anything. This did not stop the "moral crusade" against *Batllismo* from escalating at the decisive crossroads of 1933, with the coup d'état of March 31, led by President Gabriel Terra (1873–1842). Terra was a prominent *Colorado* politician, and even a rare, moderate and reluctant "*Batllista* entrepreneur", who in that critical moment was able to secure the support of the right-wing sectors of both traditional parties and the entire business community, as well as the passive acquiescence of the army, whose ranks were predominantly Colorado supporters but for the most part opposed to *Batllismo*. The year 1933 was the most propitious time for a drift towards far-right positions that could exceed the scope of the previous conservative liberalism. However, in Uruguay of the 1930s, that "impulse" to the right had its own brake too (Caetano and Jacob, 1989–1991).

In this sense, three key elements contributed decisively to determine the original prevalence of conservative liberalism among the early ranks of the Uruguayan right: (i) the failure of military putschism to gain a foothold in the country, which, as in other Latin American countries, sought to establish strong ties with the political right and the economic forces in their most radical versions; (ii) the little echo found by the first European fascism at the local level; and (iii) the scarce appeal of populist calls among a society that—across the political spectrum—tended to distrust mass and non-partisan leaderships, radically dichotomous political divisions, and corporatist and non-citizen-based configurations.[14]

Regarding the first element, while the country had its share of "military mutiny" threats, the announced "abrupt turns" to the right did not prosper. Situations such as the 1914 "Dubra plot" (an attempt at a military coup against José Batlle y Ordóñez, who was serving his second presidential term at the time),the heated debates in 1923 over military conscription (the famous "Riverós Project"), the perceived isolation among military circles and their distrust of political parties and civil society organisations, the creation in 1929 of the *Vanguardias de la Patria* (Vanguards of the Fatherland),[15] and other similar events went no further than that in this foundational period.

With respect to the second element, although the rise of European fascism and the influence of the military dictatorships that spread across the continent were felt in Uruguay,[16] they did not find much echo in the country. This is not to say that the "fascist virus" was not present as a source of inspiration among the ranks of the right in both traditional parties, in the most reactionary sectors of the business community, or in the "militaristic" embryos in the armed forces—which comprised a very small minority in the army and were almost non-existent in the other branches. "We need a Mussolini" (El País, April 24, 1924: p. 11), National Party convention member Usabiaga Salas was heard shouting in the middle of his party's 1924 convention. Five years later, another National Party member, the Herrerista legislator Rogelio V. Mendiondo, observed during a parliamentary discussion with the communist legislator Eugenio Gómez,

> I find it surprising that a Representative of the so-called progressive tendencies would come to Parliament to hurl gratuitous insults at a man of the

stature of Benito Mussolini. (*Not supported. Murmuring*). Benito Mussolini [...] is, without a doubt, the most extraordinary man of modern times.
(Diario de Sesiones, 1929: p. 510)

There were similar statements from members of the *Colorado* Party too. "I found a prosperous Italy", Pedro Manini Ríos declared from his seat in Parliament in 1929, after a recent trip to the European nation.

And apparently happy, calm, and unanimous in the support for a government that was restoring [...] not only material prosperity, but a national sentiment that was absolutely necessary to prevent it from immediately descending into social chaos. [...] Italy today is perfectly happy with the Benito Mussolini regime.
(Diario de Sesiones, 1929: pp. 512–513)

The "fascist virus" did catch on, but not too strongly. In the first place, because very few realised that the characteristics of Uruguayan society were still such that they left no room for far-right and nationalist movements with openly anti-liberal beliefs and massive projection. As the events of the following years would demonstrate categorically, the threats to the "social order" were not revolutionary in nature and the political and ideological disputes in the country did not find enough incentives to transcend the scope of the already established controversy between the ideological families of the early 1900s. The clear predominance of a basically anti-Jacobin conservative liberalism—with no operational ties to the armed forces and not articulated with a widespread ideological receptivity to the first European fascism—defined in several aspects its subsequent path.

Historical alternatives in the hegemony within the Uruguayan right: Between the electoral path and the coup

Since its foundational configuration and over the last 90 years of its history, the Uruguayan political right has seen very diverse moments and processes, a detailed examination of which exceeds the limits of this text. In more than one sense, the two great ideological families of the early 1900s have maintained, with major re-articulations and re-significations, the centrality of their historical dispute, albeit in different ways and with variations in some actors. That does not mean that liberal conservatism was always able to maintain its hegemony in the right. However, it was only when liberal conservatism prevailed among its ranks that the right was able to attain, through the electoral path, consistent government positions. In this sense, despite the corporative and fascist displays following the "palace" coup of March 1933, and even the continuing allegiance to Francoism of much of the Uruguayan right (Zubillaga, 2017), this matrix remained steadfast during the Terra years.

In contrast, a different right emerged during the 1950s and 1960s with the rural movement led by Benito Nardone (1906–1964)[17] and his *Liga Federal de Acción Ruralista* (Federal League for Rural Action), offering an alternative to conservative liberalism, with anti-liberal and populist tendencies. While it did not succeed in associating with the army, it achieved a victory at the polls and governed through a coalition with the Herrerismo sector within a reunited National Party.[18] However, the influence of Nardone's ruralism on public policies was very short-lived and weak, since he was forced to negotiate his extremist positions under democratic party dynamics, and the movement did not survive the death of its leader. The alternative to an "anti-*Batllista* revolution", loudly announced by the "*Herrerismo*-ruralism" alliance after the overwhelming victory of the National Party in the 1958 elections, quickly failed without producing the results expected by its proponents.

In the 1960s, as throughout most of Latin America, the country experienced much disruption. The social crisis and the heightened ideological confrontation of the Cold War also reached Uruguay, now devoid of its old "buffers" (a redistributive state, "Keynesian" parties, surpluses derived from favourable contexts for the export of agricultural commodities, etc.). This climate of polarisation found fertile ground in a population that was beginning to face problems previously unknown to it (pauperisation, rampant inflation, a financial speculation crisis, corruption scandals, repressive policies used to quell the growing social protest). Disloyal attitudes towards democracy and the legitimisation of political violence came from both left and right, and while these grew significantly with the impact of the Cuban Revolution, they did not start with it (Broquetas, 2014).

The late 1960s and early 1970s (1968–1973) were an ideal moment for the gradual advancement of a militaristic far right that was anti-liberal in political matters and neoliberal in economic matters, but which, nonetheless, was only able to secure government control in 1973 after a coup d'état orchestrated in two movements. Although the coup was preceded by civilian authoritarian governments, headed by Jorge Pacheco Areco (1920–1998) and Juan María Bordaberry (1928–2011) (Caetano, 2019a), respectively, which even included the first instances of state terrorism, the far right would only achieve full hegemony after the institutional breakdown. The civilian-military dictatorship ruled for over a decade and, under it, an extremist militaristic far right (with civilian involvement) was finally able to prevail. In 1974, it placed the conduct of economic policy in the hands of a techno-bureaucratic team with ties to global financial centres. Through the intensification of ruthless state terrorism practices, a strongly neoliberal economic adjustment project was implemented, which would ultimately fail spectacularly. The 1974 structural adjustment had been launched by Alejandro Végh Villegas, symbolically appropriating, as he did so, an emblematic phrase of Batlle y Ordóñez that stated that "for the poor to be less poor, the rich have to be richer".[19] When in December 1983, he again took the helm of the Ministry of Economy and Finance, his declared goal was to make sure that the economic conditions in which the dictatorship would hand the country over to democracy would not be equated with "a trash can", as he himself described them.

After the dictatorship, there was an initial period in which the *Colorado* and *Blanco* Parties ruled in a succession of four governments of coalition or agreement between the two parties, followed by 15 years of *Frente Amplio* governments. While the cycle of "deep neoliberalism" of the 1990s had a strong impact in Uruguay (Caetano, 2019a), the limits of "conservative liberalism" were not exceeded during this period with far-right positions. This means that in the history of Uruguay such positions have only been able to fully access the government via a coup (and basically only once, during the 1973–1985 civilian-military dictatorship) and have failed to secure power either through elections or through frequent coups as has been the case in other countries of Latin America.[20]

More recently, this institutional soundness exhibited by Uruguayan democracy has been confirmed both by the continuing stability of the country's institutions and by the absence of an effectively authoritarian or populist drift of the *Frente Amplio* during its 15 years of government, in what has been termed the "progressive era".

Nevertheless, the 2019–2020 electoral process put Uruguayan democracy truly to the test, namely through two key issues: (i) the hypothesis—later proven—of a "normal" acceptance of the alternation of governing parties following a long progressive cycle, something that in the rest of the continent is sadly uncommon in recent times (Caetano, 2019b); (ii) the evolution of some far-right "black swans" and their presence in the alternative government formed by the opposition. The first issue, as was foreseeable, was resolved in a completely normal way: in the runoff election in November 2019, an unexpected electoral parity between the two contending blocs was resolved without incident, ushering a transition that, as of the writing of this text, can be described as very smooth. The second issue, in contrast, represented by the rise of a far-right military tendency legitimised at the polls and its rapid naturalisation as a co-governing force, raises several doubts and uncertainties for the future.

The 2019 political shift and its uncertainties

Along with other colleagues, I have long maintained that Uruguayan democracy is *mutating*, at its own pace and with its own unique patterns, slowly but firmly accompanying other processes with a similar perspective that are unfolding more quickly and radically in Latin America (Caetano and Selios, 2016; Caetano et al., 2019).

In this context, the 2019–2020 electoral cycle[21] has seen several novel phenomena that drive this tendency to change, and which could translate into the emergence of authentic "black swans" in Uruguayan politics, associated also with far-right actors: unusual players and processes, with strong disruptive effects and difficult to predict. This type of phenomenon has been very exceptional in Uruguay's political history. Three of the most notable among these can be briefly considered here. The first is the enigmatic participation of a complete outsider—businessman Juan Sartori—in the presidential primary elections of one of the country's historical parties, the National Party.[22] Second is the presidential bid by businessman Edgardo Novick, who had previously run for mayor of Montevideo in the 2015 municipal election, under the *Partido de la Concertación* (Concerted Action Party) ticket, through an agreement with the *Colorado* and National Parties. Novick later formed the *Partido de la Gente* (People's Party), with strong anti-political and populist right tendencies.[23] Third and most especially, the meteoric rise in electoral politics of who until March of the electoral year had been commander-in-chief of the army, Guido Manini Ríos. Almost immediately after his removal from that position, he announced his intention of running for president as candidate of *Cabildo Abierto*, a far-right party with a military profile.[24]

After the June 30, 2019, primaries, the legislative election and the first presidential round were held on October 27 of that same year. From a macro perspective, there were three developments in this election that emerge as major signals in Uruguayan politics, for a number of key reasons. First, the ruling *Frente Amplio* party suffered a drop in its number of voters and the opposition succeeded in obtaining a majority of parliamentary seats. Second, the proposed constitutional amendment on security matters (known by its slogan "*Vivir sin miedo*", or "Living without Fear") lost by a small margin, having obtained almost 47% of the votes. And the third, and most significant, development was the successful results, as noted above, obtained by a far-right military-inspired partisan actor, who was rapidly accepted as a co-governing partner by *Blancos* and *Colorados*, in their almost single-minded aim of removing from government the progressive party that had ruled for the past three decades.

The *Frente Amplio*—a "coalition party" that had governed with a majority in parliament for the past three terms (2005–2020)—voted well below its expectations in the first round, losing almost nine percentage points (around 180,000 votes) with respect to the results obtained in the first round of 2014. It cost the party two senators and eight representatives. The loss of voters was greater outside Montevideo, in the interior of the country, and especially in the urban interior, where support for the *Frente Amplio* had been decisive in its 2014 victory (Caetano and Selios, 2015). This key drop in support had to do with many factors: a presidential formula that was too Montevideo-centric,[25] the lack of concrete proposed solutions for the situation of economic stagnation that impacted greatly on small- and medium-sized agricultural producers, and the importance that the population of the interior placed on the issue of insecurity (the proposed amendment received a significant percentage of votes throughout the interior, especially in the departments bordering with Brazil), among others.

Contrary to what some analysts had predicted, the issue of security "effectively moved the needle" on electoral competition, and it did so regardless of the positions adopted by the various leaders. As noted, the "*Vivir sin miedo*" reform, while not obtaining enough votes to be passed, was supported by almost 47% of Uruguayans without having been endorsed by most major leaders.[26] None of the presidential candidates backed the initiative, not even the leader of *Cabildo Abierto*, Guido Manini Ríos. However, studies conducted on the subject agree that there was a strong correlation between *Blanco*, *Colorado*, and *Cabildo Abierto* votes and the overwhelming support for the reform within the electoral base of these parties. In contrast, support for the initiative among *Frente Amplio* voters was very low (only around 10%). This means that the security factor was a decisive catalyst that played in favour of the opposition, particularly in the interior of the country (*La Diaria*, October 28, 2019: p. 4). Moreover, despite Uruguay's stability—unique in comparison to the other countries in the region—the lack of synchronicity between economic and political times also had an impact on the vote in the interior of the country. Although it was obvious that the interior was crucial for the *Frente Amplio*'s victory, its electoral strategy failed to take that importance sufficiently into account.

The leading challenger to the *Frente Amplio*, the National Party and its presidential candidate Luis Lacalle Pou, did not have a great election, falling by more than one percentage point compared to 2014, but it did successfully consolidate its candidate's electoral strategy. From the start, Lacalle Pou maintained that the National Party had to lead a "multicoloured coalition", which over the course of the campaign even incorporated *Cabildo Abierto* and the *Partido de la Gente*, along with its traditional counterparts, the *Colorado* and Independent Parties. In electoral terms it was without a doubt a winning strategy. However, effectively forming a cohesive government that does not lean heavily to the right, based on a strategy that prioritised beating the *Frente Amplio* in the November 24 runoff, as well as obtaining parliamentary majorities without having to reach agreements with it, constitutes a risky gamble. The governing coalition's acceptance of a party such as *Cabildo Abierto*, with extremist and hard-line right-wing views, has been naturalised. In the National Party there was at no time even a hint of reluctance in this regard. The warnings voiced during the campaign by *Colorado* presidential candidate Ernesto Talvi (who said, "a distance as wide as an ocean separates me from *Cabildo Abierto*") or Independent Party leader Pablo Mieres (who even went so far as to declare that he would not be part of an alliance that included *Cabildo Abierto*) were quickly brushed aside in the face of the "reality" of the results. As is well known, in several European countries, the right, the centre-right, and the centre have for decades maintained an unspoken pact (a "cordon sanitaire") with the centre-left and the left, whereby they all refuse to cooperate with the far right. In a democratically ruled Uruguay, the naturalisation of such a risky step has occurred with surprising speed and without any conditions.

The *Cabildo Abierto* factor and its leader Guido Manini Ríos

In terms of the novel developments of these elections, the most significant is that for the first time ever a completely new party, born in February of the electoral year, which absorbed the hard-line right of the traditional parties, as well as the "military family" and various anti-*Frente Amplio* reaction groups, obtained very successful results. The studies conducted thus far indicate that *Cabildo Abierto* voters (almost 11%, with just over 260,000 votes, and only 0.5% behind the traditional *Colorado* Party) included popular sectors that had previously voted for former president José Mujica, of the *Frente Amplio*, drawn by his populist appeal. Moreover, in this case, as in other experiences in Latin America and Europe, the advancement of the "charismatic leadership" of Manini Ríos accompanied the promise of a "regressive Arcadia": the return of authority and order in the face of insecurity; "normality" in the relationship between the genders, distorted by what the authorities of the new party have called "gender ideology"; an end to economic and social "*relajo*" (the "anything goes") and the "*recreo para el malandraje*" (or "playtime for hoodlums"); the affirmation of honesty over corruption; the vindication of the armed forces as an essential actor that has been under attack; the defence of a strong nationalism against the "pawns of the empires"; etc.[27]

With this deliberate and emphasised discourse, in its first electoral experience, *Cabildo Abierto* has been perhaps the most successful party in the campaign. An examination of the initial vote count of the October election shows that its growth coincides with the drop in *Frente Amplio* voters, but also with that of the two traditional parties, which saw a reduction in the number of their voters in comparison to the first round of 2014: the National Party lost more than 30,000 votes (which cost it two representatives), while the *Colorado* Party obtained practically the same number of votes as five years earlier (3,600 less, but maintaining the same parliamentary representation). From a historical perspective, both parties have failed to recover their traditional convening power, and that is particularly true for the *Colorado* Party.

For many reasons, the two traditional parties should view the successful phenomenon of *Cabildo Abierto* and Manini Ríos with concern. However, they have failed to do so, among other things, because their obsession and their maximum objective have been focused on removing the *Frente Amplio* from the government, and to do achieve that, as the very close outcome of the runoff of the November 24 election confirmed, they needed everyone in the opposition, and especially the votes of the far right.[28] As has also been noted, they need the support of *Cabildo Abierto* legislators to secure parliamentary majorities for the "Multicoloured Coalition". This, as will be seen below, is one of the most significant questions for the coming years.[29]

But what are some of the central issues at the origin of this new party? *Cabildo Abierto* was not born by spontaneous generation. As noted, it was formally created in February 2019 and its official founder, Guillermo Domenech, had until recently served as a government officer for nearly three decades.[30] The presidential candidate of the new party, as also noted, had, curiously enough, served as army commander-in-chief under two *Frente Amplio* governments, from February 2015 to March 2019, chosen by Defence Minister Eleuterio Fernández Huidobro, who had been one of the top Tupamaro leaders, no less. Why did Fernández Huidobro continue as minister of defence after José Mujica ended his term in 2015 and Tabaré Vázquez took office, when their political situation in no way seemed to merit such continuity? His political group *Corriente de Acción y Pensamiento-Libertad* (Current of Action and Thought-Liberty, or CAP-L) had practically disappeared, and what was left of it did very poorly in the 2014 elections. He clashed harshly with the human rights organisations and was strongly resisted by most of the other *Frente Amplio* sectors. Who then wanted him in that position and who continued supporting him until his death?[31]

The main legacy of Fernández Huidobro's military policy has been, precisely, Guido Manini Ríos, who in his almost five years as commander-in-chief breached constitutional and institutional norms, repeatedly voicing opinions of a political nature for which he was only recently disciplined.[32] It was also that outspoken behaviour—so unprecedented for an officer of his rank—that made him the first military leader after the end of the dictatorship. These excesses were repeatedly condoned, until President Vázquez finally removed him in March 2019, following Manini's scathing criticism of the judiciary and his obstruction of the remittance to civilian courts of a confession delivered before a military "court of honour" by a former officer who had been a notorious torturer during the dictatorship.[33]

When in March 2019, Manini Ríos left the army, he could not have done it at a better time, victimised as he was as the corporative caudillo of an institution that not only had failed to undergo a process of democratisation over the decades following the dictatorship—with the exception of the years under the first government of Tabaré Vázquez[34]—but was becoming more and more convinced as a collective body that it has been wronged, in particular, but not only, during the *Frente Amplio* governments.[35] As noted, Manini Ríos responded to his dismissal with a harsh public statement against the government, conveyed through the command's official channels, adopting an unprecedented aggressive attitude, for which he was not penalised. Within a few days, he was publicly announcing that he would be running for president as candidate of the newly formed *Cabildo Abierto* party.

From this overview of his first incursion into party politics, it would appear that Manini Ríos has executed a perfect play. It would be by no means far-fetched to speculate that in that feat he had (direct or indirect) collaborators, and that no move responded to an unforeseen coincidence. Once he had accepted the *Cabildo Abierto* presidential candidacy, Manini Ríos acted in line with other contemporary far-right players—although not as loudly as Jair Bolsonaro in Brazil or Vox leaders in Spain—not concerning himself much with moderating his most controversial aspects. In his campaign speeches he did not conceal many of his most extremist ideas, although he refused to acknowledge where he stood ideologically in the left–right spectrum. He did admit, however, that he certainly could not be considered a "centrist" regarding any issue. Neither did he attempt to hide that the people who accompanied him in his bid for president included individuals, such as Eduardo Radaelli or Antonio Romanelli, among others,[36] who had been denounced for their involvement in state terrorism practices. He was also perfectly candid about his views on the civilian-military dictatorship, which could be described as complacent at best. Nor did he hide that among the *Cabildo Abierto* candidates for parliament there were many former members of the *Juventud Uruguaya de Pie* (Standing Uruguayan Youth, or JUP), a far-right youth organisation active in the early 1970s that was accused of having ties to paramilitary groups.[37]

During the campaign, both his figure and his party attracted young naziphile extremists like magnets. These incorporations were denounced in the press. When asked about his past, in various interviews over the course of the election campaign, Manini Ríos has proudly recalled how he decided to follow his military vocation in the year 1972,[38] but has glossed over the dictatorship years, jumping forward in his recollections to the transition to democracy. To be fair, not many have asked him about what he and many of his friends and supporters were doing between 1973 and 1985. In the few occasions he has been asked, he has generally avoided giving a clear answer or has replied in a surprisingly formal way.[39] Both before and after the elections, several members of *Cabildo Abierto*, for their part, have not held back, publicly voicing their opinions on other matters—some already as acting legislators—prompting several scandals and debates.[40]

It should be noted that the appointment of Manini Ríos as army commander-in-chief in 2015 by then Defence Minister Fernández Huidobro can only be explained through the logic of the classic conception of the "meeting of combatants", that strange bond that brought together—and perhaps still does—the MLN and the most staunchly nationalist and hard-line military officers of the dictatorship, many of them members of the *Tenientes de Artigas* Lodge. The military caudillo Guido Manini Ríos—bearer of a last name with great significance in the history of Uruguay's right[41]—who grew rapidly as a successful political leader, was, in short, the product of a mistaken and extremely dangerous military policy implemented throughout much of the José Mujica administration and part of Tabaré Vázquez's second term. It was there that his political build-up began, and it continued until his consolidation as a political player in the electoral arena in October 2019.

The followers of the *Cabildo Abierto* leader have been drawn to him because he has many characteristics that are attractive to far-right positions. While he supports the market economy in very general terms, he is far from being a classic liberal in economics. He is a Catholic with quite orthodox views that exhibit a social sensitivity and popular appeal, with an inexcusable military reference. He is strongly against what he calls "gender ideology", as well as other issues on the new rights agenda. He is a "neo-patriot" of the times, questioning globalisation, invoking vague anti-imperialist slogans, and even speaking of oligarchy.[42] All these stances are very typical of some of the far-right proposals born among the higher ranks of Latin America's armed forces in recent years. This raises some important questions. Is this whole new phenomenon, which has decisive implications for the current situation, this new party that holds the key to secure parliamentary majorities and determine part of the direction of the Multicoloured Coalition government that triumphed in the 2019 elections, so predictable looking forward? Does it give guarantees in terms of regime agreement? Is it even minimally prudent to "naturalise" the incorporation of such an actor into a government that presents itself as the alternative to the *Frente Amplio* progressivism?

Colorado candidate Ernesto Talvi had said that an "ocean" separated him from *Cabildo Abierto* and its candidate, but after the election he amended his position saying that one needed to accept "reality". And what "reality" is that, exactly? That a *Blanco* and *Colorado* coalition government that also includes *Cabildo Abierto* is an alternative that veers clearly to the right and that is going to have to negotiate very controversial positions on sensitive issues. This cannot be ignored by Lacalle Pou or Talvi or anyone else. In the programme he presented in the National Party's primaries, under his sector "*Todos*" ("Everyone"), Lacalle Pou projected a centrist image.[43] But later, in the national campaign and in his strategy, he shifted towards a position more in line with liberal conservatism, the traditional ideology of the Herrerismo.

It has been held—and rightly so—that all parties and positions have the right to submit to the will of the sovereign. *Cabildo Abierto* and its leader Manini Ríos gained their power legitimately, as it responds to the will of the people. But their positions on various issues, their refusal to condemn the civilian-military dictatorship, and their demonstrated resistance to accept truth and justice in the face of the consequences of state terrorism, as well as many of the individuals in their ranks and many of their actions that barely respect the current legal framework, all of these pose, without a doubt, an undeniable risk, and position them clearly within the far right, especially with respect to Uruguay's traditional standards, as outlined above. The video Manini Ríos posted calling on the troops to vote for him and attacking the *Frente Amplio*, which coincided with serious statements issued by the Military Centre in a harshly offensive tone, and other similar episodes, in the days leading up to the November 24 runoff election, have reaffirmed the doubts and fears raised by this new actor.[44] Likewise, their requests to be appointed to certain areas and positions in the new government (the ministries of public health and housing and other positions in agencies that are clearly connected with social issues, in addition to the post of undersecretary of defence) also prompt various speculations.

As for voters of *Cabildo Abierto*, the issue merits a more in-depth study and more thorough and nuanced considerations. It is very plausible that, as pointed out above, a considerable number of people from popular sectors can be identified among *Cabildo Abierto* voters, including former voters of Mujica. These voters see in Manini a charismatic leader who gives them answers, especially on pressing security issues. But these voters are also suggesting that Uruguay, perhaps more gradually than other countries in Latin America and Europe, is experiencing in its society a shift towards views that are more critical of how democracy functions and of political parties, while, at the same time, the prestige of the armed forces is rising and a general move towards more right-wing positions appears to be confirmed, as well as an erosion of the traditional distrust of militaristic and far-right positions. That new sensibility is expressed, in part, precisely by *Cabildo Abierto*, as a true "black swan" (Caetano et al., 2019).

Some clues for a future with uncertainties

Despite its old "island vocation", fed both from within and from outside the country, Uruguay is not an island in the political and ideological context of the continent. In many aspects, it still stands out as unique in Latin America, as many international media outlets have highlighted in the weeks surrounding the elections (Colombo, 2019). However, that traditional matrix of conservative liberalism—in which the right, even with certain ambiguities, accepts a regime agreement with respect to democracy—could be challenged in the coming years more than may be expected. That recent temptation that seems to permeate many classic right-wing sectors to lean towards or flirt with these more contemporary far-right views may also be a possible path in Uruguay's future.

With the de facto power provided by its direct connections and channels of communication with the army as an institution, with enhanced appeals and complicities among several sectors of the Uruguayan electorate, with a rather loose view with respect to its integration in the alternative government coalition, and with a new type of leader, who is intelligent, cunning, and with a clear sense of strategy,[45] *Cabildo Abierto* may constitute a different inflection in the long history of Uruguayan right. The expectation that it will gradually "dissolve" within the government coalition does not seem so clear-cut. Although, as noted, the party leadership of a military caudillo is not unheard of in Uruguayan politics and although many of his actions and ideas draw on historical experiences—such as Nardone's ruralism, the more right-wing *Herrerismo*, or the *Pachequismo* of the followers of Jorge Pacheco Areco—it is perhaps the regional and historical context in which it emerges that gives the *Cabildo Abierto* phenomenon its novelty and disruptive potential.

In any case, if *Blancos* and *Colorados* (who with the emergence of this new actor have undoubtedly lost part of their traditional right-wing sectors) do not realise that their hold on Uruguayan society is still being put to the test, certain hypotheses of conflict cannot be simply discarded. If after the long-awaited victory, the traditional parties take the shortcut of accepting anything from the far right as long as they defeat the *Frente Amplio* ("with the *Frente Amplio* nothing" but with the far right "everything is tolerable"), situations such as the deepening of a "crack" in Uruguay in the manner of Argentina or scenarios of institutional instability with military involvement are indeed hypotheses that cannot be ruled out a priori. That kind of strategy may be effective for winning elections in the short term, but in the long run it can complicate any government. Much more so if in the perspective of the two great blocs in Uruguayan politics prevails a "democratic confusion", and, at the same time, the embracing of this Uruguayan far right—which is as new as it is traditional—by *Blancos* and *Colorados* is ultimately naturalised.

Notes

1 There is currently a vast literature on the subject of the political right in the world and in Latin America. Examining or even listing such works exceeds the scope of this text.

Because of its close bearing on the topic discussed here, I will only mention the recent compilation by Bohoslavsky, Motta, and Boisard (2019).
2 See, for example, *Freedom House* (http://www.freedomhouse.org/), *Polity Project* (http://www.systemicpeace.org/polity/polity4.htm), *Latinobarómetro Corporation* (http://www.latinobarometro.org/), and the *World Bank Worldwide Governance Indicators* (https://info.worldbank.org/governance/wgi/Home/Reports).
3 For a more thorough analysis, the official source at https://www.corteelectoral.gub.uy/ provides the complete and disaggregated results of the elections. For a recent biography of the president of Uruguay as of March 1, 2020, see Leonís (2019).
4 Because of its recent creation and political characteristics, conceptualising *Cabildo Abierto* as a full-fledged political party is highly debatable. It would be more accurate to describe it loosely as a political movement. Having said this, however, and for the sake of readability and to allow for comparisons with other similar national and foreign actors, the term "party" will be used here to refer to it.
5 As will be seen below, the new distribution of seats in the Uruguayan parliament does not give a majority to any one party. The country has a bicameral parliamentary system, with a senate composed of 30 members plus the vice president (who presides over it and the general assembly, which combines both chambers) and a house of representatives made up of 99 members. The distribution of seats for the legislature that began on February 15, 2020, is as follows: 13 senators and 42 representatives for the *Frente Amplio*; 10 senators and 30 representatives for the National Party; 4 senators and 13 representatives for the *Colorado* Party; 3 senators and 11 representatives for *Cabildo Abierto*; 1 representative for the *Partido de la Gente* (People's Party); 1 representative for the *Partido Independiente* (Independent Party); and 1 representative for the *Partido Ecologista Radical Intransigente* (Radical Intransigent Green Party). With the exception of this last party, the other five parties that competed against the *Frente Amplio* in the last elections formed the Coalition Multicolor.
6 A distinction is in order here between the period spanning from 1968 to 1973 (with the government of Jorge Pacheco Areco and the partial term served by Juan María Bordaberry as constitutional president) and the civilian-military dictatorship that ruled from 1973 to 1985. Although in the first period, the seeds of the coup d'état were sown and there were already far-right elements in the two administrations, including some early instances of state terrorism, the hegemony of the civilian-military far-right is only fully consolidated after the 1973 coup carried out in two stages. For a more in-depth analysis, see Caetano (2019a).
7 The term *first Batllismo* refers to the political movement founded by José Batlle y Ordóñez within the *Colorado* Party towards the end of the nineteenth century. Born on May 21, 1856, the son of Lorenzo Batlle, who served as president from 1868 to 1872, Batlle y Ordóñez first studied philosophy and journalism. In the philosophy section of the Athenaeum he developed his rationalist-spiritualist ideas and his understanding of Krausism, which he approached through the works of Heinrich Ahrens. At a young age he ventured into journalism (writing for newspapers such as *La Razón*, *La Lucha*, and *El Espíritu Nuevo*), a vocation that he would pursue throughout his life. His early political life saw him fiercely opposing the Lorenzo Latorre and Máximo Santos dictatorships. In 1886, he founded the newspaper *El Día* and fought alongside his father and brother in the *Quebracho* Revolution, before being captured by enemy forces. He backed the civilian transition headed by Máximo Tajes, who in 1887 appointed him to the position of political chief of the department of Minas. He then supported President Julio Herrera y Obes (1890–1894), with whom he would later clash strongly. He went on to lead an initiative aimed at creating a new popular and renovating sector within the *Colorado* Party. Through this effort, he developed an innovative form of political action, which involved establishing sectional clubs and selling cheaper and more accessible newspapers to reach the general public. He was elected to the House of Representatives for the department of Salto in 1890, to the national State Council that followed the anti-collectivist coup of Lindolfo Cuestas in 1898, and to the Senate for

Montevideo in 1899. Over the course of that decade, he forged an increasingly influential and controversial leadership that would take him—not without arduous political negotiations within and outside his party—to the presidency in March 1903. He served two terms as president (1903–1907 and 1911–1915) and was twice president of the National Administration Council (in 1921 and 1927) that governed the country. He died on October 20, 1929.
8 These "fellow travellers" included Emilio Frugoni's followers in the Socialist Party, many anarchists, feminists, freemasons, and liberal leaders, among others.
9 In a historical perspective, the most significant player that exercised a sort of "captainship of popular organisations" was the labour movement—especially as of the first half of the 1960s with the labour unification process. The social arm of the right has, in turn, been represented by the business chambers, which have at times constructed a unifying institutionalisation, from the *Comité de Vigilancia Económica* (Economic Monitoring Committee) in 1929–1933 to the current *Confederación Empresarial* (Business Confederation), among other examples.
10 Martín C. Martínez had an extensive career in public affairs and was a major figure in university life. He was an active member of the Constitutional Party until its dissolution and went on to join the National Party. In addition to being elected to both chambers and serving for long periods, he was twice Minister of Finance, a constituent, a member of the *Consejo Nacional de Administración* (National Administration Council), also in two opportunities, an associate justice of the Supreme Court, a member of the Board of Directors of the *Banco República*, and a national representative in diplomatic missions, among other government and state positions.
11 As a jurist, an entrepreneur with multiple business interests, the undisputed and long-standing leader of cattle-raising landowners, gathered since 1915 in the combatant *Federación Rural* (Rural Federation), of which he was a founding member and honorary president, and as the main "organic intellectual" of the ruling classes and their star speaker (penning the most important "crown speeches", as the opening addresses of the conferences of the *Federación Rural* were dubbed), José Irureta Goyena did not need to be a political leader, neither *Blanco* nor *Colorado*, to command the position of main conservative ideologue for more than half a century. It should also be noted that he was a Catholic and the author of the 1934 Criminal Code, which decriminalised abortion, if only for a brief period (the only time in the history of the country that abortion was legal until the recent law passed in 2012).
12 While over the course of his especially long political life, Luis Alberto de Herrera certainly evolved, he tended to challenge, without hesitation and in every scenario, any proposals coming from *Batllismo*. Moreover, he liked to boast that he combined the triple condition of "tolerant sceptic" when it came to religious matters, "conservative" with respect to social issues, and "calm liberal" in politics. His well-known connections with French politics and academia notwithstanding, as a politician and prominent intellectual, Herrera never concealed his ideological preference for the Anglo-Saxon school and in particular for Edmund Burke, of whom he considered himself a true disciple in the sphere of political and social ideas. On the subject of moral and citizen issues in general, he always defined himself as "liberal conservative", but at the same time a self-proclaimed irreconcilable enemy of what he termed "de-Christianizing Jacobinism".
13 The debate regarding the interpretation of the French Revolution and its impacts in Latin America was a subject in which the main proponents of liberal conservatism of the early 1900s converged. The concerns of Martín C. Martínez and José Irureta Goyena were shared, for example, by Luis Alberto de Herrera, whose most important book on political theory dealt precisely with the French Revolution and South America. This was a major work in terms of doctrine, and it was first published in Paris by the Paul Dupont publishing house in 1910. This inaugural text by Herrera established the historical foundation of his political and social ideas in an "anti-Jacobin" view of the revolution, which he used as a premise to caution against what he considered to be dangerous advances of a radical "republicanism", with strong and "dangerous" moral

implications. He referred in this way to the crux of what, in his opinion, also divided the waters in the main political and ideological dispute. For a recent and erudite study on this last subject, see Reali (2016).
14 There is a vast literature on the controversial concept of populism. The limits and scope of this text preclude an in-depth discussion of the term, so I have opted for an operational definition, in which populism as an analytical category does not identify an ideological orientation or a certain approach in public policies, but a way of doing politics that exhibits the features described in this text (among others). In this sense, while some brief 'populist moments' can be identified in Uruguay's political history, in my opinion, no such regime has ever been truly and lastingly implemented in the country.
15 This was the name of an organisation founded that year by a group of young civilians with clear far-right tendencies, who wished to receive military training in army facilities. This organisation was guided by Colonel Ulises Monegal (head of Infantry Battalion No. 4) and was denounced repeatedly by *Batllismo* politicians and left-wing parties as an "embryo of local fascism".
16 After the famous "*Cerrillada*" episode in March 1927, uncertainty regarding the final outcome of the November 1926 election prompted murmurings of military intervention and talk of a possible coup grew insistently. The rumours that circulated involved Pedro Manini Ríos, a leader of the *Riverista* sector of the *Colorado* Party. In 1927, in a personal letter to National Party leader Luis Alberto de Herrera, Jorge Ponce de León noted in this regard: "the *Riverista* sector that responds to Don Pedro [Manini Ríos] seems to be conversing in quite friendly terms with certain military officers [...] with what some say are not very reassuring intentions. Dr. Manini is said to be a great admirer of Primo de Rivera, and it is also said that he considers himself quite apt to second him in this Republic'. (Letter from Jorge Ponce de León to Herrera, dated October 18th, 1927, Museo Histórico Nacional, Archivo Dr. Luis Alberto de Herrera, vol. 26, folder 3644, doc. 52). That same year, Carlos María Morales also wrote to Herrera saying '*Riverismo* [takes every opportunity] to insist loudly with its eternal rant against the collegiate body. [...] There are those who are certain there will be a coup d'état before December 31" (Letter from Carlos María Morales to Luis Alberto de Herrera dated October 1927, op. cit. vol. 26, folder 3644, doc. 60).
17 Benito Nardone (1906–1964) was the son of Italian immigrants, born in Montevideo and originally a supporter of *Batllismo*, who later answered the call of the Bordaberry family to engage in rural activism. He became a journalist, working for *Radio Rural*, and founded the *Liga Federal de Acción Ruralista* in 1951, an association that represented rural business interests and that would go on to join forces with the National Party in the 1958 elections. In these political and radio activities, he presented himself as "*Chicotazo*", a charismatic character he had created, who spoke in a distinctly rural colloquial language. He was president of the *Consejo Nacional de Gobierno* (National Council of Government) in 1960 and 1961. Much later, through the confessions of former CIA agent Philip Agee, it was revealed that in the late 1950s he had been recruited as an "operator" by the CIA. His activities and that of his organisation during the 1950s clearly exhibited several of the new characteristics that were beginning to emerge in the Uruguayan right.
18 After insistently denying that he would ever participate in party politics, Nardone finally accepted Luis Alberto de Herrera's invitation to join the National Party ticket, which in the lead-up to the November 1958 elections also succeeded in bringing back into the party an independent group (the "*nacionalismo independiente*") that had broken away from the party with the 1933 coup.
19 The emblematic phrase of the first *Batllismo* is drawn from a fragment of a letter that Batlle y Ordóñez sent Domingo Arena, in which he explained that he was imagining a "model country", in which "the poor were less poor and the rich less rich". Végh Villegas knew very well what he was talking about, as he had been part of a circle of economists within the sector of the *Colorado* Party headed by Luis Batlle Berres (the "*Lista 15*"), also a former president of Uruguay (1947–1951).

20 As noted earlier in the text, this does not mean that the right-wing sectors of the two traditional parties, or the ruralist movement led by Nardone did not enlist far-right leaders and even organisations with fascist sympathies and even military inspiration. Most notably, in this sense, was the presidential bid in the 1971 elections within the National Party ticket of General Oscar Mario Aguerrondo (1910–1977). Aguerrondo had founded the *Tenientes de Artigas* (Lieutenants of Artigas) Lodge on August 25, 1964, and headed a military coupist faction within the armed forces in the 1960s (clashing with the leader of the constitutionalist faction, General Liber Seregni, founder of the *Frente Amplio* in 1971 and its first president). He played a major role as a guide in the 1973 coup d'état and the subsequent dictatorship. As the right-wing candidate of the National Party in the 1971 elections, he lost spectacularly within the party to another presidential candidate, Wilson Ferreira Aldunate, who received double the votes. The following year, he announced his retirement from party politics and went on to preside over the Military Centre until his death. He too failed to impose pro-fascist and militaristic far-right views via the electoral path and was later recognised by the majority of the coup generals as a true mentor of the coup and the dictatorship. This analysis should not be understood as necessarily contradicting the hypothesis of a democratic path to the dictatorship put forward by scholars such as Álvaro Rico and Mariana Iglesias. However, I insist that the hegemony of the radical far right was only secured through the coup d'état.

21 As of the writing of this text, the primary election (June 30, 2019), the parliamentary election and first presidential round (October 27, 2019), and the second presidential round or runoff (November 24, 2019) had all been held. The departmental and municipal elections, which will complete the electoral cycle, are scheduled to take place on May 10, 2020.

22 The presidential nomination of Uruguayan businessman Juan Sartori (b. 1981) within the National Party has been one of the biggest surprises of this electoral process. Unknown by the vast majority of Uruguayans until 2019, Sartori had never shown any political inclination or even voted before, and he displayed an obvious lack of knowledge of the reality of both the country and the party he joined. Very early in the electoral cycle, he began deploying a massive campaign in the media, pouring enormous funds into it and breaching electoral laws that establish start and end times for campaigns. In the June 30 primary election, he came in second, beating traditional leader Jorge Larrañaga. The reasons for his decision to run for president remain a mystery to most political leaders and analysts.

23 Edgardo Novick (b. 1956), one of Uruguay's most important businessmen, had ran for mayor of Montevideo in 2014, when the *Colorado* and *Blanco* (or National) Parties had joined forces with a number of independent citizens in an attempt to defeat the ruling *Frente Amplio* party and secure the government of the capital. In the May 10, 2015, elections, he was not only the most voted candidate in his party, but also the second most voted candidate in general, after the winning candidate, Daniel Martinez (*Frente Amplio*). After such a positive outcome, he continued in politics and went on to form the *Partido de la Gente* on November 7, 2016. Since then, he invested heavily in political publicity campaigns and has received the backing of *Blanco* and *Colorado* legislators and certain recognised political figures. A known admirer of Jair Bolsonaro, whose electoral triumph he celebrated, he had been emerging as a far-right populist candidate but fizzled out politically in 2019. In the October 27 parliamentary elections his party was only able to secure one seat in the lower chamber.

24 General Guido Manini Ríos (1958) served as commander-in-chief of the army from February 1, 2015 until March 12, 2019, the date on which he was removed by President Tabaré Vázquez for making serious public statements against the judiciary. He had been appointed by suggestion of Defence Minister Eleuterio Fernández Huidobro in the final days of the José Mujica government. Manini Ríos comes from a family of politicians with a clear right-wing political background and during his time as commander-in-chief he made numerous controversial statements on political and military issues

(including the actions of the army during the dictatorship, his opposition to the law that amended the military pension and retirement scheme, and his rejection of human rights groups and organisations of relatives of the detained disappeared). Throughout it all, he was supported by the defence minister, former Tupamaro leader Fernández Huidobro, with whom he had forged a friendship. In September 2018, he was placed under rigorous arrest for a period of 30 days for his harsh critical statements against the official bill for the amendment of the military pension fund.

25 The *Frente Amplio* formula was formed by Daniel Martínez, former mayor of Montevideo, as the presidential candidate, and Graciela Villar, former head of the legislative body of the department of Montevideo, as vice presidential candidate.

26 This proposed constitutional amendment, initially furthered only by National Party senator Jorge Larrañaga (who came in third in his party's primary election) included the following measures: the creation of a National Guard of up to 2,000 soldiers, to support domestic law enforcement efforts; the obligation to complete jail sentences (prohibition of early release for certain serious crimes); reviewable life sentences for very serious crimes; and night raids by court order (Uruguay's Constitution only allows day raids, even with a court order).

27 Immediately after he was terminated as commander-in-chief, Manini took to the command's official channel to deliver a message to the army. Dressed in military fatigues and speaking in a very aggressive tone, he lashed out against 'the falsehoods of bureaucrats incapable of seeing reality, blinded by their arrogance, or trapped in their ideological prejudices, and the actions of those who profit from confrontation, turning into well-paid pawns of the centres of world power, always ready to act out a perverse script that leads to the destruction of our institutions and leaves Uruguayans in the most absolute state of helplessness' (Montevideo Portal, March 13, 2019).

28 The difference was just 37,402 votes, 1.5% of the total votes cast, with 48.8% for the Lacalle-Argimón winning formula and 47.3% for the Martínez-Villar formula.

29 The statements and complications arising during the initial appointment process for the new government's cabinet in November and December 2019 clearly point in that direction.

30 Guillermo Domenech (b. 1950) is a lawyer and notary public who held the position of official notary of the state from 1990 to 2019, spanning several governments. He was a member of the National Party, in the *Herrerismo* sector, until he founded *Cabildo Abierto*. He was chosen by Manini Ríos as his running mate and his campaign was characterised by his attacks against "gender ideology" (famously saying, "Next thing you know they will be imposing a law making homosexuality compulsory") and his claim that God has guided party politics to Manini Ríos as a "reincarnated Artigas".

31 Eleuterio Fernández Huidobro (1942–2016) was one of the top leaders of the *Movimiento de Liberación Nacional-Tupamaros* (National Liberation Movement-Tupamaros, or MLN-T), a guerrilla group that was active during the 1960s and 1970s. He was imprisoned a year before the coup and held by the dictatorship as one of the Tupamaro hostages, under inhumane prison conditions and subjected to horrific torture. Following the dictatorship, he was elected senator under the *Movimiento de Participación Popular* (Popular Participation Movement, or MPP) ticket for two periods, and again for a third period under the CAP-L ticket. After resigning from his seat as senator in May 2011, over differences with a bill presented by the *Frente Amplio* that sought to annul three articles of the Expiry Law, he was appointed *Frente Amplio* defence minister in July of that same year. Although his actions as minister caused much controversy within the *Frente Amplio*, he was confirmed in that position by Tabaré Vázquez when he took office as president in 2015. On many occasions, it became obvious that he had the support of a significant part of the officers of the armed forces, who even came to consider him 'the best defence minister' since the transition to democracy. He died in office on August 5, 2016, and the wake was held at the Defence Ministry headquarters, where the main speaker was, precisely, Guido Manini Ríos, the commander-in-chief who had been appointed at his suggestion in February 2015.

32 During the almost five years that he served as commander-in-chief, Manini Ríos was involved in numerous incidents that caused a strong political impact. He used social media continuously to issue messages that criticised the government's human rights policy and the trials against military officers accused of state terrorism practices during the dictatorship. He delivered speeches haranguing his troops with a clear political tone. In the performance of his duties, he regularly flaunted the strict rules of secularism he was expected to abide by. He harshly confronted the organisations of relatives of the disappeared, who repeatedly accused him of obstructing the search for remains, and he clashed publicly with other government ministers and legislators in his defence of the demands posed by the army, in particular regarding the changes made to the military pension and retirement scheme, among other issues.

33 The final reason for his termination was a document he sent the president making serious accusations against the judiciary and how it handled the trials against former military personnel accused of state terrorism, compounded by his delay in submitting to the courts the record of a confession by José Gavazzo (a notorious agent of repression who was serving a sentence under house arrest for his crimes during the dictatorship), heard by a court of honour formed by generals. The Prosecutor's Office later brought a criminal action against Manini Ríos for his failure to refer that information to civilian courts. That action is currently pending. After he was elected senator in 2019, Manini Ríos announced that he would not hide behind his parliamentary privileges and would answer to justice. He has also accused the prosecutors of acting against him "mandated by political powers".

34 Between 2005 and 2010, the defence ministers under the first Vázquez administration, Azucena Berrutti, Gonzalo Fernández, and José Bayardi, implemented a policy that has been described as "democratising" by various analysts and actors. This policy was discontinued under the Mujica administration, whose defence ministers were Luis Rosadilla and Eleuterio Fernández Huidobro.

35 Although relations were less conflictive than during the *Frente Amplio* governments, there were also particularly tense moments during the first and second administrations of Julio María Sanguinetti (1985–1990 and 1995–2000), during the government of Luis A. Lacalle Herrera (1990–1995), and during the Jorge Batlle administration (2000–2005). The two presidencies of Tabaré Vázquez (2005–2010 and 2015–2020) were more conflictive than that of José Mujica (2010–2015), and this is largely explained by what is noted above regarding the connections between Tupamaro leaders and members of the *Tenientes de Artigas* Lodge.

36 Eduardo Radaelli was one of the Uruguayan military officers prosecuted and convicted in Chile for the kidnapping and disappearance of the chemist Eugenio Berríos in 1991. Berríos had served in the repressive services of Augusto Pinochet and escaped from Chile to Uruguay in 1991. His remains were later found buried in a Uruguayan beach in 1995. Antonio Romanelli, who served as a custodian at the Libertad Prison during the dictatorship and is today one of *Cabildo Abierto*'s leading men on security issues, has been denounced by several dozen former political prisoners who accuse him of torture, abuse, and anti-Semitism.

37 One of Guido Manini Ríos's older brothers, Hugo, was one of the main founders of the JUP in 1970. See Bucheli (2019).

38 Besides being the year before the dictatorship, 1972 was the moment of greatest military confrontation between the MLN-T and the armed forces. In November of that year, the latter announced the military defeat of the *Tupamaros*.

39 In September 2019, after the court action had been brought against him, Manini Ríos responded to a question from a journalist who asked him how he would define a military man who kills a person and buries them in military grounds, by saying simply, "He erred". When asked to elaborate, the retired general and candidate said that those were events that occurred "half a century ago and in which there were many who erred. We cannot go on picking at a scab day in and day out".

40 To avoid such situations in the future, Manini Ríos has provided *Cabildo Abierto* legislators with a good conduct "manual" or "guide" that they are to follow in their public activity.
41 As noted earlier, Pedro Manini Ríos, Guido's grandfather, was a very prominent *Colorado* politician who broke with President José Batlle y Ordóñez in 1913, proclaiming, "we are *Colorados*, not socialists". He served as legislator and minister and was for decades the leader of the *Colorado* Party's right-wing sector, known as "*Riverismo*", with strong ties to anti-*Batllista* generals. Guido's father and uncle, Alberto and Carlos Manini Ríos, respectively, also had prominent political careers. The newspaper *La Mañana*—founded in 1917 by Pedro Manini Ríos, among others, and reappearing in 2019 after going out of circulation in the late 1990s—has been and currently is the traditional media outlet of the Manini Ríos family.
42 On several occasions Manini Ríos has defined himself as an admirer of the work of Alberto Methol Ferré. With respect to his geopolitical perspective, the only trip he made abroad during his campaign was to Brasilia, where, among other activities, he met with retired general Hamilton Mourão, Bolsonaro's running mate and then vice president of Brazil.
43 See the campaign programme "*Lo que nos une*" at https://lacallepou.uy/descargas/programa-de-gobierno.pdf.
44 Just minutes before the ban on political campaigning began, Manini Ríos issued a message to personnel telling them not to vote for the *Frente Amplio*: "The same people", he said, "that have questioned the very need for the existence of the armed forces, which only a year ago passed a pension law that primarily affected the lower ranks and this year an organic law that ignores the characteristics of the role of the military, who have not tired of insulting the men in uniform and went as far as disparagingly calling them 'meat with eyes,' those same people are today asking for your vote. They are ultimately, once again, mocking the men who wear the uniform of our fatherland. To them, we soldiers now say, 'we know who you are'". This message came out simultaneously with the publication of an editorial piece in *Nación*, the official magazine of the *Cooperativa de Ahorro y Crédito de las Fuerzas Armadas* (Armed Forces Cooperative of Savings and Credit, or CAOFA), which was distributed through the Military Center. Retired colonel Carlos Silva Valiente heads both institutions and is also an active member of *Cabildo Abierto*. The editorial—strongly offensive towards the government and the *Frente Amplio*—concludes: "Next Sunday, we must pave the path to a new dawn. We must begin to remove Marxism from the horizon of our national destiny once and for all. Long live the fatherland!"
45 In recent statements, the Uruguayan researcher on military issues, Dr Julián González Guyer, has hypothesised that Manini Ríos should be considered an officer trained during the dictatorship and that, as such, he is highly inclined in his political attitude to strategic thinking and the need to construct an enemy.

References

Azúa, C. R. de (1985) *Uruguay: ¿una sociedad amortiguadora?* Montevideo, Banda Oriental-CIESU.
Bohoslavsky, E., Motta, R. P. S., & Boisard, S. (eds.) (2019) *Pensar as direitas na América Latina*. São Paulo, Alameda.
Broquetas, M. (2014) *La trama autoritaria. Derechas y violencia en Uruguay (1958–1966)*. Montevideo, Banda Oriental.
Bucheli, G. (2019) *O se está con la patria o se está contra ella. Una historia de la Juventud Uruguaya de Pie*. Montevideo, Fin de Siglo.
Caetano, G. (2017a) El impacto de la Revolución Rusa en Uruguay (1917–1923). *Estudios. A cien años de la Revolución Rusa: Legados, significados y miradas en clave*

latino-americana/ Universidad Nacional de Córdoba-Centro de Estudios Avanzados 37, 47–67.
Caetano, G. (2017b) Emilio Frugoni y la Revolución Rusa. *Prismas. Revista de Historia Intelectual / Universidad Nacional de Quilmas* 21, 219–224.
Caetano, G. (2019a) *Historia mínima de Uruguay*. Mexico City, El Colegio de México.
Caetano, G. (2019b) Las izquierdas y la confusión democrática. *Nueva Sociedad* 281, 104–116.
Caetano, G., & Jacob, R. (1989–1991) *El nacimiento del terrismo*, 3 vols. Montevideo, Banda Oriental.
Caetano, G., & Selios, L. (2016) El ciclo electoral 2014 en Uruguay: ¿todo igual? In Mayorga, F. (ed.), *Elecciones y legitimidad democrática en América Latina*. La Paz, UMSS-IESE-CLACSO-Ed. Plural, pp. 95–138.
Caetano, G., & Selios, L. (2017) Análise do ciclo eleitoral 2014 en Uruguai e dos erros das enquisadoras. *Tempo Exterior. Revista de análise e estudos internacionais (IGADI)* 15 (1), 79–107.
Caetano, G., Selios, L., & Nieto, E. (2019) Descontentos y 'cisnes negros': Las elecciones en Uruguay en 2019. *Araucaria. Revista Iberoamericana de Filosofía, Política, Humanidades y Relaciones Internacionales* 21 (42), 277–311.
Cámara de Representantes. (1929) *Diario de Sesiones*, 4 January, vol. 350, p. 510.
Cámara de Representantes. (1929) *Diario de Sesiones*, 1 April, vol. 350, pp. 512–513.
Colombo, S. (2019) No perdamos este Uruguay. *New York Times*, 10 December. https://www.nytimes.com/es/2019/12/10/espanol/opinion/uruguay-lacalle-pou.html [Accessed 30 October 2022].
Freedom House. (n.d.) *Freedom House*. http://www.freedomhouse.org/ [Accessed 30 October 2022].
Goyena, J. I. (1948) *Discursos del Dr. José Irureta Goyena. Homenaje a su memoria*. Montevideo, Tipografía Atlántida.
Herrera, L. A. de (2009) *La Revolución Francesa y Sudamérica*. Montevideo, Instituto Manuel Oribe/ARCA.
Herrera, L. R. (2016) *La revolución en el orden (1897–1929)*. Montevideo, EBO.
Latinobarómetro Corporation. (n.d.) *Latinobarómetro: Opinión Pública Latinoamericana*. http://www.latinobarometro.org/ [Accessed 30 October 2022].
Leonís, E. (2019) *Luis Lacalle Pou. Un rebelde camino a la presidência*. Montevideo, Planeta.
Martínez, M. C. (1885) Valor teórico y práctico de la soberanía popular. *Anales del Ateneo del Uruguay* 8 (44), 307–318.
Political Instability Task Force. (n.d.) *Polity IV Project*. http://www.systemicpeace.org/polity/polity4.htm [Accessed 30 October 2022].
República Oriental del Uruguay. (n.d.) *Corte Electoral*. https://www.corteelectoral.gub.uy/ [Accessed 30 October 2022].
Traverso, E. (2018) *Las nuevas caras de la derecha*. Buenos Aires, Siglo Veintiuno Editores Argentina.
World Bank Worldwide Governance Indicators. (n.d.) *Worldwide Governance Indicators*. https://info.worldbank.org/governance/wgi/Home/Reports [Accessed 30 October 2022].
Zubillaga, C. (2015) *Una historia silenciada. Presencia y acción del falangismo en Uruguay (1936–1955)*. Montevideo, Ediciones Cruz del Sur-Linardi y Risso.
Zubillaga, C. (2017) *Una historia silenciada. Las relaciones diplomáticas de España y Uruguay durante el primer franquismo (1936–1955)*. Montevideo, Ediciones Cruz del Sur-Linardi y Risso, 2017.

PART III
Contemporary expressions of the right

8
BRAZIL

The New Right and the rise of Jair Bolsonaro[1]

Camila Rocha, Esther Solano and Jonas Medeiros

Introduction

Years before the ascension of Jair Bolsonaro, a far-right Congressman, to Brazil's presidency, New Right activism had occupied the Brazilian streets and social networks, taking by surprise political analysts accustomed to associate social movements and street protests with leftist groups. Some claimed that, despite the use of updated activism techniques, the ideas defended by the militants were the same as the ones championed by the country's traditional right: neoliberalism and conservatism.[2] Thus, it did not make sense to call it a New Right movement. However, despite this continuity of ideas and political actors, it is indeed possible to identify the development of a New Right in Brazil. This process involved the emergence of new leaders and new forms of expression and organisation, as well as new ideas that recently started to circulate with greater strength in the Brazilian public sphere: libertarianism and the denunciation of a "leftist cultural hegemony" in the country.[3]

In the first section of this article, we describe right-wing activities in Brazil in the previous decades, considering their links to the actions of the New Right that would emerge years later. In the second and third sections, we indicate how, amid the political transformations that occurred in the country, a new constellation of actors and ideas had been formed which then greatly contributed to Brazil's political shift to the right and Bolsonaro's rise to power.

The Brazilian traditional right

The existing ties between the leaders of the New Right and those of the traditional Brazilian right were built mainly from the contact network fostered over time by national and international pro-market organisations known as

DOI: 10.4324/9781003352266-12

think tanks.[4] At the end of the 2000s, the circuit of think tanks founded in the 1980s and 1990s expanded, uniting those from anarcho-capitalists to monarchists, and in which older generations of intellectuals and businesspeople met the young militancy that acted on social networks, in student movements, and street protests.

The formation of the first pro-market think tanks in Brazil is intimately related to the dissemination of neoliberalism around the world through the activity of intellectuals, militants, politicians, and business people in the 1930s (Cockett, 1995; Stedman-Jones, 2014). In Brazil, the promotion of neoliberalism began between the 1940s and the 1950s through a strong campaign against the left that united conservative Catholics and anti-communist businesspeople, who committed themselves to the preservation of private property.

In 1946, Austrian economist F. A. Hayek's *The Road to Serfdom*, published originally in 1944, was translated into Portuguese with the support of the businessman Adolpho Lindenberg. Lindenberg, along with Plinio Corrêa de Oliveira (who happened to be Lindenberg's cousin), was one of the main founders of the TFP in 1960, which was intimately related to members of the Brazilian royal family and operated across Latin America.[5] At the time, there were many groups and organisations committed to the fight against communism (Motta, 2002). The appeal of such anti-communist discourse may be observed in the massive adherence to the *Marcha da Família com Deus pela Liberdade* protests, which, organised by conservative Catholic women, was attended by around 300,000 people in the city of São Paulo in 1964 (Cordeiro, 2009).

However, if Catholic conservatism captivated a significant share of society at the time, neoliberalism was confined mainly to the elites who, like Lindenberg, were also concerned with what they viewed as substantial advances of the left. Among them, there were Eugenio Gudin, the economist who participated in the ninth meeting promoted by the Mont Pèlerin Society in Princeton, New Jersey, in 1958 (Boianovsky, 2018),[6] and the businessman Paulo Ayres Filho, whose work with the Foundation for Economic Education began in 1959, and who would later join the Mont Pèlerin Society (Spohr, 2012).[7]

Ayres Filho was a leading figure in the civil-military coup against President João Goulart in 1964, also backed by Gudin. In 1961, he founded the *Instituto de Pesquisa e Estudos Sociais* (IPES) in São Paulo, which brought together businesspeople, politicians, military, and intellectuals to resist the advance of the left.[8] Among those, there were Catholics and conservative intellectuals linked to the *Instituto Brasileiro de Filosofia* (IBF) and the *Sociedade de Convívio*.[9]

Although there were neoliberal intellectuals inside IPES, its objective was not to make its ideology known beyond the elite, just as it was not the goal of the economists gathered together in the *Associação Nacional de Programação Econômica e Social* (ANPES), founded in 1964 by the economist Roberto Campos. Despite being responsible for the visit of foreign economists to Brazil, such as Milton Friedman in 1973, ANPES was exclusively concerned with designing public policies for the country and not with the dissemination of neoliberalism to a wider public (Aranha, 2016; Boianovsky, 2018), whereas the main aim of IPES was to overthrow João Goulart.

After the military coup in 1964, most of the Brazilian neoliberals supported or participated directly in Marshal Humberto Castelo Branco's administration (1964–1967). Roberto Campos, Minister of Planning of the military government, and Octávio Gouveia de Bulhões, Minister of Finance, were among them. However, with the end of Castelo Branco's mandate and the onset of developmentalist, anti-liberal military governments, the neoliberals lost their recently gained space in the government. In their place, conservative, anti-communist cadres linked to the IBF and the *Sociedade de Convívio* were appointed to government posts. Since the civil organisations that fostered the neoliberals had shut down, neoliberals started to act on their own in civil society. That was the case of the businessman Henry Maksoud, owner of companies in various fields, such as the contractor Hidroservice and the luxury hotel Maksoud Plaza.

Maksoud was one of the pioneers in the dissemination of Hayek's and Friedman's original ideas beyond the elite circles in Brazil, through the publication of the magazine *Visão*, book translations, and the TV show *Henry Maksoud e você*, trying to influence a group formed by what Hayek called "second-hand dealers of ideas" (Fonseca, 1994). The Austrian economist came to Brazil three times between 1976 and 1981, at Henry Maksoud's invitation (Gross, 2003). During his last visit, Hayek gave a lecture at the University of Brasilia attended by Eugenio Gudin, Roberto Campos, and Octávio Gouveia de Bulhões. Nonetheless, the activities promoted by Maksoud were never related to a specific organisation and did not have specific aims. Neoliberal organisations only became formalised in the 1980s, during the country's re-democratisation process.

In this period, conservative ideologists that had supported the military regime slowly lost their influence. During the transition to democracy, conservative discourses, characterised by aggressive anti-communist rhetoric, lost their appeal due to dwindling public and private support. The fight against communism was not a priority any longer. In fact, the idea of being a rightist was out of fashion at the time since it linked right-wing people and organisations to the military regime. For similar reasons, political scientist Timothy Power (2010) coined the epithet "the ashamed right" to characterise the Brazilian right after the end of the dictatorship.

The unfavourable scenario prompted conservatives, who were saddled with a frayed discourse and could not rely on great funding for their organisations, to defend free markets more organically and less pragmatically than in the 1950s and 1960s. Conservative intellectuals started to attend the circuits formed by the *Instituto Liberal*[10]–founded in 1983 in Rio de Janeiro by the Canadian-Brazilian businessman Donald Stewart Jr. and José Stelle, Hayek's translator and chief editor at Henry Maksoud's magazine *Visão*–and by the *Instituto de Estudos Empresariais* (IEE), created in 1984 by the businessmen Winston Ling and Willian Ling. The Liberal Institute had eight branch offices scattered across Brazil by the beginning of the 1990s, and in 1993 hosted the Mont Pèlerin Society's annual meeting in

Rio de Janeiro. About the same time, other pro-market think tanks were created, such as the *Instituto Atlântico*, founded by old members of the *Câmara de Estudos e Debates Econômicos e Sociais* (CEDES)[11] and headed by the economist Paulo Rabello de Castro, who had graduated from the Chicago School of Economics.

Most of the organisations founded at the time had an important interlocution with the *Partido da Frente Liberal* (PFL), now renamed *Democratas* (DEM), which housed politicians that used to be linked to the military regime's party, the *Aliança Renovadora Nacional* (ARENA). Roberto Bornhausen, whose brother, Jorge Bornhausen, was a politician affiliated to the PFL, presided the São Paulo chapter of the *Instituto Liberal and the Instituto Atlântico*, which was responsible for elaborating the party's political programme. Intellectuals linked to the former *Sociedade de Convívio*, such as Antonio Paim and Ricardo Vélez Rodríguez, also circulated in those think tanks and actively sought to influence it ideologically, ministering many formation courses to their members.

However, after sociologist Fernando Henrique Cardoso, affiliated to the *Partido da Social Democracia Brasileira* (PSDB), was elected to be President of Brazil in 1994 and after the end of hyperinflation, the institutes started to face increasing difficulties in keeping their sponsors. Many businesspeople believed it was no longer necessary to finance the dissemination of pro-market ideas since the federal government had already implemented these ideas in practice. Stewart Jr.'s death in 1999 accelerated the process, and, at the beginning of the 2000s, almost all branch offices of the liberal institutes had shut down. Amid the decline of the Instituto Liberal, the IEE focused on promoting the *Fórum da Liberdade*, that gathers right-wing leaders from different areas in the city of Porto Alegre, and the *Instituto Atlântico*, after approaching the PFL in the 1990s and supporting Roseana Sarney, the party's pre-candidate in the 2002 general elections, temporarily distanced itself from direct activity in national politics.

The Brazilian New Right

In 2003, amid the withering of Brazil's pro-market organisations, former union leader Luiz Inácio "Lula" da Silva's first presidential term started. Despite his leftist origins, the PT's leader adopted a more orthodox economic orientation than that of President Cardoso, with the objective of not upsetting the country's economic elites, especially those related to the financial markets.[12] However, the outbreak of a corruption scandal known as *mensalão* in 2005 altered this perspective.

The scandal was named after the monthly instalments paid to deputies in exchange for their votes in favour of projects which were of interest to the Executive branch, and it became one of the most known corruption episodes in Brazil.[13] It received wider media coverage than previous corruption scandals (Miguel and Coutinho, 2007), and it involved high-rank government officials. In June 2005, Lula's chief of staff, José Dirceu, resigned from his office and, months later, had his parliamentary mandate revoked. In March 2006, Antonio Palocci, then Minister of Finance, also resigned from his post, despite having become the main actor for the maintenance of the orthodox economic policy of the government, and his successor, Guido Mantega, soon adopted a more heterodox approach.

In addition to the changes that occurred in government, the *mensalão* scandal also negatively affected the image of the PT, which had historically championed ethics in politics, and contributed to an increase in distrust in the political system as a whole (Venturi, 2006; Carreirão, 2007; Paiva et al., 2007). Amid such a negative impact, the first movement linked to the New Right, the *Movimento Endireita Brasil* (MEB), was founded in 2006 in São Paulo by young lawyers led by Ricardo Salles (President Bolsonaro's Minister of Environment).[14]

Like the MEB members, most political pundits and opposition politicians affirmed that, after the *mensalão*, Lula would lose political and electoral support. However, the ex-union leader got re-elected due to the economic improvement and the expressive electoral support of the lowest social strata (a phenomenon the political scientist André Singer (2012) called *Lulismo*).[15] Still, he also finished his mandate with a popular approval rate of 80%. Therefore, during his second term (2006–2010), there was a broad political consensus around the "Lulist" regulation,[16] and disgruntled voices, from both the left and right, were rare. The existing right-wing parties (such as Bolsonaro's party at the time, the *Partido Progressista*, PP, ARENA's political heir) were part of the government's legislative alliance and other opposition leaders, from PFL/DEM or PSDB, did not seem to have great differences with the government's agenda.

In civil society, dissonant voices also had little support. In 2007 there were some manifestations of the movement *Cansei!*,[17] created after an aeroplane crash to protest against what its members viewed as an "aerial chaos" due to the bad management of airports by the PT government. However, the movement was ridiculed by the media and even by right-wing politicians such as the former governor of São Paulo Cláudio Lembo (PFL/DEM), who declared that the movement was composed of "silly rich ladies". Opposition to the government in the public sphere was limited to the activity of a few journalists in newspapers, magazines, and books criticising Lula and the PT (Chaloub and Perlatto, 2015), and people who decided to express their frustration and resentment in online forums.

At the time, the Internet became a refuge for anti-PT right-wingers or those who did not see their demands reflected in Lula's policies. Feeling cornered in mainstream publics, these individuals turned to the digital space to explore and sympathise with strangers through forum interactions, blogs, websites, and digital communities, encouraging the creation of discursive spaces that existed outside the dominant pro-government currents. Thus, in addition to the subaltern counterpublics that were active at the time, such as those formed by feminist activists (Medeiros, 2017), LGBT+ and queer people, for example, there were also non-subaltern counterpublics formed by traditionalists, anti-globalists, supporters of the military regime, among others, who influenced the formation of the Brazilian New Right (Rocha, 2021).

Whether or not counterpublics are subaltern, they all use counterpublicity: a radical counter-hegemonic political strategy based on intentional shock and disruptive performances. This occurs when members of specific audiences think that their ideas do not circulate in dominant audiences and the very manifestation of their worldviews and lifestyles are at risk. It is also possible to say that counterpublics not only resignify identities and social positions by creating contradictions but also affect negotiation contexts, given their contradictory and ambivalent nature at the same time. As far as ambivalence is concerned, it is plausible to argue that counterpublics can democratise the dominant public sphere when they point out the lack of plurality in public debate and point out social suffering that is seldom or not at all considered by dominant publics.

At the same time, however, counterpublics also stimulate sociocultural fragmentation and sociopolitical polarisation. In particular, political polarisation is fuelled by counterpublics since they operate according to the logic that there are only political enemies to be destroyed, and no legitimate political opponents who could be co-opted or defeated. For the members of counterpublics the impossibility of debate rests on the perception that their enemies always act maliciously, that they are perverts, "fascists", have no humanity nor rationality, or have been submitted to "brainwashing" and indoctrination that lead them to defend evil ideas, which makes any rational debate impossible. Thus, even if members of counterpublics have rational-critical arguments to support their positions, they prefer to refuse the discussion. Moreover, they stigmatise other people who do not share their worldviews and seek to debate their ideas with political opponents.

The paradoxical character of counterpublics, on the other hand, lies in how they relate to conflict. Counterpublics not only establish the conflict between the dominant cultural horizon and an alternative horizon; they also make it possible to name the conflict and outline their views for the reorganisation of public life. In general, dominant publics rationalise their cultural horizons and present them as consensual, or free from conflict, to perpetuate the dominance of their culture, codes, performances, ideas, and social structures. Counterpublicity denaturalised these false consensuses. Its paradoxical dimension, though, lies in the difficulty of overcoming pure conflict and fabricating new, more inclusive, and reflective consensuses and forms of coexistence (Rocha and Medeiros, 2020).

The emergence of the online social network Orkut was crucial in the emergence of right-wing counterpublics. In 2004, the network eventually became one of the main spaces for forming the New Brazilian Right. The first step in this direction was taken in the 1990s by philosopher Olavo de Carvalho, who, by the early 2000s, stopped writing for mainstream media outlets and focused only on his online activities. In 2002 he created a collaborative website called *Mídia sem Máscara*. In 2004 there were already two Orkut forums dedicated to the discussion of Carvalho's ideas. Two years later, he started broadcasting a podcast, and in 2009, he began offering online philosophy lessons for a fee.

Significantly influenced by a marginal, esoteric, and anti-modern current of thought called traditionalism, also shared by Steve Bannon and Aleksandr Dugin

(Teitelbaum, 2020), Carvalho argued that the left had established a cultural hegemony in Brazil through the more or less conscious adoption of a political strategy developed by the Italian communist intellectual Antonio Gramsci. Such a process supposedly began during the re-democratisation era in the mid-1980s. It involved the activity of mainstream media outlets, NGOs, publishers, universities, organisations that operated in the arts and humanities field, and international entities that defended progressive agendas like feminism, LGBT+ rights, and human rights in general. All those organisations were, according to Carvalho, part of an ongoing worldwide revolutionary process called "globalism". For globalists, only the intervention of a global authority, invested in an unprecedented power concentration could solve the main contemporary issues, hence Carvalho's (2009) call for liberals and conservatives to unite in the fight against the leftist cultural hegemony and the upsurge of a "universal Leviathan".

Today, references to globalism and leftist cultural hegemony can be found in most discourses associated with contemporary right-wing leaders and groups, especially in the United States. In Brazil, these references were incorporated by readers of foreign authors and users of American internet forums, then readapted to the national context, and eventually shared with a larger audience through the translation of texts into Portuguese and dissemination in national digital forums. In this sense, Olavo de Carvalho's activity was fundamental for the emergence of the New Right in Brazil. Around 2010, when Facebook became a popular social network in Brazil, Carvalho's ideas had been circulating on the internet for some years, and it was possible to find four communities that bore his name.

Initially designed for the American public, Orkut rapidly became popular in Brazil. It is estimated that in January 2006, 75% of all its users were from Brazil (Fragoso, 2006), which indicated an early engagement of Brazilians in this type of social network in comparison to people of other countries. Between the years 2005 and 2007, the peak of Orkut's popularity in Brazil, internet access was limited largely to groups formed mainly by educated young people and adults, in its majority from middle and upper classes, and located primarily in the southern and south-eastern regions of the country (Comitê Gestor da Internet no Brasil, 2007). Using Orkut, one could create communities about the most varied subjects, in which internet users could interact with each other through conversation topics. However, the use of fake profiles was quite common, and it contributed to the chaotic and sometimes violent development of debates (Fragoso, 2006).

The environment provided by Orkut ended up fostering the constitution of right-wing counterpublics – debate arenas characterised by disruptive and indecorous language in detriment of rational-critical arguments, which are the basis of dominant publics' legitimacy (Warner, 2002). Olavo de Carvalho used this kind of language consciously, to call attention through shock and indecorous behaviour and counteract the rational-critical argumentation used by dominant publics through the defence of the use of swear words.

Not only was the language disruptive, but the very ideas that circulated in such forums were also so conflictive to the dominant horizon that, if they were uttered without qualifications in dominant publics, they were very likely to cause hostile reactions. Among the most recurrent ones was Carvalho's idea that Brazil was dominated by a "Communist Gay dictatorship", that the Brazilian military dictatorship and its fight against so-called terrorists should be praised, and the idea expressed by young libertarians that "taxation is theft".

Although there were glaring differences and acute tensions between groups that met in those forums, they shared the fight against globalism and "left-wing cultural hegemony" in Brazil to a lesser or greater degree. Thus, although the defence of traditionalist and anti-modern ideas was restricted to a small group, Olavo de Carvalho created a shared political language and constituted a broader discursive field (Alvarez, 1990) that could unify different groups that had strong tensions among themselves, such as Brazilian libertarians.

Libertarianism, which promotes free-market capitalism more radically than neoliberals linked to the Chicago School such as Ludwig von Mises and Murray Rothbard, was almost non-existent in Brazil until then. However, it was through Orkut that university students and independent professionals would be able to contact each other to share ideas, translate, and share texts and get influenced by Carvalho's ideas.

The right-wing counterpublics, however, did not limit themselves to the Internet. On June 2, 2006, the businessman Hélio Beltrão Filho created the online community "*Liberalismo Verdadeiro*" for discussing economic liberalism on Orkut and gathering people to establish a new organisation inspired by the American Mises Institute. In 2007, one year after the digital community was founded, the *Instituto Mises Brasil* (IMB) was established through the reunion of prominent libertarian activists on the Internet, such as the brothers Cristiano and Fernando Chiocca.[18]

At the time of the creation of the IMB, another initiative started to take shape in the Orkut communities: the formation of *Liber*, a Brazilian political party inspired by the American Libertarian Party.[19] In 2009, *Liber* already had an official website, a political programme, Twitter and Facebook accounts, and 500 members that paid annual fees to the party. But the organisers failed to gather the 500,000 signatures necessary for the registration of a political party, and the initiative was scrapped.

Nevertheless, people who orbited around IMB, or actively participated, to a bigger or smaller degree, in *Liber*'s institutionalisation attempt, played an essential role in fostering a new libertarian militancy in Brazil, breaking with the high degree of elitism and centralisation of the traditional right. Highly active on the internet, the militants started to promote their ideas on YouTube channels, forums, blogs, and social networks. This strategy, combined with the creation of study groups and participation in student movements and organisations throughout Brazil, ended up aggregating a growing number of like-minded people.

Simultaneously, militants also circulated in older forums and organisations, such as the *Fórum da Liberdade*, promoted annually by the IEE. The contact between different generations provided access to already established pro-market contact networks inside and outside the country and new sources of funding. The example of the *Instituto Ordem Livre* illustrates this. Created officially in 2009, it fostered *Liberdade na Estrada*, sponsored by car rental giant *Localiza*, Salim Mattar's company, a businessman who supported the diffusion of pro-market ideas since the 1980s. *Liberdade na Estrada* promoted libertarian lectures in universities throughout Brazil. Its five first editions reached 50 universities in more than 30 cities (*Instituto Ordem Livre*, n.d.).

Eventually, the militancy in higher education became more articulated and institutionalised with the creation of *Estudantes Pela Liberdade* (EPL). Inspired by its American namesake, it favoured efforts for coordinating students who wanted to organise study groups and run for students' committee elections in different states.[20] Since its establishment, the EPL has organised 650 events across public and private universities, supported the founding of more than 200 study groups, and, in 2014, had 600 voluntary leaderships that helped to forge new community bonds (Polletta and Jasper, 2011).

At that time, pro-market and libertarian ideas dominated the then-emerging New Right. However, by the end of Lula's second term, in 2010, the "pro-market and libertarian hegemony" of the New Right gave way to the conservatives. In the 1960s, conservative organisations such as TFP had an important impact on civil society, mobilising the anti-communist discourse and supporting the civil-military coup of 1964 (Motta, 2002). But after re-democratisation and the decline of communism in the 1980s, both older leaders and organisations linked to the Catholic Church, and more recent ones related to evangelical churches, started to focus on issues concerning the emerging feminist and LGBT+ agenda.

There was a very slow progress under both the FHC and Lula administrations, especially regarding abortion laws.[21] In this sense, it is important to emphasise that Lula, a former union leader, was elected with conservative voters' support. At the time, there was still a dissociation between defending a conservative agenda and voting on left-wing candidates for the presidency (Nishimura, 2004). However, during Lula's second term, bills like the Maria da Penha Domestic Abuse Law, proposed in 2004 and adopted in 2006 (Senado Federal, 2006a), and the criminalisation of homophobia, proposed in 2006 (Senado Federal, 2006b), marked a big change.

Bolsonaro's rise to power

After 30 years as a legislator, former army captain Jair Bolsonaro appeared on the political scene as a palatable leader for the emergent New Right in 2014, when he received a record 464,000 votes in Rio de Janeiro's legislative elections, four times the amount he obtained in the previous election. In the same year, one of his sons, Eduardo Bolsonaro, was elected as a Rio de Janeiro federal representative for the first time, with 82,000 votes. The vast difference in the number of votes comes from two main factors: the early engagement in social networking[22] and an emphasis on consistently defending conservative values, especially from 2011 onwards.[23]

Bolsonaro historically has always sought to meet the demands for better wages from the low-rank military, his electoral base, and position himself frontally against human rights, not afraid of asserting himself as an anti-communist, right-wing politician. In the 1990s, he asserted that Congress should be closed down and that President Fernando Henrique Cardoso should be shot dead. However, in 2002, when he lobbied to nominate the communist Aldo Rabello to the Ministry of Defence, he claimed that he had voted for Lula. In an interview, he ironically stated that communists nowadays drink whisky and live well (Folha de São Paulo, 2002). At the time, Bolsonaro's party was part of the PT's coalition, and political pragmatism spoke louder than ideologies.

But things changed in Lula's successor Dilma Rousseff's first mandate. In only four years, Brazilian society went through a "progressivist shock". In 2011, the *Comissão Nacional da Verdade* was created to investigate the State's crimes during the military dictatorship. The same year, the *Superior Tribunal Federal* (STF) recognised the right to same-sex marriage. The following year, the STF also recognised the right to abortion in foetal anencephaly cases and confirmed the validity of the racial quota system in public universities. A project for a constitutional amendment to widen labour rights to domestic workers, known as *PEC das Domésticas*, and a law prohibiting physical punishments and cruel and degrading treatment to children and adolescents, known as *Lei da Palmada*, were promulgated in 2013 and 2014, respectively. Simultaneously, Brazilian versions of the Canadian Slut Walks popped up throughout the country between 2011 and 2012, popularising feminism among young women and fostering new feminist activism on the streets and social networks (Medeiros and Fanti, 2019).

Facing such a scenario, Bolsonaro did not hesitate to lead the reaction to the so-called progressivist shock. Flanked by other conservative legislators, he managed to bar the printing of leaflets of the programme *Escola sem Homofobia*, formulated as early as 2004 and derogatorily called Gay Kit (Soares, 2015). However, he was unsuccessful in his attempt to bar the installation of the *Comissão Nacional da Verdade* and the approval of same-sex marriage bill. And there was still the possibility that Dilma Rousseff, if re-elected, would dedicate herself to the legalisation of abortion, once she had claimed in 2007 that such practice should be decriminalised (Pires, 2010).

Due to Bolsonaro's activity during this period, which was extensively publicised in his social media accounts, many conservatives, previously more dispersed in forums and free-market organisations, started to flirt with the former army captain. At the same time, Orkut libertarians began labelling themselves liberal-conservatives, pointing to a historical tendency of free-market defenders who adhered ideologically or pragmatically to conservatism (Constantino, 2018).[24] Such positioning caused discomfort among the militancy for some time, as the label liberal-conservative seemed like an oxymoron,[25] and, eventually, caused tensions in various groups,[26] especially in and around matters such as abortion rights.

In 2014 Bolsonaro had established himself as one of the leaders of the conservative reaction that had taken over the country. In the following years, his political projection reached new heights, peaking during the protests for the impeachment of Dilma Rousseff. During the presidential elections of 2014, the militants of the emerging New Right pragmatically campaigned for PSDB candidate Aécio Neves, and they all supported him in the runoff. At the time, Rousseff's defeat was taken for granted by the opposition due to the report of a corruption scandal related to the most prominent state company in the country, oil giant *Petrobrás* (Singer, 2018). Thus, the shattering of expectations with the announcement of her re-election was such that soon it was suggested that the election was rigged. Opponents of the PT began to express outrage, which provided a welcoming environment for anyone who wanted to protest against the situation.

The first pro-impeachment protest was called only six months after the re-election of Dilma Rousseff. The call for the protest was made on the Facebook page of Paulo Batista, a state legislator candidate from São Paulo also known as *Raio Privatizador*. His campaign was coordinated by libertarian militants and members of the *Movimento Brasil Livre* (MBL), the main pro-market movement in the country.[27] In humorous videos shared on YouTube, Batista was shown firing "privatising rays" on supposedly communist cities. Although Batista was not elected, around 2,500 people attended the protest, which was supported by Olavo de Carvalho. For the first time, it gathered all the representatives of New Right groups in the streets of São Paulo, including legislator Eduardo Bolsonaro. The protests continued being called by different movements, until March 15, 2015, when, according to *Datafolha* Institute polls, more than 250,000 people, bearing the national flag's colours, filled the streets of São Paulo to demand Rousseff's impeachment, encouraging the organisers to call new protests later in the year.

According to opinion research conducted by Esther Solano, Márcio Moretto Ribeiro, and Pablo Ortellado during the protests in São Paulo in August 2015, 96% of the protesters were dissatisfied with the political system. Seventy-three per cent said they did not trust political parties, and 70% claimed that they did not trust politicians (Rossi, 2015). Thus, beyond sharing the rejection of the PT and its leaders (Telles, 2016), rejection of the political system as a whole was widespread among protesters, probably due to the generalised perception that the political system was corrupt.

After the 2005 *mensalão* scandal, which affected the PT's leadership, only 5% of the population considered corruption the country's main problem. However, in October 2015, these numbers had increased to 34% (Singer, 2018). This increase resulted from a series of protests against corruption that took place between 2011 and 2012, after the *mensalão* scandal trial, and especially after the massive street protests of June 2013. The 2013 uprisings, started by the *Movimento Passe Livre* (MPL), demanded reduced public transportation fares and were violently repressed by the police. They gathered millions of people throughout Brazil in dozens of protests that, despite their several demands, turned against the political system as a whole, perceived as impermeable to the population's appeals (Nobre, 2013).

The outrage against the political system increased the following year due to the beginning of a huge anti-corruption operation, responsible for the imprisonment and condemnation of several politicians and businesspeople. Initiated in March 2014 with a money laundering report at *Petrobrás*, and inspired by the Italian *Mani Puliti*, the *Operação Lava Jato* soon gained wide mainstream media coverage and rapidly made one of its architects, Judge Sérgio Moro, the most prominent symbol of the fight against corruption in the country.

Thus, amid a crisis in public trust aggravated by the worsening economic situation, it is understandable that 56% of the protesters agreed with the statement "someone outside of the political system would solve the crisis". For 64% of the interviewees, this person could be an "honest judge", and for 88% an "honest politician". When asked who inspired more trust, 19.4% affirmed that they strongly trusted Jair Bolsonaro, who headed the list. Only 11% said they trusted PSDB, the party most of them had voted for in 2014, and only 1% said they trusted the *Movimento Democrático Brasileiro* (MDB), the party of the then Vice-President Michel Temer, who would occupy the presidency if the impeachment demanded by protesters was successful.

Bolsonaro was one of the few politicians who could participate in the anti-impeachment demonstrations and be applauded by the crowds, unlike other opposition leaders. Thus, at the end of 2015, the former military captain, considered by part of the population as one of the few honest politicians in the country, became a natural presidential candidate by defending law and order, advocating anti-system rhetoric, and attacking the PT and the left in general. His military background and consistent support for the death penalty, the reduction of the age of criminal responsibility for minors, and the injunction of forced labour among prisoners were seen as some positive attributes among his supporters. He was regarded as the only one capable of reducing violence through repressive measures and disciplining society in the face of moral degradation in a country where the rights of leftists, gays, and Black people were supposedly better protected than those of the "ordinary citizen".

The former army captain, who married an evangelical woman in a ceremony presided by the conservative televangelist pastor Silas Malafaia in 2013, gained prominence for opposing "gender ideology" and supporting discipline in schools. His appeal to the conservative Christian public would increase when, in March 2016, Bolsonaro formally joined the *Partido Social Cristão* (PSC), which gathered a significant part of the conservative Christian leaders in Brazil, and was baptised in the Jordan River by Pastor Everaldo, the party's candidate in the 2014 presidential elections.

However, Everaldo's presidential campaign became less known by its exaltation of Christian values than by the exhaustive repetition of the motto "let's privatise everything". The motto was a brainchild of Bernardo Santoro, director of the *Instituto Liberal* at the time, who was Liber's ex-president and an active participant in Orkut counterpublics in the mid-2000s. Santoro joined PSC in 2014 and became a self-styled "liberal-conservative". He focused on actively influencing

Jair Bolsonaro and his sons to embrace free-market radicalism. In his own words, Santoro intended to diffuse free-market radicalism to broader sections of the population, such as members of the impoverished middle class and "Uberized" labourers.[28]

Santoro's mission was a tough one. At the time, free-market defenders saw Bolsonaro as an adept of national developmentalism, a set of State-centred economic policies advocated by the military dictatorship in the 1970s. Santoro did not give up, and his efforts soon started to pay off. In March of that year, Jair's son Eduardo Bolsonaro enrolled in a course on Austrian economics offered by the *Instituto Mises Brasil*, established by Hélio Beltrão Filho, the creator of the Orkut community "True Liberalism". His brother, who served as a municipal councillor in Rio de Janeiro, decided to run for mayor in the elections of that year with a message strictly aligned with the agenda of Santoro.

Bolsonaro seemed less inclined to market radicalism than his sons, although he decided to participate in events promoted by the market circuit as a presidential pre-candidate. In 2017, he was introduced to Paulo Guedes by Winston Ling, founder of the IEE. Guedes, a Chicago School graduate and a well-known figure of the financial market circuits, founded the *Instituto* Millennium in 2006, a pro-market think tank based in Rio de Janeiro, with Rodrigo Constantino and Hélio Beltrão Filho.

But the pro-market milieu was initially suspicious of Bolsonaro and tensions grew among his new party's political leaders, whose extreme political pragmatism often sacrificed the right-wing public agenda. The last straw was PSC's alliance with the *Partido Comunista do Brasil* (PC do B) in the 2016 gubernatorial elections in Maranhão, forcing Bolsonaro and his sons, staunch anti-communists, to search for a new party.[29] In August 2017, the Bolsonaros announced their affiliation with the *Partido Ecológico Nacional* (PEN). To house the former captain's presidential aspirations, the party changed its name to *Partido Patriota*. As General Secretary of the party, Bernardo Santoro introduced Bolsonaro to a young economist called Adolfo Sachsida, a University of Brasilia PhD and analyst at the federal government's *Instituto de Pesquisas Econômicas Aplicadas* (IPEA). Sachsida, at Santoro's request, formed a group of 11 economists that met weekly with Bolsonaro.

The opposition of free-market defenders to Bolsonaro seemed to decline gradually. In December 2017, Rodrigo Constantino publicly suggested that Paulo Guedes should be the Minister of Economy in a future Bolsonaro government. However, in early 2018, the pre-candidate decided to leave the *Partido Patriota* and affiliate to the *Partido Social Liberal* (PSL). The sudden change in affiliation to a new party quickly caused discomfort among the libertarian militants of PSL that had gathered since 2016 at the group LIVRES. Staunch anti *Bolsonaristas*, LIVRES militants left the party shortly after Bolsonaro joined it, adhering to the *Partido Novo*.

The pre-candidate eventually caused another shock when he shunned participation in the presidential debate organised by the *Fórum da Liberdade*, which gathered right-wing leaders and ideologues yearly. In order to end once and for all lingering suspicions due to his erratic political movements, Bolsonaro decided to seal his alliance with the pro-market defenders by announcing in the first semester of 2018 that Paulo Guedes would be his Minister of Economy. Despite all sorts of suspicions, tensions, and resentments, most market fundamentalists actively supported Bolsonaro's presidential campaign, bringing together the New Brazilian Right around a libertarian-conservative amalgam.

In addition to the support of market fundamentalists, Bolsonaro soon became a strong candidate for presidency by adopting an anti-system rhetoric, aggressively attacking the Worker's Party and the left as a whole. His defence of conservative Christian values, the traditional family, hierarchy, and order resonated well among conservative sector of Brazilian society to whom the agendas of feminist, black and LGBT+ movements were part of a widespread moral degradation related to a high rate of violent crimes and youth's "bad behaviour", considering the words of Bolsonaro's core voters:[30]

> I am a good citizen who works, pays taxes, has a decent life and is unprotected. Where's the victim's human rights? Human rights end up being bad because it's for bandits, for criminals, for lefties, for feminists ... What about us? The State does not protect us, but Bolsonaro will change this situation PT has created. He will protect good honest citizens.
>
> (Interview 1)

> I'm against race quotas for public universities. What about poor white people? There are rich black people. There is less and less racism now. There are many people who want to take advantage of being black. Slavery was a long time ago, you don't have to remember that all the time. There is racism on both sides.
>
> (Interview 2)

> That homophobia thing we didn't have before. Now it's homophobia everywhere. Before there wasn't so much violence against gay people, but now it seems that they show off too much. Partially, they are guilty of the violence against them because they show themselves too much.
>
> (Interview 21)

> What we have today is a total crisis of values. Everything's backwards. It's all wrong. Television teaching you how to be gay. Kids don't have the values we had ... You should have religious education in schools, yes, to learn ethics, to know what is right and what is wrong.
>
> (Interview 23)

> I vote for Bolsonaro because he defends our families, he's on the religious side. The PT wanted to make our kids gay, it was going to release the

prisoners, and also the children could choose in the birth certificate if they want to be boys or girls. PT would destroy families. They don't respect religion. (...) These people think only about sex, prostitution, orgies. ... Bolsonaro took an attitude, had courage. We are in a battle, God against the demons. This time God won".

(Interview 11)

The kids don't care about anything now. We used to be raised with discipline at home and at school. It was "yes, sir", it was respect, it was authority. I am in favour of military school, yes, singing the anthem, the flag, because we have to teach children to have responsibility, discipline, if not it is a mess.

(Interview 16)

They're all the same. PT, PSDB. Power is power. They don't care about us. It's all corrupt, dirty (...) Oh, I think Bolsonaro is different and can change all that. We believe in him. We have faith in him, hope, he is not the same.

(Interview 15)

Conclusion

After the first round of the elections ended in October 2018, Bolsonaro had collected more than half of the valid votes in 12 states and the Federal District, which surprised many political analysts. Bolsonaro was disappointed by the results, as he felt he could win the elections in the first round. On the other hand, the counterpublic militants were impressed by the votes he had received and leaders of the pro-impeachment protests, such as law professor Janaína Paschoal, journalist Joice Hasselmann, and then federal legislator Eduardo Bolsonaro, all PSL candidates, received more than one million votes each. The party became the second-largest parliamentary bench in Congress, with 52 members, increasing six times its presence in the federal lower legislative house.

Bolsonaro's victory, as well as that of many New Right activists, was a result of a long political and social process that can be traced back to the *mensalão* corruption scandal in 2005 and culminated with a firm electoral rejection of the PT and Lula's arrest in 2018. Even though many factors explain Bolsonaro's victory—economic and social crisis, rampant violence and crime, Lula's imprisonment, and the disappointment with the PT and the political system as a whole, including the intense political content sharing through social networks (Brito Cruz, 2019)[31]—it is of paramount importance to consider the formation of emerging New Right militancy networks which diffused new ideas during a series of critical moments between 2011 and 2016: the progressivist shock (2011–2014), the protests against corruption (2011–2012), the *mensalão* scandal trial (2012), the uprisings of June 2013, the *Operação Lava Jato* (2014), Dilma Rousseff's re-election (2014), and pro-impeachment protests (2014–2016).

Bolsonaro came to symbolise the burgeoning outrage against the PT and the political system, and the desire for law, order, and discipline in Brazilian society. His closeness to evangelical leaders, Olavo de Carvalho's followers, and radical pro-marketeers delivered him a wide-ranging mixture of personnel ready to serve in government, apart from those recruited into the army that also exalted the military dictatorship. The disruptive and indecorous language characteristic of counterpublic discourse became frequent in official communications, as in Donald Trump's administration (Thimsen, 2017), contrary to Michael Warner's hypothesis that the counterpublics would normalise if their members became part of dominant publics.

However, there are significant tensions between the new right-wing groups. In this sense, the first two years of Bolsonaro's government were a game changer for the New Right, which subsequently has begun to show signs of division between unconditional Bolsonaro supporters that still employ disruptive and indecorous language, that we understand as a *dominant counterpublicity* (Rocha; Medeiros, 2021).

While the emergence of counterpublics facilitated by digital media (Downey and Fenton, 2003) points to increased representation of certain groups in the public sphere, to the extent that it allows more people to participate and influence the public debate, it can also have harmful effects. The increased fragmentation of the public (Sunstein, 2017) and the formation of the so-called 'bubble effect', a process of feedback of ideas and information by internet users through filters and algorithms (Pariser, 2011), may lead to the intensification of political radicalisation (Downey and Fenton, 2003), and counterpublicity may facilitate the popularisation of authoritarian ideas incompatible with the democratic regime.

Notes

1 This chapter draws on a modified version of a Working Paper written by Camila Rocha: The New Brazilian Right and the public sphere. *Mecila Working Paper Series, No. 32.* São Paulo, The Maria Sibylla Merian International Centre for Advanced Studies in the Humanities and Social Sciences Conviviality-Inequality in Latin America. http://dx.doi.org/10.46877/rocha.2021.32. The arguments presented here are further developed in Rocha, C., Solano, E. Medeiros, J. (2021) The Bolsonaro paradox: The public sphere and right wing counter publicity in contemporary Brazil. Springer-Nature.

2 Neoliberalism is a set of social, political, and economic ideas and practices whose onset goes back to an attempt to rehabilitate the old laissez-faire, which had acutely decayed after the 1929 crisis. The use of the prefix *neo* highlights an important change in relation to the nineteenth-century laissez-faire (Boas, 2009; Gans-Morse, 2009; Jackson, 2010). Different from the liberal laissez-faire, neoliberalism defends an active role of the State as a promoter of free markets. In other words, if the State should have no role in regulating the economy for the adepts of laissez-faire, neoliberals believe that the State should act in an active manner in its regulation, in the sense of creating a legal-juridical apparatus to foster the good functioning of the free market (Morresi, 2008; Dardot and Laval, 2016). It is possible to say that, over the last decades, neoliberalism acquired such importance that, in the words of Pierre Dardot and Christian Laval (2016), it became the world's new zeitgeist. Thus, the existence of progressivist neoliberals, such as Bill Clinton and Tony Blair (Fraser, 2017), and conservative

neoliberals, as Ronald Reagan and Margaret Thatcher. For this reason, considering the arguments developed in this article, it is important to point out the differences between neoliberalism and libertarianism, which came to influence significantly the formation of a New Right in Brazil. Economists Milton Friedman and Friedrich von Hayek can be classified as neoliberals, while it is more adequate to consider Ludwig von Mises as a libertarian, as is proposed by the libertarian journalist Bryan Doherty (2009). By contrast, conservatism is not so much a political philosophy as an attitude towards the world that is necessarily reactive to progress in the realm of values and customs. According to the conservative philosopher Roger Scruton (2015), due to their denial of abstraction, conservatives tend to "wail" as they try to maintain traditions in view of their impending substitution by something considered worse. This necessity of keeping certain traditions is anchored on the understanding that these are not arbitrary customs, but a condensation of the knowledge originated by a long learning process that favours the reproduction of society. Thus, conservatism can also be described as the feeling of responsibility for the dead, the living, and those that are yet to be born, in the formulation of the great critic of the French Revolution Edmund Burke.

3 Libertarianism stands for the radical defence of the free market without any restrictions and is also associated with the defence of the moral and political liberty of human beings of not being coerced one by another (Doherty, 2009). Libertarians usually do not like to be labelled as either left or right. Murray Rothbard's book notwithstanding, empirically they tend to connect with right wing leaders and parties. In Brazil they mostly lean to the right. Although there is a small political group that refers to themselves as left-libertarians, they are gathered under a right-wing party called the New Party (*Partido Novo*).

4 In general, think tanks can be defined as permanent organisations, responsible for research and/or diffusion of the ideas related to the proposition of public policies. Considering this, most pro-market think tank activities are classified by the specialised literature as political and ideological advocacy (Desai, 1994; Cocket, 1995), based particularly on the diffusion of market freedom, sometimes combined with conservative values, and of public policies in accordance with such orientation. In practice, in the words of Mike Caroll, Heritage Foundation's CEO, the business of this type of organisation is "people", that is, the gathering of cadres ready to influence and, eventually, act directly in governmental instances. For more information about the operation of think tanks in Brazil after the re-democratisation process, see Gros (2003), Casimiro (2011), Hauck (2015), and Rocha (2017).

5 Lindenberg is the acting president of the *Instituto Plinio Corrêa de Oliveira* (IPCO), founded in December 2006. For more information, see: https://ipco.org.br/quem-somos/#.W-27UnpKhmA.

6 The Mont Pèlerin Society was founded in 1947 by Hayek with the intention of stimulating the exchange of ideas between intellectuals familiar with the theses outlined in *The Road to Serfdom* such as Ludwig von Mises, Milton Friedman, Karl Popper, Wilhelm Röpke, Lionel Robbins, Walter Eucken, Walter Lippmann, Michael Polanyi, Salvador de Madariaga, and others (Cocket, 1995; Stedman-Jones, 2014).

7 The Foundation for Economic Education (FEE), founded in March 1946 in the city of Irvington-on-Hudson, New York, was idealised by the businessman Leonard Read and was supported for many years by a fund with a multimillion-dollar balance, the Volker Fund, created by the magnate William Volker and managed by a free-market enthusiast. Thus, the institution had a relative autonomy in face of immediate political interests and aspired to educate American people for the advantages of free-market capitalism (Doherty, 2009).

8 Later, between the 1960s and the 1970s, IPES managed to have branches in other Brazilian capitals. For more information, see Dreifuss (1987) and Ramírez (2007).

9 The IBF was founded in 1949 in São Paulo and was initially headed by the Brazilian jurist and philosopher Miguel Reale. The institution had in its cadres Luis Washington Vita, Vicente Ferreira da Silva, Renato Cirell Czerna, Heraldo Barbuy, Vilém Flusser,

Leônidas Hegenberg, Roque Spencer Maciel de Barros, Ubiratan Borges de Macedo, Antonio Paim, and Ricardo Vélez Rodríguez. Between the 1960s and the 1980s, IBF operated with the Catholics of the Sociedade de Convívio, created in 1961 in São Paulo by Father Adolpho Crippa, from the Order of Salvatorians, with the active participation of Paulo Mercadante, Creusa Capalbo, Antonio Paim, Nelson Saldanha, Ricardo Vélez Rodríguez, and Ubiratan Borges de Macedo (Gonçalves, 2017).

10 Liberal in Brazil stands mainly for pro-market currents, being less associated to the defence of progressivist values than liberal groups in the Anglo-Saxon context.

11 CEDES was composed by a group of academics who, in its majority, were alumni of University of São Paulo, especially from the *Fundação Instituto de Pesquisas Econômicas* (FIPE). The group had great liberty to elaborate public policy proposals, despite the Chamber being sheltered in what Rabello de Castro referred to as "the national temple of conservatism", the *Sociedade Rural Brasileira*, an entity that was, in his view, profoundly anti-neoliberal. At the time, however, the *Sociedade Rural* was presided over by Renato Ticoulart Filho and other directors who, according to Castro, were more intellectual and open to innovations. The group also relied on bankers, such as then-president of Unibanco Roberto Bornhausen, and the Andrade Vieira family, owner of Bamerindus, a bank strongly linked to the state of Paraná's rural elites. According to the historian René-Armand Dreifuss, CEDES was maintained by 50 national and international companies and associations. Renato Ticoulart, in his own words, defined it as limited to "academic visions, of an absolute apoliticism", even if their aim was to "gather the business community in the sense of showing that neoliberalism is not equal to savage capitalism, to a misery producer order, but a leverage towards social development" (Dreifuss, 1989: pp. 52–53).

12 This argument was developed in Lima (2016).

13 In an opinion research survey conducted in 2006 by *Fundação Perseu Abramo*, the PT's think tank, 76% of the population affirmed that the *mensalão* had occurred, which indicated low adherence to the party's official version of the scandal, according to which the financial transactions which were the original focus of the scandal were campaign money that was not accounted for by the PT's former treasurer, senator Delúbio Soares (Venturi, 2006).

14 "*Endireita*" means literally to straighten something up, and figuratively, a right turn in politics.

15 For Singer, Lulismo constituted a particular phenomenon of Brazil's political history, a political programme that combined economic orthodoxy with the fight against inequalities through public policies focused on the poorest part of the population. Due to its difficulties in self-organising, the poorest people of Brazil, which Singer calls the "sub-proletariat", would form the social basis of lulism, and would be represented, initially, by Lula and, afterwards, by the PT. The traditional middle class was opposed to this sub-proletariat, and after the *mensalão* scandal would become the social basis for anti-lulism, having as its main political expression, at the time, the PSDB.

16 The economist Leda Paulani defines the mode of regulation as "institutions, norms, calculus modes and procedures that ensure capital reproduction as a social relation" (Costa, 2018).

17 In a loose translation, "Enough!" expressing the discontent of the group with the current political situation.

18 In 2015, a few years after the foundation of IMB, the Chiocca brothers left the institution and decided to found their own organisation, the Rothbard Institute.

19 Founded in 1971 by David Nolan in the state of Colorado, United States, the Libertarian Party promotes libertarian ideas.

20 More information on the operation of the EPL can be found in Silvia (2017).

21 The Draft Bill 1131/1991, elaborated by the then PT federal representatives Eduardo Jorge and Sandra Starling, which proposed decriminalising abortion, was tabled in 1999 during FHC's second term. In 2003, 2007 and 2011, during the PT administrations, it was once again tabled (Câmara dos Deputados, 1991).

22 Jair Bolsonaro created a Twitter account in 2010 and a Facebook fan page in 2013.
23 As pointed out by research conducted by BBC Brazil based on more than 1,500 speeches given by the then representative at the Deputies' Chamber plenary for 27 years: "Bolsonaro from the start of his career was more concerned with the defence of military interests [his electoral basis] than arguing with the PT and the left. [...] In his first mandate as a representative, from 1991 to 1994, words such as 'military', 'armed forces', 'benefits', 'salary' and 'pensions' appeared 702 times in the abstracts and key-words of the 279 speeches he gave in the Chamber's Plenary. During his current mandate, from 2015 until now, the same set of sixteen words have appeared only 110 times, in a total of 143 speeches. Over time and with the increase in his national projection, the corporative issues of the Army, the Navy and the Air Force receded. Bolsonaro's time in the tribune started to be occupied with issues that 'appealed' to the deputy's new public, who knew him mainly from the internet, and a new set of 16 terms, such as 'human rights', 'PT', 'torture', 'Cuba', 'left', and 'gays' had a peak in his last mandate (2011 to 2014), appearing 297 times in this period, while they were only cited 41 times in Bolsonaro's first mandate (1991-1994)" (Shalders, 2017).
24 As with the support of American libertarians for the conservative Senator Barry Goldwater in the 1960s (Doherty, 2007), and the support of F. Hayek for the British conservative leader Margaret Thatcher (Cockett, 1995): in each of these cases, support was mixed with important ideological and identity tensions.
25 "Some people think that the expression liberal-conservative is an oxymoron. The confusion starts at the beginning of everything, when Burke himself, the great conservative, became a member of the Whig Party, which was a Liberal party that opposed the Tories. So what was he: liberal or conservative? I think these words have different meanings according to place and time, and ideological interests. Those who say that the label liberal-conservative is semantically impossible say this out of ideological interests. They are, above all, Libertarians, which want to distance themselves from values such as order or traditions, so I will not grant them the right to define liberalism. I believe that the liberal-conservative thought exists and it is not only used in Brazil, but also abroad. [...] I believe that the boundaries of these terms are ill-defined. The polemic on its use is open, but I do not see anybody in authority to solve it. To settle the polemic, I would say the following: I am an old Burkean Whig, with national colours" (Interview with Lucas Berlanza, March 2017).
26 "The (Liberty) Express was created in 2012, but it was not well delineated as to being either liberal or conservative. Instead, it orbited a common place of these two philosophies, which is the Natural Law triad of life, freedom and property. Liberals and conservatives shared those views. Over time, all the remaining liberals left. Because those who called themselves liberals were, in fact, I would say, pseudo-liberals, because everyone called themselves liberals [but] were liberals of conservative hues, they had emerged under the sign of some conservative group. So I saw the liberal world under the blessings of Nelson Rodrigues, someone else under the blessings of Ortega y Gasset, who is a conservative and aristocratic liberal, another by a monarchist author, culturally very conservative. So, at the end of the day, other issues of society were discussed and it ended up taking a conservative form" (Interview with Lourival de Souza, April 2017)
27 Founded initially by a group of friends led by Fábio Ostermann as a Facebook page to coordinate the pro-market militancy during June 2013, MBL was recreated by the activist Renan Santos on November 15, 2014. Since then, it has served as the main pro-market movement in the country, and one of the groups that led Dilma Rousseff's pro-impeachment campaign.
28 According to sociologist Ludmila Costhek Abílio (2017), "uberization consolidates the passage from a worker statute to one of nano businessperson, permanently available for work, removing minimum working guarantees while maintaining workplace hierarchies; yet, it appropriates, administratively and productively, a loss of publicly established working forms. However, this appropriation and subordination may operate on

new logic. We can understand uberization as a possible future for companies in general, which become responsible for providing infrastructure for their 'partners' to execute the work; it is not difficult to imagine hospitals, universities, and companies in a wide range of fields adopting this model and using the work of their 'just-in-time collaborators' according to their needs".

29 When Bolsonaro left the PSC, Paulo Rabello Castro, founder of the Atlantic Institute in 1992, became the party's candidate in the 2018 election. However, in the same year, he withdrew his candidacy and started to figure as candidate for vice-president on presidential candidate Álvaro Dias's *Podemo*'s ticket.

30 These interviews were conducted before and after Bolsonaro's election. In August 2018 Esther Solano conducted seven in-depth interviews with seven Bolsonaro supporters who were residents of the city of São Paulo and were selected in order to include diverse economic positions, professions, ages, and genders. In 2019 Camila Rocha and Esther Solano also conducted many more interviews with Bolsonaro supporters as part of research sponsored by Tide Setúbal Foundation and Friedrich Ebert Stiftung Brasil that are available for download at their respective websites.

31 Leticia Cesarino (2019) proposes an interesting discussion about digital populism based on Bolsonaro's use of WhatsApp in his campaign.

References

Abílio, L. C. (2017) Uberização do trabalho: Subsunção real da viração. *Passa palavra*, 2 February. https://passapalavra.info/2017/02/110685/ [Accessed 21 September 2020].

Alvarez, S (1990) *Engendering democracy in Brazil: Women's movements in transition politics*. Princeton, Princeton University Press.

Aranha, F. A. (2016) *Tecnocracia e capitalismo no Brasil num estudo de caso: A Associação Nacional De Programação Econômica e Social (Anpes) (1964–1967)*. Master's dissertation. Universidade Federal De Goiás.

Boas, T., & Gans-Morse, J. (2009) Neoliberalism: From new liberal philosophy to antiliberal slogan. *Studies in Comparative International Development* 44 (2), 137–161.

Boianovsky, M. (2018) *The Brazilian connection in Milton Friedman's 1967 presidential address and 1976 Nobel lecture*. Duke University Center for the History of Political Economy Working Paper, (2018–11).

Brito Cruz, F. (2019) *Definindo as regras do jogo: As regulações da campanha política e a internet*. Doctoral thesis. Faculdade de Direito da Universidade de São Paulo.

Câmara dos Deputados. (1991) *PL 1135/1991*. https://www.camara.leg.br/proposicoesWeb/fichadetramitacao?idProposicao=16299 [Accessed 11 September 2020].

Carreirão, Y. (2007) Identificação ideológica, partidos e voto na eleição presidencial de 2006. *Opinião Pública* 13 (2), 307–339.

Carvalho, O. de (2009) *A revolução globalista*. http://olavodecarvalho.org/a-revolucao-globalista/ [Accessed 23 September 2020].

Casimiro, F. H. (2011) A dimensão simbólica do neoliberalismo no Brasil: o Instituto Liberal e a cidadania como liberdade de consumo. *Cadernos de Pesquisa do Cdhis* 23 (1), 227–250.

Cesarino, L. (2019) On digital populism in Brazil. *PoLAR: Political and Legal Anthropology Review*, 15. https://polarjournal.org/2019/04/15/on-jair-bolsonaros-digital-populism/ [Accessed 23 September 2020].

Chaloub, J., & Perlatto, F. (2015) Intelectuais da 'Nova Direita' brasileira: Ideias, retórica e prática política. In *Anais dos Encontros da Associação Nacional de Pós-Graduação*

e Pesquisa em Ciências Sociais, 39° Encontro, 26–30 October 2015, Caxambu. São Paulo, Anpocs.
Cockett, R. (1995) *Thinking the unthinkable: Think tanks and the economic counter-revolution 1931–1983.* London, HarperCollins.
Comitê Gestor da Internet no Brasil (2007) *Indicadores de uso da internet no Brasil, 2005/2006.* https://www.cetic.br/media/docs/publicacoes/10/pal2007ofid-11.pdf [Accessed 23 September 2020].
Constantino, R. (2018) *Confissões de um ex-libertário: Salvando o liberalismo dos liberais modernos.* São Paulo, Record.
Cordeiro, J. M. (2009). *Direitas em movimento: a campanha da mulher pela democracia e a ditadura no Brasil.* Editora FGV.
Costa, H. (2018) *Entre o lulismo e o ceticismo.* São Paulo, Alameda.
Dardot, P., & Laval, C. (2016) *A nova razão do mundo: Ensaio sobre a sociedade neoliberal.* São Paulo, Boitempo.
Desai, R. (1994) Second-Hand dealers in ideas: Think-Tanks and Thatcherite hegemony. *New Left Review* 203, 147–155.
Doherty, B. (2009) *Radicals for capitalism: A freewheeling history of the modern American libertarian movement.* New York, PublicAffairs.
Downey, J., & Fenton, N. (2003) New media, counter-publicity and the public sphere. *New Media & Society* 5 (2), 185–202.
Dreifuss, R. A. (1987) *1964 – A conquista do Estado: Ação política, poder e golpe de classe.* Rio de Janeiro, Vozes.
Dreifuss, R. A. (1989) *O jogo da direita na Nova República.* Rio de Janeiro, Vozes.
Folha 2002 link: https://www1.folha.uol.com.br/folha/brasil/ult96u43699.shtml
Fonseca, F. (1994) *A imprensa liberal na transição democrática (1984–1987): Projeto político e estratégias de convencimento (Revista Visão e Jornal O Estado De São Paulo).* Master's dissertation. Universidade Estadual De Campinas.
Fragoso, S. (2006). Eu odeio quem odeia... Considerações sobre o comportamento dos usuários brasileiros na 'tomada' do Orkut. In E-Compós (Vol. 6).
Gonçalves, R. J. M. (2017) *História fetichista: O aparelho de hegemonia filosófico Instituto Brasileiro De Filosofia Convivium (1964–1985).* Anápolis, Editora da Universidade Estadual de Goiás.
Gros, D. (2003) *Institutos liberais e neoliberalismo no Brasil da Nova República.* Doctoral thesis. Fundação de Economia e Estatística Siegfried Emanuel Heuser.
Hauck, J. (2015) *Think tanks: Quem são, como atuam e qual seu panorama de ação no Brasil.* Master's dissertation. Universidade Federal de Minas Gerais.
Instituto Ordem Livre. (n.d.) *Liberdade na estrada.* http://ordemlivre.org/lne [Accessed 23 September 2020].
Jackson, B. (2010) At the origins of neo-liberalism: The free economy and the strong state, 1930–1947. *The Historical Journal* 53(1), 129–151.
Lima, F. (2016) PT e PSDB já foram ortodoxos e heterodoxos, aponta estudo. *Valor Econômico,* 8 April. https://valor.globo.com/brasil/noticia/2016/04/08/pt-e-psdb-ja-foram-ortodoxos-e-heterodoxos-aponta-estudo.ghtml [Accessed 11 September 2020].
MEDEIROS, J.; FANTI, F. (2019) Recent Changes in the Brazilian Feminist Field: The Emergence of New Collective Subjects. In: FERRERO, Juan Pablo; TATAGIBA, Luciana; NATALUCCI, Ana (Ed.) *Socio-Political Dynamics within the Crisis of the Left Turn in Argentina and Brazil.* Lanham: Rowman & Littlefield.
Miguel, L. F., & Coutinho, A. (2007) A crise e suas fronteiras: Oito meses de 'mensalão' nos editoriais dos jornais. *Opinião Pública* 13 (1), 97–123.

Morresi, S. (2008) *La nueva derecha argentina y la democracia sin política*. Los Polvorines, Universidad Nacional de General Sarmiento: Buenos Aires, Biblioteca Nacional.

Motta, R. P. S. (2002). *Em guarda contra o perigo vermelho: o anticomunismo no Brasil, 1917-1964* (Vol. 180). São Paulo: Editora Perspectiva.

Nishimura, K. (2004) Conservadorismo social: Opiniões e atitudes no contexto da eleição de 2002. *Opinião Pública* 10 (2), 339–367.

Nobre, M. (2013) *Imobilismo em movimento: Da abertura democrática ao governo Dilma*. São Paulo, Companhia das Letras.

Paiva, D., Braga, M. do S. S., & Pimentel, J. (2007) Eleitorado e partidos políticos no Brasil. *Opinião Pública* 13 (2), 388–408.

Pariser, E. (2011) *The filter bubble: How the new personalized web is changing what we read and how we think*. London, Penguin.

Pires, C. (2010) Em carta, Dilma assina compromisso contra o aborto. *O Estado de São Paulo*, 15 October. https://politica.estadao.com.br/noticias/geral,em-carta-dilma-assina-compromisso-contra-o-aborto,625257 [Accessed 17 September 2020].

Polletta, F., & Jasper, J. M. (2001). Collective identity and social movements. *Annual review of Sociology*, 27(1), 283–305.

Polletta, F., & Jasper, J. M. (2011) Collective identity and social movements. *Annual Review of Sociology* 27 (1), 283–305.

Power, T. (2010) *Political right in postauthoritarian Brazil: Elites, institutions, and democratization*. Pennsylvania, Penn State University Press.

Ramírez, H. (2007) *Corporaciones en el poder: Institutos económicos y acción política en Brasil y Argentina: Ipes, Fiel y Fundación Mediterránea*. Buenos Aires, Lenguaje Claro Editora.

Rocha, C. (2017) O papel dos think tanks pró-mercado na difusão do neoliberalismo no Brasil. *Millcayac – Revista Digital de Ciencias Sociales* 4 (7), 95–120. http://revistas.uncu.edu.ar/ojs/index.php/millca-digital/article/view/1020.

Rocha, C. (2021). *Menos Marx mais Mises. O liberalismo e a nova direita no Brasil*. São Paulo: Todavia

Rocha, C., & Medeiros, J. (2020) 'Vão todos tomar no...': A política de choque e a esfera pública. *Horizontes ao Sul*. https://www.horizonteSãosul.com/single-post/2020/04/27/VAO-TODOS-TOMAR-NO-A-POLITICA-DO-CHOQUE-E-A-ESFERA-PUBLICA [Accessed 9 August 2020].

Rocha, C., & Medeiros, J. (2021) Jair Bolsonaro and the dominant counterpublicity. *Brazilian Political Science Review* 15 (13), 1–20. https://doi.org/9.1590/1981-3821202100030004.

Rossi, M. (2015) Perfil de quem foi à Paulista destoa de lideranças e não poupa ninguém. *El País*, 18 August. https://brasil.elpais.com/brasil/2015/08/18/politica/1439928655_412897.html [Accessed 18 September 2020].

Scruton, R. (2015) *Como ser um conservador*. São Paulo, Editora Record.

Senado Federal. (2006a) *Projeto de Lei da Câmara n. 37*. https://www25.senado.leg.br/web/atividade/materias/-/materia/77244 [Accessed 23 September2020].

Senado Federal. (2006b) *Projeto de Lei da Câmara n. 122*. https://www25.senado.leg.br/web/atividade/materias/-/materia/79604 [Accessed 23 September 2020].

Shalders, A. (2017) Como o discurso de Bolsonaro mudou ao longo de 27 anos na câmara? *BBC News Brasil*, 7 December. https://www.bbc.com/portuguese/brasil-42231485 [Accessed 11 September 2020].

Singe, A. (2018) *O lulismo em crise: Um quebra-cabeça do período Dilma (2011–2016)*. São Paulo, Companhia das Letras.

Singer, A. (2012) *Os sentidos do lulismo: Reforma gradual e pacto conservador*. São Paulo, Companhia das Letras.
Soares, W. (2015) Conheça o 'kit gay' vetado pelo governo federal em 2011. *Nova Escola*, 1 February. https://novaescola.org.br/conteudo/84/conheca-o-kit-gay-vetado-pelo-governo-federal-em-2011 [Accessed 11 September 2020].
Spohr, M. (2012) O empresariado e as relações Brasil-Estados Unidos no caminho do Golpe de 1964. *Confluenze. Rivista Di Studi Iberoamericani* 4 (2), 45–62.
Stedman Jones, D. (2014) *Masters of the universe: Hayek, Friedman, and the birth of neoliberal politics*. Princeton, Princeton University Press.
Sunstein, C. (2017) *#Republic*. Princeton, Princeton University Press.
Teitelbaum, B. (2020) *War for eternity: Inside Bannon's far-right circle of global power brokers*. London, HarperCollins.
Telles, H. (2016) A direita vai às ruas: O antipetismo, a corrupção e democracia nos protestos antigoverno. *Ponto-e-Vírgula: Revista de Ciências Sociais* 19, 97–125.
Thimsen, A. F. (2017) Did the Trumpian counterpublic dissent against the dominant model of campaign finance? *Javnost-The Public* 24 (3), 267–283.
Venturi, G. (2006) A opinião pública diante da crise. *Teoria e Debate* 66, 20–26.
Warner, M. (2002) Publics and counterpublics. *Public Culture* 14 (1), 49–90.

9
CHILE
Orthodoxy and heterodoxy on the right[1]

Stéphanie Alenda, Carmen Le Foulon and Julieta Suárez-Cao

Introduction

Any analysis of the right is inevitably confronted with a problem of conceptualisation. Like the left, the right has historically taken on very diverse and heterogeneous sociological, organisational, and ideological forms and expressions, hindering a clear and perennial distinction among different notions that are often confused, if not contradictory: conservatism, liberalism, nationalism, fascism, populism, social Christianity, corporatism, and neoliberalism, among others. These numerous terms, as well as their spatially and historically variable character, frustrate attempts unequivocally to define "the" right. This ambiguity is reinforced by political actors' own frequent tendency to deny an existing right-wing identity, due to its stigmatising character.[2]

In the face of these difficulties, the expert literature has sought to contribute to the categorisation of political tendencies in several ways. One of the first approaches sought to identify the sociological differences between left and right. Mainly following this approach, the right was assimilated to the defence of a dominant class position, preservation of the capitalist system, and maintenance of the established order, on the one hand, and the incarnation of a traditional national and/or religious identity (albeit one questioned by the liberal right), on the other. The distinction between left and right then weakened as a result of cleavages'—particularly class cleavages'—decline as stable predictors of electoral behaviour. In his own way, Edward Gibson, one of the leading scholars of the Latin American right, confirmed the inability of sociological variables to account for the left/right partition. In his book dedicated to conservatism in Argentina, he thus stressed the need for the right to expand its traditional bases of support (made up of the upper strata of society), through the constitution of multiclass coalitions (Gibson, 1996: pp. 7–8).[3]

DOI: 10.4324/9781003352266-13

A second approach to distinguishing the right from the left consisted of classifying political parties according to their forms of organisation in an effort to identify a scheme characteristic of the right. This approach proved no more successful. The seminal typology of Maurice Duverger (1951) showed that the right had adopted the model of the "cadre" party, one structured in a loose and decentralised way, rather than adopting a "mass" party model. However, both the organisational heterogeneity of right-wing partisan formations and the collapse of the kind of active membership traditionally characteristic of left parties have since blurred the organisational distinction. In general terms, research on the internal structure of political parties has been scant, especially research in comparative terms (Panebianco, 1990: p. 492), on Latin America (Wills-Otero, 215; Wills-Otero, 2009), and specifically concerning parties from the right (Sajuria, Dosek, and Alenda, 2020).

The most fruitful classification efforts have focused on the ideas guiding political behaviour. These efforts were pioneered by political historian René Rémond (2005, 1982). This third approach refers to value systems developed prior to ideas. As a cultural approach, it allows for addressing the heterogeneity of right-wing formations through attention to the families or traditions that together make up the right. This approach marks a counterpoint to the sociological and organisational approaches. Rémond (2005: p. 14), in contrast, defends the importance of the left-right cleavage and argues that the right, like the left, cannot be reduced to a simple reflection of sociology, thus neglecting the study of political membership on its own terms.

We take this thesis as a starting point for thinking about the diversity of the right within Chile today and ask what this diversity owes to the 'existence and permanence of some sort of archetypes that over time acquire a coherence that allows them to subsist' (Rémond, 1982: p. 39). To that end,[4] in light of the results of a survey of the leaders of *Chile Vamos*,[5] we examine the convictions rooted in fundamental values that underpin "sensibilities" and are reflected in given ideological tendencies. We begin from the premise that "all political ideology organises a particular historical form of political sensibility" (Ansart, 1982: p. 143). Based on this proposition, we seek to highlight the nuances of values that give shape to various political sensibilities within the current Chilean centre-right.

In the first part of this chapter, we return to the existing theoretical discussion about defining and classifying the right. The second part then addresses the stages of its construction in Chile since the nineteenth century. Rather than defending the idea of traditions of thought that have adapted over time, or of stable and institutionalised "tendencies" (Sartori, 1992), we advocate an approach based on the idea of political sensibilities based on fundamental values. As we will see, these do not operate as invariant universals. Rather, they become meaningful and are resignified and used by actors themselves within particular historical contexts of political competition. The third part of the chapter analyses the position of the leaders of *Chile Vamos* on three dimensions: economic (role of the market versus the State), political (replacing the constitution inherited from the dictatorship), and cultural (abortion and same-sex marriage). We maintain that the current centre-right cannot be understood as the product of evolution and adaptation of conservative doctrine alone. Instead, it must be understood, on the one hand, in light of its ideological reconfiguration during the military dictatorship and, on the other hand, as a result of more recent ideological transformations that attest to a diversification of *Chile Vamos* leaders' sensibilities.

Essentialist versus constructivist understandings of the right

To solve the problem of defining the right, essentialist approaches propose to determine the universal and timeless characteristics of the values and behaviours of the right, leaving aside both contextual considerations of time and place and ideological nuances. In Europe, the right has from this perspective traditionally figured as associated with notions of authority and elitism, in contrast to a left presented as essentially democratic and participatory (Alexandre-Collier and Jardin, 2004). Resistant to the ideologies of change proper to the left, the right has also been thought naturally to defend the established order, whether in its social, political, or economic dimensions.[6]

In the case of Chile, conservative historiography has also contributed to the centrality of these notions, both for intellectuals following this essentialist approach to the right and for political actors themselves. These intellectuals and political actors have all highlighted an obsession with the principle of authority and attachment to order running through cultural "right-wing" politics.[7] In their book on the right in Latin America, Luna and Rovira (2014) emphasise another feature distinguishing the left from the right, one previously noted by Norberto Bobbio (1995): "Whereas the right conceives most inequalities as natural and difficult (or even inconvenient) to eradicate, the left conceives most inequalities as socially constructed and as a target for progressive social change" (p. 3). For the authors, this minimal "ideological definition", stable in time and space, is linked to the actors' positions on the State–market axis and their degree of support for redistributive policies aimed at correcting extreme levels of inequality. The focus of their analysis thus shifts towards the strategies that the right has had to develop in order to survive in adverse contexts marked by demands for redistributive policies, while also safeguarding its economic interests. Central to these strategies have been representation of interests through non-electoral strategies allowing the right to exert influence, adoption of electoral strategies directed against the political establishment, and organisation in political parties.

However, although this proposed minimal definition does take into account the convictions that allow us to understand how political identities are forged, it is both too specific and too general to have heuristic value. It is too reductionist in that it refers to a broader doctrinal corpus consisting of the defence of a natural order rooted in a traditionalist and/or religious vision of the world, of which the understanding of inequalities is only one dimension. That defence also refers to other distinctive markers, such as the protection of life, or the cult of the family, traditionally considered by the right as the repository of moral values and a privileged site of their transmission as well as for the education of individuals. It is also too general in that, although these markers appear as universal invariants that lend themselves to defining the right altogether independently of given historical situations, they are actually the product of history, as well as of the trajectory of certain ideas initially demarcating left and right, before later being claimed by the right. Such is the case of the notion of "freedom", which motivated all the nineteenth century's revolutions against absolutism and authority, yet from the twentieth century onwards became the banner of the right's struggle against the totalitarian power of communist regimes, left-wing leaders, and state intervention in the economy (Rémond, 1982: p. 23). Luna and Rovira's analysis notes these contextual variations, but without giving them sustained attention.[8] The essentialist approach they privilege thus dodges the eminently relational character of the notions of left and right, as well as the way that, as ideas circulate over time, the lines of demarcation between left and right shift, and positions on issues of so-called values—such as marriage, family, abortion, or the role of the state—evolve, with each side adopting sometimes previously inconceivable positions.

Breaking with this view, among other things, René Rémond (2005) proposes to distinguish "families of thought" characterised by sharing "a global project; a vision of the ideal society; philosophical references; a history; memories, some happy and others less so; a particular sensibility" (p. 82). Distinguishing three, distinct right-wing political families in France,[9] Rémond maintains that their continuity has inherited in the stability of certain key ideas and each family's combination of particular principles and values. Yet, he does not exclude the possibility of these traditions' adapting to specific, contingent situations or deny the possibility of their evolving.[10] Although Rémond's original typology can hardly be exported to contexts other than France,[11] it invites identification of lasting historical traditions equally present at other latitudes, albeit defined according to their own unique circumstances and problems. Various typologies for classifying European rights succeeded that of Rémond.[12] Recently, his nomenclature was also adapted for application to the Argentine right (Morresi, 2015).[13]

Most such typologies agree on the existence of a liberal and a conservative right, although the characteristics attributed to each vary depending on the national contexts considered. However, the proposed categorisations do not always distinguish rigorously between filiations, which are, in any case, difficult to establish, and underlying resemblances between two currents of thought. That distinction is often particularly relevant in the case of countries that have experienced a breakdown of the democratic system. Should the parties inherited from authoritarian regimes be thought of as breaking from or continuing with the old regime? Although taxonomic efforts highlight the recurrence of doctrinal traditions that contribute to establishing the "identity" of the right, they are less pertinent for thinking about moments when political landscapes are reconfigured. At such moments, it is often difficult to discern between rupture and continuity, between historical filiations and mere similarities.

We will therefore investigate the historical traditions of thought that have shaped the Chilean right since the nineteenth century. In this section, we give particular emphasis to the ideological influences that were consolidated during the military dictatorship. The right was reconfigured around these influences, and the Chilean centre-right is currently developing various forms of internal differentiation in relation to them.

As we will see, the different historical traditions of political thought on the Chilean right translate into distinct sensibilities rooted in key values. Their empirical manifestations take on different expressions united by a logic of family resemblance. These sensibilities make sense, are given new meanings, and are used by actors themselves in particular historical contexts of political competition.

The political and ideological field of the Chilean right

What history shows is that Rémond's classification of political forces does not sufficiently emphasise the fact that ideological categories are above all objects of symbolic struggles taking place within a political field in which they are mobilised. In turn, these political forces evolve under the effect of both endogenous dynamics and exogenous influences. They may therefore sometimes compete and seek to differentiate themselves from one another, while other times they manage to form alliances and cooperate (Gaxie, 2004; Le Bohec and Le Digol, 2012).

It should be noted that the question of the traditions of thought proper to the Chilean right has taken on renewed interest lately for intellectuals seeking to contribute to the "renewal of their narrative" (Verbal, 2017: p. 62). Hoping to overcome the "intellectual crisis" of the Chilean right today, philosopher Hugo Herrera has proposed rescuing two currents usually considered secondary in Chilean historiography (Correa Sutil, 2004): the national-popular[14] and social Christian traditions, which he favours adding to the historical depiction of the right in Chile, placing them alongside conservatism and liberalism (Herrera, 2014: p. 120). Rehabilitating these two additional, statist, traditions[15] allows him to formulate a criticism of the economistic excesses of the liberal tradition within the right. Herrera also accounts for the existence of an intellectual right,[16] which he describes as "anti-oligarchic"—in the sense that it cannot be reduced to the defence of the economic interests of an oligarchy—and "specifically political", due to its links to politics (2014: pp. 114, 117). The nature of this conflict within the right, as presented by Herrera, is not unlike that sketched by Correa Sutil (2004), who, albeit from the opposite political-theoretical vantage point, likewise points to a tension running through the history of the Chilean right: one between "liberal capitalism" and what she calls "social-Christian populism" (a "danger" the liberal right seeks to combat) (pp. 111–143).

Taking part in the fight for the definition of the current right, historian Valentina Verbal (2017) maintains, on the contrary, that its historical-ideological anchorage is found in classical liberalism and is shared by liberals and conservatives.

She thereby questions the relevance of the social Christian and national-popular currents for the Chilean right. Regardless of its conservative roots, she argues that the former was given expression principally by the *Falange*, a political party formed in 1935 by a group of younger social Christians, which split off from the Conservative Party in 1938 and struck a path to the left merging into the Christian Democratic Party in 1957. As for the latter, it lacked political representation and did not qualify as a formation on the right due to its rejection of economic liberalism (Verbal, 2017: p. 64).[17]

However, Chilean historiography shows that conservatives and liberals did not always share the same vision regarding defence of economic freedom. A social Christian sensibility was present within the elite of the Conservative Party starting from the end of the nineteenth century, and that sensibility remained alive after the separation from the *Falange* (Pereira, 1994: p. 131).[18] In fact, "at the 1901 Convention, chaired by Carlos Walker Martínez, the Conservative Party had incorporated the Christian social order into its program" (Pereira, 1994: p. 117). At the time, Conservatives perceived the solution to the "social question" as laying in Christian social doctrine, not liberal individualism, or other ideologies. Regardless of that long past influenced by Social Christianity, Verbal (2017) considers the "marked anti-capitalist discourse" of Eduardo Cruz-Coke, who represented that camp in 1946, as sufficient to disqualify Social Christianity as a tradition of right-wing thought (p. 64). The truth is that this more economically liberal form of right discourse became pronounced only once "an affirmation of the importance of capital and a gradual opposition to the growing intervention of the State" had been installed within conservative thought (Pereira, 1994: p. 173).[19]

This displacement of the dividing lines between conservatives and liberals is part of the aforementioned dynamics of the political field. That displacement resulted from three central events: the separation of Church and State sanctioned by the 1925 Constitution, which enabled the two camps to overcome their theological differences; the right's shared opposition to the left ideology of communism and the Popular Front; and the *Falange*'s irruption into the political game, with the subsequent rise of Christian Democracy. With the emergence of a party that was clearly centrist on socio-economic matters (Valenzuela, 1995: p. 47), the Conservative Party was pushed further to the right. This evolution led to the merger of the two parties in the National Party (1966), while the Christian social programme that consisted of purging capitalism of its "vices and injustices" (Pereira, 1994: p. 370) gradually lost relevance as a distinctive position.

In short, the question of the number of traditions of thought within the Chilean right—much less that of what, precisely, defines the right—cannot be answered univocally. Rather, the issue invites attention to the controversial uses of certain categories in the context of symbolic struggles to endow the right with an identity. Above all, it implies historically reconstructing the processes through which party organisations and their doctrines adapt to changing conditions of electoral competition and given inflections in political life. Despite its gradual constitution in a centrist ideology, social Christianity was one of the currents of thought rooted in the Conservative Party; in turn social Christianity gradually became a party family. In 1949, differences dividing them came more clearly to light, as the Conservative Party split into the Conservative Traditionalist Party, which was favourable to strengthening ties with the Liberal Party, and the Conservative Christian Social Party, which was opposed to doing so. That split notwithstanding, rather than artificially dissociating social Christianity from conservatism, it is worth highlighting their historical overlap and interactions, sometimes competitive, sometimes collaborative.

From these historical evolutions, we can thus discern the emergence and clarification of three different traditions of thought. First, there is a tradition of value conservatism, marked by iron-clad opposition to everything that could contribute to licence in customs and stalwart support for the family as the "primary cell of the society, with rights and duties prior to and superior to the State" (Pereira, 1994: p. 192). The second tradition favoured a moderate conception of State–market relations as one requiring a "proper balance", with the State playing a regulatory role to correct market errors in pursuit of greater social justice.[20] Finally, there was economic liberalism, characterised at least until the mid-1920s by its orthodoxy.[21]

The 1950s and 1960s marked the gestation of a "new right". Two ideologies[22] contributed to its construction: corporatism and nationalism, which were expressed through the National Party and the *gremialista* movement[23] (Valdivia, 2008). This stage has been analysed as a moment of "rupture" (Benavente and Araya, 1981) or "historical discontinuity" (Moulian and Torres, 1988: p. 79). First, it marked the decline of the nineteenth-century oligarchic right represented by the Conservative and Liberal Parties. What is more, it also prevented the development of close relations between those two older parties, and the swarm of currents and political organisations[24] that then appeared in conflict. According to specialists, the novelty of this "new" right lay in its being "nationalist";[25] "profoundly anti-Marxist", and/or "open to the middle strata" (Valdivia, 2008: pp. 80–81).[26] It also set itself apart from the traditional right's adherence to liberal ideology and largely rejected dictatorial regimes. Corporatism and nationalism thus shared a fundamental idea: society needed to be depoliticised in the face of what was then perceived as an excessive influence of parties and ideologies.

During those decades, corporatism became consolidated as the right's alternative to liberal thought, which, like socialism and social Christianity, was in crisis. Recognising this influence implies qualifying the unanimity of adherence to the project of capitalist modernisation (Correa Sutil, 2004: p. 141) by a traditional business community that, for the most part, remained statist. It also helps to explain the ideological onslaught of corporatism during the 1960s, in a context of widespread popular mobilisation during the government of Eduardo Frei Montalva.

However, it should be underlined that this corporatist set of ideas never succeeded in becoming a tradition of right-wing thought on a par with conservatism, liberalism, or social Christianity.[27] Indeed, it was first of all a phenomenon inseparable from expressions of fascism elsewhere in the world.[28] It sought to deactivate social classes by giving direction of the economy to a series of intermediate associations—corporations—and returning to a traditionalist Catholic order threatened by what was then perceived as a crisis of essential Catholic values.[29] Second, corporatism was not defined by any particular partisan or political tradition. Rather, it permeated different parties and movements like the *Falange*. Members of the *Falange* begin to espouse this ideal of "conservative renewal", whether within the Conservative Party (Ruiz, 1992a: p. 101),[30] the National Party, or *gremialismo*. Likewise, it was incorporated into the principles of military government (Cristi and Ruiz, 1992: p. 13), although it was abandoned early. Finally, it fed twentieth-century Chilean nationalism (Valdivia, 2008: p. 112), without allowing clear lines to be drawn between corporatism and nationalism. Towards the end of the Popular Unity government, the right was thus characterised by the diversity of its ideological currents, projects, and organisational expressions. Within this diversity, two general approaches could be distinguished: one favouring a minimal state, and another that favoured a corporate organisation of the State and social life in general while opposing all liberal and democratic forms of political participation.

Gradually, the corporatist argument would be displaced by the neoliberal doctrine of Friedrich Hayek and the Chicago School of Economics. That substitution was facilitated by both currents sharing the same principle of defence of the natural order,[31] part of the right's traditionalist and religious worldview. But, more than constituting a universal invariant, we maintain that this principle and the doctrinal corpus to which it was linked were revitalised in the face of the communist threat and a crisis of Catholic values.[32] This convergence was also reflected in the principle of *subsidiarity*. This principle was understood in two ways: one Francoist and critical of political parties, which emphasised a conception of politics as a natural phenomenon,[33] and another neoliberal, which advocated for the end of state intervention in the economy and became hegemonic only at the end of the 1970s (Ruiz, 1992a: pp. 109, 120). The principle of subsidiarity, which has its origin in the social doctrine of the Church, circumscribes the intervention of the State to situations in which the capacities of individuals, families, groups, or intermediate associations are inadequate for them to be self-sufficient in their respective fields. The connection of *gremialismo* with neoliberal theses passed through a traditionalist interpretation of that doctrine, one materialised in the notion of "Catholic subsidiarity".[34] Presenting it as a response to statism, Jaime Guzmán, the founder of the *gremialista* Movement and main editor of the Declaration of Principles of Military Government, defined this notion as a "metaphysics of the person", a being "created in the image and likeness of God" who precedes society (Guzmán, 1965; Cristi, 2000: p. 69). After the coup, several other political-intellectual contributions sought to harmonise the neoliberal option with Christian morality based on their common concern with safeguarding the natural order (Alenda, Gartenlaub and Fischer, 2020). This project was facilitated by the influence within the new business elites acquired by Opus Dei, in which neoliberal doctrine and conservative Catholic thought converged (Montero, 1997;

Thumala, 2007; Romero and Bustamante, 2016). During the 1980s, neoliberal ideology thereby became hegemonic within a right-wing political field divided into many competing political organisations. On the State–market axis, the clearest gap was between "pure" liberals[35] and statist nationalists—of orthodox corporatist orientation—who were critical of neoliberalism. Their position sharpened during the economic crisis of the early 1980s. In practice, they adhered to a principle of subsidiarity applied through targeting public spending to the neediest sectors, that is, the use of criteria of economic efficiency in social policy. According to this economistic approach, which applied to all areas of social life, the role of the State is restricted to guaranteeing full exercise of entrepreneurial freedom without restricting individual liberty, while the market becomes the main mechanism for allocating resources (Allamand, 1993: p 37; Montero, 1997: pp. 162–163). During that period, the nationalists ended up represented by two competing groups: *Avanzada Nacional*, founded in 1983, and the National Action Movement (MAN), which was created in 1987; the scant influence that this current achieved revealed the already anachronistic character of its corporatist-inspired economic proposal. Consensus instead developed in favour of defending a "free society", which was to be the founding principle of National Renewal (RN) in 1987.[36]

During the 1980s, being liberal thus referred to defence of political liberties. Unlike the more monolithic UDI (Alenda, 2014), whose ideological roots date back to Guzmán's *gremialista* movement, RN was internally divided between "conservatives" and "liberals". The latter sought to strengthen democracy and open up to the political centre (Cañas, 1992; Cornejo, 2001; Godoy, 2005; Mackinnon, 2005). Cultural liberalism emerged later. Only after the adoption of key amendments to the 1980 constitution, the differences between "conservatives" and "liberals" began to shift to cultural issues (divorce, same-sex marriage, etc.) (Díaz, 2016: p. 489), a change attesting to the contingent nature of political sensibilities.

Since then, political sensibilities have continued to evolve, even while the Chilean right's competing currents have each maintained a family resemblance to one of the earlier three historical traditions (conservatism, social Christianity, and liberalism). The next section will examine how the complex map of historical traditions and ruptures traced in the previous section has been updated in the twenty-first century. To empirically apprehend political sensibilities, we will take as a point of reference the positions of leaders on the current Chilean centre-right on three dimensions: State–market relations, cultural and "value" issues, and political order.

Current political sensibilities within *Chile Vamos*: Orientations transversal to the parties

To update the traditions of thought and political sensibilities that can be traced in the positions of the leaders of the *Chile Vamos* centre-right coalition, composed by UDI, RN, and *Evópoli*[37] and the PRI,[38] we use the responses of leaders of the UDI, RN, *Evópoli*, and the PRI to a survey carried out between November 10, 2015 and October 31, 2016.[39] The advantage of investigating sensibilities lies in the possibility of transcending party divisions and delving into other dimensions of the centre-right. This new centre-right, our results show, is marked by three distinct sensibilities concerning State–market relations, each associated with one of the previously described traditions of thought. First, there is what one could call a "subsidiary sensibility", which is a direct heir to the neoliberal-Catholic confluence of the dictatorship. Second, there is a "solidary sensibility", which is mainly related to the social Christian and conservative tradition. And finally, there is what we call a "libertarian sensibility" with orthodox liberal roots that was reconfigured during the Chilean dictatorship.[40] The divisions among supporters of these three distinct sensibilities within the centre-right do not run along simple party lines. Thus, while 12% of the leaders of the UDI can be categorised as libertarian, 14% of RN leaders and 17% of *Evópoli*'s are libertarians as well. The proportion of libertarians within each of the main three centre-right parties was thus statistically indistinguishable.[41]

The sensibility most influential among current centre-right leaders was the subsidiary one: 59% of UDI leaders, 57% of those from RN, and 47% of those in *Evópoli* fell into this group. The differences between *Evópoli* and UDI are statistically significant (99% confidence level), whereas the one between *Evópoli* and RN is significant at 85% confidence level. *Evópoli* is the party with the smallest proportion of leaders who present the characteristic sensibility of the post-dictatorship right, one marked by *gremialista* doctrine. Finally, although the percentage of leaders exhibiting the solidarity sensibility is higher in *Evópoli*, 36% of its leaders, followed by 31% of RN's, and 29% of UDI's fell into that group. The difference between *Evópoli* and RN does not reach statistical significance at conventional levels, and only at 85% level of confidence in the case of *Evópoli* and UDI. As for the percentage of libertarians, there are no statistically significant differences between parties. In short, UDI has more leaders with a subsidiary sensibility and less with a solidary or libertarian one than *Evópoli*, with differences that are statistically significant, but not substantial. It should therefore be emphasised that, in practice, the distribution of these three distinct sensibilities among the leaderships of the different centre-right *Chile Vamos* coalition parties is remarkably homogeneous (Figure 9.1).

We also examined whether there are variations in the distribution of sensibilities associated with individual characteristics of the leaders other than their party affiliations such as the leaders' religiosity, age, and gender. In view of the possible Christian social root of the group of solidary sensibility, we examined the effect of leaders' religiosity. All of the leaders were classified into four groups according to whether they claim to belong to any religion and how often they attend religious services.[42] As shown in Figure 6, although there are certain differences, they are neither substantively nor statistically significant.[43] The percentage of libertarians ranges from 12% among those with low religiosity, to 13% among those with medium religiosity and 15% among those without any religion, reaching 16% among those who declare themselves highly religious. The percentage of those with a subsidiary sensibility varies even less, coming in between 54% and 56% for leaders at all levels of religiosity. As for the solidary sensibility, it figured

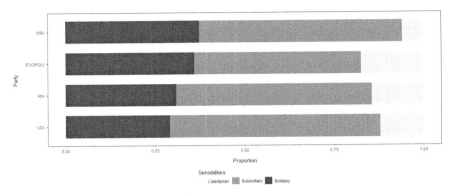

FIGURE 9.1 Chile: Sensibilities by party. Source: Authors' elaboration.

among 28% among those of high religiosity, 30% of those not professing any religion, 31% of those with medium religiosity, and a full 34% of leaders of low religiosity. It is observed, then, that there are no substantial differences in the distribution of sensibilities according to religiosity.

Possible differences according to age groups were also explored. We were particularly interested in determining whether there might be significant generational differences. As seen in Figure 9.2, although certain differences can be seen, there is no evidence of a strong generational cleavage where these sensibilities are concerned. The percentage of libertarians is higher among the youngest leaders: 18% among those under 30 and 17% among those 30 to 45 years old. This percentage drops to 13% among those aged 46 to 60, and a mere 9% among those over 60. However, the pattern is not so linear where the other two sensibilities are concerned. The percentage of those with a subsidiary sensibility was lowest among those under 30 and those between 46 and 60 years old (49% and 51% respectively). By contrast, it was somewhat but not greatly higher among those between 30 and 45 and those over 60 (59% and 60%). As for leaders with a solidary sensibility, it was most common among those between 46 and 60 years old (36%), while the next lower age group had the lowest percentage (24%). Within other age groups, it ranged from 31% to 33%.

Similarly, it is possible to ask whether gender differences are related to the sensibilities surveyed. Figure 9.2 shows the distribution of sensibilities by gender. Here again, there were no large discrepancies. The percentage of libertarians is the same in both groups (13%). There were, however, other slight differences. A higher percentage of female leaders supported a more solidary role for the State (35% versus 30%). In contrast, male leaders were slightly more favourable to the subsidiary model (57% versus 52%). However, neither of these differences was statistically significant.

In sum, the sensibilities inherited from the right's three distinct historical traditions of thought are transversal to the political parties. Moreover, with few

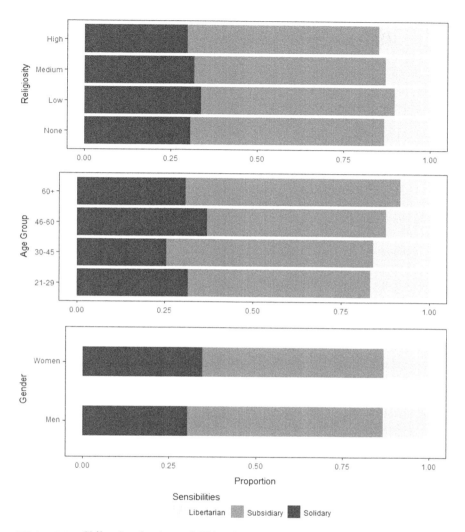

FIGURE 9.2 Chile: Leaders' sensibilities by degree of religiosity, age group, and gender. Source: Authors' elaboration.

exceptions, leaders' distribution among them did not substantially vary by individual characteristics such as religiosity, age, or gender.[44]

This near-absence of variation seems to corroborate the premise from which we began: certain affective orientations persist over time based on values that underlie political sensibilities. The bulk of these originated from the military regime, during which the subsidiary approach developed. That sensibility is still predominant among centre-right leaders regardless of age. Meanwhile, the libertarian sensibility, more marked among young people and within *Evópoli*, recalls initiatives of the "pure" liberals during that same period.[45] Finally, the solidary sensibility represents an updated version of the statist tradition present both in social Christian conservatism and in the national-popular current.

In this way, examination of leaders' orientations on the State–market axis reveals the transversality of a vision that is fundamentally economistic (subsidiary or libertarian). That economistic orientation contributes to cementing the coalition, despite the co-existence of three distinct sensibilities within each party. Conversely, as we will see in the next section, it is where it comes to value issues that the three parties differ most.

Values positions: The apple of discord within the coalition?

Until now, the sensibilities and positions of party leaders have been analysed with a focus on issues associated with the traditional left-right cleavage, such as debate about the desirable role of the State in the economy and the market's advantages as a mechanism for allocating resources. However, this portrait would be incomplete without analysis of leaders' attitudes concerning value issues of increasing relevance in Chilean political debate in recent years. This section therefore examines their attitudes regarding abortion, civil union, and same-sex marriage.

With regard to the issue of rights to sexual dissent, we distinguished among those against granting any such rights, those in favour only of civil union, and those also supporting equal marriage. Figure 9.3 shows how attitudes regarding civil union and equal marriage are distributed by sensibility and party. Paradoxically, the economic libertarians seem to be the most conservative group in value terms. Fifty-four per cent of them opposed both kinds of reforms. By contrast, 48% of those favouring a subsidiary economic role of the state and 40% of those favourable to a solidary role of the state did. The difference between the two extremes (54% and 40%) was statistically significant at 90% confidence levels. However, there are no differences by sensibility in terms of support only for civil union. Support for that position ranges from 26% to 29. Finally, the three groups' differences in support for same-sex marriage were marked. Only 18% of the libertarians are in favour of both civil unions and same-sex marriage, the most culturally liberal position. By contrast, a quarter (24%) of leaders supportive of a subsidiary state and a third (34%) of those standing up for a solidary state favoured it.[46]

Positions regarding the rights of sexual minorities, with the exception of support for equal marriage, varied relatively little from one sensibility to another. It is interesting to analyse the same responses in terms of which party these leaders came from. As can be seen in Figure 10.3, there are important divergences in that regard. Although the UDI and RN have very similar and statistically indistinguishable distributions, *Evópoli*'s is radically different. Thus, while 56% of UDI leaders and 53% of RN leaders oppose both civil union and same-sex marriage, only 8% do so in *Evópoli*. Conversely, while only 12% of the leaders of the UDI and 16% of the RN are in favour of both, three quarters (77%) of the leaders of *Evópoli* are.

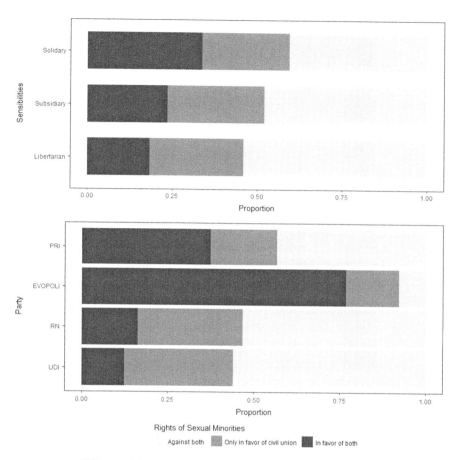

FIGURE 9.3   Chile: Positions on rights of sexual minorities by sensibility and party.
Source: Authors' elaboration.

Another area in which reform was being debated at the time of our survey was that of abortion. As in the case of sexual minority rights, differences of position concerning abortion proved not to differ substantially, or statistically significantly, depending on leaders' underlying sensibilities about the State–market axis. However, here again, the parties proved much more notably different from one other, even though their leaders in all cases overwhelmingly declare themselves against the decriminalisation of abortion (Figure 9.4). That opposition held true even for *Evópoli*, despite its claim to be a liberal party.

In short, in terms of value issues, leaders' positions did not differ greatly according to their sensibilities concerning the State–market axis. That lack of variation by economic sensibility could reflect the general weight of moral conservatism, which also contributes to cementing the centre-right coalition. Moral conservatism

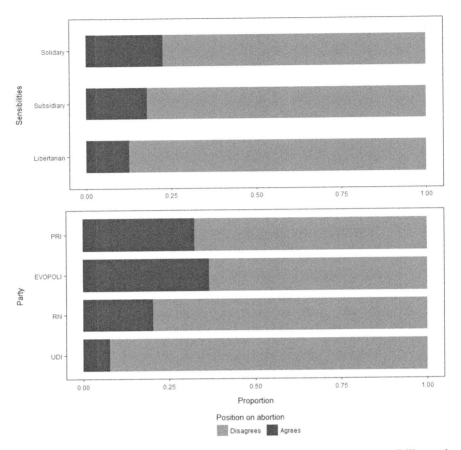

FIGURE 9.4 Chile: agreement with decriminalisation of abortion by sensibility and party. Source: Authors' elaboration.

is particularly notable in relation to abortion, but also continues to guide responses related to sexual minority rights. There are, nonetheless, significant variations across parties. In particular, *Evópoli* party leaders assume substantially, and statistically significantly, more liberal positions than others. On decriminalisation of abortion, a post-material issue that remains fundamental for the Chilean right in general, there was even a noticeable difference between RN and the UDI.[47]

Chile Vamos: Right or centre-right?

Based on analysis of the empirical results of our survey of the leaders of *Chile Vamos*, one can discern the presence of a new centre-right space within the coalition. The average leader does continue to favour a subsidiary state role and to oppose both abortion and the rights of sexual minorities. Nonetheless, one cannot ignore the fact that a considerable proportion of the current right favours a more solidary state role and the emergence of centre-right leaders holding more liberal positions on issues related to the cultural-moral order. These lines of dissent within the coalition point to a consolidation of a centre-right space. The present section examines leaders' answers to questions on two current issues.

The two current issues we examined were the elimination of profit in education and the need to reform the current Constitution, which dates back to the dictatorship. Both are considered demands that emerged from outside the right in Chile. The discussion about ending profit in education was defended on the streets by student movements and presented as a leftist issue. In theory, one might therefore expect to find little support for this measure within *Chile Vamos*. As for constitutional reform, it was triggered by supporters of the centre-left government of Michelle Bachelet. Moreover, it symbolises conflict concerning the legitimacy of the institutions inherited from Augusto Pinochet. One would therefore expect to find little support from the right for a change of constitution.

As shown in Figure 9, while only 25% of the libertarians agree or strongly agree with eliminating profit in education, 43% of those favouring a subsidiary state and 58% of those favour a solidary one. These differences are all statistically significant at 99% confidence levels. This question also allows for validating our distinction among leaders in terms of three sensibilities: libertarian, subsidiary, and solidary. If those categories really capture distinct attitudes regarding the desirable degree of state intervention in the economy, then leaders' positions on eliminating profit in education should vary accordingly. Those favouring a solidary role for the state should be most supportive of such reform, whereas libertarians should be least supportive. And indeed, that proves to be the case, with substantial and statistically significant differences in this regard between leaders with each of those sensibilities.

However, as Figure 9.5 also shows, there are no substantive, or statistically significant, differences between the political parties. Thus, in all parties a little more than 50% of the leaders disagree with eliminating profit in education. The coalition thus appears more or less evenly divided on this issue, including within each of the three main parties.[48]

Finally, leaders' agreement with establishing a new Constitution is analysed. As Figure 9.6 shows, the level of agreement varies substantially according to the sensibility and the party of the leaders. While only 15% of libertarians agree with establishing a new Constitution to replace that of 1980, 29% of those with a subsidiary sensibility and 46% of those with a solidary one did, all differences statistically significant at 1%.

The differences across parties are even greater. As one would expect, UDI leaders agreed least with such reform (21%), whereas those of *Evópoli* are most apt to agree with it (61%). RN leaders come in between these two extremes (35%). All of these differences are statistically significant.

The results of this section are surprising in several ways. First, they show that there is significant support among centre-right leaders for eliminating profit in

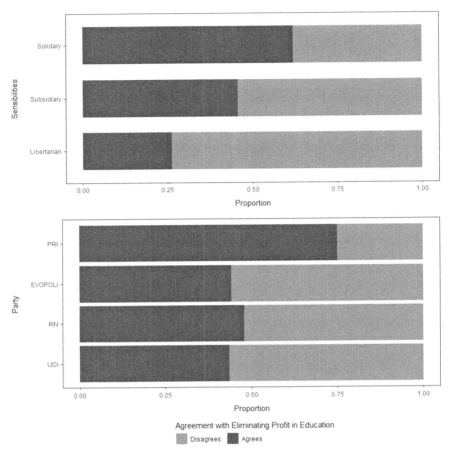

FIGURE 9.5 Chile: Agreement with eliminating profit in education by sensibility and party. Source: Authors' elaboration.

education. One may conclude that belief in the market as the best mechanism for adjudicating distribution of resources in all social spheres is subject to some degree of challenge within the right.

Second, our results show greater agreement with establishing a new constitution for Chile than one might expect within the right. Rejecting a new constitution implies defending the legitimacy of the existing Constitution of 1980. Therefore, those who are open to replacing it can be understood as having a more critical vision of the Pinochet regime.[49] These findings, confirmed by the estimations that in the October 25, 2020, national plebiscite, between 32% and 50% of centre-right voters approved drawing up a new Constitution (Alenda, 2021), make it possible to speak of the *Chile Vamos* coalition as a space within which leaders with different sensibilities coexist. A not insignificant minority now espouses

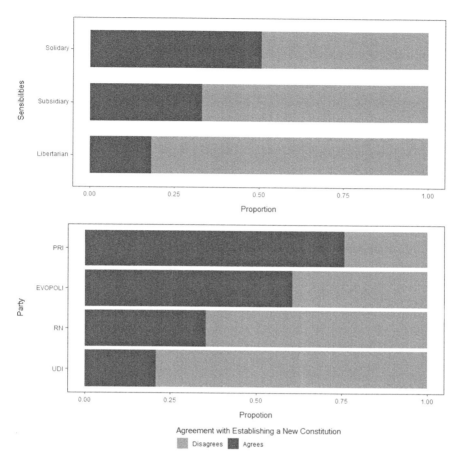

FIGURE 9.6   Chile: Agreement with establishing a new constitution by sensibility and party. Source: Authors' elaboration.

positions close to the centre of the political spectrum. That holds not only for so-called "cultural" issues, or issues of post-material values, but also where it comes to greater regulation of the economy and critical views of the dictatorship's institutional legacy.

Conclusion: *Chile Vamos* as a centre-right coalition

Theoretically, we have suggested that there is a preservation of political sensibilities over time. Without assuming that the affective modes of positioning around the values grounding these sensibilities are invariable, we have analysed them as "sorts of archetypes that over time acquire a coherence that allows them to subsist", in the words of Rémond (1982: p. 39). We do not, however, assume that such affective modes of positioning are invariable. Rather, through our empirical findings concerning political sensibilities concerning the desirable role of the State in the economy, we sought to explore and update this complex map of traditions, which we have traced back to the nineteenth century and the historical rupture that occurred in the twentieth.

The current three sensibilities on the right retain a family resemblance with the three nineteenth-century traditions of thought, despite various changes and adjustments to them over time. The liberal sensibility, which was inherited from the tradition of more orthodox liberalism, acquired a radicalised expression during the Chilean dictatorship through the dismantling of the state and imposition of neoliberal economic policies. As for the subsidiary sensibility, it is the successor of the particular liberal-Catholic confluence that took form in nineteenth-century Chile. The solidary sensibility, finally, can be traced back to a more statist-conservative and social Christian tradition.

We also show that the current centre-right must be understood in light of its ideological reconfiguration during the military dictatorship and also as a result of more recent ideological adaptations. These more recent adaptations have given rise to greater diversification of right-wing Chilean sensibilities, and greater influence of a culturally liberal current. Consequently, the current Chilean right's positions are far from univocal.

Indeed, the current Chilean right's multivocality extends to current notions of liberalism itself. Not only does liberalism contain different nuances when considering the role assigned by the leaders to the market, from those who reject any kind of interference by the state in the economy (libertarians), to those supporting limiting its role to a subsidiary one focused on questions of social need, up to the solidary sensibility favourable to a greater individual contribution to the public coffers. Also, the polysemic nature of the notion of liberalism gives rise to different uses. Which components or interpretation of liberalism are emphasised varies depending on historical context and the conditions of political competition. It is in this sense that the notion of political sensibility turns out to be particularly valuable heuristically: it allows for studying these ascriptions ("to be liberal", "to be a liberal party") while taking into account the contextual fluidity and variability of their contours.[50]

The results presented demonstrate the existence of different sensibilities in relation to the State–market axis within the Chilean right. These sensibilities coexist within each of the centre-right parties and are thus transversal to them. Moreover, the empirical data show that there are not even any important differences in the distribution of these sensibilities among the largest parties in the coalition. In all three parties, the subsidiary sensibility is most prevalent, and in each case the percentage of leaders with a solidary sensibility is actually double the percentage of libertarians.

The greatest differences observed across parties are on the so-called values axis, especially regarding attitudes towards same-sex marriage. Within *Evópoli*, the vast majority of leaders are in favour of equal marriage and civil union (77%).

In marked contrast, only 12% of the leaders of the UDI and 16% of those of RN are. As expected, differences regarding support for decriminalising abortion are attenuated. In all three parties, an overwhelming majority opposes decriminalisation. However, important differences between parties are nonetheless evident on abortion. While a third of the leaders of *Evópoli* support decriminalisation, 20% in the RN and only 8% in the UDI do.

In sum, we found a considerable proportion of centre-right leaders with attitudes favourable to state regulation of the economy, liberal on value issues, and critical of Pinochet's legacy. Although the bulk of the elites, mainly from traditional parties (RN and UDI), maintain classical right-wing attitudes, a substantial percentage of leaders have more moderate centre-right positions. Our results reveal that the coalition between new and conventional parties from the right, *Chile Vamos*, finds itself at odds between an orthodox pole of market-centred and morally conservative attitudes, and a heterodox pole of state-centred and morally liberal stances.

Notes

1 This is an improved and updated version of an article that was published in Spanish in *Anatomía de la derecha chilena: Estado, mercado y valores en tiempos de cambio*. Santiago, Fondo de Cultura Económica, 2020. Translation credits: Dr. Elaine Thomas.
2 In Latin America, this rejection can be explained by the historical connection of the right (whether movementist, partisan, or represented by interest groups) with authoritarian governments. This stigma is reminiscent of that weighing on the right-wing formations of European countries after the Second World War. In this sense, we can consider that Chile, where identification with the right by both citizens and political elites is more accepted than in Brazil or Argentina, constitutes an exception to the prevailing tendency in Latin American countries.
3 In the case of Chile, Correa Sutil (2004) agrees both with the high social origin of the "hard core" of the right and with its tendency to become multiclass within the framework of electoral competition. Along the same lines and on Latin America more generally, see Monteforte Toledo and Villagrán Kramer (1968).
4 For more details on the methodology of this survey and the questionnaire applied to the leaders of Chile Vamos, see Le Foulon et al. (2020).
5 As François Goguel (1958) pointed out early on, behind ideas, there is "a background of feelings, almost instinctive, in any case irrational, feelings about the meaning of life, the nature of man, the ends of society" (p. 54).
6 For a list of the features of the European right, see Scruton (1982).
7 For a comprehensive review of this historiography, see Alenda et al. (2018). In relation to this political culture of order, the authors write: "The order is there, whether because it is understood as a Hispanic and colonial heritage or as a product of the State responsible for forming the nation; whether because it is dimly perceived in the institutional channels that Salvador Allende intended to engrave on the socialist revolution, or, in a radically opposite way, because it is defined in the new Constitution sanctioned during the dictatorship. During the transition to democracy, it also returns through elite pacts or in the figure of technopols" (p. 138).
8 In fact, a minimal definition establishes a concept by identifying attributes that are necessary and sufficient for classifying, in this case, a party as on the right (Sartori, 1970). In contrast, a conceptualisation more amenable to spatiotemporal variations could instead follow a "family resemblance" strategy of definition, in which a concept's defining attributes may vary according to context (Goertz, 2006).

9 These were, first, a counter-revolutionary or traditional right originating from visceral rejection of the Revolution and calls for the restoration of the Old Regime; a liberal or moderate "Orleanist" right that originally proposed to reform the monarchy by incorporating modern principles of parliamentarism; and a Caesarean, "populist", or Bonapartist right not rejecting of the achievements of the Revolution but characterised by high valuation of the authority of the leader and ideological ambiguity.
10 The Orleanism of the nineteenth century was born of a "modern and secular notion of monarchy" (Rémond, 1982: p. 87) having little to do with democracy, a political liberalism that at the same time advocates for social conservation. During the twentieth century, this conciliatory doctrine of a "proper balance" oscillating between liberal and conservative values was more clearly advanced by the centrist Union for French Democracy (UDF).
11 The typology's relevance for accounting for French political history not limited to the nineteenth century was also questioned (Rémond, 1982: p. 38). That criticism led the author to update it (2005), adding to the initial inventory other families: the Christian Democrats, the radical current, and the extreme right.
12 An exhaustive review of each of these typologies—including Eatwell et al.'s (1989) distinction between reactionary right, moderate right, radical right, extreme-right, and new right, or Alexandre-Collier and Jardin's (2004) position in favour of distinguishing just three traditions (conservatism, liberalism, and Christian democracy)—lies beyond the purview of the present chapter.
13 In Latin America, Michael Coppedge (1997) has made a similar attempt at classification, distinguishing four types of right-wing formations. A first, conservative type has its roots in the oligarchic parties of the nineteenth century and did not moderate its doctrine in response to the extension of suffrage. His second type is characterised by its adherence to fascism, while a third is made up of parties supporting authoritarian regimes. Finally, "centre-right" parties seek to broaden the right's traditional bases of support by promoting ideas related to strategic cooperation between the private and public sectors, public security, and morality, while prioritising economic growth over redistribution.
14 The categorisation of "national-popular" is still questionable considering that the sectors to which Herrera alludes in no case claimed to represent the "popular sectors". They were, in fact, more inclined to open distrust of the popular sectors, which they regarded from a perspective that oscillated between paternalism and calls for authoritarian discipline.
15 On this point, we refer to the work by Fernández and Rumié (2020).
16 As instances of this intellectual right, Herrera (2014) refers primarily to Francisco Antonio Encina, Alberto Edwards, Mario Góngora, and Jaime Guzmán.
17 Beyond this argument, the ideological ambiguity of the small parties that have been grouped under the name of national-popular makes it difficult clearly to differentiate them from the conservatives, liberals, and social Christians. Correa Sutil (2004), for her part, characterises them as "anti-communists, nationalists and corporatists" (p. 50).
18 In 1946, Cruz-Coke stated that social Christianity was 'the most authentic expression of the old Conservative Party and unites a tradition-which made the Republic great during the last century—a permanent revision of our social economic postulates to achieve greater social justice, always bearing in mind the maintenance of the rights of the human personality' as cited by Pereira (1994: p. 132). Returning to the roots of this current, after losing its position as sole defender of Christian to the *Falange*, the Conservative Party in the 1950s continued to dispute the Christian Democrats' positioning as the most authentic representatives of the social-Christian current (Pereira, 1994: p. 355).
19 However, it should be noted that conservatives' position in the 1920s regarding "individualistic economic liberalism" (Pereira, 1994: p. 165) still reflected the influence of social Christianity. At the 1929 Convention, in the context of the global economic crisis, the party defended a vision of the State as a "regulator to avoid the rampant

economic struggle in which all the nations of the world are participating" (Pereira, 1994: p. 166).

20 The "national-popular tradition" rescued by Herrera (2014) would be subsumed within this second conception due to its statist character, despite its failing to meet two of the characteristics highlighted by Rémond as necessary to qualify as a family of thought (historical duration and coherence allowing it to subsist). Indeed, on the one hand, the "attempt at nationalist renewal of the right"—see Fernández and Rumié (2020)—was mainly an intellectual movement, with low representation and, on the other hand, it tended to lack its own identity as it became mixed up with corporatism, as we will see later.

21 However, it should be noted that, despite changing the character of society by promoting its secularisation and laicisation (Cavieres, 2001), the different disaggregations of the Liberal Party assumed a moderate position on anti-clericalism in cultural matters after the promulgation of the Constitution of 1925. In socio-economic matters, too, Liberals drew closer to the Conservatives, never questioning the economic structure or prevailing social order (Valdivia, 2008: p. 17).

22 Following Stoppino (1991), by ideology we refer here to a "set of ideas and values concerning the political order that have the function of guiding collective political behaviours" (p. 755). Stoppino goes on to distinguish two meanings of the word: one "weak", which we use here, and another "strong", in the line of Marx.

23 *Gremialismo* is a political ideology inspired in the social doctrine of the Catholic Church that conceives every correct social order should rely on depoliticised intermediary bodies (corporations) managed in freedom. In Chile, it refers to the liberal-conservative movement created in the second half of the 1960s, which opposed the University Reform of the Catholic University.

24 Within the National Party alone, Valdivia (2008) distinguishes three projects: the neoliberal, the authoritarian liberal, and the nationalist, none of which managed to prevail completely until 1970 (p. 113). She views "ideological mixture" as responsible for the dissolution of the PN in 1973 (Valdivia, 2006: pp. 15–47).

25 Unlike Herrera (2014), who places the "national-popular" within a tradition of thought on the right, Valdivia maintains that "the oligarchic right, in general, was sceptical of nationalism and remained distant from it in political-ideological terms" (Valdivia, 2008: p. 86).

26 On this point, other historians establish fairly definite lines of continuity between the Conservative and Liberal Parties and the current UDI and RN, respectively (see Correa Sutil, 2004; Fernández and Rumié, 2020). If we consider that similarity is not synonymous with filiation, the two perspectives become complementary.

27 Social Christianity was reactivated with the foundation of the Christian Social Movement in 1983. Led by Juan de Dios Carmona, it regrouped Christian Democratic militants expelled from Christian Democratic Party for their support of the military regime.

28 Moulian and Torres, however, emphasise that Chilean corporatism was not inspired by fascism, but rather by Spanish traditionalist theorists (1988: p. 21).

29 In Chile, the conservative Catholic historian Jaime Eyzaguirre, among others, develops this approach in the text "Our Tragic Social Reality" (1938).

30 According to Pereira, in the mid-1940s, one of the 24 points of the *Falange's* programme called for fostering "corporate organisation that allows for giving direction to economic life. The State must be inspired by an organic, authoritarian democracy respectful of freedom" (1994: p. 154).

31 Cristi and Ruiz characterise this as "the Hayekian notion of 'spontaneous order', which sums up the typical conservative rejection of the artificial, resulting from the mere agency of the human will" (1992: p. 12).

32 It is not by chance that the Opus Dei began to settle in Chile from the 1950s onwards, increasing its presence during the 1960s in order to contribute to the fight against Frei's reformist programmes and counter the currents inspired by Marxism, such as

the theology of liberation at the continental level. In 1982, during the period of the dictatorship in Chile, Opus Dei was granted its own bishop by Pope John Paul II, stimulating its expansion in the 1980s and 1990s (Mönckeberg, 2016: p. 245). On the convergence between Opus Dei and neoliberalism, see Romero and Bustamante (2016) and Bustamante (2010).

33 Ruiz (1992b) writes in this regard: "What constitutes the socio-political body's head properly speaking, the political power, must not intervene in society, but rather provide a "subsidy" for the weaknesses or incapacities of intermediate bodies, since each of them has natural ends to fulfil" (p. 120).

34 On the evolution of Jaime Guzmán's thinking in relation to economic liberalism, see Cristi (1992) and Mansuy (2016), among others.

35 Most of Hayek's postulates are collected by the Corporation for Contemporary Studies, a centre founded in 1978 and is dedicated to promoting a "new liberal right" (Benavente and Araya, 1981: pp. 302–310; Moulian and Torres, 1988: p. 18). *Nueva Democracia*, a movement founded by *gremialistas* in 1979 before the birth of the UDI—like other institutional initiatives of the time, such as the Centre for Public Studies—shares this economistic vision, but from a conservative traditionalist starting point (Benavente and Araya, 1981: p. 334).

36 That party was born from the unification of several different right-wing groups: the National Union Movement (MUN) and Independent Democratic Union (UDI), both created in 1983; the Labour Front, founded in 1985, of which the Christian Social Movement was then part; and Social Democracy, with its anti-liberal position regarding economic management. See point 4 of the declaration of principles of National Renewal: "Principle of subsidiarity and free society".

37 Political Evolution (Evópoli) was founded in 2012 as a centre-right liberal platform (Alenda et al., 2020).

38 The Independent Regionalist Party was initially founded in 2006 as a centrist force that took part of *Chile Vamos*. It was dissolved in 2018.

39 This survey was conducted as part of FONDECYT Project # 1151503. For more details on the survey methodology and the questionnaire applied to the leaders of *Chile Vamos*, see Le Foulon et al. (2020).

40 Although the results of the PRI are reported in this graph, given the difficulties in generating the sample, it cannot be considered random. The interpretation is therefore based on the three main parties of the coalition, and figures do not include data on PRI, except in cases where we analyse by party. In addition, it is worth noting the party's loss of registration after the 2017 elections and its subsequent merger with a party outside the coalition.

41 Even the difference between the UDI and Evópoli, greater than that of each of those parties with RN, was only statistically significant at 10%.

42 We asked them if they had any religion and asked those professing a religion about their frequency of church attendance. Those who attended religious services never or almost never, or once or twice a year were classified as displaying low religiosity; their religiosity was classified as medium if they attended once a month or every 15 days, and high if they attended one or more times a week.

43 As explained in Le Foulon et al. (2020), calculations of the standard errors and, therefore, of the statistical significance of the differences between parties include a correction by finite sample. This correction was used since the population under study—leaders of the *Chile Vamos* parties—was relatively small, making it necessary to adjust downward the calculation of standard error. Although this correction is used in the analysis by party, it does not apply to the analyses taking all the leaders together. Thus, the standard errors used in those analyses may be overestimated, yielding more conservative conclusions regarding the statistical significance of the differences.

44 The individual characteristics of the leaders are more distinguishable by the party organisation to which they belong. As expected, Evópoli is the party that groups the

highest percentage of young people, with 83% under 45. In contrast, for the UDI and RN, that proportion falls to less than 37%. At the other pole of the spectrum, RN shows the highest percentage of those over 60: 30%, versus 18% for the UDI and 4% for Evópoli. Likewise, Evópoli is the most secular party, while the UDI is the most religious. More than 35% of the leaders of Evópoli do not profess any religion, whereas only 12% of RN and 7% of the UDI do not. The same pattern obtains for high religiosity, which characterises 42% of UDI leaders, 26% of those from RN, and only 16% of those in Evópoli. Finally, regarding gender, the three parties are all overwhelmingly masculinised organisations: on average, only a quarter of their leaders are women.

45 See note 36.
46 These differences are statistically significant at 95% confidence levels.
47 For reasons of space, graphs of these responses by age, gender, and religiosity are not included, but the results on those dimensions generally conform to what one would expect. Thus, as the religiosity and age of the respondents increase, so too does their opposition to extending rights to sexual minorities. These differences between groups are, for the most part, statistically and substantively significant. The effect of gender is different. While the same proportion of women as men say they are against both measures, a higher percentage of men agrees only with civil union, whereas a higher percentage of women favours both rights. Regarding agreement with the decriminalisation of abortion, religiosity behaves as expected, with greater acceptance among those who do not profess any religion (44% in favour), similar levels of support among leaders with low and medium religiosity, and least acceptance among those with high religiosity (8%). On the other hand, age does not behave in a linear way: both younger and older adults are more favourable to decriminalisation. Surprisingly, there were no significant differences of opinion on this question between men and women.
48 For RN, the null hypothesis that the proportion is 50% in favour and 50% against cannot be rejected. In the case of the UDI and Evópoli, although the differences between the two groups are small and similar, the proportion is statistically different from 50% with 95% confidence.
49 These discrepancies have not been long in surfacing. A few months into the second Piñera government, the statements of Congressional Deputy Ignacio Urrutia (UDI) characterising the victims of the dictatorship as "terrorists with a Christmas bonus" caused the Secretary of Human Rights, Lorena Recabarren (*Evópoli*), to reject these statements (Undersecretary of DD.HH. suggests sanctions for Urrutia and receives criticism from the UDI and RN, *La Tercera*, April 20, 2018). Noting revealing discrepancies within the coalition parties, the Secretary General of the UDI, Issa Kort, also distanced his party from Urrutia's controversial remark. Subercaseaux, A. (2018) *Chile Vamos* and DDHH: Pending task. *El Mostrador*, 28 April. http://www.elmostrador.cl/noticias/opinion/2018/04/27/chile-vamos-y-ddhh-tarea-pendiente/ [Accessed 22 October 2022].
50 As Ansart (1982) writes: "A political sensibility is not a permanent set of attitudes and affective reactions of which it would be enough just to determine the definitive contours. It is, on the contrary, a place of conflicting undertakings, a place of daily rivalries" (p. 152).

References

Alenda, S. (2014) Cambio e institucionalización de la 'nueva derecha' chilena (1967–2010). *Revista de Sociologia e Política* 22 (52), 159–180.

Alenda, S. (2021) Prácticas y avatares de la derecha chilena: ¿de la moderación programática a la renovación? *Puntos de referencia Humanidades y Ciencias Sociales* 571, 1–15.

Alenda, S., Pelfini, A., López, M. A., & Riveros, C. (2018) El estudio de las élites políticas en Chile: Los sostenes del orden. In Vommaro, G. & Gené, M. (eds.), *Las élites políticas en el Sur. Un estado de la cuestión de los estudios sobre Argentina, Brasil y Chile.* Buenos Aires, Universidad Nacional de General Sarmiento, pp. 138–190.

Alenda, S., Gartenlaub, A., & Fischer, K. (2020) 'Ganar la batalla de las ideas': El rol de los *think tanks* en la configuración de la nueva centro-derecha chilena. In Alenda, S. (ed.), *Anatomía de la derecha chilena. Estado, mercado y valores en tiempos de cambio.* Santiago, Fondo de Cultura Económica, pp. 119–156.

Alexandre-Collier, A., & Jardin, X. (2004) *Anatomie des droites européennes.* París, Armand Colin.

Allamand, A. (1993) *La centro-derecha del futuro.* Santiago, Editorial Los Andes.

Ansart, P. (1982) Pour l'analyse des sensibilités politiques. In *Études dédiées à Madeleine Grawitz: liber amicorum.* Paris, Dalloz, pp. 141–152.

Benavente, A., & Araya, E. (1981) *La derecha política chilena y el régimen militar. Entre la independencia y la subordinación, 1973–1981.* Santiago, ILADES.

Bobbio, N. (1995) *Derecha e izquierda. Razones y significados de una distinción política.* Rome, Donzelli.

Bustamante, F. (2010) La formación de una nueva mentalidad religiosa de la elite empresarial durante la dictadura militar, 1974–1990. El catolicismo empresarial del Opus Dei. *Revista Cultura y Religión* 4 (1), 105–124.

Cañas, E. (1992) Los partidos políticos. In Castillo, C. T. & Parada, E. L. (eds.), *Chile en los noventa.* Santiago, Dolmen, pp. 53–90.

Cavieres, E. (2001) Anverso y reverso del liberalismo en Chile, 1840–1930. *Historia* 34, 39–66.

Coppedge, M. (1997) *A classification of Latin American parties.* Kellogg Institute Working Papers 244.

Cornejo Irigoyen, R. (2001) *Origen y evolución histórica de la nueva derecha en Chile. Relaciones de cooperación/conflicto entre Renovación Nacional y la Unión Demócrata Independiente (1983–2000).* MA thesis. Pontificia Universidad Católica de Chile.

Correa Sutil, S. (2004) *Con las riendas del poder. La derecha chilena en el siglo XX.* Santiago, Sudamericana.

Cristi, R. (2000) *El pensamiento político de Jaime Guzmán.* Santiago, LOM.

Cristi, R., & Ruiz, C. (1992) *El pensamiento conservador en Chile.* Santiago, Universitaria.

Díaz, N. (2016) Una travesía inconclusa: Divisiones en Renovación Nacional durante el gobierno de Sebastián Piñera. *Revista de Ciencia Política* 36 (2), 481–502.

Duverger, M. (1951) *Les partis politiques.* París, Armand Colin.

Eyzaguirre, J. (1938) Nuestra trágica realidad social. *Estudios* 65, 2–7.

Fernández, J., & Rumié, S. (2020) Las transformaciones de la derecha chilena: Desafíos, adaptaciones y renovaciones (1932–2010). In Alenda, S. (ed.), *Anatomía de la derecha chilena: Estado, mercado y valores en tiempos de cambio.* Santiago, Fondo de Cultura Económica, pp. 43–85.

Gaxie, D. (2004) *La democracia representativa.* Santiago, LOM.

Gibson, E. (1996) *Class and conservative parties: Argentina in comparative perspective.* Baltimore, The Johns Hopkins University Press.

Goertz, G. (2006) *Social Science concepts: A user's guide.* Princeton, Princeton University Press.

Godoy, O. (2005) Horizontes futuros de la derecha chilena. *Revista Política* 45, 207–214.

Goguel, F. (1945) *La politique des partis sous la IIIe République.* Reprint, Paris, Seuil, 1958.

Guzmán, J. (1965) El capitalismo y los católicos de tercera posición. *Revista Fiducia* 20, 4–5.
Herrera, H. (2014) *La derecha en la crisis del bicentenario*. Santiago, UDP.
Le Bohec, J., & Le Digol, C. (eds.) (2012) *Gauche/Droite. Genèse d'un clivage politique*. Paris, Presses Universitaires de France.
Le Foulon, C., Valenzuela, P., Alenda, S., & Espinosa, A. (2020) Metodología de la encuesta a dirigentes de Chile Vamos. In Alenda, S. (ed.), *Anatomía de la derecha chilena: Estado, mercado y valores en tiempos de cambio*. Santiago, Fondo de Cultura Económica, pp. 347–369.
Luna, J. P., & Kaltwasser, C. R. (eds.) (2014) *The resilience of the Latin American right*. Baltimore, The Johns Hopkins University Press.
Mackinnon, I. (2005) *Renovación Nacional: Entre conservadores y reformistas*. BA thesis. Pontificia Universidad Católica de Chile.
Mansuy, D. (2016) Notas sobre política y subsidiariedad en el pensamiento de Jaime Guzmán. *Revista de Ciencia Política* 36 (2), 503–521.
Mönckeberg, M. O. (2016) *El imperio del Opus Dei en Chile*. Santiago, Penguin Random House.
Montero, C. (1997) *La revolución empresarial chilena*. Santiago, CIEPLAN Dolmen.
Morresi, S. D. (2015) 'Acá somos todos democráticos'. El PRO y las relaciones entre la derecha y la democracia en la Argentina. In Vommaro, G. & Morresi, S. D. (eds.), '*Hagamos equipo'. PRO y la construcción de la nueva derecha argentina*. Buenos Aires, Universidad Nacional de General Sarmiento, Prometeo, pp. 163–201.
Moulian, T., & Torres, I. (1988) *La reorganización de los partidos de la derecha entre 1983 y 1988*. Working paper. Programa Flacso-Chile, no. 388.
Panebianco, A. (1990) *Modelos de partido: Organización y poder en los partidos políticos*. Madrid, Alianza Universidad.
Pereira, T. (1994) *El Partido Conservador 1930–1965*. Santiago, Fundación Mario Góngora.
Rémond, R. (1954) *Les droites en France*. Reprint, Paris, Aubier, 1982.
Rémond, R. (2005) *Les droites aujourd'hui*. Paris, Louis Audibert.
Renato, Cristi. and Carlos, Ruiz. (1992) *Les droites aujourd'hui*. Santiago de Chile, Editorial Universitaria, S.A.
Romero, J., & Bustamante, F. (2016) Neoliberalismo, poder y religión en Chile. *Revista latinoamericana de investigación crítica* 5, 79–100.
Ruiz, C. (1992a) Corporativismo e hispanismo en la obra de Jaime Eyzaguirre. In Cristi, R. and C. Ruiz (ed.), *El pensamiento conservador en Chile*. Santiago de Chile, Editorial Universitaria, pp. 67–102.
Ruiz, C. (1992b) El conservatismo como ideología. Corporativismo y neoliberalismo en las revistas teóricas de la derecha. In Cristi, R. and C. Ruiz. (ed.), *El pensamiento conservador en Chile*. Santiago de Chile, Editorial Universitaria, pp. 103–123.
Sajuria, J., Dosek, T., & Alenda, S. (2020) Ciclo de vida y diferencias organizacionales en los partidos de la centro-derecha chilena. In Alenda, S. (ed.), *Anatomía de la derecha chilena: Estado, mercado y valores en tiempos de cambio*. Santiago, Fondo de Cultura Económica, pp. 227–268.
Sartori, G. (1970) Concept misformation in comparative politics. *The American Political Science Review* 64 (4), 1033–1053.
Sartori, G. (1992) *Partidos y sistemas de partidos*. Madrid, Alianza.
Scruton, R. (1982) *A dictionary of political thought*. London, Pan.
Stoppino, M. (1976) Ideología. In Bobbio, N., Matteucci, N., & Pasquino, G. (eds.), *Diccionario de Política*. Madrid, Alianza, 1991.

Thumala, M. A. (2007) *Riqueza y piedad. El catolicismo de la élite económica chilena*. Santiago, Penguin Random House.

Toledo, M. M., & Kramer, F. V. (1968) *Izquierdas y derechas en Latinoamérica*. Buenos Aires, Pleamar.

Valdivia, V. (2006) 'Crónica de una muerte anunciada': La disolución del Partido Nacional, 1973–1980. In Valdivia, V., Alvarez, R., & Pinto, J. (eds.), *Su revolución contra nuestra revolución. Izquierdas y derechas en el Chile de Pinochet (1973–1981)*, vol. 1. Santiago, LOM.

Valdivia, V. (2008) *Nacionales y gremialistas. El 'parto' de la nueva derecha política chilena, 1964–1973*. Santiago, LOM.

Verbal, V. (2017) *La derecha perdida. Por qué la derecha en Chile carece de relato y dónde debería encontrarlo*. Santiago, Libertad y Desarrollo.

Wills-Otero, L. (2009) From party systems to party organizations: The adaptation of Latin American parties to changing environments. *Journal of Politics in Latin America* 1 (1), 123–141.

Wills-Otero, L. (2015) *Latin American traditional parties, 1978–2006. Electoral trajectories and internal party politics*. Bogota, Uniandes.

10
VENEZUELA

Democracy as market, or how the right-wing opposition confused the two in its quest for power

Barry Cannon and Ybiskay González

Introduction

This chapter on Venezuela will be concerned primarily with those groups who are opposed to the Bolivarian order installed by the late president Hugo Chávez from his election in late 1998 and continued by President Nicolas Maduro after the death of the *comandante* in 2013 until the present, collectively known as the Opposition. It will seek to show, first, that the Opposition uses a "democracy/dictatorship" dichotomy in their discursive practice to help foster unity among its different factions and supporters, perpetuating an atmosphere of polarisation in Venezuelan society to help it obtain power, and second, that this helps to obscure the right-wing, neoliberal order which it seeks to install once it achieves that goal. This second contention will then be analysed in more detail, using policy documents and primary research with opposition spokespeople to show that the Venezuelan Opposition is, generally speaking, rightist in orientation, conservative in instinct, and neoliberal in policy direction, despite disagreements over strategy and the speed of transition to a market-led economy between its different factions.

The chapter will proceed as follows. First, we will present a brief overview of the Venezuelan Opposition, arguing that it has mostly common roots in the pre-Chávez, Punto Fijo regime (1958–2000). Additionally, we argue that it is heterogeneous in composition and divided over the prevalence of institutionalist or extra-institutionalist strategies to defeat *Chavismo*, vacillating between these two, seemingly opposed strategies. Nevertheless, we argue here that these two strategies, rather than opposed, should be viewed as one unified overall strategy, parts of which can be activated or given greater salience, depending on the national and international context. Second, and despite the ever-presence of extra-institutional practices as part of their strategic repertoire, the Opposition privileges a "democracy/dictatorship" dichotomy in its discursive practices, with

DOI: 10.4324/9781003352266-14

the Opposition occupying the democratic space and dictatorship referring to the governing Socialist Party of Venezuela (PSUV). This polarising discourse helps obscure and excuse Opposition use of undemocratic practices while maintaining unity in its disparate coalition.

Moreover, a brief examination of key socio-economic policy documents, augmented by material from interviews from 2012 with a variety of Opposition-linked personalities, will highlight three key points: first, that market freedoms are privileged as the core meaning of freedom; second, that state intervention in the economy, denoted as socialism, is equated with tyranny; and, third, that social inequalities, of gender and to a lesser extent, ethnicity, are recognised, but their origin and urgency questioned. Hence, the Venezuelan Opposition can be characterised as right-wing, neoliberal, and relatively conservative in orientation, following the classifications offered by Castro-Rea and Solano for this volume. The "democracy/dictatorship" discourse, however, helps obscure these policy orientations, which are in general a difficult sell to the majority of Venezuelans reluctant to accept severe social inequality. In this way, the Opposition diverts attention from the neoliberal underpinnings of its socio-economic policy orientation and its own undemocratic strategic behaviour, while simultaneously drawing attention to and underlining that of the PSUV.

Background to and characterisation of the Venezuelan Opposition

Towards the middle of the twentieth century, after the 1958 Punto Fijo Pact put an end to the preceding dictatorship of Marcos Perez Jiménez, the Venezuelan political system was configured as a democratic bipartisan system with no significant opposition. Both leading parties, AD (Democratic Action) and COPEI (Social Christian Party), agreed on the need for increased private sector activity and state intervention, funded by abundant oil revenue, to help grow the economy, resulting in little ideological differentiation between the two (Villaroel, 1996). Left-wing guerrilla insurgencies and right-wing-inspired military coups, taking place in the 1960s, failed because the main political parties carried out important social reforms that benefitted a large part of the population (Straka, 2017: p. 85). This led to an ideological blurring (Ramos, 1997) similar to what Whitehead (2002) describes as the adaptation of elites to democracy. As Bresser Pereira (2006: p. 123) observes, right-wing political actors understood the need to brand themselves as centrist to achieve power.

This ideological blurring, however, became unsustainable during the economic crisis that Venezuela suffered in the 1980s. The crisis led to the introduction of neoliberal policies in 1989, blunting and reversing the previous expansionist economic and social regime, which most Venezuelans had enjoyed to that date. By 1993, citizens had become more polarised along left-right lines, making it possible to identify two distinct ideologically defined political blocs (Molina and Álvarez as cited by Magallanes, 2007). Those on the right were identified as seeking free-market solutions to the socio-economic crisis, whereas those who sought to continue the old model of wealth distribution were regarded as of the left. Little was said, however, of political liberalism as a system of rights, tolerance, or deliberation. As Coronil (1997) points out, throughout the Punto Fijo period, historical legacies of colonialism, such as formal systems of race, class, and gender sociocultural divisions, continued unquestioned, and indeed were sometimes defined as "civilisation" itself.

Within this historical context, the dominant Venezuelan political parties had to face the electoral success of Hugo Chávez in 1998. New political parties emerged after this event, such as PJ (First Justice) and ABP (Brave People's Alliance), founded in 2000 from excisions of COPEI and AD, respectively. Although these parties consider themselves on the "centre-left", their discourse, in fact, positions them on the right (Cannon, 2014). Later, VP (Popular Will), to which former Venezuela's so-called "acting" President Juan Guaidó belongs, was founded in 2009, as well as VV (Come Venezuela), founded in 2012. VP positions itself as social democratic, but in fact is quite radically liberal in its orientation, while VV is much more openly right-wing. As a result, a new conservative radicalism emerged similar to ideologically demarcated party dynamics found in other countries (Duno-Gotberg, 2020). These new and old political actors have grouped together to oppose *Chavismo* but without a consensus on how to carry this out.

Cannon (2014) identifies three approaches to the Venezuelan Opposition in the literature. First, there is a dominant orthodox approach, as Corrales and Penfold (2007) exemplified, privileging institutions by presenting these as the norm by which other political regimes are measured. *Chavismo*, in this account, has undermined institutions and hence democracy itself, creating the conditions for a democratic Opposition to have no choice but to use extra-institutional methods to restore democracy. Hence the norm by which the Bolivarian regime is measured is liberal democracy itself, and it is found wanting in the extreme. Dominguez (2011), on the other hand, emphasises structural power as the key area where battle lines are drawn, with institutions barely mentioned. Furthermore, it is the Opposition, rather than *Chavismo*, which has acted undemocratically, and can do so again, as Opposition strategies are unified in purpose and intent, not ad hoc responses to rule-bending by the incumbent as Corrales and Penfold (2007) contend. Finally, García-Guadilla (2005) emphasises civil society's role as both victim and progenitor of such political and ideological polarisation. In her account, the increased social differentiation, which developed during the pre-Bolivarian period known as Punto Fijo, has consolidated itself into mutually exclusive political positions, neither of which seems capable of creating a unifying alternative.

Despite these differences, all three approaches agree on the multivariate nature of the Venezuelan opposition, drawn from a variety of organisational backgrounds, and locked into a protracted battle with a government and state system which it views as inimical to its interests and objectives. Those objectives are seen implicitly or explicitly as fundamentally to construct, or, as the Opposition would argue, restore, a liberal-democratic politico-institutional regime (liberty) and a market-based socio-economic regime (property rights). Both are in turn considered essential to protect the interests of the social and corporate groups within the Opposition and hence restore Venezuela to its "natural" economic, social, and political trajectory.

These characterisations can be seen in the development of the Venezuelan Opposition from the emergence of *Chavismo*, which primarily shows an apparent alternation between institutional and extra-institutional opposition strategies. Initially, after Hugo Chávez was inaugurated as President in 1999, some opposition groups cooperated with the new government, responding to its perceived moderation (Cannon, 2009: p. 80). This changed in 2001, however, with the granting of emergency powers to the President by the new National Assembly, allowing him to pass 49 laws on major issues, including education, land reform, oil, and fishing, among others, without having each of them approved by the National Assembly (Cannon, 2009: p. 80). This signalled the beginning of a new more radical phase in government policy (Ellner, 2008: p. 112), which led to a bitter and pronounced confrontational stage between Opposition and government. The confrontation persisted until 2006 and included a coup in April 2002, a debilitating oil strike in late 2002/early 2003, a recall referendum against Chávez's mandate in 2004, and an electoral boycott in 2005 (Domínguez, 2011).

This confrontational stage was marked by the establishment of the CD (Democratic Coordinator), a heterogeneous grouping of political parties, NGOs, the business association *Fedecámaras*, and the trade union confederation, the CTV (Venezuelan Workers Confederation) with the support of the Catholic Church and private media. Lasting from October 2002 to August 2004, its disappearance was attributed to its very heterogeneity. However, it was said to have laid the basis for the emergence of later unity strategies, as it created basic structures and decisions on which the later Opposition Democratic Unity Roundtable (MUD) coalition could build (Cannon, 2014). In 2006, however, there was a notable shift to a more electoralist strategy, although without abandoning confrontation entirely. The emergence of this second phase in Opposition unity began to gain momentum when their electoral candidate Manuel Rosales officially accepted defeat in the 2006 presidential elections, "the first time an opposition politician had recognized a Chavista victory" (Domínguez, 2011: p. 125). In this phase, politics and political parties would dominate, although extra-political tactics would continue to play an important part in Opposition strategy.

This move to a more institutionalist, party-based stage consisted of three elements reached through various agreements: the formation of the MUD in January 2008, with around 30 parties becoming affiliated eventually, but with a variety of ideological and programmatic positions and regional spreads (MUD, 2008); a unified candidate system; and the beginnings of a unified policy discourse. This latter element was expressed most notably in the "Guidelines for the Government of National Unity Programme, (2013-2019)" (*Lineamientos para el Programa de Gobierno de Unidad Nacional, (2013-2019)* (MUD, 2012). These moves in the direction of unity and constitutionalism initially resulted in a run of electoral successes, most notably the legislative elections of September 2010, with the MUD winning only 1% less votes (47.7%) than the PSUV (48.9%). Although still in a minority in the National Assembly, it allowed the Opposition to deprive the government of the two-thirds majority needed to select officials with constitutional powers and to grant the president enabling powers allowing him to enact extraordinary legislation.

However, it was the ill-fated 2014 general elections, following on from Chávez's death in March 2013, with Henrique Capriles Radonski as the Opposition candidate against Chávez's successor, Nicolás Maduro, which inaugurated a return to prominence of extra-institutional strategies, and which persisted right up until 2020. In those elections, Maduro's slim majority (a mere 1.5%) was contested, with US support, by Capriles and the MUD, leading to violent Opposition-led protests (Hetland, 2016: p. 8). While these eventually abated, a fresh wave of protests seeking Maduro's removal erupted in early 2014 following the ruling PSUV's strong showing in municipal elections in December 2013 (Hetland, 2016: p. 9). Maduro survived these protests, which resulted in the deaths of 43 people, including opposition and government supporters along with members of the security forces. Cyr (2013) and Sagarzazu (2014) note, however, that the MUD had made considerable advances in these elections, losing key seats by small margins, and beating the PSUV in areas where before Chávez had won easily. This tendency came to spectacular fruition in the December 2015 parliamentary elections when the PSUV was soundly beaten by the MUD, which gained a two-thirds supermajority in the National Assembly (AN)—the first time the Opposition had achieved an AN majority since Hugo Chávez came to power in 1999. This resounding majority, in theory, would have allowed the Opposition-controlled legislature to change some fundamental laws and even aim for the removal of Maduro. In this deeply polarised scenario, with the PSUV controlling the other four of Venezuela's five state "powers" (executive, judiciary, electoral, and citizens' powers), the political impasse deepened profoundly.

Political activity since has been characterised by a variety of actions on the part of both government and Opposition aimed at neutralising, preventing, or reversing the actions of the other, most notably Opposition attempts to remove Maduro from power and government reactions to these moves. On the government side, there were judicial, institutional, and electoral attempts to neutralise the National Assembly Opposition majority. The National Assembly's legislative power was neutralised by the Supreme Court in 2016, and in 2017 the Opposition boycotted elections for regional governments and the newly created Constituent Assembly, which then came to replace the National Assembly as the state's supreme legislative body (Pantoulas and McCoy, 2019: p. 392). Instead, the Opposition pursued a sustained and relatively successful street protest strategy, followed by another (partial) boycott of the 2018 presidential elections, which Maduro won, albeit on one of the lowest electoral turnouts in Venezuelan history at just 46.1% (Pantoulas and McCoy, 2019: p. 400).

This closing down of political space for the Opposition, and the arrival of Donald J. Trump to the presidency of the United States in January 2017, eventually led to a radicalisation of Opposition strategy once again and a hardening of polarisation regarding the country at the geopolitical level. Led by the United States, which extended sanctions against Venezuela, especially on its all-important oil industry, deepening an already profound economic and humanitarian crisis (Weisbrot and Sachs, 2019), in January 2019 around 50 countries, mostly in the Americas and Europe, recognised Juan Guaidó, a hitherto unknown VP (Popular Will) National Assembly deputy, as the de jure President of Venezuela, although with little de facto power (Buxton, 2019). Guaidó, with US support, then went on to attempt an ostensibly "humanitarian" relief operation from neighbouring (and right-wing-led) Colombia and Brazil, and to support two coup attempts against Maduro in April 2019 and 2020, all of which failed in their objectives largely due to the Venezuelan Armed Forces remaining loyal to the government. Despite some attempts at mediation by the Vatican, Mexico, Uruguay, Norway, and the European Union, among others, Opposition strategic policy remains one of confrontation with the government, including keeping open the possibility of a US invasion to dislodge Maduro. Despite this, the political impasse seems to remain firmly in place, even though there seems to be a lessening of street support for the Opposition as millions of Venezuelans, including many Opposition supporters, flee the worsening socio-economic crisis in the country (Buxton, 2019). While the main demand of the Opposition is elections in the context of an Opposition-led "interim" government, this polarised impasse looks set to continue for the foreseeable future, although US President Joe Biden, Trump's successor, seems to be prioritising a negotiation strategy, coordinated with the European Union and others, which depending on progress, mostly measured by "free and fair" elections, could see sanctions lessening (Monge, Moleira and de Miguel, 2021).

Hence, to conclude this section, the Venezuelan Opposition seems to have moved from a confrontational to a largely electoral power strategy, returning to a deepened confrontational one, this time set within a much more favourable geopolitical context for them. While the confrontational strategy remains unsuccessful in that it has not resulted in the removal of *Chavismo* from power, due, in particular to its failure to peel of the Armed Forces from the government, it has achieved more electoral strength, at least up until the last elections. With its abandonment of the electoral arena since the 2018 presidential election, and with the Opposition dominated by more radical sectors, such as the Leopoldo López led VP, to which Guaidó belongs, this confrontational strategy remains the dominant one at the time of writing (early 2021), although increasing strategic disagreement in the Opposition (Rodriguez, 2021) and the arrival of Joe Biden to the US presidency in 2021 seem to be prompting a return to negotiations. Nevertheless, democracy remains the key identificatory slogan of the Opposition, as both its umbrella organisation incarnations suggest (Democratic Coordinator and Democratic Unity Roundtable), juxtaposing their democratic vocation with the "authoritarian", "autocratic" nature of its Socialist rival. Indeed, one of its first strategic objectives is the "democratic reconstruction" of Venezuela.

Democratic "reconstruction"

The Opposition discourse of "recuperating democracy" has two main aims. First, it aims to create unity within the Opposition's disparate groups and to extend its reach to include anti-*Chavistas* from the centre-left and right spectrum, and indeed from within *Chavista* ranks themselves. To the Opposition, any supporter is welcome as long as they reject *Chavismo*; what matters is to create a coalition big enough to demonstrate its legitimacy against the government. This is because the Opposition's identity must be created and settled as the clear anti-thesis of *Chavismo*, presenting it with narrow parameters in which to create its coalition. This is largely forged through the creation of an attractive and convincing discourse for rejecting *Chavismo* to counter the high levels of support the latter had, at least until Chávez's untimely death in 2013. This discourse centres on defending democracy from the *Chavistas*, hence fostering unity among its different factions and supporters. Democracy then is a master signifier because of its ability to act as a sponge due to its multiplicity of interpretations (Solomon, 2015: p. 39).

Filling "democracy" with a meaning helps create a dominant "common sense" understanding of what democracy is. As in other Latin American countries, democracy comes to represent a societal reality organised logically and systematically as "modernisation" (Ferrero, 2014: p. 11). Latin American states privilege discourses around development and modernisation over liberal values such as respecting difference and guaranteeing rights for all citizens. Democracy, thus, comes to constitute the promise of a fullness-to-come, which normalises a lifestyle and a particular understanding of politics in which only those groups that are able to advance capitalist modernisation can legitimately govern. Thus, when the traditional powerful groups could not influence the law-making process during the first year Chávez was authorised to legislate by decree (2001), the first cycle of protest against the government began (Garcia-Guadilla, 2005: p. 114; Corrales, 2011). The idea that the government did not play by the rules of the game was immediately assumed, experienced, and represented as authoritarianism. As Chomsky (1999, p. 8) says, "any activity that might interfere with corporate domination of society is automatically suspect because it would interfere with the workings of the free market, which is advanced as the only rational, fair and democratic allocator of goods and services".

The Opposition articulated two discursive formations as the obstacles preventing the achievement of democracy. First, between 2000 and 2001, expressions of backwardness and representations of Chávez as mestizo, non-elite, and military (González, 2021a) were circulated widely in the media, creating an image of Chávez as a danger to democracy. Second, the Opposition forged a narrative that any sociocultural divisions within Venezuelan society were originated by the government, rupturing the heretofore secure and stable sense of "consensus" in the nation (Cannon, 2004). What is missing from this account, however, was that in the pre-Chávez, Punto Fijo era in Venezuela, as noted above, there was no political opposition to speak of (Zahler, 2017) and social divisions were minimised in the representation of a prosperous petro-state (Tinker-Salas, 2009). Democracy, thus, invested with a promise of modernisation helped the formation of the Opposition identity and its practices. By self-representing as defenders of democracy, the Opposition could present themselves as modern civil society in contrast to the "populistically" manipulated followers of Chávez. Their actions were "right" because the "other wrong" was causing the division of Venezuelan society.

In order to demonstrate *Chavismo* as wrong, the media became the essential expression of the Opposition at the beginning of the conflict (Pérez-Liñán, 2007: p. 83). The media was the space for professionals in Venezuelan society to represent themselves as reliable and accurate in telling Venezuelans what democracy means, and how wrong the government was. By portraying the Opposition as legitimate while "the other" is considered "illegitimate" and dangerous, the Opposition reproduced an "Us/Them" discourse, which is curiously similar to that associated with populist leaders. This construction facilitates increasing activism to support and defend what one values as truth while reproducing a dominant form of exclusionary politics that vests political power in the elite and demonises left-wing and racialised groups. What makes this form of exclusion invisible and legitimate is the normalised understanding of social divisions by which "dangerous" groups are excluded from politics. As Venezuelan history has demonstrated, the deeply ingrained suspicion of mass politics made possible an understanding of democracy that favoured elitism (Rhodes-Purdy, 2017). Moreover, the focus on the populist style of Chávez made another form of exclusion more invisible as the negative connotations of populism for governance has been increasingly recognised in the media and in academia (Lara, 2018). In this way, the pernicious polarisation visible in Venezuela (McCoy, 2017) is not just reproduced by the government, as most accounts insist, but also by the Opposition (González, 2021b).

If the signifier democracy has been central to fostering unity among its different factions and supporters, polarisation has been the dynamic by which the Opposition obscures its unwillingness to compromise through dialogue. The war against *Chavismo* is an assertion of the old norm by which liberal democracy reduces the possibilities of political transformation, guided by an understanding of politics whereby "conflict" is acceptable only if the rules of the democratic game are observed. In this way, the war against non-liberal power is explained and justified while producing a "war without ends" of liberal powers (Reid, 2004: p. 78). In other words, the interpretation of subjects claiming for political transformation as problematic, although they are "free" to do so, makes the subordination of conflict a constant end. The inclusion of this war is not to present a dichotomy between liberal and illiberal forces; rather, it represents the difficulties in dealing with forms of thought based on a principle of difference (or pluriverse) (Escobar, 2017) rather than contradiction. The Opposition thereby is rewriting the dominant historical narrative within which they become the legitimate subjects to govern, and dialogue is impossible with the "wrong other". A kind of authoritative/monological moralism justifies the Opposition's actions rather than a recognition of differences, toleration, and deliberation. As González (2021a) demonstrates, the Opposition has never represented the conflict as an interplay between them and the government, but rather as the result of the "inferior" and illegitimate actor either in the government or supporting the government. Consequently, a central discourse emerging from the Opposition is the need to "reconstruct" the country's institutions, seen as dominated by Chávez and used for his own personal, party political, and ideological ends. Opposition policy documents reiterate this position incessantly.

In the above-mentioned "Guidelines for a Government of National Unity Programme (2013-2019)" (MUD, 2012) (here known as the *Lineamientos*), for example, this is seen as necessary to ensure personal and social liberty and because the "possibility of success for the economic system critically depends on the solidity of institutions" (p. 304). In Cannon's (2014) overview of this document, he identified five main objectives within an overall aim of democratic "reconstruction". These are remarkable not just as a statement of intent, but also as an exercise in claiming to be *Chavismo*'s negation. Thus the Opposition claims that, in power, they will fully adopt the terms of the 1999 Constitution, most notably ensuring human rights and constitutional guarantees are respected; "strengthen and promote" spaces for consensus building, participation, and social dialogue, as well as guaranteeing access to justice; invigorate and remodel the public powers, including promoting the independence and autonomy of each branch of government at the national, state, and municipal levels; restore powers to states and municipalities taken from them under the present government; and undertake the "professionalisation" and "modernization" of state bureaucracies, in order to "adapt them to the needs of a modern State" (Cannon, 2014, pp. 13–14). The implication here is that no PSUV government respected or fulfilled the norms of the Constitution in any of the areas mentioned, and these can only be fulfilled by the removal of the PSUV, its replacement with an Opposition-led government, and a reconstitution of the pre-Chávez politico-institutional order, the only one technically capable of ensuring "modernity".

Similarly, this dichotomisation between illiberal *Chavismo* and the "democratic" Opposition is equally salient in a law passed by the National Assembly in February 2019, then under Opposition domination, the cumbersomely named "Statute that Governs the Transition to Democracy to Restore the Validity of the Constitution of the Bolivarian Republic of Venezuela" (Asamblea Nacional Venezolana, 2019). This law aims to set out an "efficient path to return to democracy" (III) from the present "illiberal" order. This order is directly associated with "real socialism", which has "produced persecution, chaos and misery" (I), and therefore the "urgent need to return to constitutional democracy" (I). The Opposition's various campaigns, both electoral and extra-constitutional, are presented as a "democratic struggle" (II) leading to the present "liberational conjuncture" initiated by the May 20, 2018, elections. These elections, the document asserts, were held without Opposition agreement and therefore are regarded as "unfree". President Maduro has thus become a "usurper" as, for the document reasons, the constitutional order has collapsed. The law identifies three progressive phases to recuperate "democracy" (IV): the cessation of the usurpation (i.e., the removal of Maduro from the presidency); the installation of a provisional government; and, the realisation of "free, transparent and competitive elections". The main aim of this process is to achieve the "full re-establishment of the constitutional order, the rescue of popular sovereignty through free elections and the reversal of the complex humanitarian emergency" (Asamblea Nacional Venezolana, 2019, Cap 1, Art 3). The situation of polarisation is therefore entirely blamed on *Chavismo*, which is portrayed as socialist and, therefore, authoritarian, and autocratic. The Opposition, conversely, is entirely constitutional and democratic, even in its extra-institutional actions, which are the result of the government's autocracy rather than its wilful choice. Yet, the equation of "socialism" with "autocracy" denotes an "equation" between "democracy" and "market", with the government's "socialism" seen as retrograde and backward, and the "market" as "democratic" and "modern".

The impossibility to dialogue in the normative framework of liberal democracy not only demonstrates features of intolerance and imposition but also obscures any political project behind the signifier "democracy". Political projects seek to secure forms of consensus by establishing a strategic order of economic, political, and social relations. It is possible, thus, to observe modern democracies as guided by the economic rationalities of liberalism and the system of hierarchical social differentiation between those who are called to govern and those who are governed. The Opposition, while constructing its identity based on "democracy", is reproducing a strategic order without revealing its position on issues such as privatisation, liberalisation of the economy, and dismantling of public education and other social services. In other words, by identifying as democrats, the Opposition can get enough support that otherwise might be minimal due to the limited appeal of their pro-market, neoliberal policy proposals in Venezuelan society. Moreover, since polarisation facilitates a process of identification that tells individuals that their identities and the Other's identities are mutually exclusive, the Opposition's identity as the opposite to *Chavismo* helps to shape the process of creating a right-wing identity. Whereas the *Chavistas* are represented as lacking any morality because of their wrongdoing, the Opposition as "the correct" one seeks to hold a positive representation in Venezuelan society. Such a valued representation is based on social stereotypes that recognise White-modern-North knowledge, behaviours, and actions as the only legitimate ones. Without questioning such knowledge, for example, the Opposition assumes and trusts that those in the North know what to do, even when the structural problems in the South can radically differ. In this way, no discussion outside the dominant neoliberal economic policies is possible, whereas social policies are reduced to a top-down approach that considers the market as the best solution to get the poor out of poverty. As Dagnino (2007, p. 553) argues, neoliberalism has created "an alluring connection between citizenship and the market" and has essentially resulted in the emergence of "earned citizenship"—i.e., something acquired when a person participates as both consumer and producer within the economy.

Opposition economic and social policy

Opposition oscillation between institutionalised and radical strategies is mirrored in economic and social policy, which moves between a more centrist, gradualist approach to change, to a more radical, abrupt, "shock doctrine" approach. Both, however, are ideologically unified in that they seek to impose a market-based socio-economic system, which reifies individual effort within a privatised economic system as the only possible path to prosperity and growth, in a word, neoliberalism. Cannon (2014) concludes that Opposition economic policy could be characterised by two main elements: a pre-eminence given to the private over the public—with a pivotal role envisaged for private property seen as the principal, if not only, means to economic progress, and an acceptance that the state oil company, PDVSA, would maintain its present condition as a state-owned company, but removed from immediate governmental control, by opening it up to wider private sector involvement and hence national and global competitive pressures. He termed Opposition economic policy as "gradual, pragmatic productivism" (Cannon, 2014): while the endpoint was to establish a market-led regime, there were clear discrepancies among the Opposition as to the extent of privatisations, particularly of the all-important state oil industry.

In terms of Opposition social policy Cannon (2014) concluded it had several notable characteristics, all of which are guided by a principle of state subsidiarity to the market. First, it was anti-poverty, in that it aimed to concentrate, according to one (social democratic) interviewee, on those seen as "most in need ... because the state cannot maintain all of society" (García, 2012 as cited by Cannon, 2014). It was also ultimately oriented at creating opportunities to achieve individual autonomy, with a leading Opposition politician from Capriles's First Justice Party (PJ), Julio Borges (2012) as cited by Cannon (2014), arguing that the ultimate aim of social policy is "that the country does not need social policy", but rather that the market will ultimately provide thorough "productivity, investment, diversification of the economy". Second, while the state is envisioned as having a role, this would be largely as a coordinator of private provision of such services, linked to a policy of decentralisation of these services to the regional and municipal level. Third, social policy success is based on "quality" and "efficiency" rather than on supposed partisan criteria, and policies of "depoliticisation" are signalled in all these areas, a charge levelled at existing social policy programmes installed by the Chávez government. These, while being continued, will nonetheless be tied to other services, "professionalised" and integrated into the pertinent ministries and their existing service provision. Hence, one could summarise Opposition social policy as social market policy in the sense that social services are provided in function of people's participation in the labour market, which is viewed as the ideal path to achieve individual autonomy equated, in the final analysis, to an absence of state social provision. Moreover, while some level of continuity is suggested with an emphasis on poverty and assurances that some of the more important existing social services will be maintained, this may be more in appearance than in substance.

Finally, it is interesting to note attitudes to ethnic and gender inequalities among Opposition spokespeople interviewed by us in 2012. In general, interviewees did show some concern for these issues, but with distrust among some as to the government's motivations in highlighting such inequalities. Indeed, some thought that these issues were problematic or demagogic tactics on the part of *Chavismo* to maintain power. Regarding ethnic inequalities, for example, some interviewees, such as Botti (2012), then president of the business federation, *Fédecamaras*, did acknowledge that "black people got fewer opportunities" in Venezuela, or Schafriker (2012), who pointed out that there were too few Black people in government. However, others claimed that while "there is a colour barrier … it is a colour barrier that is not an obstacle to social benefits" and that "the theme of Afro descendants was just revolutionary nonsense" (España, 2012), a perspective also expressed by Schafriker (2012). Others still argued that Venezuela was a *mestizo* (mixed race) country, and for that reason, race was not an issue.

There is more awareness on gender issues, with many recognising that women have fewer opportunities in many fields than men. Consequently, Marino González (2012), then policy coordinator of the MUD, recognises that the Opposition needs to give more thought to gender issues. Maldonado (2012), however, also argues that, like racism, many people do not regard it as a problem, and indeed, Guijarro (2012) insists that gender equality is not a great theme for debate in Venezuela as "we have other more important priorities". Such disputes in the importance of such social inequalities were also translated to policy documentation where they receive only token consideration, if at all. Hence, Opposition attitudes to social inequalities, such as race and gender, range from a mild concern for such inequalities to a refusal to recognise their existence, indicating an essentially conservative attitude to such issues.

The Venezuela to come, or the Venezuela that has already been?

Socio-economic policy positions were updated in a January 31, 2019, PowerPoint presentation made to the world's media at the Central University of Venezuela (UCV), by Juan Guaidó, the former self-proclaimed "interim" president of Venezuela, entitled *Plan País: La Venezuela que Viene* (Country Plan: The Venezuela to Come) (Guaidó, 2019).[1] While the event itself was widely reported in the international media, the actual contents of the presentation received very little attention, indicating, perhaps, a shared acceptance of those contents as unremarkable common sense by the assembled media with the Opposition. Yet, Guaidó's presentation deepens the Opposition's commitment to market-led policy preferences, as well as furthering its thinking on the future of the Venezuelan oil industry. The policy ideas for the latter, indeed, are drawn from a document entitled *Venezuela Energética* (Energized Venezuela), a plan for the nation's hydrocarbons industry co-authored by Guaidó's VP party leader Leopoldo López in 2017 (López and Baquero, 2017).

The presentation begins by outlining the Opposition case for Venezuela as a "failed state", providing an account, compiled from various sources, on the country's economic and social implosion. The plan is presented as the antidote to this catastrophic situation, which is blamed squarely on the "failed economic system of Socialism of the XXI century" by "destroying the country's productive apparatus, [with] arbitrary regulations and controls leading to appropriations which are then corruptly plundered" (Guaidó, 2019). State interventionism, therefore, is cast as inherently retrograde as it hampers individual effort, destroying the "citizen's capacity to stand on their own two feet" by "punishing anyone who looks to provide for their family in a dignified manner" (Guaidó, 2019). Three strategies are offered to remedy this situation: "recover the State for people (*gente*)"; "empower Venezuelans so that they can liberate their creative and productive forces" (Guaidó, 2019); and reinsert Venezuela in "the concert of free nations of the world" (Guaidó, 2019). Hence, once again, Socialism is equated with retrograde tyranny, and democracy with a modern "free market"-producing "individual autonomy" (Guaidó, 2019).

Regarding the first task, among other measures, democracy and the state should be put at people's (*gente*) service, so that "society can develop itself freely and with dignity" to help "promote entrepreneurship [and] competition" (Guaidó, 2019). Empowering Venezuelans means their having "capacities to structurally overcome poverty and generate opportunities for themselves, for their loved ones and for society as a whole" (Guaidó, 2019). This implies "[r]e-establishing market mechanisms and economic liberties which permits society to organise itself in an autonomous manner to solve its problems", which will be achieved by the removal of the existing system of state controls on private property, "recreating an independent judicial system which guarantees private property, the rule of law and protects the citizen", and "a policy of social solidarity which will solve the emergency and contribute to Venezuelans reaching their potential" (Guaidó, 2019). Finally, reinserting Venezuela in "the concert of free nations of the world" is necessary primarily to "attend to the Complex Humanitarian Emergency (CHE) which is punishing our country" and to restore the country's supposedly lost sovereignty, although no mention is made in this context of the impact that punishing Opposition-supported US sanctions have had on this situation (Guaidó, 2019).

There are, however, a few short-term priorities to help achieve these larger goals. These are to: stabilise the economy; attend to the CHE; reactivate the oil industry; and assure universal access to quality public services, among others. To achieve these aims, "massive" financing will be attained from four fundamental sources: "multilateral finance organisations and countries interested in the restoration of democracy and development in Venezuela" (Guaidó, 2019); a "profound" debt restructuring; macro-economic and regulatory restructuring to attract international investment; and recuperation of illegally sourced wealth.

Stabilising the economy will be achieved by a variety of measures, all of them with a decided market orientation: anchoring the exchange rate to slow inflation, dismantling systems of state control and regulations, recapitalising the banks, and reactivating the capital markets, promoting international investment including in public companies and in the provision of public services. There is an emphasis throughout on the involvement of the private sector through competitive tendering in the provision of public services, and the state will only "be responsible for the regulation and strict fulfilment of contracts" [while] "maintaining the ownership of the assets" (Guaidó, 2019). Direct subsidies for utilities will be provided initially, "according to the payment capacity of the different sectors of the population" (Guaidó, 2019), but the aim will be to eventually eliminate all subsidies, meaning in all probability higher bills to access these basic goods.

Absolutely central to this programme is the "reactivation" of the oil industry. This will be achieved through the approval of a new Hydrocarbons Law, which will include "preserving the property of the Nation over the oil fields" (Guaidó, 2019); permitting private capital as majority shareholder in oil projects; designing a "competitive" fiscal regime; maximising the production of gas and oil; and creating a Venezuelan Hydrocarbons Agency (AVH) to "administer the oil fields, and regulate and supervise the sector" (Guaidó, 2019), among other measures. These plans for the oil sector are drawn from the above mentioned, *Venezuela Energética* by Guaidó's party leader, Leopoldo López, along with Gustavo Baquero (2017), a Harvard trained professor in the elite Caracas business school, IESA. The new Hydrocarbons Law will "ensure appropriate profits for the Venezuelan people and competitive income for investors" (p. 4), and a new "independent" regulatory entity, the AVH mentioned above, to help restore confidence among Venezuelans and the international community.

The most interesting and innovative aspect of the proposals comes under the heading "democratising the oil" (López and Baquero, 2017). Here, each Venezuelan citizen over 18 years old will receive direct benefits from the oil through a new Assets Fund for Venezuelans (FPV), based, the document reassuringly states, on Norway's Oil Fund, one of the richest sovereign wealth funds in the world. Of particular note is the correlation of "direct ownership" of the oil by "the people", with each Venezuelan citizen, on becoming 18 years old, obtaining a personal account in the FPV, with "directly owned shares which will grow based on oil and gas sales" (López and Baquero, 2017: p. 10). This personal fund can only be used to finance "essential needs" (López and Baquero, 2017: p. 10), i.e., medical insurance, mortgages, and education costs, and will also be the basis of future pension entitlements. The individual citizen then becomes an asset manager, using their FPV funds to finance his or her own principal asset—themselves. The fund will be "totally transparent" in that monthly statements on personal accounts will be provided to each citizen, who will also be able to access a webpage to monitor the daily activity of the fund, and it will be controlled by an "independent board without governmental interference" (López and Baquero, 2017: p. 10). Under such a schema, however, citizens will have no ability to influence decisions regarding "how information is shared, goals, and policies are set, tax resources are allocated and how programs are operated" (Arnstein, 1969: p. 216). Instead, citizens remain passive recipients of the consequences of decisions made by unnamed others. State financing through taxation is not envisaged as progressive, as there will be a flat rate of 50% tax on each citizen's fund, regardless of income (López and Baquero, 2017), with no indication if this will be additional to existing taxes on income or replace them.

Through this fund, *Venezuela Energética* seems to propose that the final two objectives will be achieved, that is, diversifying the economy and the transition to energy renewables. The FPV will finance the development of new industries and a "robust service sector" (López and Baquero, 2017: p. 14), again citing Norway as an example, including "hundreds of small businesses" (López and Baquero, 2017: p. 14), although, in fact, Norway very rarely uses its oil fund for these purposes. Similarly, while most of the oil would be exported, these sales would finance the development of Venezuela's hydroelectric, solar, and wind energy sources. The document, however, is not clear through what mechanisms either of these objectives will be achieved.

The "Venezuela to come", then, is dominated by three recurrent discursive tropes: an anti-socialism equating the "Socialist State" with tyranny, economic and social desolation, and death; the urgent and complete replacement of the "Socialist State" by a "modern", marketised, regulatory state guided by the "rule of law" and the "traditions" of Venezuelan society, surmised as an innate entrepreneurialism; the "unleashing" through this state of these "natural" entrepreneurial energies of a repressed Venezuelan people, who will then be in a position to provide socially for themselves and their families, with minimum intervention from the state. Ideological and political polarisation, therefore, is deeply entrenched into Opposition political imaginaries of a future non-*Chavista* Venezuela, leaving little room for the continuation of the latter political project in such a future.

Conclusion

In this volume, Castro-Rea and Solano conceive of the right as aiming to further a meritocratic social milieu, governed by the equal opportunity to compete. Only such a system can ensure that each individual's natural talents can flourish and be rewarded adequately. The role of the state here is to "simply create the conditions for fair competition to occur: maintain order and stability, enforce law, protect private property, etc." and a low-tax fiscal environment to ensure just reward, in other words, state–society relations are governed by the principle of state subsidiarity. Moreover, neoliberalism is considered as a system where economic logics prevail over social and political logics, as economic freedom is equated with political liberty. Finally, conservatism "means a disposition to conserve" (as explained in this book's introduction by Castro-Rea and Solano), which involves the acceptance of the existing sociopolitical order as in essence unchangeable, as any attempts to do so most probably would deepen instability and risk chaos. This position precludes any radical attempts at eradicating existing social inequalities.

The above account of the Venezuelan Opposition aims to draw attention to the underlying right-wing, neoliberal, and conservative aspects of its nature. While the Opposition is indeed a heterogeneous alliance of parties that consider themselves anything from social democratic to conservative or libertarian, our review of Opposition policies demonstrates its overall right-wing orientation. Policies outlined in Opposition documentation underline its neoliberal orientation through its unwavering faith in market-based freedoms as the only possible solution to the country's current crisis. The source of this crisis is identified primarily as due to state interventionism in the economy affected by the PSUV, which, by extension, undermines democratic freedoms. The solution is a reduction of state roles to that of guarantor of such freedoms, principally through its juridical institutionality, sufficiently reformed, that is, as one interviewee, the radical libertarian politician Maria Corina Machado (2012) expressed to us as "a strong, but restricted state". The Venezuelan Opposition can also be seen as right-wing due to the reluctance in some quarters to recognise the existence of social inequalities. Nowhere in Opposition discourse is there a concern expressed for class inequalities. Rather, these are displaced by the concept of "poverty", which is in effect simply a symptom of socio-economic and, therefore, class inequality. Moreover, there is a conservative tendency within the Opposition, not only due to its refusal to acknowledge class inequalities, therefore seeking to restore pre-Chávez structural inequalities, but also due to its reluctance to recognise gender or race inequalities, these being seen as primarily the result of the existing government's policies and its social interventionism. The solution lies in Venezuela's returning to an Arcadian pre-Chávez era, where such divisions were at best unproblematised or, at worst, ignored or repressed.

Overall, we recognise that there are differences within the Opposition coalition with respect to the level of privatisation of state enterprises, particularly that of the oil industry, and in recognition by some of race and gender inequalities. Additionally, there is a concern for the issue of poverty, albeit within a charity conception of those who deserve state help as opposed to most who must find security in the market. Overall, however, all Opposition actors unanimously endorse market mechanisms to overcome all inequalities, including those of class, with the State creating a legal context in which competitive individualism can flourish. In this way, even the most left-leaning Opposition groups seek to restore traditional social hierarchies in Venezuela to the pre-Chávez state, thus ignoring the original egalitarian demands of the Venezuelan people, which led to the emergence of Chávez in the first place.

Note

1 A later published version of this plan in English, Spanish, and French can be found here: https://www.planpaisvzla1.com/.

References

Arnstein, S. (1969) A leader of citizen participation. *Journal of the American Institute of Planners* 35 (4), 216–224.
Asamblea Nacional Venezolana. (2019) *Estatuto que rige la transición a la democracia para restablecer la vigencia de la constitución de la República Bolivariana de Venezuela.* http://asambleanacionalvenezuela.org/documentos/botones/boton_1559953972.pdf [Accessed 19 January 2020].
Borges, J. (2012) *Leader, First Justice Party.* Interview with authors, 28 February.
Botti, J. (2012) *President, Federación de Cámaras y Asociaciones de Comercio y Producción de Venezuela (FEDECAMARAS).* Interview with authors, 13 February.
Bresser-Pereira, L. (2006) Izquierda nacional y empresarios en América Latina. *Nueva Sociedad* 202, 121–132.
Buxton, J. (2019) The missteps of Venezuela's opposition—again. *NACLA Report on the Americas* 51 (2), 130–133. https://doi.org/9.1080/10714839.2019.1617472.
Cannon, B. (2004) Venezuela, April 2002: Coup or popular rebellion? The myth of a United Venezuela. *Bulletin of Latin American Research* 23 (3), 285–302.
Cannon, B. (2009) *Hugo Chávez and the Bolivarian revolution: Populism and democracy in a globalised age.* Manchester, Manchester University Press.
Cannon, B. (2014) As clear as MUD: Characteristics, objectives, and strategies of the opposition in Bolivarian Venezuela. *Latin American Politics and Society* 56 (4), 49–70.
Chomsky, N. (1999) *Profit over people: Neoliberalism and global order.* New York, Seven Stories Press.
Coronil, F. (1997) *The magical state: Nature, money, and modernity in Venezuela.* Chicago, University of Chicago Press.
Corrales, J. (2011) Why polarize? Advantages and disadvantages of a rational-choice analysis of government-Opposition relations under Hugo Chávez. In Ponniah, T. & Eastwood, J. (eds.), *The revolution in Venezuela: Social and political change under Chávez.* Cambridge, MA, Harvard University Press, pp. 67–90.
Corrales, J., & Penfold, M. (2007) Venezuela: Crowding out the opposition. *Journal of Democracy* 18 (2), 100–113.
Cyr, J. (2013) Que veinte años no es nada: Hugo Chávez, las elecciones de 2012 y el continuismo político venezolano. *Revista de Ciencia Política* 33 (1), 375–391.
Dagnino, E. (2007) Citizenship: A perverse confluence. *Development in Practice* 17 (4–5), 549–556.
Dominguez, F. (2011) Venezuela's opposition: Desperately seeking to overthrow Chávez. In Dominguez, F., Lievesley, G., & Ludlum, S. (eds.), *Right-wing politics in the New Latin America: Reaction and revolt.* London, Zed, pp. 113–130.
Duno-Gottberg, L. (2020) El campo transversal de la política venezolana: ¿Hacia una Derecha (post)Bolivariana? In Chaguaceda, A. & Duno- Gottberg, L. (coords.), *La derecha como autoritarismo en el siglo XXI.* Ciudad Autónoma de Buenos Aires, Fundación Cadal, México, Centro de Estudios Constitucionales Iberoamericanos, AC, Houston, Texas, Rice University, pp. 303–324.
Ellner, S. (2008) Rethinking Venezuelan politics: Class, conflict, and the Chávez phenomenon. *Journal of Latin American Studies* 41(1), 186–188.
Escobar, A. (2017) *Designs for the pluriverse: Radical interdependence, autonomy, and the making of worlds.* Durham, Duke University Press.
España, L. P. (2012) *Academic, Universidad Católica Andrés Bello (UCAB).* Interview with authors, 17 February.

Ferrero, J. (2014) *Democracy against neoliberalism in Argentina and Brazil: A move to the left*. New York, Palgrave Macmillan.

García, I. (2012) *Leader, PODEMOS Party*. Interview with authors, 28 February.

García-Guadilla, M. P. (2005) The democratization of democracy and social organizations of the opposition: Theoretical certainties, myths, and praxis. *Latin American Perspectives* 32 (2), 109–23.

González, M. (2012) *Public policy coordinator, Mesa de Unidad Democrática*. Interview with authors, 27 February.

González, Y. (2021a) 'Democracy under threat': The foundation of the opposition in Venezuela. *Bulletin of Latin American Research* 40 (1), 69–83.

González, Y. (2021b) *The Confrontational 'Us and Them' Dynamics of Polarised Politics in Venezuela: A Post-Structuralist Examination*. London: Rowman & Littlefield.

Guaidó, J. (2019) *Plan País: La Venezuela que viene*. http://s3.amazonaws.com/semanaruralvzla/carpeta_ckfinder/files/Mafe/Docs/Plan%20Pais%20-%20Juan%20Guaido.pdf [Accessed 19 January 2020].

Guijarro, R. (2012) *Director, CEDICE*. Interview with authors, 8 February.

Hetland, G. (2016) Why is Venezuela in crisis? *The Nation*, 17 August. https://www.thenation.com/article/why-is-venezuela-in-crisis/ [Accessed 19 January 2020].

Lara, M. P. (2018) A conceptual analysis of the term 'populism'. *Thesis Eleven* 149 (1), 31–47.

López, L. (2018) *Venezuela Energética: El régimen abre las puertas para liquidar a PDVSA*. http://www.leopoldolopez.com/venezuela-energetica/ [Accessed 19 January 2020].

López, L., & Baquero, G. (2017) *Venezuela Energética: Propuesta para el bienestar y el progreso de los venezolanos*. Caracas, Editorial Dahbar.

Machado, M. C. (2012) *Independent Public Representative*. Interview with authors, 17 February.

Magallanes, R. (2007) El debate político en Venezuela a inicios del siglo XXI. *Politeia*. 30 (38), 27–57.

Maldonado, V. (2012) *Director, Camara de Comercio, Industria y Servicios*. Interview with authors, 7 February.

McCoy, J. (2017) Lessons from Venezuela's pernicious polarization. *LASA Forum XLVIII* 1, 53–57.

Mesa de Unidad Democrática (MUD). (2008) La alternativa para el cambio. *Globovision*, 23 January. http://www.globovision.com/news.php?nid=76943 [Accessed 4 April 2012].

Mesa de Unidad Democrática (MUD). (2012) *Lineamientos para el Programa de Gobierno de Unidad Nacional (2013–2019)*. https://docs.google.com/file/d/0B9pllLm3e0NmV3o3d09Ddm5fWm8/edit [Accessed 19 January 2020].

Monge, Y., Moleira, A., & de Miguel, B. (2021) The European Union and United States move closer on Venezuela policy. *El País*, 9 July. https://english.elpais.com/usa/2021-07-09/the-european-union-and-united-states-move-closer-on-venezuela-policy.html [Accessed 18 August 2021].

Pantoulas, D., McCoy, J. (2019) Venezuela: Un equilibrio inestable. *Revista de Ciencia Política (Santiago)* 39 (2), 391–408.

Pérez-Liñán, A. (2007) *Presidential impeachment and the new political instability in Latin America*. New York, Cambridge University Press.

Ramos, M. L. (1997) Creencias y valores de los parlamentarios en Venezuela. *Nueva Sociedad* 148, 44–50.

Reid, J. (2004) War, liberalism, and modernity: The biopolitical provocations of 'Empire'. *Cambridge Review of International Affairs* 17 (1), 63–79.

Rhodes-Purdy, M. (2017) *Regime support beyond the balance sheet: Participation and policy performance in Latin America.* Cambridge, Cambridge University Press.

Rodriguez, F. R. (2021) The loser's curse. *Francisco R. Rodríguez.* https://franciscorodriguez.net/2021/05/12/the-losers-curse/?emci=b8d1be8a-afb4-eb11-a7ad-0050f271b5d8&emdi=eabdda87-b0b4-eb11-a7ad-0050f271b5d8&ceid=4620321 [Accessed 14 May 2021].

Sagarzazu, I. (2014) Venezuela 2013: Un país a dos mitades. *Revista de Ciencia Política* 34 (1), 315–328.

Schafriker, B. (2012) *Rector, Universidad Metropolitana.* Interview with authors, 23 February.

Solomon, T. (2015) *The politics of subjectivity in American Foreign Policy discourses.* Ann Arbor, University of Michigan Press.

Straka, T. (2017) Leer el Chavismo: Continuidades y rupturas con la historia Venezolana. *Nueva Sociedad* 268, 77–86.

Tinker Salas, M. (2009) *The enduring legacy: Oil, culture, and society in Venezuela.* London, Duke University Press.

Villarroel, G. (1996) Democracia sin consenso: Los valores confrontados de la cultura política venezolana. *Espacio Abierto: Cuaderno Venezolano de Sociología* 5 (2), 223–248.

Weisbrot, M., Sachs, J. (2019) Economic sanctions as collective punishment: The case of Venezuela. *Center for Economic and Policy Research,* April. http://cepr.net/images/stories/reports/venezuela-sanctions-2019-04.pdf [Accessed 19 January 2020].

Whitehead, L. (2002) *Democratization: Theory and experience.* New York, Oxford University Press.

Zahler, R. (2017) Medium- and short-term historical causes of Venezuela's crisis. *LASA Forum XLVIII* 1, 3–6.

PART IV
Conclusions

11

THE RIGHT IN THE AMERICAS

Concluding remarks

Julián Castro-Rea and Esther Solano

This volume accomplished a vast exploration of the origins, development, and current state of the political right and conservative movements in ten countries in the Americas. It bore testimony to the diversity of national experiences in that respect, although it also unveiled some important parallels among them, as well as their transnational dimensions.

At the outset, we showed the existence of a hemispheric political dimension favouring right-wing actors, propelled by the United States. This dimension has been in place since the nineteenth century, yet in other analyses of the right it is usually an afterthought, an aspect that is fully acknowledged only in extreme situations like military interventions. The subtle, everyday presence of this conservative force pushing all countries in the Americas in the right-wing direction must be incorporated, we believe, to a more comprehensive understanding of domestic politics.

The six historical case studies showed us that conservative and right-wing ideologies and political organisations in the Americas do indeed have a long pedigree; usually reaching back to the early nineteenth century when most countries in the Americas achieved independence. Reactionary ideologies and traditionalist reforms guided by conservative and right-wing principles were blended into largely coherent political narratives. Under different forms and names, political actors across the hemisphere advocated for the preservation of traditional structures of authority and/or for the reorganisation of society along the premises of right-wing ideologies.

Another regularity seen across cases is that the social bases of conservative and right-wing movements include, but are not limited to: large business and landowners, churches, middle classes, and the military brass. It is only natural that elites in a given society have a vested interest in the preservation of the status quo, or its reorganisation to enshrine and protect inequalities. It is more puzzling when

DOI: 10.4324/9781003352266-16

the masses, comprising both middle and working classes, endorse and promote such approaches. Here, we must acknowledge the cunning political ability of the right, with the help of populism, to get the active support of people who inevitably stand to be negatively affected by its programme and policies.

We also found that conservative and right-wing actors are generally wary of democracy, to the extent that in contexts of open competition they struggle to gather enough votes to be elected. Therefore, they prefer some kind of guided democracy (limited competition, banning some parties, an institutional body that oversees and even fixes electoral results, etc.) or outright authoritarian regimes that guarantee the defence of their interests and principles, by force if necessary. This has been an unfortunate, recurring historical reality, in particular in Latin America. Because despite the application of clever political strategies it is not always possible to guarantee the endorsement of the masses to right-wing options, privileged actors may choose to make use of violence to protect their status; flexing their economic (business), social (aristocracy), or ideological (Churches) muscle to ensure also political predominance. This is why the existence of viable conservative and right-wing parties is important, in order to offer a peaceful avenue for the expression of elite interests, which may otherwise put democracy at risk.

Consistently, economic and social inequalities increased under right-wing governments throughout the twentieth century. Historical periods where the right has prevailed coincide with the rise of socioeconomic disparities. It only makes sense, as the right believes that inequalities are natural, innate in any society, and even positive, to the extent that they give an incentive to people to work harder and be creative in order to be more competitive in the marketplace. Redistribution policies are frowned upon by conservatives and the right, because they are deemed to be distortions of the natural order of things, where winners and losers in the social ranking are determined by either tradition or spontaneous human interaction.

The rebirth of democracy experienced across most Latin American countries by the end of the twentieth century offered the right a new opportunity to be electorally competitive. Neoliberalism became both the mantra, the main guide for public policy, and the right's best cohesive ideological core. The end of the Cold War opened a window of opportunity for the rhetorical and indeed political conflation of democracy with open markets, a credo imported straight from the neoliberal playbook. Ordinary people, parties, and other political actors were then convinced that opening the political sphere for competition also meant opening the economic space. Even some parties and leaders who were elected with left-wing credentials ended up implementing neoliberal policies, yielding to the prestige of this ideology in the post–Cold War era. The promise of economic prosperity brought in by the neoliberal discourse became a convenient argument to win elections and form governments, before voters realised the actual consequences of unrestrained economic freedom.

This way, negative impacts of neoliberalism temporarily shut down right-wing actors from power. They managed to survive thanks to their ability to adapt to non-electoral interest representation, the support of media conglomerates praising the glories of free markets and international organisations and networks with ideological affinity. The right's transnational connections were a supplementary factor in the past, but became crucial in the twenty-first century. These international links managed to make a difference in the preservation of conservative and right-wing political options during their "Pink Wave" dark times, in the early 2000s. A new dimension of political advertising and campaigning was consolidated with the determinant role that think tanks and their social media presence acquired in the political debate.

In time, right-wing actors were able to return to power thanks to the crafty use of post-ideological, pseudo-democratic, and populist strategies, thus creating a competitive right-wing movement adapted to the twenty-first-century realities. In a context of democracy uncertainty, erosion, and rejection of traditional politics, right and extreme-right actors were capable of misguidedly offer answers and hope to a significant part of a country's population, who would trust their promises and bring them to power with their vote. Conservatism and the right take advantage of times of crisis to propose easy fixes and reach control of political institutions. The political right has been able to present an alternative vision that, be it momentarily, is given credibility by the voters or other actors holding political power and is thus able to form governments and/or dominate the political conversation.

Discussion of specific national cases makes us believe that this return to power is only temporal, as eventually the flaws and biases in the right-wing political agenda will call alternative political options to the rescue, thus engaging most countries in the region to a periodical left-right political pendulum. By 2022, this dynamic seems to be already in motion, with electoral victories of the left in Mexico, Honduras, Peru, Chile, Argentina, Bolivia, and Brazil. Meanwhile, leftist governments managed to remain in power in Venezuela and Cuba.

Of course, there are important differences of degree from one country to the next one, ranging from the brutal military dictatorships experienced in South and Central America in the 1970s and 1980s, to the calm evolution of conservatism and the right in Canada and the comparatively benevolent neoliberal regimes that prevailed in the hemisphere in the 1990s, with the end of the Cold War and beyond. Recent right-wing populism experiences, such as Bolsonaro's Brazil and Trump's United States, sit somewhere in between these extremes.

In sum, we believe that our exploration of these variegated cases of study is a valuable contribution to the comparative understanding of conservatism and the right in the Americas from a scientific, balanced perspective, a contribution that may be useful for further study of the cases considered, for comparison with other political contexts beyond the Americas and for unveiling the transnational dimension of this vast ideological movement.

INDEX

Note: Page numbers in *italics* indicate figures, **bold** indicate tables in the text

Abascal, S. 131
Aberhart, W. 81
Afghanistan 27
Africa 37
Alberdi, J. B. 116
Alfonsín, R. 67
Alsogaray, A. 67
Anaya, R. 136
Andino, Gen. T. C. 118–119
Añez, J. 30–31, 36
anti-liberalism 63, 93
anti-Sandinista 32
anti-Semitism 63, 93, 129
Arango, A. P. 94
Arboleda, S. 94, 98, 103, 104
Areco, J. P. 147, 155–156
Argentina 1–3, 10, 30, 35, 45, 155, 190, 209, 241; *'Alianza'* (Alliance) 67; *Alianza de Centro* (Centre Alliance, AC) 67; *Alianza de la Juventud Nacionalista* (Nationalist Youth Alliance, AJN) 63; *Cambiemos* 69–70, 72; 1853 Constitution 61, 71; coups 58, 61, 71; dictatorships 59, 64, 65, 70; *federales* 60; free elections in March 1973 64; golpe in 1976 65; *golpe* of September 1930 61; Kirchnerism 69–70; May Revolution (1910) 60; *Movimiento por la Dignidad y la Independencia* (Movement for Dignity and Independence MODIN) 67; "National Security Doctrine" 61; occupation of the Malvinas/Falkland Islands 66; *Partido Autonomista Nacional* (National Autonomist Party, PAN) 60; *Partido Justicialista* (Justicialist Party, PJ) 57; Patriotic League (*Liga Patriótica Argentina*, LPA) 62; Peronism 59, 63–70; Peronist 57–59, 63–69, 71–72; "Proceso de Reorganización Nacional" (National Reorganisation Process, 1976–1983) 65; *Propuesta Republicana* (Republican Proposal, PRO) 68; *Recrear Argentina* (Recreate Argentina) 68; "Sepoy oligarchy" 63; *Unión Cívica Radical* (Radical Civic Union, UCR) 57; *Unión del Centro Democrático* (Union of the Democratic Centre, UCEDE) 66; *unitários* 60
Aspe, P. 134
Ayres Filho, P. 168
Azúa, C. R. de 142–143

Bachelet, M. 28, 205
Bailleres, R. 132
Bannon, S. 172
Baquero, G. 230–231
Barragán, E. M. 137
Barrios, F. G. 134
Barrios, J. R. 116

244 Index

Batista, P. 177
Batlle y Ordóñez, J. 142, 147, 156, 158, 162
Beltrão Filho, H. 174, 179
Bennet, R. B. 79
Bernier, M. 85
Bertrand, F. 118
Betancur, B. 91
Biden, J. 222
Bilderberg Group 40
Black people 178, 180, 228; black movement 180; black population 93
Blumenthal, M. 31
Bobbio, N. 58, 192
Bolivia 61
Bolsonaro, E. 175, 177, 179, 184
Bolsonaro, J. 12–13, 30, 152, 168, 171, 175–186, 241
Bonilla, M. 118
Bonilla, P. 118–119
Bordaberry, J. M. 147, 156, 158
Borges, J. 227
Bornhausen, J. 170
Bornhausen, R. 170, 184
Brazil 1–2, 10–13, 24, 30, 34–35, 61, 152, 162, 222; *Aliança Renovadora Nacional* (ARENA) 170–171; *Câmara de Estudos e Debates Econômicos e Sociais* (CEDES) 170, 184; civil-military coup of 1964 175; *Comissão Nacional da Verdade* 176; counterpublics 171–174, 178, 182; dominant counterpublicity 182; *Estudantes Pela Liberdade* (EPL) 175; *Fórum da Liberdade* 170, 174, 179; *see also* Brazil, *Instituto de Estudos Empresariais* (IEE); the Foundation for Economic Education 168; *Instituto Atlântico* 170; *Instituto Brasileiro de Filosofia* (IBF) 168–169, 183–184; *Instituto de Estudos Empresariais* (IEE) 169, 170, 174, 179; *Instituto de Pesquisa e Estudos Sociais* (IPES) 168–169, 183; *Instituto de Pesquisas Econômicas Aplicadas* (IPEA) 179; *Instituto Liberal* 169–170, 178; *Instituto* Millenium 179; *Instituto Mises Brasil* (IMB) 174, 179; *Instituto Ordem Livre* 175; *Lulismo* 171, 184; Magazine *Visão* 170; *Marcha da Família com Deus pela Liberdade* 168; Mensalão 170–171, 177, 181, 184, 187; *Movimento Brasil Livre* (MBL) 177, 185; *Movimento Democrático Brasileiro* (MDB) 178; *Movimento Endireita Brasil* (MEB) 171, 184; *Movimento Passe Livre* (MPL) 177; *Operação Lava Jato* 178, 181; *Partido Comunista do Brasil* (PC do B) 179; *Partido da Frente Liberal* (PFL)/ *Democratas* (DEM) 170–171; *Partido da Social Democracia Brasileira* (PSDB) 170–171, 177–178, 181, 184, 187; *Partido Ecológico Nacional* (PEN) 179; Partido Patriota 179; *Partido Progressista*, PP 171; *Partido Social Cristão* (PSC) 178; *Partido Social Liberal* (PSL) 179; Petrobrás 177–178; PT 170–172, 176–177, 180–182, 184–185; Rousseff's impeachment 177–178, 181, 185; the *Sociedade de Convívio* 168–170, 184; TFP 168, 175; University of Brasilia 169, 179
British: colonialism 21, 37; economic global networks 60; empire 33, 37, 46–47, 77–79, 144; imperialism 63; intelligence 33
Buchanan, J. 22
Buckley, W. F. 23
Builes, Msgr. M. A. 98
Bulhões, O. G. de 169
Bush, G. W. 25, 29, 33, 39, 47–48

Cabal, Sen. M. F. 95
Cabrera, L. 129
Calderón Hinojosa, F. 135
Calhoun, J. C. 21–22
Calles, P. E. 129
Cambridge Analytica 27
Cámpora, H. 61, 64
Campos, R. 168–169
Canada 3–4, 10–11, 241; Air Canada 80; Alberta 81, 83–85; the Bank of Canada 79; the Blue Book 81; Calgary 82; Canada-US Free Trade Agreement *see* Free Trade Agreement with North America (NAFTA); Canadian Alliance 82; Canadian flag 79; Canadian Radio Broadcasting Commission 79; CBC 79, 81; *Coalition Avenir Québec*, CAQ 84; the *Common Sense Revolution* 83; Conservative Party 81–82, 85; Democratic Action of Quebec 84; Francophone culture 84; *Lament for a Nation* 78; Liberal Party of Canada (LPC) 76, 78; Maritime provinces 81; Ontario 82–85; *Parti Québécois* 84; People's Party of Canada 85; Petro-Canada 80; Progressive Conservative

Party 82; Quebec 82, 84–85; Reform Party 81–82; Saskatchewan 83, 85; second referendum on Quebec sovereignty (1995) 84; the Tory tradition 77
Caro, J. E. 92
Carvalho, O. de 172–174, 177, 182
Castelo Branco, Mah. H. 169
Castro, P. R. de 170, 184, 186
The Catholic Church 43, 45, 61, 63, 96, 98–99, 104, 106, 126–127, 220; Catholic militants 64; Catholicism 58, 61, 77, 84, 96, 98–99, 134; Catholics 61, 92, 98, 106, 119, 128, 130–131, 133, 168, 184; 1968 CELAM meeting 99; *see also* the General Conference of the Latin American Episcopate of 1968; the Episcopate 64; the Eucharistic Congress in 1934 63; the General Conference of the Latin American Episcopate of 1968 131; ISD 133; Jesuits 128; the Mexican Episcopate Conference 136; Opus Dei 197, 211–212; *Rerum Novarum* of 1891 127; Second Vatican Council (1962–1965) 61, 99, 131; Social Doctrine of the Church (DSI) 127, 137; *see also* Episcopate of 1968, ISD; Thomist philosophy 93; ultramontanist Catholics 142; Vatican 61, 98, 106, 222
Cedillo, S. 129
Central American Federation 113
Cerrato, Pr. S. C. 30, 32
Chamorro, J. S. 30, 32
Chávez, H. 36, 217, 219–221, 223–225, 227, 232
Chicago School of Economics 77, 170, 174, 179, 197
Chile xviii, xix, 1–3, 10, 13, 28, 30, 34, 63, 241; *Avanzada Nacional* 198; Chilean people 63; *Chile Vamos* 191–192, 198–199, 204–207, 209, 212–213; Conservative Christian Social Party 196; Conservative Party 195–197, 210; Conservative Traditionalist Party 196; Constitution 191, 195, 198, 205–207, 209, 211; 1901 Convention 195; Declaration of Principles of Military Government 197, 212; dictatorship 191–192, 194, 199, 205, 207–209, 212–213; Evópoli 198–199, 201–205, 208–209, 212–213; *Falange* 195, 197, 210–211; *gremialista* movement 196–198; Liberal Party 196, 203, 208, 211; military government 197; military regime 201, 211; the National Action Movement (MAN) 198; National Party 195–197, 211; the National Renewal (RN) in 1987 198–199, 202, 204–205, 209, 211–213; Popular Unity government 197; PRI 198, 212; UDI 198–199, 202, 204–205, 209, 211–213
China 23
Chomsky, N. 40, 48, 223
Chrétien, J. 81
Climate change 24–26, 46, 137
Clouthier, M. 134
The Cold War xx, 4, 22, 29, 61, 121, 130, 147, 240–241
Colindres, V. M. 118
Colombia 2, 10–11, 30, 35, 222; Armed Forces Revolutionaries of Colombia (FARC) 90–91, 100, 105–106; Christian "MIRA" party 101, 106; "Colombia Justa Libres" 100–101, 106; Colombian Catholic Action (ACC) 99, 106; the Colombian Conservative Party 90–91, 93–94, 96–99, 105–107; Colombian Federation of Ganaderos 102; the Colombian Liberal Party 92, 94–95, 98–99, 102, 105, 107; 1887 Concordat 96; 1973 Concordat 98–99; 1991 Constitution 99, 103, 106; the Constitution of 1886 96, 103; Democratic Centre Party (CD) 88, 91, 95–97, 101–102, 104–105; Evangelical Council of Colombia (Cedecol) 99; "Great Alliance for Colombia" 101; Internal Armed Conflict (CAI) 90; "La Regeneración" 93; "*La Violencia*" 91; Medellín Cartel 102; M-19 guerrillas 102; "*Muerte a Secuestradores*" (MAS) 102; National Front (1958–1974) 94; National Liberation Army (ELN) 90; the National Party 92–93; National Union Party (De la U) 91, 95, 105; *Partido Centro Democrático* 95; the Radical Change Party 95; separation of Panama 90–93; *see also* Panama, independence of; the Social Party of National Unity (U Party) 95–97, 105; "United Self-Defence Forces of Colombia" (AUC) 102; *Uribistas* 91; "War of thousand days" (1889–1902) 90
Colosio, L. D. 134
Communism 22, 30, 38, 59, 63, 94, 98, 128, 132, 143, 169–175, 195; anti-communism 23, 63, 66, 93, 130–132;

Index

anti-communist 31, 99, 102, 130–132, 134, 168–169, 175–176, 179; communist 69, 71, 131, 145, 173, 174, 176, 177, 193, 197, 210
Comte, A. 116–117
Conason, J. 20
Constantino, R. 176, 179
Corrales, J. 219, 223
Cruz, Sen. T. 31
Cruz-Coke, E. 195, 210
Cuba 29, 34–35, 70, 241; Castro's Cuba 131; the Cuban Revolution 130, 147
Cyr, J. 221

Darwin's evolutionism 111
Dávila, M. 118
De la Rúa, F. 67
De Maistre 5, 92
Diefenbaker, J. 78, 82
Dirceu, J. 170
Domenech, G. 151, 160
drug: activity 121, 123; anti-drug operations 31; cartels 90; drug-free consumption 95; trafficking 90, 101–102, 123–124, 135
Dugin, A. 170
Duque, I. 95, 101–102
Duverger, M. 191

Ebrard, M. 137
Echeverría, L. 131
Echeverrista 132
ECLAC 101
El Salvador 35, 122
ethnic inequalities 228
Europe 10, 92, 116, 151, 192, 222
European 43, 79; countries 209; enlightenment 111; experience 1, 130; Middle Ages 5; migrants 61; national-populist right 69; nation-states 82; philosophers 111; right(s) 193, 209; totalitarian ideologies 128; *see also* Fascism, European
The European Union 222
Evangelism 43; Charismatic Evangelical 106; Evangelical Christian 106; evangelical churches 99, 107, 108, 175; evangelical leaders 182; evangelical woman 178; evangelicals 43, 136; Jehovah's Witnesses 43, 45; Mormons 43, 45; Neo-Pentecostals 99; Pentecostals 99
Everaldo, Pr. 178

Facebook 27, 32, 173–174, 177, 185
fascism 20, 158, 189, 196, 210–211; European 145–146; fascist 20; "post-fascism" 140
Fox, V. 134
France 7, 143, 193; French right 77
Franco, F. 63, 66, 93, 128
Francoism 146; Francoist 197
Free Trade Agreement with North America (NAFTA) 38, 80
The French Revolution 92, 144, 157; anti-Jacobin 12, 146, 157; anti-Jacobinism 140–142; Jacobin 92, 144; Jacobinism 92, 142–143, 157
Friedman, M. 168–169, 183
Frondizi, A. 61
Fujimori, A. 30
Fulbright, Sen. J. W. 36; *see also* United States, Fulbright Programme

G20 60
Gaitán, J. E. 98
Gamboa, L. 91, 96
gender issues 68, 228; abortion 6, 24, 70, 81–82, 95, 100, 135–137, 157, 175–176, 184, 192–193, 202–204, 213; civil union 202, 208, 213; feminism 136, 173, 176; gay rights 6, 24; LGBT+ 171, 173, 175, 180; Maria da Penha domestic abuse law 175; PEC das domésticas 176; same-sex adoption 95, 136; same-sex marriage 68, 81–82, 176, 192, 198, 202, 208; sexual minorities 202–203, 213
Gibson, E. L. 102, 190
globalism 173–174
Goldwater, B. 23
Gómez, E. 145
Gómez, L. 93–95, 98, 100
González, F. 91, 98
González, M. 228
Gortari, C. S. 134
Goulart, J. 168–169
Goyena, J. I. 143–144, 157
Gramsci, A. xviii–xx, 73
Grenada 29, 34
Guaidó, J. 30, 36, 219, 222, 228–230
Guatemala 34–35, 61, 110, 114, 116, 122; The University of San Carlos de Borromeo 110
Gudin, E. 168–169
Guedes, P. 179–180
Gutiérrez, R. L. 118
Guzmán, J. 197–198, 210

Harper, S. 76, 82
Harris, M. 83
Hasselmann, J. 181
Hayek, F. A. 22, 82, 168–169, 183, 185, 197, 212
Hayekian 77, 211
Heilman, L. 31
Henríquez, Gen. 133
Hernández, J. O. 123
Herrera, A. 137
Herrera, H. 194
Herrera, L. A. de 143, 144, 156–158, 161
Hobbesian 77
Hofstadter, R. J. 20
Honduras 10, 12, 32–35, 47, 241; the Central University 116; David's Manifesto 114; Economic Societies of Friends of the Country 110; the Liberal Party 118, 120–121, 123; *Libertad y Refundación* Party 123; National Party 119, 121, 123
Horwitz, R. B. 22–23
Huidobro, E. F. 151–153, 159–161
Humala, O. 28
Hurtado, A. G. 94

Igartua, J. E. 79
Illia, A. 61
immigration 6, 69, 79; European immigrants 142; Italian immigrants 60, 158; Spaniard immigrants 60; see also migration
indigenous: groups of the Pampa 60; people 98; "problem" 128; women in Peru 29
International Monetary Fund, IMF 38–39, 69, 121–123
Iraq 27, 29, 47
Israel 32

Jaramillo, G. R. 94
Jiménez, M. P. 218
Justo, A. 61

Kauth, R. 88
Kennedy, J. F. 29, 38, 47–48
Keynesianism 22; Keynesian 23, 77–80
Kirchner, C. F. 68–69; see also Argentina, Kirchnerism
Kirchner, N. 68–69; see also Argentina, Kirchnerism

Lacalle Pou, L. A. 140, 150, 154, 160
Laguado Duca, A. 92, 102

Lastarria, V. 116
Laurier, W. 78
Lewis, S. 20
libertarianism 12, 23, 167, 174, 183
Lindenberg, A. 168, 183
Ling, Willian 169; see also Brazil, *Instituto de Estudos Empresariais* (IEE)
Ling, Winston 169, 179; see also Brazil, *Instituto de Estudos Empresariais* (IEE)
Locke 116
López Murphy, R. 68
"Lula" da Silva, L. I. 170–171, 175–176, 181, 184; see also Brazil, *Lulismo*

Macdonald, J. A. 77
Machado, M. C. 232
Macri, M. 68, 71
Madison, J. 21
Maduro, N. 217, 221–222, 225–226
Maksoud, H. 169
Malafaia, S. 178
Manning, P. 81
Mantega, G. 171
Martínez, C. W. 195
Martínez, M. C. 143, 157, 159
Martínez, M. E. 65
Marxism 61; anti-Marxist 196; *Communist Manifesto* 1; "Gramscian Marxism" xx; Judeo-Marxist internationalism 63; Marxist activism 99; Marxist intellectuals xx
Masons 119
Mate, A. 31
Mattar, S. 175
Meade, J. A. 135–137
Mendiondo, R. V. 145
Menem, C. 67–68, 71
Mexico 7, 10, 12, 29, 32, 35, 47, 115, 222, 241; the Agua Prieta rebellion 127; the Allies 128; the Autonomous Technological Institute of Mexico (ITAM) 132; Business Coordinating Council (CCE) 133; the Communist League September 23, 132; Confederation of Employers of the Mexican Republic (*Coparmex*) 129; the Constitution of 1917 127–128, 136; *Cristero* War 127; El Bajío 135; Federal Security Directorate 134; Free School of Law 129; Fundación Azteca 137; Institutional Revolutionary Party (PRI) 127, 130, 133–136; Maya train 36; the "Mexican miracle" 130,

133; Monterrey 129, 133; Monterrey Group 132–133, 137; National Action Party (PAN) 128, 130, 131, 133–137; National Autonomous University of Mexico (UNAM) 129; National Confederation of Popular Organisations (CNOP) 131; the National Preparatory School 129; National Regeneration Movement (MORENA) 136–137; *neo-panismo* 133–134; Party of the Mexican Revolution 130; PRD 136; *Salinista* 134; Social Encounter Party (PES) 136; Sonoran group 127; State Institutes of Sciences 129; *Synarchism* 128; Technological Institute of Superior Studies of Monterrey (ITESM, 'Tec de Monterrey') 132; the University of Mexico 129
Middelbrook, K. 103
The Middle East 31
Mieres, P. 150
migration 136; European migrants 60; undocumented migrants 26; waves of migrants-Central Americans, Caribbean, Africans 136; White migrants 117; *see also* immigration
Mises, L. von 174, 183
Mitre, B. 60
Mont Pèlerin Society 168–169, 183
Montalva, E. F. 196
Montesquieu 111, 124
Montoya, J. C. 134
Morales, E. 31
Morazán, F. 112–116
Morín, M. G. 130–131
Moro, S. 178
Mossadegh, M. 33
Mujica, J. 151, 153–153, 159, 161
Mulroney, B. 79–81, 83
Mussolini, B. 145–146

Napoleon 110, 143
Nardone, B. 147, 155, 158–159
Nicaragua 30–31, 34–35, 122; Comayagua 114; Léon 114; the University of León 110
Nixon, R. 22, 46
Norton, B. 31
Norway 222, 231; Norway's Oil Fund 230
Novick, E. 149, 159
Núñez, R. 92, 102, 105

Obrador, A. M. L. 136–138
Ochoa, F. 102
Oliveira, P. C. de 168, 183
Ortega, D. 31–32
Ortellado, P. 177
Ortiz, R. 61

Palacios, M. 101
Palocci, A. 170
Panama 29, 34–35; independence of 93; separation of 90, 93
Paschoal, J. 181
Paul II, PP. J. 133–134
Pearson, L. B. 79
Peña Nieto, E. 135–136
Perón, J. 61, 64–65, 71; *see also* Argentina, Peronism; Argentina, Peronist
Peru 1–2, 28, 30, 34–35, 45, 241
Pinilla, Gen. G. R. 94
Pinochet, A. xviii, 205–206, 209
Pliego, R. S. 137
populism 19, 25–26, 66, 105, 190, 224; digital 186; "Intelligent" 85; national-populism 59, 70; Peronist 65; political 59; "social-Christian" 194
Powell Jr., J. F. 23–24, 26, 46
Protestantism: historical 99; Protestant 43, 103, 106, 130; Protestant churches 99; Protestant Congregations 106; Protestant pastors 100
Pumarejo, A. L. 98

Quigley, C. 37

racism 19, 180, 228
Radonski, H. C. 221
Reagan, R. xviii, xx, 34, 47–48, 80, 134
Reaganomics 80
Reid, B. 24
religious freedom 24, 92
Rémond, R. 191, 193–194, 207, 210–211
Reyes, R. 103
Rhodes, C. 36–37, 47; *see also* Rhodes Scholars programme
Rhodes Scholars programme 36, 46–47
Ribeiro, M. M. 177
Ríos, Gen. G. M. 141, 149–155, 158–162
Ríos, P. M. 146, 162
Robertson, P. 24
Rockefeller, D. 38
Rockefeller, J. D. 39
Rodríguez, M. O. 92, 94
Rodríguez, R. V. 170, 184
Romo, A. 137
Rosa, R. 112, 116–117

Rosales, M. 220
Roth, P. 20
Rothbard, M. 174, 183–184
Rousseau 83, 110
Rousseauist optimism 77
Roussef, D. 176–177, 181, 185
Russel, P. H. 82
The Russian Revolution of 1917 144

Sada, E. G. 133
Sagarzazu, I. 221
Salas, U. 145
Salles, R. 171
Samper, E. 99, 106
Samper, J. M. 102
Santoro, B. 178–179
Santos, J. M. 91, 95, 100
Sarmiento, D. F. 60, 116
Sarney, R. 170
Sartori, J. 149, 159
Serra Puche, J. J. 134
Sierra, J. 129, 137
Sierra, T. 118
Singer, A. 171, 184
Smith, A. 110, 124
socialism xix, 4, 63, 143–144, 196, 226, 229; anti-socialism 231; "real socialism" 225; "socialist education" 128; the Socialist Party 157; socialist revolution 209; socialist/socialists 92, 123, 143, 162, 222, 226; "Socialist State" 231
Solís, M. C. 134
Soto, M. A. 116
The Soviet Union xix, 23, 122; *see also* The USSR
Spain 43, 63, 110; Falangist Hispanicism 128; Franco's government in 63; *see also* Franco, F.; Francoism; Hispanicism 93; independence of 115; "Indies Christianity" of the Spanish empire 142; Napoleon's invasion of 110; separation of 112; Spanish Civil War 93; Spanish colony 110; Spanish Crown 60, 93; Spanish *Falange* 63; the Spanish Republic 128; Spanish State 110; Viceroyalty of the River Plate 60; Vox leaders in 152
Stelle, J. 169
Strauss, L. 25
Sydnor Jr., E. B. 23

The Taliban 27
Talvi, E. 150, 154

Temer, M. 178
Terra, G. 145–146
Thatcher, M. xxi, 134, 183, 185
think tanks xviii, xxi, 24–25, 40–41, 43–44, 46, 168, 170, 183, 241
Torres, C. 99
Traverso, E. 140
Trudeau, J. 76
Trudeau, P. E. 79
Trump, D. xxi, 1, 10, 19–20, 23, 25–27, 29, 31, 46, 48, 140, 182, 221–222, 241
Turner, J. 80

UNESCO 27
United Nations Conference on Environment and Development (1992) 24
United States xx, xxi, 1, 4, 10, 77–81, 102, 118, 121–122, 131, 133, 137, 140, 173, 221–222, 239, 241; American Enterprise Institute 24–25; The Americas Society (AS) 38; Atlas Foundation 43; Atlas Network 46; backlash politics 23–35; Bill and Melinda Gates Foundation (BMGF) 41; CAFTA 38; The Carnegie Endowment 41; The Central Intelligence Agency (CIA) 33; Centre for International Private Enterprise (CIPE) 36; Christian Coalition 24; Constitutional fundamentalism 19, 25; the Council of the Americas (COA) 38; Council on Foreign Relations (CFR) 39; Democrats 28, 33, 38–39; Department of Defense 33; exceptionalism 19, 25; Ford Foundation 39, 41; Freedom House 31; FTAA 38; The Fulbright Program 36–38; Koch Foundation 24, 41; McCarthyism 23; Monroe Doctrine 27; Moral Majority movement 24; NAFTA 38, 80; the National Endowment for Democracy (NED) 34–35; nGOS 24, 28, 36, 38, 40, 46; Office of Strategic Services (OSS) 33; Operation Mockingbird 40; Republicanism 22; Republicans 28, 33, 38–39; "Revolution of Independence" 21; the Rockefeller foundation 38–39, 41; State Department 26, 32, 47; State Policy Network 46; Tea Party movement 25–26; Trilateral Commission 40; the United States Chamber of Commerce (USCC) 23–24; the University of Chicago 22; University of Virginia 22; the US Civil

War 22; US Constitution 19–21, 25; USAID 29–32, 37
Uruguay 10–12, 222; armed forces 141, 145–146, 151, 153, 159–162; *Batllismo* 142, 144–145, 156–158; *Blancos* 141–142, 149, 155; *Cabildo Abierto* (Open *Cabildo*) 141, 149–155, 161–162; *Coalición Multicolor* (Multicoloured Coalition) 140; *Colorados* 141–142, 149, 155, 162; *Corriente de Acción y Pensamiento-Libertad* (Current of Action and Thought-Liberty, or CAP-L) 152; Coup of March 1933 145–146, 157–158; *Frente Amplio* (Broad Front) 148–152, 154–156, 159–162; Herrerismo 147, 154–155; Independent Party 150, 156; *Juventud Uruguaya de Pie* (Standing Uruguayan Youth, or JUP) 153; liberals 142; *Liga Federal de Acción Ruralista* (Federal League for Rural Action) 147, 158; Montevideo 142, 149, 157–160; the National or *Blanco* Party 140–143, 145, 147–151, 154, 156–160; *Pachequismo* 155; *Partido de la Concertación* (Concerted Action Party) 149; *Partido de la Gente* (People's Party) 149–150, 156, 159; republicans 142; *Tenientes de Artigas* Lodge 153, 161; Tupamaro 151, 160–161; *Vanguardias de la Patria* (Vanguards of the Fatherland) 145
The USSR 135; *see also* The Soviet Union

Valdés, M. A. 131
Valencia, G. L. 103
Valladares, P. 119
Valle, J. C. del 110–116, 124–125
Vázquez, T. 141, 151–153, 159–161
Vélez, A. U. 91, 95, 100, 102–103, 105–107
Venezuela 2, 10, 13, 30–36, 45, 48, 70, 241; ABP (Brave People's Alliance) 219; AD (Democratic Action) 218–219; Assets Fund for Venezuelans (FPV) 230–231; Bolivarian regime 217, 219, 225; Capriles's First Justice Party (PJ) 219, 227; Caracas business school, IESA 230; CD (Democratic Coordinator) 220, 222; Central University of Venezuela (UCV) 228; *Chavismo* 217–220, 222–228; Complex Humanitarian Emergency (CHE) 226, 229; 1999 Constitution 225; COPEI (Social Christian Party) 218–219; coup, coups 218, 220, 222; CTV (Venezuelan Workers Confederation) 220; democracy 217, 222–229; dictatorship 217–218; *Fedecámaras* 220, 228; Opposition Democratic Unity Roundtable (MUD) 220; PDVSA 227; PJ (First Justice) 219–227; polarisation 217, 219, 222, 224, 226, 231; Punto Fijo 217–219, 223; Socialist Party of Venezuela (PSUV) 218, 221, 225, 232; *Venezuela Energética* 229–231; Venezuelan Armed Forces 222; Venezuelan Hydrocarbons Agency (AVH) 230; VP (Popular Will) 219, 222, 229; VV (Come Venezuela) 219
Vietnam War 39

Warner, M. 182
Washington Consensus 122
Welfare State 22, 79
WHO 27
Wikileaks 40
Wilson, W. 39
Working classes 64, 240
The World Bank 30, 38
The World Trade Organization 38
World War II xx, 31, 33–34, 36, 45, 60

Xenophobia 19, 25, 62, 69

Yocupicio 129
Yrigoyen 61